Methods of Exploring Emotions

Gathering scholars from different disciplines, this book is the first on how to study emotions using sociological, historical, linguistic, anthropological, psychological, cultural, and mixed approaches. Bringing together the emerging lines of inquiry, it lays foundations for an overdue methodological debate.

The volume offers entrancing short essays, richly illustrated with examples and anecdotes, that provide basic knowledge about how to pursue emotions in texts, interviews, observations, spoken language, visuals, historical documents, and surveys. The contributors are respectful of those being researched and are mindful of the effects of their own feelings on the conclusions. The book thus touches upon the ethics of research in vivid first person accounts.

Methods are notoriously difficult to teach—this collection fills the gap between dry methods books and students' need to know more about the actual research practice.

Helena Flam received Fil.Kand. from Lunds Universitet, Sweden, and her PhD in Sociology from Columbia University, US. Since 1993 she has been Associate Professor of Sociology at the University of Leipzig, Germany. She has published on emotions, social movements, organizations, and discrimination. She is a founder and a past convener of the European Research Network on Emotions affiliated with the European Sociological Association.

Jochen Kleres, PhD, has used emotions analysis in his research on civil society, AIDS, migration, and organizations. He is currently pursuing a post-doctoral project at the University of Gothenburg, Sweden. Presently serving as the convener of the European Research Network on Emotions, he is the author of the very first methods text discussing how to identify and analyze emotions in autobiographic narratives.

Methods of Exploring Emotions

Edited by Helena Flam and Jochen Kleres

LONDON AND NEW YORK

First published 2015
by Routledge
2 Park Square, Milton Park, Abingdon, Oxon OX14 4RN

and by Routledge
711 Third Avenue, New York, NY 10017

Routledge is an imprint of the Taylor & Francis Group, an informa business

British Library Cataloguing-in-Publication Data
A catalogue record for this book is available from the British Library

Library of Congress Cataloging in Publication Data
Methods of exploring emotions / edited by Helena Flam, Jochen Kleres.
pages cm
1. Emotions. 2. Emotions–Social aspects. I. Flam, Helena. II. Kleres, Jochen.
BF531.M48 2015
152.4072–dc23 2014042042

ISBN: 978-1-138-79869-4 (hbk)
ISBN: 978-1-315-75653-0 (ebk)

Typeset in Baskerville
by Wearset Ltd, Boldon, Tyne and Wear

Printed and bound in the United States of America by Publishers Graphics, LLC on sustainably sourced paper.

Contents

Figures

Tables

Contributors

Stina Bergman Blix is Assistant Professor in Sociology at Stockholm University, Sweden. Her research focuses on the professionalization of emotions and the relationship between emotional experience and expression, particularly its bodily manifestations. Her dissertation scrutinized dramaturgical theory through close observation of the rehearsing process of professional stage actors, resulting in the development of concepts such as decoupling and habituation of professional emotions.

Julien Bernard is a senior lecturer at the Department of Sociology of the University Paris Ouest Nanterre la Défense, and a member of the laboratory Sophiapol (sociology, philosophy and political anthropology), where he leads the research network Socioanthropology of Emotions. His PhD focused on *Emotions and Rituals in Undertakers' Work*. His research has since dealt with industrial risks, death, and family.

Thomas Burkart is a trained psychologist and sociologist, practicing as a psychotherapist in Hamburg, and has held lecturing positions at the University of Hamburg and Berliner Methodentreffen. His dissertation was on *Consulting for the Solving of Complex Problems*. Since 1997 he has been a member of the interdisciplinary Hamburger Forschungswerkstatt. His research focuses on qualitative methods, introspection, problem-solving, and emotion/emotional experience.

Barbara Czarniawska holds a Chair in Management Studies at the University of Gothenburg, Sweden. A *Doctor honoris causa* at Stockholm School of Economics, Copenhagen Business School and Helsinki School of Economics, she is a member of the Swedish Royal Academy of Sciences, the Swedish Royal Engineering Academy, the Royal Society of Art and Sciences in Gothenburg, and Societas Scientiarum Finnica. She takes a feminist and constructionist perspective on organizing—recently exploring the connections between popular culture and practice of management—and the organization of news production. She is interested in methodology, especially in techniques of fieldwork and in the application of narratology to organization studies.

Nicole Doerr holds a PhD from the European University Institute. After concluding her Marie Curie Fellowship at Harvard University she started as Assistant Professor in International Relations at Mount Holyoke College. Doerr has published in *Mobilization, Globalizations*, the *Feminist Review, Social Movement Studies*, and the *European Political Science Review*. Her co-authored book, *Advances in the Visual Analysis of Social Movements* (with Alice Mattoni and Simon Teune), appeared in *Research in Social Movements, Conflicts and Change*.

H. Julia Eksner is an anthropologist (MA, Free University of Berlin, 2001) and a learning scientist (PhD, Northwestern University, 2007), thus connecting socio-cultural and developmental perspectives in the study of emotion. She is currently Professor of Education at the Frankfurt University of Applied Sciences, and a lecturer in the international MA-programme for Visual and Media Anthropology at the Freie Universität, Berlin.

Francesca Falk studied history and political theory at the universities of Basel, Zurich, Geneva, and Freiburg/Breisgau. She works at the University of Fribourg as a senior lecturer and research scholar, holds a PhD from the University of Basel—with a thesis entitled *Borders: Where Liberalism Reaches its Limits*—and was a visiting scholar at UC Berkeley. Her areas of special interest include: the history of modern Europe and its global contexts, (post-)colonialism, protest, migration, visual culture, and political theory.

Helena Flam, Fil.Kand. from Lunds Universitet, and PhD in sociology from Columbia University, has been Professor of Sociology at the University of Leipzig since 1993. She has published in the areas of social movements, emotions, and discrimination. She is a co-founder and a former convener of the European Research Network on Emotions affiliated with the European Sociological Association.

Yiannis Gabriel is Professor of Organizational Theory at the School of Management of Bath University. Previously, he held chairs at Imperial College and Royal Holloway, University of London. He has a PhD from the University of California, Berkeley. He is well known for his work on leadership, management learning, organizational storytelling and narratives, psychoanalytic studies of work, and the culture and politics of contemporary consumption. He is co-founder and co-ordinator of the Organizational Storytelling Seminar series.

Benno Gammerl is a post-doctoral researcher at the Max Planck Institute for Human Development, Center for the History of Emotions in Berlin.

His fields of interest range from comparative to oral history and from imperial formations to queer settings. He is currently working on homosexuality and emotional life in rural West Germany 1960–90.

Deborah Gould was involved in ACT UP for many years, as well as the Chicago activist group, Queer to the Left; and is a founding member of the art/activism/research collaborative group, Feel Tank Chicago. She is Associate Professor of Sociology at the University of California, Santa Cruz. Her scholarly interests are contentious politics and political emotion. Her book, *Moving Politics: Emotion and ACT UP's Fight Against AIDS*, has won two awards.

Bettina Hitzer is a Minerva research group leader at the Max Planck Institute for Human Development, Center for the History of Emotions in Berlin. Her research focuses on the history of emotions, medical history, urban history, and religious history. Her current project examines the shifts of illness-induced body-fears, especially in the context of cancer.

Ishan Jalan is currently Assistant Professor at the Department of Management Learning and Leadership, Lancaster University Management School. He holds a PhD in Organization Studies from the University of Bath; and a post-doc from Lund University. Ishan is passionate about studying the dark side of organizational life. His research interests concern the various nuances of emotions at work; leadership studies; identity; and using psychoanalytic approaches to studying organizational life.

Claudia Jarzebowski is Assistant Professor of Early Modern History and the History of Emotions at the Free University, Berlin. Before this she was a senior lecturer in early modern history at the Free University, Berlin; and a Feodor Lynen Fellow at the University of Pennsylvania (Alexander von Humboldt Foundation). She is a partner investigator of the Center of Excellence for the History of Emotions (Australian Research Council, University of Western Australia/Perth). Her PhD was entitled *Incest. Kinship and Sexuality in the 18th Century*. She is currently doing research for a book, *Childhood and Emotion, 1450–1700.*

Tamar Katriel is Professor of Communication and Education at the University of Haifa. She has authored the following books: *Talking Straight: Dugri Speech in Israeli Sabra Culture* (1986); *Communal Webs: Communication and Culture in Contemporary Israel* (1991); *Performing the Past: A Study of Israeli Settlement Museums* (1997); *Dialogic Moments: From Soul Talks to Talk Radio in Israeli Culture* (2004). Her recent research centers on grassroots activism in the Israeli context.

Jochen Kleres holds a PhD in sociology from the University of Leipzig, Germany. His dissertation was on dissolution processes in AIDS organizations. He was a research assistant in a comparative EU project on institutional discrimination against migrants. He is currently a post-doctoral researcher at the University of Gothenburg, Sweden, and serves as a convener of the Emotions Network within the ESA. His fields of interests are social movements, NGOs and civil society, AIDS, migration, and the role of emotions in these fields.

Helmut Kuzmics was Professor of Sociology at the University of Graz, Austria, until his retirement in May 2013. He is a member of the ESA Research Network Sociology of Emotions. His research interests are: historical and comparative sociology, figurational sociology, fiction, and sociology.

Gada Mahrouse is Associate Professor at the Simone de Beauvoir Institute, Concordia University, Montreal, where she teaches and researches in the areas of critical race studies, cultural studies, transnational feminist, and post-colonial/decolonizing theories. She recently published a book entitled *Conflicted Commitments: Race, Privilege and Power in Transnational Solidarity Activism*, which focuses on the challenges of solidarity across asymmetrical power relations (McGill-Queens University Press, 2014).

Alberto Martín Pérez is Assistant Professor in the Department of Sociology and Analysis of Organizations of the University of Barcelona. He holds a PhD in sociology from the Ecole des Hautes Etudes en Sciences Sociales of Paris, and has been post-doctoral Fellow at the Institute of Public Goods and Policies of the Spanish National Research Council (CSIC). His current research centers on the access of immigrants and full citizens to welfare provision and public services. He is mostly interested in the social construction of citizenship in contemporary democratic societies.

Jean Nizet is a philosopher and sociologist, and is Professor at the University of Namur and the University of Louvain. His main research themes are the sociology of organizations, human resource management, adult aducation, and, with Denise Van Dam, organic farmers. He has published several books and articles on these topics.

Jocelyn Pixley is currently Honorary Professor in Sociology at Macquarie University, Sydney; and Professorial Research Fellow at the Global Policy Institute, London Metropolitan University. Her research includes emotions in the financial world, which she has been investigating empirically for years.

Cristina Soriano is senior researcher at the Swiss Center for Affective Sciences of the University of Geneva, Switzerland. She studied English philology at the University of Murcia (Spain), where she also obtained a PhD in linguistics. She further studied at Hamburg University and the University of California, Berkeley, where she specialized in cognitive linguistics. She conducts interdisciplinary research on cross-cultural emotion semantics, the metaphorical representation of concepts (including experimental research), and the affective meaning of color.

Sylvia Terpe is a sociologist and post-doctoral Research Fellow at the Max Planck Institute for Social Anthropology in Halle, Germany. Her main research interest is in the sociology of morality and values, in particular regarding the role of emotions in morality; as well as morality and values in bureaucratic settings, in the economic sphere and in business firms.

Denise Van Dam is a psychologist and sociologist and works as Assistant Professor at the University of Namur. Her research interests include organic farming, social movements, professional practice, and qualitative methodology. She has set up several interdisciplinary research projects about organic farming in different regions of France, and in Belgium.

Dunya Van Troost is a PhD candidate at the VU-University, Amsterdam. Her dissertation, *The Emotional Side of the Appeal*, explores how demonstrators express emotions on the issue they are protesting about, and how these vary and originate in the socio-political factors that surround demonstrations. This research is part of a collaborative project "Caught in the Act of Protest: Contextualizing Contestation" (see: www.protest-survey.eu). She holds master's degrees in political science and social psychology from Leiden University.

Eda Ulus is a senior lecturer in organization studies in the Bristol Leadership Centre, Bristol Business School. Her research interests include workplace emotions, narrative methods, psychoanalytic approaches, learning, gender, race, and social justice. Eda immensely enjoys fieldwork, particularly meeting with individuals and learning about their work experiences. She has published in *Organization* and is currently working with Inge Aben (on a grant awarded by the *British Academy of Management*) to study introversion in learning and management. At the time of publication she was due to take up a position at Leicester University.

Jenny Weggen is a PhD candidate at the Institute for Sociology of the University of Hamburg. Her research deals with emotions in organizations, especially third sector organizations. Her research interests include the sociology of emotions, organizational theories, methods of qualitative social research, and the sociology of religion. She is a member of the Hamburger Forschungswerkstatt, and spent a research period at the University of Queensland Business School in Brisbane, Australia.

Åsa Wettergren is Assistant Professor at the Department of Sociology, University of Gothenburg. She has published pieces on the topic of humor and irony in culture jamming, and emotions in social movements generally; emotions in migration; bureaucratic emotions; and emotions in politics. After having completed a project on the credibility assessments of asylum seekers to Sweden, she currently directs (together with Stina Bergman Blix) a project on lawyers and emotions.

Michalinos Zembylas is Associate Professor of Education at the Open University of Cyprus. His research interests are in the areas of educational philosophy and curriculum theory, and his work focuses on exploring the role of emotion and affect in curriculum and pedagogy. He is particularly interested in how affective politics intersect with issues of social justice pedagogies, intercultural and peace education, and citizenship education.

Preface

Jochen Kleres

The sociology of emotions looks back on more than 30 years of history. It has experienced exponential growth as a research field in recent years (see overviews in, for example, Flam 2002; Turner and Stets 2006). Parallel advances in psychology, philosophy, history management, and other fields have produced a broad range of substantive knowledge about emotions (Greco and Stenner 2008). As compelling as some of the approaches in sociology, management, and history are, they do not offer much on methods, leaving practitioners and converts restless.

To date, the "emotional turn" has been unaccompanied by explicit methodological debates. This disregard of methodological issues has produced a significant gap in how to expand our knowledge about emotions. At the same time, there is a burgeoning interest in methods. Conference sessions on methodology enjoy much attention, while reviewers call for methodological reflection. The aim of this volume is to address this tangible demand.

This groundbreaking book raises, as the first of its kind, the question of how to do empirical research on emotions using sociological, historical, linguistic, ethnographic, psychological, and mixed approaches. It not only brings together emerging lines of inquiry. It also lays foundations for the methods field and its takeoff. It presents both fairly standard qualitative methods fine-tuned to deal with emotions, as well as a number of methodological innovations, often embedded in the critique of the standard methods. Moreover, a couple of the contributions discuss quantitative methods that help to unearth and explore emotions.

The contributors in this volume briefly report on the how-to aspects of doing research, and illustrate it richly with examples and anecdotes. They discuss how to bring emotions into relief—relying on visuals; various types of interviews; participant and non-participant (ethnographic) observation; metaphors and emotion words, conversations, discourses, narrative, and literary text analysis; and self-observation.

Contributions in this volume cover a wide range of methodological issues: one of them being the problem of bringing emotions into relief, given their often low visibility and the fact that their expression may be socially discouraged or tabooed. This includes emotions experienced by the researcher. Finding emotions is another central issue relating to both data collection and analysis: how does one identify, collect, sort, and interpret material on emotions?

Contributors explore this by using a range of standard and innovative approaches. The chapters also demonstrate that classical investigative methods are in fact themselves rife with emotions. The research process itself is emotionally structured since research subjects and researchers interact through their emotions. While standard methodologies call for value neutrality and scientific rationality, arguing for the necessity to neutralize or void emotions, the chapters in this volume show that this is not only unrealistic but that the emotional dimension of doing research offers tremendous heuristic potential. Emotions can help develop new insights and even devise new methods, thus pushing research projects forward. Importantly, this argument extends to the emotions of the researcher as well. While emotions can block research too, the pertinent issue is when and how to reflect on the emerging emotions in order to let them make research more constructive.

The present volume is an outcome of the publication efforts of the Research Network Sociology of Emotions affiliated with the European Sociological Association. It adds a novel research focus to an entire range of publication topics covered by the network thus far. These have addressed emotions in theorizing (Hopkins *et al.* 2009), organizations (Sieben and Wettergren 2010), friendship (Holmes and Greco 2011), finance (Pixley 2012), power (Flam and Heaney 2013), politics (Demertzis 2013), and the internet (Benski and Fisher 2013). This very broad range of research foci aptly testifies to the high relevance of emotions to all spheres of social life, as well as to the fundamental significance of emotions to sociology at large. By offering the reader an answer to how-to questions, we hope to make the exploration of emotions even more enticing.

References

Benski, T. and E. Fisher (eds). 2013. *Internet and Emotions.* New York: Routledge.

Demertzis, N. (ed.). 2013. *Emotions in Politics: The Affect Dimension in Political Tension.* Basingstoke, New York: Palgrave Macmillan.

Flam, H. 2002. *Soziologie der Emotionen. Eine Einführung.* Konstanz: UVK Verlagsgesellschaft (UTB für Wissenschaft).

Flam, H. and J. G. Heaney (eds). 2013. *Journal of Political Power*, special issue on "Power and Emotion," 6 (3).

Greco, M. and P. Stenner (eds). 2008. *Emotions: A Social Science Reader.* London, New York: Routledge.

Holmes, M. and S. Greco (eds). 2011. *Sociological Research Online*, special issue on "Friendship and Emotions," 16 (1).

Hopkins, D. R., J. Kleres, H. Flam, and H. Kuzmics (eds). 2009. *Theorizing Emotions: Sociological Explorations and Applications.* Frankfurt am Main, New York: Campus Verlag.

Pixley, J. (ed.). 2012. *New Perspectives on Emotions in Finance. The Sociology of Confidence, Fear and Betrayal.* New York: Routledge.

Sieben, B. and Å. Wettergren (eds). 2010. *Emotionalizing Organizations and Organizing Emotions.* Basingstoke: Palgrave Macmillan.

Turner, J. H. and J. E. Stets. 2006. "Sociological Theories of Human Emotions," *Annual Review of Sociology*, 32: 25–52.

Acknowledgments

Helena Flam would like to express her deep gratitude to Gerhard Boomgaarden for taking on an unusual book proposal. Also, thanks to Allie Hargreaves at Wearset for her expertise, efficiency, and generosity as project manager and Peter Kenyon for his great patience and skill in copyediting. They helped turn it into a wonderful book.

Chapter 1

Introduction

Methods of exploring emotions

Helena Flam

When I entered the world, monads were self-contained and autonomous. Economists often referred to monads in support of theoretical and methodological individualism. Today monads are social: scientists discovered that they communicate. They decide when to engage in exchange processes with their friends and in conflicts with their foes. When I entered the world, there were no homosexual giraffes and finance was neither sexy nor dangerous. Today homosexuality is a challenging fact. Deregulated finances both seduce and endanger—nations, enterprises and households.

Needless to say, the world has undergone massive changes in many other respects. My point merely is that today the world of "nature" as we know it, even the monads, question methodological individualism. They call for acknowledging diversity, sociality, and enmity. The world of finance both ignores borders and refutes methodological nationalism. Leaving individualist and nationalist methodologies behind, the contributors to this volume acknowledge sociality and diversity, not just in substance but also in methods. They offer exciting insights into how one generates methodological relationism and interactionism.

This volume explores human sociality and diversity through the specific prism of emotions. It posits human beings as inherently social, connected to each other and larger collectivities by innumerable feelings. It imagines societies as the criss-crossing of emotions webs. It differs from its predecessors in its methodological focus and its objective to demonstrate—even to the skeptics—that emotions are in fact researchable: one only needs to push standard investigative methods beyond their current limits. This entails forcing the usual research instruments, such as observation, interview, survey, text, or visual analysis, to adapt to new research questions, so as to yield new, "emotion data."

Even researchers not interested in emotions per se might find this collection interesting. The volume consists of entrancing short essays, richly illustrated with examples and anecdotes, that provide basic knowledge about how to pursue emotions. The contributors are respectful of those being researched and are mindful of the effects of their own feelings on the conclusions. They also share with the readers how it feels to do research by recalling their moments of joy, sorrow, disappointment, and fear. The book thus touches upon the ethics and emotional experience of research in vivid first person accounts.

A few contributors to this volume recount how they joined the ranks of those who forsook standard positivist precepts of how to approach the interview persons (IPs) and data. They revive their very first realization that not only face-to-face bodily and verbal communication—but also potent, yet unacknowledged, individual and circulating, emotions—played a key role in the encounters they observed between public servants and their clients (Martín Pérez); the interviews they conducted with organic farmers (Van Dam and Nizet); or, finally, responses to a questionnaire concerned with how the privileged people of the North negotiated their power positions during visits to the South (Mahrouse). They also describe the methods they generated to catch the dynamics of their own and others' emotions as these developed during the encounters in which they participated. Other contributors tell of how their own unacknowledged expectations interfered with the autobiographic, narrative interview about emotions (Gammerl), or caused deep prolonged upset—stopping the process of document analysis in which they were engaged (Gould). Their argument is that only once acknowledged and critically reflected upon do emotions help generate new substantive insights and a new mix of—even innovations in—investigative methods.

Most contributors in this volume go well beyond reporting hitherto unacknowledged fieldwork-related emotions, or pinpointing their innovative, research-enriching potential. They share their knowledge about, and experiences of, how to go about observing, interviewing and surveying, visual- or text-reading emotions. Each chapter includes a brief statement describing the research goals, or a specific research project for which the emotion-exploring instruments presented in the text were developed and employed. This volume testifies, and is dedicated to, very diverse ways of pursuing emotions, without claiming that it is exhaustive. In personalized accounts the contributions show that explicating emotions makes for more reflective and more ethical—and simply better—research.

Most authors in this volume are explicit about their definitions of emotions, and the methodological issues which follow. This applies particularly strongly to the first part of the volume in which experts in the sociology of literature (Kuzmics), contributors to the "narrative turn" in the studies of work organizations (Czarniawska; Gabriel and Ulus), pioneers in linguistic ethnography (Katriel) or bottom-up elite studies (Pixley), present their approaches to the study of emotions.

Three contributions to this volume address the issue of status and power differentials between IPs and their interviewer. While one study looks at top-down interviewing, in which the IPs have less status and power than the interviewer (Wettergren) and about which a fair amount has already been written, two others discuss bottom-up interviews in which researchers have lesser status, power and knowledge than the IPs (Kleres; Pixley).

Although the volume has a clear qualitative profile, it nevertheless includes two contributions on surveying emotions. These discuss procedures that facilitate the application of quantitative methods in the study of emotions. The first contribution addresses the question of how to combine a survey with narratives about emotions. It argues for moving between—for example—emotional averages and the semantics of individual feelings, to generate potent data interpretations; and offers rich advice on how to quantize qualitative and qualiticize quantitative data (see Terpe's Q&Q of emotions). Another contribution engages in a critical extension of the burgeoning research on protest emotions (Van Troost). It reveals that missing data on emotions are patterned—explained by socio-demographic factors as well as nationality. It makes a good case for including more questions about emotions in the surveys.

This collection emerged from the growing interest in taking stock of the extant working methods within the Emotions Network affiliated with the European Sociological Association—which includes a fair number of ethnographers, historians, linguists, and psychologists, as well as Argentinian, Australian, Canadian, Israeli, and US scholars. It also constitutes an attempt to respond to the skeptics who commented that our theoretical books on emotions are interesting, but who challenged us to show how one actually does research on emotions.

It is worthwhile to stop to comment on the specific verbs and expressions that various contributors to this volume tested, played around with, rejected, and in the end adopted, to depict what they do to, or with, emotions, while engaging in research. Among these verbs we find, for example: acknowledging, pursuing, eliciting, releasing, unearthing, unveiling, explicating, exploring, or dissecting emotions; as well as collecting, surveying, and categorizing emotion data. This act of trying out, or playing around with, verbs and expressions—and the verbs themselves—communicate some uncertainty about what it means to do research on emotions, on the one hand, and, on the other, whether we merely acknowledge and explicate or in fact prompt and press our "objects of study" to reveal their emotions. The verbs depicting our practices are themselves borrowed from medicine, mining, cartography, chemistry, and rhetoric, thus implying that we see emotions akin to body parts—substances to be examined, extracted, or dissected, gases to be released, mines or landscapes to be explored or surveyed, and texts to be analyzed or interpreted. Seen from this point of view our own roles appear akin to those of doctors, miners, topographers, chemists, or (political) philosophers. The verbs and professions reveal a clear bias towards the normal science that marks our own efforts, even though we aim at leaving it behind. Indeed, the researchers in this volume do their best to collect and make sense of the emotion data they collect. As this volume shows, together we acknowledge, unearth, explicate and much more—each author taking a slightly different position on how to define, and thus how to do, research on emotions.

Matching approaches with methods of exploring emotions

Although the texts in this volume are grouped by the methodological instruments used to address emotions, this introduction aligns these texts according to their epistemology and ontology. It takes on the task of presenting a few well-known approaches to emotions in order to match them with the methodological instruments on which they rely or which they imply.

The view that emotions are at the center of human sociality—and therefore deserve to command our attention—is central to this volume. It is a view that defies positivism and behaviorism—the hard currency of the social and behavioral sciences—which claim that only observable, measurable, and unambiguous phenomena can and should be subject to scientific investigation. To behaviorists, inner states cannot be observed or measured, and therefore should be left alone—best treated as the black box.

The shared position of departure of this volume is indeed that the role of the researcher is to take note of emotional expressions, treating them initially at face value, as data. However, the contributors part ways as soon as they have agreed that specific bodily expressions, utterances, or images, inform about emotions. Some take the view that, in principle, emotions have a physical, expressive, and cognitive dimension (Kuzmics). Even though not all three are accessible or visible to an outsider—leaving room for interpretation—it is possible and necessary to zoom in on, interpret, and contextualize interacting individuals and their emotions in order to develop or refine specific theses. Others take the position that experienced emotions are irrelevant, while emotional expressions per se are equally or less important than what those co-present make of them—how they are interpreted is crucial for the definition of the situation (Czarniawska; Eksner). Yet others, in contrast, argue that the capacity to express compelling emotions is far from easy—almost impossible in fact—if the expression is not underpinned by the "right" emotions. In fact, only when an emotional constellation is "true to itself" can an individual put on a convincing performance and those co-present have little choice but to accept this performance at its face value (Bergman Blix).

A pioneering sociologist of emotions, Arlie Hochschild (1979: 557–8), dubbed mere emotional expression, "surface acting." Stress on emotional expression had been focal in Goffman's (1967) earlier dramaturgical approach. She, however, wished to probe deeper. Hochschild explored attempts to align feelings with the expected emotional expression, thereby bringing into relief the efforts at "deep acting" or "emotions management" for the sake of conformity. Hochschild argued, and proved via empirical research, that individuals are, in principle, capable of making a distinction between what they feel and what they *should* feel, even though capitalist management and traditional gender ideologies undermine this capacity. Responding directly to Hochschild's theses, Bogner and Wouters (1990) pinpointed that it was not capitalism but much older "Eliasian" civilization processes that called for emotions management. This centuries-long emotions management made it impossible to posit any clear-cut difference between "authentic," subjective feelings, and the prescribed emotions.

The position that it is possible to diagnose one's own "authentic" feelings is countered from one more perspective that holds that emotions are inherently ambivalent. Not only do feeling rules often call for what one does not feel—a cause of much tension and short-circuited reflection patterns (Flam 2008; 2010). To make the situation more complex, emotions run in groups and their shapes are nebulous. This leaves much room for guesswork and interpretation—in real life as well as in research—for working out for oneself and for others which emotions should become operative (Gould; Flam). On the part of researchers, this calls for openness and attention to this very multilayered and multivalent ambivalence and, when necessary, for specifying the conditions under which it becomes reduced (Mahrouse; Gould 2009). Finally, those interested in proscribed or taboo emotions show that these can be released by methodological subterfuge (Gabriel and Ulus; Jalan; Pixley) or, alternatively, offered by or deciphered via narratives (Flam; Kleres; Gammerl; Terpe).

To locate the contributions of this volume in a larger field of research on emotions, and to pay heed to the fact that quite a few contributions to this volume report on participant or non-participant observations, let me start by positioning them in relation to two contrasting approaches in ethnography. Burawoy's (2003) prescription for "reflexive ethnography" will stand here for a "standard" approach to theoretically informed field research. In contrast, Taylor and Rupp's (2005) discussion of some central issues posed by ethnography will illustrate its "feminist-queer" variant. Together they demarcate the contours of the field of ethnographic research.

Observing emotions

Burawoy's critical review of his own, as well as many other well-known sociological and ethnographic studies—most of which entailed participant observation—serves to buttress a twofold claim about what constitutes rigorous ethnographic research. From a constructivist perspective, he calls for much more reflection about the limiting and distorting effects of one's own embodied participation[1] in the field, as well as one's own theoretical lenses on the research outcomes. From a realist perspective, he calls for research not only focusing on the "internal" processes of change, but also on the "external" forces of change in which the "internal" processes are embedded and which they necessarily reflect.

Of immediate relevance here is that he hardly pays any attention to emotions. When considering how his own theoretical lenses influenced what he saw during his doctoral research on factory work regimes, he admits that he "was guilty of reifying 'external forces' "; and, in a by-the-way fashion when discussing his findings, refers to both workers' fears underwriting their games with management, and the distinction he made between industrial relations generating either hostility or amicability (Burawoy 2003: 651, 654). Apart from these and two other scattered remarks,[2] in Burawoy's 34 pages of text emotions—even his own feelings of guilt—are a sleeping beauty. He mentions that he did not notice, and therefore did not reflect upon, the fact that his fellow workers were black. Arguably, not only his Marxist lens—but also his emotionally intense dream of "interracial solidarity"—kept him both color- and tension-blind.

Burawoy argues for "standard" research methods, relying on systematic, intensive observations, and communication. He vehemently rejects ethnography focused on the inner worlds. He not only rejects dialogic ethnography—which "reduces everything to the mutual orbiting of [a single] participant and [a single] observer," and makes four dimensions of his own prescription for "reflexive ethnography" fold "into an auto-centric relation of ethnographer to the world"—he also clearly positions himself against the "cultural turn" in anthropology in which it "becomes a mesmeric play of texts upon texts, narratives within narratives" (Burawoy 2003: 674). I take this to mean that he would not even take a look at Denzin's *Interpretive Ethnography*.[3]

Taylor and Rupp's (2005) feminist-queer ethnography, in contrast, focuses explicitly on the question of how gender, sexuality, and power differentials affect field research. Both authors have become known, among others, for their research on emotions in diverse social movements. Yet reflections on the role of emotions in participatory observation are absent from their 24-page text, and emotion words appear as seldom as in Burawoy's text. The most striking are the pages reporting the power "negotiations" between the researchers and the drag queens they studied. In detail, Taylor and Rupp describe what to many would be humiliating and angering provocations to which their "study objects" resorted. In reading the text I admired the authors' willingness to share the painful anecdotes—but at the same time wondered if and how they reflected and felt about "having to accept" unwanted touches, groping, and slaps, or their breasts suddenly exposed on stage. The text says that the researchers, as feminists, would never allow other men to engage in such expressions of male dominance, but that "[w]ithout quite knowing it, we accepted these actions as part of a leveling process, even though they also made us angry" (Taylor and Rupp 2005: 2123).[4] The text does not pose or answer the question of why they did not decide to stop the research project, or negotiate—again and again—their power position with the actors they studied. Reading the text I felt embarrassed, humiliated, frustrated, and aggravated, and wondered whether they did too. Was it—as in Burawoy's case—a falsely understood sense of solidarity that kept them going? A deep devotion to social science? Or was it anxiety about having one's professional reputation tainted if the project was abandoned? Was keeping feelings of anger unacknowledged or undiscussed a way of avoiding exploring these possibilities and thus the difficult compromises?

As just shown, in both the texts which discuss ethnographic research, there was no explicit link made between the method and the fieldwork emotions. In contrast, several contributors to this volume have as an explicit goal to be inquisitive and critical about one's own and others' emotions in the field. Yet their approaches vary greatly—some equate emotional expression with emotion, while others see it as mere performance of "justificatory emotions"; some argue that bodies in space co-determine emotions, while others, in contrast, show that emotions move and position bodies in space; a final group struggles with accessing taboo emotions.

Emotional expression and emotions

Several contributors take the position that knowledge about the observed emotions can be derived by closely observing one's own feelings in relation to others, feeling the emotions of others and, finally, co-feeling with others when collective emotions emerge (Bernard; Bergman Blix; Wettergren). Czarniawska's position is that observing emotional expressions and emotion attribution—that is, how the co-present interpret the emotional expressions of others—is necessary and sufficient. One's own emotions or views on displayed emotions are irrelevant.

However, both these positions admit the possibility of narrowness, or even error, in the researcher's own interpretation. To minimize these, they recommend engaging in comparisons across cases and settings, consulting practitioners in (and experts on) the particular research field, or drawing on popular art, and, finally, relating the findings to the pertinent theories of emotions if these are available. This research program does not privilege theory-derived value- and emotion-free systematic observation as the only source of scientific knowledge, but instead recognizes that different types of actors with their different positioning in and outside a research field possess insights into, experience of, and theories about emotions that are essential to the generation of scientific knowledge.

Depending on the research question, different investigative strategies can be employed and observations collected with more or less rigor. So, for example, Van Dam and Nizet while conducting—as they come to realize—very emotionalized interviews with farmers about their conversions from regular to organic agriculture, decide to supplement these with observations of emotion data. For this purpose they develop a coding sheet to note down emotional expressions of all participants involved in the interview. Bernard, who is interested in the rituals, their participants, phases, and their emotional determinants, strictly follows the call of normal science for systematic, meticulous observational notes and careful analysis. He engages in a two-year participatory ethnographic research project in the same setting, taking copious notes in his diary. Step by step, he develops categories to systematically capture his own feelings, and the feelings of different—lay and professional—participating actors; carefully noting disparate markers of key emotions they display during various sequences of a shared ritual. Wettergren and Czarniawska identify power differentials and expressions of humiliation as a key issue. Wettergren stays a few months in the same setting, so she is able to compare similar situations/instances of it in this setting, over time. Moreover, she "checks" her observations against what the participants in the research field tell her in the interviews, against related observations made in other settings in similar situations and against pertinent theorizing. Czarniawska, having accidentally witnessed a puzzling scene and defined it as her additional research preoccupation, remains on alert, looking for more such scenes, where and when they develop. In analyzing and framing her findings she draws on scientific theories as well as popular art.

In all these cases one's everyday lay knowledge about emotional expressions helps note, select, and interpret what one considers as research-relevant data. But this lay knowledge is played out against theory, the knowledge of the regular participants in the field, and/or those who possess expert knowledge about—or special insights into—this field. Thus, the emerging research-based knowledge about the emotional expressions of the participants in the field acquires inter-subjective elements, yet is offered from a unique vantage point—that of a knowledge-amassing and knowledge-sifting researcher.

With one notable exception, the basic assumption of this research is that for the most part the observed emotional expressions correspond to specific inner emotional states, and that bodily and symbolic communication, if subject to careful, systematic, analysis, can pry open the black box, throwing light on how minds, emotions, and bodies work—often, although not always, in unison. Specific theories behind this assumption may vary, but they all heed culture and its capacity to bring individuals to adopt specific ways of feeling, expressing, and interpreting emotions.

Staging and performing emotions

Goffman's (1967) dramaturgical approach suggests that we should not make such a straightforward assumption. We should not be so naïve as to take appearances for reality. The dramaturgical approach cautions us against equating specific emotional expressions with the corresponding individual feelings. It proposes instead that we all stage and put on performances in our everyday encounters with others, following fairly standard scripts. People play-act for a great number of reasons: to avoid embarrassment of losing "face," to prove their social competence or good will, to pursue their strategic goals, or to avoid the abyss resulting from interaction breakdowns. Most of all, by relying on "impression management," they wish to impose a specific conception of their selves on others. As the father of ethnomethodology, Harold Garfinkel (1967)[5] simultaneously pointed out, it takes a lot of training and an intricate, sustained performance to credibly establish oneself in a social role. His study of "Agnes"—a transgender person who had been brought up as a boy but aspired to learn the minutiae of staging a compelling performance as a woman—gave rise to the much used concept of "doing gender" (Kessler and McKenna 1978; West and Zimmermann 1987). Following the example of Judith Butler (1990), other authors in the fields of critical philosophy, and literary, cultural, gender, and race studies, have taken to exposing the oppressive aspects of discourses (performativity) and practices (performances) that press human beings into preset heterosexual social categories of class, gender, and "race." They share with Goffman's dramaturgic and Garfinkel's ethnomethodological approach the view that there is a principle disjuncture between the self-reducing performance of social roles and the multifarious "true" self. From this it follows that we should assess and interpret performances without drawing overconfident conclusions about the attendant "true" feelings.

Seen from this perspective, Czarniawska's research agenda follows a mixed behaviorist-"attributive" approach: behaviorist when she asserts that the human mind is a black box, and attributive when she consents to accept that only when the observers following a familiar script assign specific attributes to the performance and the performer(s), does it/do these acquire a specific substance (see Kessler and McKenna 1978). If the observers see an enacted power differential effecting humiliation, then it has to be understood as such, irrespective of what performers actually feel. A researcher cannot know what a woman shedding a tear, or blushing, actually feels. Nor whether the boss who has just reprimanded her in public actually feels anger or contempt. However, by looking at the reactions of the witnesses a researcher can conclude that the performance was understood as an angry staging of power, resulting in a teary public humiliation (for a contrasting "interactive" approach to performance, see West and Zimmerman 1987; 1995).

Eksner's study of Turkish-German boys' "angry talk" seems to fit, yet questions this particular version of the dramaturgical, performance-stressing approach. It reveals that the boys resort to an assertive mode of speaking that is meant to confirm their definition of masculinity and to evoke fear, when, for example, engaging in territorial disputes with their German peers. What is put on, however, comes across as authentic anger—in the context of racialized German discourses concerning the need for discipline and control of Turkish juvenile aggression. Importantly, this contribution posits the disjuncture between the intentions behind a performance and the reading of this performance, as a research and social problem.

Similarly, the Israeli soldiers that Katriel studies stage "authenticity" when they prepare the set and the props for the videos in which they quietly speak about the feelings of humiliation and helplessness they witness and experience as soldiers tasked with disciplining and fighting Palestinians. These emotions serve as weapons aimed at the Israeli state, the army, and their parents' generation, all of whom, in their view, wage an unjust, unfair, even criminal, war. The Turkish-German boys' displays of anger fit with their own culture of masculine assertion, but not with the peaceful self-image of the larger German society in which they live. The Israeli soldiers' display of "defeatist" emotions, and their seeming lack of blinding patriotic love, clearly challenge the ideal of an Israeli citizen-soldier, as well as the militarized status quo.

Strangely enough, there is a deep connection between the Israeli soldiers and Sweden's Queen Christina. Both seem to reveal their innermost personal secrets when they speak of their own vulnerability and pain. But—as Katriel and Jarzebowski show—these involve staged performativity. The purpose of engaging "justificatory emotions" is to legitimize highly unusual, illegitimate, or even illegal courses of action. Jarzebowski tells us to read the pages of Christina's memoir as a performance in a staged drama in which the language of extraordinarily intense emotions, and prescient tears, serves the purpose of justifying her highly unorthodox ascent to the Swedish throne and her subsequent—until the present day much-debated—decision to abdicate, leave the Protestant Church, and become a Catholic.

The labor emotions do in space

In contrast to this performative view on emotions, Bergman Blix argues that a compelling performance cannot take place until the multi-layered emotions true to the situation, relationship, and context, underpin it (see also Kuzmics). Reflecting in particular upon the English librettist William Gilbert (of Gilbert and Sullivan), and his practice of "blocking" during rehearsals, Bergman Blix (2010: 77–80) asks how the setting, positioning, distance, and the movements of the bodies in relationship to each other affect how each individual, separately and in interaction with others, feels. In paying attention to how bodies moving or blocking each other in space enable a convincing sliding in and expression of specific emotions, her research program reverses that developed by Sara Ahmed (2004)—only Bergman Blix's "moving bodies" not only feel or talk, but also reflect upon and contextualize their mutual emotions and relations.

A major advocate of attention to emotions in critical cultural and race/gender studies, Ahmed (2004) is interested in exploring what emotions do. In her approach to the world, it is not so much actors or discourses that perform, but rather emotion words. In *The Cultural Politics of Emotions* (2004), she focuses on selected emotions to explicate their singular logics and implications. Her argument (2004: 13) is that "[t]he replacement of one word for an emotion with another word produces a narrative. Our love might create the condition for our grief, our [envisioned] loss could become the condition for our hate." The emotions linked in this way, along with the narratives of causation they imply or explicate, become attached and stick to specific groups/figures or objects, bringing into relief their contours while designating them as friends or foes. Hers is an investigation of power relations via the prism of emotions and bodies. The bodies which become designated as loved, become objects of love, while those which become designated as disgusting or hateful, become objects of disgust and hate.[6]

This is borne out by Zembylas' contribution. In contrast to Ahmed, who at times reifies emotions to the point that it seems they do all the work, Zembylas' chapter clearly posits elite actors and their top-down racist public discourses as a cause of how members of a society think, feel, and talk about—as well as position their bodies in relationship to—each other. His field notes evoke a class break during which a Turkish-Cypriot girl cautiously approaches a small group of Greek-Cypriot girls who abruptly tell her to leave; his interview with the class teacher confirms that this is a standard in the lower grades; and a conversation with some pupils from this class reveals that Greek-Cypriot children wish to keep the Turkish-Cypriot children at a distance because they think of them as Black/black, dirty, and disgusting. The Turkish-Cypriot children, in turn, either tentatively—or violently—attempt to cross the invisible borders generated by disgust. Using triangulation as a method—highlighting a phenomenon using at least two different research instruments—Zembylas "proves" that in the lower school grades, disgust establishes and enforces apartheid.

Zeroing in on taboo emotions

Criticizing Goffman's dramaturgical approach for its programmatic—but as I show (Flam 2009), not actual—unwillingness to dwell upon what people really feel, Hochschild (1979) introduced the distinction between the displayed emotions corresponding to the societal norms about emotions, and individual feelings. The norms about emotions she names "feeling rules," and insists that capitalists, managers, male-dominated culture, as well as the women's movement are their architects. Feeling rules tell us what to feel, when to feel it, and with what intensity and duration. Similarly, Reddy (1997; 1999) introduced the concept of the "emotional regime," with political-cultural elites as its architects. He emphasized that those suffering under such a regime might seek emotional refuge and develop their own dissenting emotional cultures. James Scott (1990) stressed the difference between the oppressive, surface, official political culture, and the hidden scripts of the oppressed which harbor pent-up explosive anger.

They all focused on the difference between the imposed, prescribed, obligatory, displayed emotions, and the actually felt feelings. These they defined as unfit for the occasion in the eyes of the power-holders—and therefore taboo. In contrast—as the Freudian version has it—banned or taboo "dark" affects express basic drives, potentially threatening the very foundations of a social order. They therefore become repressed by social institutions, turning un- or subconscious.

Hochschild (1979; 1983) has opted against doing research on affect in Freud's sense of the word.[7] She was instead interested in the individual feelings unfit for the occasion, but ones which individuals are quite aware of and can communicate about. Her research showed that more often than not individuals are willing to generate expected feelings, while putting aside what they really feel, either because they do not want to lose their jobs or upset the people they love. On important issues, however, when emotions management acquires permanency, this happens at the cost of pent-up, random bouts of seemingly uncalled for intense anger (see, for example, Hochschild 1989: 35–61) akin to Freud's affect.

Drawing explicitly on the psychoanalytical perspective, various authors pick up on the idea that societies, with their regulatory institutions, suppress a great number of affects. These taboo affects remain beyond conscious control and thus cannot be managed easily, or even at all. They seep out in seemingly unrelated contexts, often resulting in acts of destruction (Shepherdson 2008). In particular, damaging, oppressive, and totalitarian institutions take—or enable the taking of—command of taboo affect to release it at the designated targets (Bird 2007). To Bird (2003), Ahmed (2004), and Berlant (2011)—critical literary, cultural, and gender and "race" scholars—the challenge is to show in meticulous text or in film analyses how affect generated by these institutions interacts with values and norms prescribed by the dominant political culture embedded in nationalism, consumerism, fascism, or the neoliberal capitalist economy. They argue that the affect interacting with the embedded cultural *desiderata* generates unrealizable, and thus self-destructive, attachments that imprison the self. Even if the protagonists try to break free by critical reflection, or through unusual engagements, or seek distantiation in humor and satire, they hang suspended in the cage. Others bang their heads against its walls (Ahmed 2014). Most are in pain.

Some instruments designed for empirical social research help to reveal this pain. They achieve the articulation of proscribed emotions and affects. In contrast to focus group interviews (Frith and Kitzinger 1998; but see also Gabriel and Ulus), autobiographic narrative interviews—as well as scenarios, metaphors and (un)solicited anecdotes (Gabriel and Ulus; Jalan)—are well suited for this purpose, although of course fiction and poetry can be engaged as well (Elias 1982; Kuzmics).

Earlier autobiographic narrative interviews have been used, for example, to address emotions felt by different types of Austrians when their country was first annexed by Germany and later liberated by the Allies (Ziegler and Kannonier-Finster 1991); or to highlight regime-related fears and anxieties in socialist Poland and Germany before 1990 (Flam 1998). Since autobiographic narrative interviews put IPs under pressure to tell an intelligible, compelling, and detailed story within a short period of time (Schütze 1982, 1983), as an interview type they prompt Freudian slips, self-contradictions, speech and story disruptions, revealing metaphors, and even lies, when unfit or taboo affect/topics/emotions threaten to surface (Ziegler and Kannonier-Finster 1991). Inner dialogues reproduced in these interviews reveal much about the inner struggles between the prescribed and proscribed moral principles and emotions (Flam 1998). Moreover, as Kleres (2011) argues, emotions of the person as expressed in an autobiographical narrative can be read by inspecting the pacing and segments of the narrative, as well as by zooming in on the choice of expressions, words, and sentences used to convey one's experience. When properly contextualized, they can disclose much about the shifting pressures to adopt specific emotional styles (Gammerl 2009, 2012).

Autobiographic narrative interviews offer much valuable insight into the contextualized symbolic worlds, orientation patterns, and emotion-laden expectations of the IPs. They tell whether, how, and why these changed as a result of their lived—reflected and felt—experiences. The well-known shortcoming of this type of interview is that the single opening, life-story triggering question, in allowing the individual narrators plenty of time and space in which to assert their individuality by reliving and telling their life stories, deprives the interviewer of any control— thus generating much material which upon closer analysis might turn out to be simply irrelevant.

The introspective interview method presented here by Burkhart and Weggen combines an individual with a group interview. It does not offer a comparable narrative luxury to single individuals. They are instead offered

Table 1.1 Approaches and research methods for exploring emotions

(Unorthodox) positivist-expressionist dramaturgical	Observing/noting which emotions an actor expresses, treating expression as emotion data (observation logs and text/visual analysis, categorizing, "checking" against expert opinions, fiction, theory).
Attributionist dramaturgical	Observing/noting which emotions are attributed to an actor/actors/by other actors (observation logs and text/visual analysis, categorizing, "checking" against expert opinions, fiction, theory).
Interactionist dramaturgical	Observing/noting which emotions are expressed and attributed by actors to each other, noting one's own concurrent emotions, as well as when relevant circulating and shared emotions emerge (observation logs or text/visual analysis, supplemented by interviews and documents, and compared to expert opinions, other settings, fiction, theorizing).
Emotional regime: feeling rules, costs of conforming, departing	Triangulation to reveal the obligatory feeling rules, paying attention to how they position and shape bodies in space as well as to the (embodied, emotional) costs of departing from the feeling rules, and the potential suffering caused by trying to conform to them (for example, painful emotions management or somatic and psychic disorders); not forgetting "justificatory emotions" or "escapist emotions" legitimating (individual and collective) departures from the prescribed feeling rules.
Emotional ambivalence	Triangulation, and, when possible, "checking" against theory to tease out under which conditions ambivalent emotions are generated and transformed, and some become dominant—starting by looking for emotional exaggeration, denotative hesitancy, mixed metaphors, irony, the Janus face of each emotion (see also taboo emotions and affect).
Taboo emotions and affect	Eliciting responses to scenarios, vignettes, metaphors, anecdotes; asking for examples of (day)dreaming; relying on autobiographic narrative interviews and even carefully designed introspective focus group and expert interviews; fiction, poetry, etc.; in the text analysis looking for (dramatic, comic or satirical) anecdotes, narrator's metaphors, narrative breakdowns, slips, etc.

a few minutes to recollect their experiences on a specific topic, write down these recollections, and then share what they choose with others in the group. The short time, the specificity of the topic, and the co-presence of others, may cut into the ability to recollect or recount more fully. It is very likely that taboo emotions will be bypassed. However, the gain is that the material is manageable and that hearing the reported recollections of those who are co-present may help a particular individual to remember and report more—or with greater precision—in the second round.

From a Freudian perspective Gabriel and Ulus, as well as Jalan—all of whom have much experience in conducting expert interviews—argue for using scenarios as interview props. By prompting the IPs to take recourse to fantasy, these help circumvent the punitive superego, and let "true," socially undesirable emotions—such as envy or rage—surface. In this manner, much normally censored information about organizations and issues can be gathered. These contributors share with us their know-how about how to construct such scenarios, and when in the interview to employ them. Pixley makes no explicit reference to Freud, but has similarly found—while interviewing financial elites—that scenarios free her conversation partners from the professional straightjacket of rationality. It seems, then, that calling for scenario elaboration helps the IPs surmount their moral qualms, professional standards, or societal norms—the usual barriers to honesty, even with oneself—allowing the IPs to reveal their unfit, or even "dark" emotions. In such cases we can indeed speak of unearthing, unveiling, or uncovering emotions which normally remain hidden below the surface, undiscovered.

To assure the success of any expert interview, it is not only necessary to take heed of the power and status differentials between the IP and the interviewer, but also of any paternalistic, iceberg, cathartic and interview reversal effects that, if not counteracted, might subvert the interview (Vogel 1995). As Kleres points out, we should also pay attention to a variety of unspoken (or even taboo) emotions that the power differentials generate. To gain knowledge about various fields of activism and policy, interviewing "experts" on the constitutive elements in these fields has become a widespread research practice. As Kleres points out, the very same experts constitute the "emotions experts" who can offer valuable insights about the emotions that operate in these fields, some of which might be "dark" ones.

Standard emotions research at its limits

Hitzer's contribution on the history of cancer since World War II counters any heroic narrative about having discovered the secret of accessing taboo or individual emotions. Her travels across a sea of documentation, and her reading of the contradictory messages such documentation sends, make it clear just how hard it is to find out "what they [the cancer patients] really felt." Press reports, professional medical records, patient journals, and critical sociologists all seem to tell a different story. Hitzer's chapter evokes sociological discussions about whether triangulation is in fact a useful methodological device at all: while proponents argue that it helps gain insight into a phenomenon by highlighting its various aspects, opponents argue that different methods and research instruments generate data that address different phenomena—there is no shared essential object behind them.

Hitzer is seconded by Pixley, who points out that research sometimes has to face its own limitations: some members of financial elites are willing to say that their occupational field is uncertainty-, even fear-ridden. They tell of others feeling anxious about the risks associated with handling enormous financial sums. But as far as they are all concerned—"one just gets used to it." Perhaps an autobiographic narrative interview might capture better than a scenario one the critical point at which anxiety about risk-taking becomes suppressed?

But even this research instrument is at its limits when the cultural-political and emotional regimes exact their toll by wiping out any type of emotion or emotional expression. As Wouters has pointed out, in the 1950s and into the 1960s the norm was emotionlessness or keeping emotions under control, even when faced with severe illness and death (Wouters 2002). Even a highly motivated, hard-working researcher will not accomplish much with those who deeply internalize this norm, although asking about day-dreaming in addition to the lived experience might help (Gammerl in this volume; also 2008, 2012).

As a sociologist I am out of my depth when faced with a metaphor or a visual, not to mention metonymy (Ahmed 2004)—but this is the point at which linguists (Soriano) or interpreters of the visual (Falk; Flam and Doerr) come to our rescue. All three chapters show that there are sedimented iconic figures and metaphorical or discursive worlds associated with each emotion word and each visual—all waiting to be discovered and explored. As lay speakers and onlookers we are unaware of these worlds, even though they affect us. It is exactly for this reason—because they affect us without us being aware of it—that we should acquire pertinent interpretative skills and knowledge. Iconography teaches us, for example, just why it is that our first impulse is to feel pity and concern when we see a human being helped up to his feet (Falk). Conceptual Metaphor Theory tells us, *inter alia,* that anger in English culture is viewed as dangerous as fire or wild animals or natural elements. Like pressurized liquids, or weapons, it has to be kept under control—it reminds of illness and insanity (Soriano). Visual analysis, finally, reveals what to look for to discover how and what (un)intended message(s) associated with specific emotions a visual can communicate. Literacy in visuals and metaphors will help us to become better interpreters of the maladies of the world, and, perhaps, of its joys as well.

In closing

Georg Simmel, a classic figure of sociology and cultural studies, engaged in the phenomenology of emotions. Max Weber sometimes cited a piece of empirical evidence in support of his theses on emotions, while Emile Durkheim employed both statistics and ethnographic evidence to address emotions. Norbert Elias (1978), Carol Zisowitz Stearns and Peter Stearns (1986) and Cas Wouters (2004; 2007) established a tradition of mining the manners books for emotions. Relying on these books they developed theories about how and why emotions norms had changed over time; but, since manners books only propose specific conduct rules as desirable, these theories can say little about whether the norms the books recommended became internalized and put into practice.

Broader methodological forays into the realm of emotions occurred when Arlie Hochschild started asking people about their emotions on good and bad days, or how they felt on the day of their birthday or graduation. For her first book (1983) on emotional labor she also relied on non-participant observations, interviews, and documents to establish not just what people say they should feel and actually feel, but also how they act with regard to their feelings. To trace the twists and shifts in American love ideals and practices, Francesca Cancian (1990) combined history with a survey and qualitative data. Eva Illouz (1997) delved into history, ads, ideals, dating, and the decision-making patterns of the middle class to inspect the state of the romantic utopia; while Charlotte Bloch (2002a, 2002b, 2012) employed phenomenological and group interviews to highlight experiences of flow and stress, and to find out about envy in academia. Helmut Kuzmics (1994, 2013; Kuzmics and Haring 2013) made forays into fiction as well as officers' and soldiers' diaries. Added to Jack Katz's (1999) observing, recording and videotaping—whether of children in kindergarten, or of police interrogations—to theorize about emotions and sociality, the sociologists of emotions proved that as far as methodological creativity is concerned the sky is the limit.

The contributions towards the pursuit and exploration of emotions in this volume point to methods for empirical studies developed mainly in the field of sociology—but also to ones in history, linguistics, ethnography, social psychology, and other disciplines. Together they constitute only the tip of the iceberg, but they demonstrate that ever more methodological instruments are being tried out in an effort to catch emotions *in flagrante.*

Acknowledgments

I would like to thank Nils Kumkar, Jochen Kleres, and Joc Pixley for their encouragement, and Stina Bergman Blix and especially Benno Gammerl for their very useful criticisms of the first draft. I am grateful to Helmut Kuzmics for his critical reading of the final version, and thank Joc, Jochen, and Gada Mahrouse for their suggestions as well. Thank you too to Stephanie Bird.

Notes

1 In this sense Burawoy acknowledges feminist and post-colonial, but not queer, discussions about how one's (unreflected) standpoint or position as an observer generates situated and partial knowledge. For a useful overview see Denzin (1997: 217–23).

2 When reflecting upon his initial indifference to gender, "race," and class, and its blinding consequences, Burawoy speculates that perhaps another male researcher, who had completed earlier research at the same factory, experienced things differently since his "blue-collar pride flared up more easily at managerial edicts" (Burawoy 2003: 651). Furthermore, when addressing how returning to the original research site might advance science, Burawoy cites an example of a hostile community—which prompted the returning scholar to qualify her old findings and reflect upon the effects of historical change (ibid.).

3 On advice of several commentators the third key author, Denzin, whose work also allows for a good demarcation of the field of ethnography, was removed from the main text to simplify the exposition. Denzin's (1997: 206–16) dense reading of the feminist, post-colonial, borderline, and queer ethnography, is an unmistakable product of the 1980s and 1990s—a period in which the breaking of silence about the suffering of various oppressed and vulnerable groups entered center stage. Denzin engages even with single autobiographic narratives, anecdotal accounts, and poems—as long as these reveal something new about (the intersectionality of) the body, lived experience, and culture. The book is an exploration of how the voices, in particular those addressing human suffering, have shaped scientific reporting, harnessing art—poetry, prose, performance, theater, film, video—and quasi-journalistic accounts, for this purpose. By introjecting new voices, by performing the range of emotions associated with their lived experience, those who spoke out revolutionized the art of reporting ethnographic research results. More importantly, some of these voices overturned the established truths about the societies or social groups they depicted and addressed. The message of Denzin's book is, however, that even when the artistic-interpretative reporting has fairly "normal science" research at its base, this type of reporting conceals the research processes, builds in an idiosyncratic bias, is egocentric, and blends out what it aims to criticize—suffering-imposing discourses, structures, and institutions (Denzin 1997: 123, 216–18). Denzin joins those who criticize much of the interpretative ethnography for revealing so little about how to actually do research on emotions. This is where the present volume steps in, even though it offers "merely" a gateway to full-length studies.

4 The authors-ethnographers also describe a hole that a drag queen deliberately burned into a tank top one of the ethnographers was wearing; how they (that is, the authors-ethnographers) were on occasion presented to theater audiences as "the professors of lesbian love" or "the pussy lickers"; and how they were called

on stage to have to say to the audience: "I love to lick pussy" (Taylor and Rupp 2005: 2123). Taylor and Rupp say that this was in keeping with the politics of vulgarity employed by the drag queens to build up complicity with the audience—necessary to start their work of gender and sexuality deconstruction—but also that they, as researchers, at some point realized that the drag queens' actions actually aimed at "leveling," i.e., placing them in the same "queer" boat.

5 While Goffman proposed that play-acting individuals can read each other's clues, and are at all times cognizant of mishaps in play-acting as well as the attempts to correct these—thus making play-acting actors all-knowledgeable and empathetic, if not always necessarily sympathetic—Garfinkel proposed that people engage in much communication precisely because they cannot read each other's clues and find it necessary to engage in a communication effort to clarify to each other "what was really meant." Several contributors to this volume adopt a Garfinkelian position on emotions, when they argue that to know "what was really felt" requires not just observing, but also engaging in communication with the participating actors as well as experts in the field in which they act.

6 Ahmed defines each emotion and its logic, and then follows its permutations. This she combines with poignant anecdotes about racism and snippets of racialized public discourses to deepen our understanding of the ostracizing labor these emotions do when they create communities of belonging. The message is that the bodies which become designated as loved and admired, turn into privileged bodies treating as self-evident their right to occupy and expand in space. They also block or diminish—whether by imposing self-doubt, fear, pain, or a sense of humiliation—the bodies of others. Ahmed shows how various emotions constitute, position, align, and stabilize privileged white, Western bodies within the (local or national) borders of "their" communities of belonging, while they legitimate their shared hatred and fear of the other. Emotions also posit other—non-Western, Muslim, terrorist, foreign, migrant, female, or homosexual—bodies, as mobile and thus untrustworthy, fear-inspiring, disgusting, and threatening. These bodies are to be kept out, or, alternatively, to be kept in but on condition that they will lovingly embrace the very community of love that causes their discrimination, exclusion, and pain.

7 Shepherdson (2008) argues that Freud often reserved (and when he did not, should have reserved!) the concept of affect for the unconscious-destructive expressions of the suppressed libido/*Lustprinzip*. He criticizes American feminists for mixing up, and using interchangeably, emotions and affect.

References

Ahmed, S. 2004. *The Cultural Politics of Emotion*. New York: Routledge.

Bergman Blix, S. 2010. *Rehearsing Emotions*. Stockholm: Stockholm University.

Berlant, L. 2011. *Cruel Optimism*. Durham, NC: Duke University Press.

Bird, S. 2003. *Women Writers and National Identity: Bachmann, Duden, Özdamar*. Cambridge: Cambridge University Press.

Bird, S. 2007. "Norbert Elias, the Confusion of Törleß and the Ethics of Shamelessness" in M. Fulbrook (ed.) *Uncivilizing Processes? Excess and Transgression in German Society and Culture: Perspectives Debating with Norbert Elias*: 203–23. Amsterdam: Rodopi.

Bloch, C. 2002a. "Moods and Quality of Life," *Journal of Happiness Studies*, 3: 101–128.

Bloch, C. 2002b. "Managing the Emotions of Competition and Recognition in Academia" in J. Barbalet (ed.) *Emotions and Sociology*: 113–31. Oxford: Wiley-Blackwell.

Bloch, C. 2012. *Passion and Paranoia: Emotions and the Culture of Emotion in Academia.* Surrey, UK: Ashgate.

Bogner, A. and C. Wouters. 1990. "Kolonialisierung der Herzen? Zu Arlie Hochschilds Grundlegung der Emotionssoziologie," *Leviathan*, 18 (2): 255–79.

Burawoy, M. 2003. "Revisits: An Outline of a Theory of Reflexive Ethnography," *American Sociological Review*, 68 (5): 645–79.

Butler, J. 1990. *Gender Trouble.* New York: Routledge.

Cancian, F. 1990. *Love in America.* Cambridge: Cambridge University Press.

Denzin, N. 1997. *Interpretative Ethnography.* London: Sage.

Elias, N. 1978 [1939]. *The Civilizing Process.* New York: Urizen Books.

Elias, N. 1982. *Über die Einsamkeit der Sterbenden in unseren Tagen.* Frankfurt a.M.: Suhrkamp.

Flam, H. 1998. *Mosaic of Fear: Poland and East Germany Before 1989.* New York: East European Monographs distributed by Columbia University Press.

Flam, H. 2005. "Emotion's map: a research agenda" in H. Flam and D. King (eds) *Emotions and Social Movements*: 19–40. London, New York: Routledge.

Flam, H. 2008. "The Sentient 'I': Emotions and Inner Conversation" in J. M. Domingues and F. Vandenberghe (eds) *Theory*, the Newsletter of the Research Committee on Sociological Theory, International Sociological Association, Spring/Summer: 4–7.

Flam, H. 2009. "Extreme Feelings and Feeling at Extremes" in D. Hopkins, J. Kleres, H. Flam and H. Kuzmics (eds) *Theorizing Emotions: Sociological Explorations and Applications*: 73–93. Frankfurt a.M., New York: Campus Verlag.

Flam, H. 2010. "Emotion, and the Silenced and Short-Circuited Self" in M. Archer (ed.) *Conversations About Reflexivity*: 187–205. London, New York: Routledge.

Frith, H. and C. Kitzinger. 1998. "'Emotion Work' as a Participant Resource: A Feminist Analysis of Young Women's Talk-in-Interaction," *Sociology*, 32 (2): 299–320.

Gammerl, B. 2009. "Diskussionsforum Erinnerte Liebe: Wie kann eine Oral History zur Geschichte der Gefühle und der Homosexualität beitragen?" *Geschichte und Gesellschaft*, 35 (2): 314–45.

Gammerl, B. 2012. "Emotional Styles: Concepts and Challenges," *Rethinking History*, 16: 161–75.

Garfinkel, H. 1967. *Studies in Ethnomethodology.* Engelwood Cliffs, NJ: Prentice-Hall.

Goffman, E. 1967. *Interaction Ritual.* New York: Pantheon Books.

Gould, D. 2009. *Moving Politics.* Chicago: The University of Chicago Press.

Hochschild, A. 1979. "Emotion Work, Feeling Rules, and Social Structure," *American Journal of Sociology*, 85: 551–75.

Hochschild, A. 1983. *The Managed Heart.* Berkeley: University of California Press.

Hochschild, A. 1989. *The Second Shift.* New York: Penguin. With Anne Machung.

Illouz, E. 1997. *Consuming the Romantic Utopia.* Berkeley: University of California Press.

Katz, J. 1999. *How Emotions Work.* Chicago: The University of Chicago Press.

Kessler, S. J. and W. McKenna. 1978. *Gender: An Ethnomethodological Approach.* Chicago: The University of Chicago Press.

Kleres, J. 2011. "Emotions and Narrative Analysis: A Methodological Approach," *Journal for the Theory of Social Behaviour*, 41 (2): 182–202.
Kuzmics, H. 1994. "Power and Work: The Development of Work as a Civilizing Process in Examples of Fictional Literature," *Sociological Perspectives*, 37 (1): 119–54.
Kuzmics, H. 2013. "Emotions and Habitus of Officers as Reflected in Great Literature: The Case of the Habsburg Army from 1848 to 1918," *Human Figurations*, 2 (1), available online at: http://hdl.handle.net/2027/spo.11217607.0002.105 (accessed July 7, 2014).
Kuzmics, H. and S. A. Haring. 2013. *Emotion, Habitus und Erster Weltkrieg. Soziologische Studien zum militärischen Untergang der Habsburger Monarchie.* V & R Unipress: Göttingen.
Reddy, W. M. 1997. "Against Constructionism: The Historical Ethnography of Emotions," *Current Anthropology*, 38 (3): 327–51.
Reddy, W. M. 1999. "Emotional Liberty: Politics and History in the Anthropology of Emotions," *Cultural Anthropology*, 14 (2): 256–88.
Schütze, F. 1982. "Narrative Repräsentation kollektiver Schicksalbetroffenheit" in E. Lämmert (ed.) *Erzählforschung*: 568–90. Stuttgart: J. B. Metzlersche Verlagsbuchhandlung.
Schütze, F. 1983. "Biographieforschung und narratives Interview," *Neue Praxis*, 13: 283–93.
Scott, J. 1990. *Domination and the Arts of Resistance.* New Haven: Yale University Press.
Shepherdson, C. 2008. "Emotion, Affect, Drive" in C. Shephersson (ed.) *Lacan and the Limits of Language*: 81–100. New York: Fordham University Press.
Taylor, V. and L. Rupp. 2005. "When the Girls are Men: Negotiating Gender and Sexual Dynamics in a Study of Drag Queens," *Signs*, 30 (4): 2115–39.
Vogel, B. 1995. "Wenn der Eisberg zu schmelzen beginnt…" in C. Birkmann, A. Deeke, and B. Völkel (eds) *Experteninterviews in der Arbeitsmarktforschung*: 73–83. Nürnberg: Institut für Arbeitsmarkt und Berufsforschung der Bundesanstalt für Arbeit.
West C. and D. H. Zimmermann. 1987. "Doing Gender," *Gender and Society*, 1 (2): 125–51.
West C. and D. H. Zimmermann. 1995. "Doing Difference," *Gender and Society*, 9 (1): 8–37.
Wouters, C. 2002. "The Quest for New Rituals in Dying and Mourning: Changes in the We–I Balance," *Body & Society*, 8 (1): 1–27.
Wouters, C. 2004. *Sex and Manners.* London: Sage.
Wouters, C. 2007. *Informalization. Manners & Emotions Since 1890.* London: Sage.
Zisowitz Stearns, C. and P. N. Stearns. 1986. *Anger.* Chicago: The University of Chicago Press.
Ziegler, M. and W. Kannonier-Finster. 1991. *Österreichisches Gedächtnis: Über Erinnern und Vergessen der NS-Vergangenheit.* Wien: Bohlau.

Part I

Emotions—a legitimate object of study

Chapter 2

Using fiction as sociology

How to analyze emotions with the help of novels

Helmut Kuzmics

Introductory remark

Before the development of sociology as a science in its own right, the art of observing people and reporting their behavior was largely confined within the boundaries of fictional literature. Lepenies (1985) reserved the term "proto-sociology" for the "realist" classical novel of the nineteenth century (Balzac, Flaubert, Zola, Dickens, etc.). "Sociology" proper was thought by many to replace the novel's function to inform about society and also to criticize it by doing all this in a more neutral, objective, and "scientific" way. But "good" sociological writing has never ceased to be associated with a "good" literary style, and, likewise, novels have not ceased serving the function of describing and explaining the social world around us (Kuzmics and Mozetic 2003; Edling and Rydgren 2011).

The focus here is on "emotions." We may distinguish three aspects of emotions: somatic (the physical—acceleration of the heartbeat, sweating, trembling, etc.); behavioral (flight or attack, including the expressive aspect, functional in group communication); and the feeling-component (i.e., panic) in the narrower, culturally variable sense of the term "emotion" (see Elias 1987). The best possible data are those which allow us simultaneously to identify the emotion and the corresponding behavior that can be seen as the result of that initial emotion (for instance, panic followed by a silly decision to flee in the face of an overestimated danger). These data will be rare, since this would mean having an observer (or honest self-reporter) present both at the location where the emotion occurs and where the action takes place. (Collins (2008) seems to believe that "real" empirical studies of violence can only be found since the invention of photography and video technology.) Moreover, emotions can evade both the observer and the consciousness of the actors themselves: in the case of bypassed, unacknowledged shame, Scheff and Retzinger (1991) have demonstrated the absence of all normally reliable "markers" of shame. This means that every attempt to interpret fiction, sociologically, will also have to be based on theory.

This paper will focus on three examples of how emotions and their experience are part and parcel of sociological explanation via fiction: Jane Austen in *Pride and Prejudice* described how socially inferior women preserved their pride in the gentry-milieu of early nineteenth century England; Len Deighton (*Close-Up*, 1972) portrayed a vivid picture of the emotional dynamic of Americanization and the creation of marketing egos shaped by Hollywood; Siegfried Sassoon, meanwhile, can be treated as an author writing about soldiers' fears and emotions related to courage in the Great War. With the help of these examples, the methodology of selecting, highlighting, and analyzing emotions will be explained, and its main problems outlined.

Examples

Jane Austen's "Pride and Prejudice" and the emotion of shame

Jane Austen can be seen, fundamentally, as a sociologist of the English family; or to be more precise, of the upper class English family during a phase of growing individualization at the time of the turn of the eighteenth to the nineteenth century. The novel also contains a sociology of the relations between a (rising) middle class and the old aristocracy, and entails a minutely detailed analysis of power resources and power relationships between representatives of these groups.

Elizabeth's over-eager and foolish mother presses much too hard to secure a wealthy marriage for her daughter Jane. The lack of self-control she displays during a conversation at a ball is extremely embarrassing.

> In vain did Elizabeth endeavour to check the rapidity of her mother's words, or persuade her to describe her felicity in a less audible whisper; for to her inexpressible vexation, she could perceive that the chief of it was overheard by Mr. Darcy, who sat opposite to them. Her mother only scolded her for being nonsensical.
>
> [...]
>
> Her mother would talk of her views in the same intelligible tone. Elizabeth blushed and blushed again with shame and vexation. She could not help frequently glancing her eye at Mr. Darcy, though every glance convinced her of what she dreaded; ...
>
> (Austen 1988 [1813]: 99–100)

Elizabeth does all she can to redeem her family's honor—and her sister's happiness—after the proud Mr Darcy torpedoes Jane's union with his friend Mr Bingley. She accuses Darcy of unfeeling arrogance. Darcy's letter, motivated by his affection for Elizabeth, shows her that she too has been prejudiced and that his accusations were justified.

In the quotation above, reference is made to "shame." We see very clearly how the mechanism of "class marriage" functions. First, Elizabeth identifies spontaneously and entirely, and without further rational evaluation, with the honor or disgrace of her family. Whatever one might say about the individualization—the "affective individualism" (Stone 1977) of the English family on the threshold of modernity—this is the point where it stops: this disgrace is a group disgrace, just as family honor is shared by all its members. Second, the heroine shares the standards of the evaluation; it is typical in a relatively stable, vertically organized society, for the "inferiors" to consent to a yardstick that makes them inferior. I used this novel in order to shed light on two sociological puzzles. First, it seemed to me that Jane Austen's observations might help to describe and explain the English national habitus of "proud distance" (Kuzmics and Axtmann 2007), in sharp contrast to the Central European, Austrian, disposition towards courtly flattery and servility. Her observations might also be used to better understand the more general psychodynamics of uneven relationships between men and women separated by rank (Kuzmics 2007) at the crossroads of class and gender—which may have become more common in a present society where male superiors regularly meet female employees in the workplace environment.

The gulf between appearance and reality in the production of behavior and expression of emotion: the case of the film industry in Len Deighton's "Close-Up"

The book's English hero, Marshall Stone, an actor who is soon to become a Hollywood star, promises his equally English colleague (and rival) that he will refuse to accept the lead role they are both auditioning for unless he feels he has won it "fair and square" (Deighton 1972: 43). But at the same time, Stone offers his rival a dangerous mixture of coffee and alcohol: "He took a hip flask from his jacket and poured both coffee and brandy. 'And stop looking so bloody worried, Edgar. We English have got to stick together. Am I right? Stick together and we can beat the bastards.' " (Deighton 1972: 44). It is at this moment that the young Edgar Nicolson realizes the man opposite him is a rival who will stop at nothing, and who certainly intends to beat him to the part at any cost. Reeking of alcohol at the interview stage would not be advisable, yet Nicolson shows only indirectly that he has seen through the ruse:

> Nicolson said, "Yes, we must all stick together," and then he pushed the coffee to the far side of the table.
> [...]

> "Don't feel like it, eh?"
> "I get tense," said Nicolson, "and then my stomach just rejects everything."
> "I understand," said Stone. He understood.
>
> (Deighton 1972: 44–5)

At first sight, this appears to be a relaxed, friendly conversation between colleagues—both maintain this impression. The moment of truth comes much later.

I used this scene in a paper on Americanization (Kuzmics 2006) and the creation of a so-called "Marketing Personality" via the "soft power" of the US entertainment industry. The book allows us to see how the boundaries between acting on stage and acting in the competition of real life can become blurred. Using Goffman's dramaturgical model makes it possible to study the formation of a "social habitus" by the daily reproduction of interaction-routines. The novel adds to these "interaction-rituals" the corresponding emotions—quite special fears (tenseness) that result from the danger of suffering defeat at the hands of clever rivals.

Heroism and suppressed fear in the Great War: Siegfried Sassoon

Not many famous war novels place fear at the center of their stories. In the second volume to his war trilogy (*Memoirs of an Infantry Officer*, first published 1930 and based on diaries), Siegfried Sassoon gives a lively example of a behavior that could qualify as "reckless," and yet we find here scarcely any hint of the fear he must have faced. But the story helps one to understand another further, important, aspect of "heroism"; namely, that not all forms of courage qualify for heroic behavior. Following the sudden death of the friend and lance-corporal he took with him on his daring expedition, Sassoon seeks revenge and launches a one-man campaign against the German trenches, furiously throwing hand grenades and causing the enemy to abandon their position. Unable to secure the victory by consolidating this territorial gain with the help of his men, he has to retire ("Having thus failed to commit suicide") and must reflect upon the fact that his behavior was actually rather foolish:

> Little Fernby's anxious face awaited me, and I flopped down beside him with an outburst of hysterical laughter.
>
> (Sassoon 1997 [1930]: 59)

> I was both exhausted and exasperated. My courage was of a cock-fighting kind.
>
> (Ibid.: 60)

> Obviously I had made a mess of the whole affair.
>
> (Ibid.: 61)

The language of fear is only indirect—but from his state of exhaustion and hysteria we can guess that this had to do with an anxiety he did not want to admit to.

I selected this scene from numerous others in order to highlight the complexity of the notion of "heroism" and its relationship with fear. While Sassoon's alter ego, Sherston, admits to the ambiguity his demonstration of "courage" (or better "folly") leaves in the eyes not only of the reader but foremost of his comrades and superiors, the corresponding fear is indicated only by "hysterical laughter" after his successful return to the trenches. Examples like these help to refine our understanding of conventional concepts like heroism and fear, and to be able to contrast them with more legitimate, "official," accounts.

Methodology

Selection of literary sources

The relationship between literature and sociology can be manifold—referring to its descriptive function, fiction can serve either as a confirming, falsifying or illustrating source, or as sociological reasoning itself. If one is to treat literature as sociology, then one also has to show that novels can predate sociological concepts and explanations. If fiction is only used as a mechanism for delivering sociological evidence, one has to find out whether the textual units regarded as "sources" can be treated as simple "observations," rather than as evidence for more complex notions of social reality. But novels also have to entertain, to move, and to create tension in order to appeal to a broader audience—poetic truth is often rather different from plain truth. Since sociology, too, often has aims and styles that transcend mere social reporting and interpretation (accusing and excusing; expressing urgent needs for political change, or the opposite), the difference between sociology and fiction is often one of degree rather than of kind: the element of tragedy, satire, comedy, or romance (Northrop Frye 1990; White 1975) can also be detected in sociological prose.

What does this mean for the selection of fiction texts? (I do not work with lyrics, and only casually with drama—poetry tells us a lot about emotions, but only rarely describes the social context; while plays give the characters their voice, but do not contain descriptive information.) The first decision is: do we focus on "high" literature, ordinary fiction, or even "trash"? The examples illustrated above are well-known novels of remarkable literary quality. They were chosen because of their authors' particular ability to observe and interpret social phenomena sharply, and using a refined vocabulary. Of course, we can also analyze other types of fiction—they tell us at least as much about society as the language of architecture or art, but probably not more.

The second decision we face is this: systematic search or following the traces of "serendipity" (Merton and Barber 2006)? The selection of the Jane Austen novel and of Sassoon's war trilogy was the result of systematic research guided by the research questions pursued by, and with the help of, several guides and monographs on English literature (or, more particular, on war fiction). Len Deighton's *Close-Up*, in contrast, was selected as a result of quite ordinary personal reading, reading carried out with the aim of entertainment and pleasure but with a theoretical eye which allowed me to see its sociological value. In any case, working with novels requires a love of fiction and a desire to read a lot of it.

Method of interpretation

But once we have decided to use a certain text, what should be the textual units appropriate for sociological interpretation? The scale of options includes units (like words or sentences) that can be counted by way of a quantitatively oriented type of content analysis; but also much bigger units like whole scenes in which the author describes characters and dialogues, and delivers interpretations in a way that leads to ideal-types quite similar to those used by sociologists themselves. For the qualitative interpretation of such larger textual units, various methods have been developed that strive to secure standards of scientific objectivity by providing detailed coding instructions. Among these methods, the strategy to develop a "Grounded Theory" (Strauss 1987) has attracted considerable attention. "Grounded Theory" was developed from the analysis of qualitative interviews designed for scientific purposes and research questions. Literary texts lack this design and the author (either as internal or first-person narrator, as omniscient, or as limited or external subjective narrator) does not only seek to inform his/her readers about society (and about his/her own theories), but also seeks to entertain, thrill, move, and so on.

A sociology of literary expression is needed which deals with the problem: what kind of audience was addressed, and by what kind of message? Since exaggeration, colorization, suppression, and invention are common elements of literature, the social scientist must have a theory of this—or at least a suspicion about the intentions of the author and their effects on the subject; as well as how his/her position is related to the interests, attitudes, and expectations that are shared by members of those social strata in which the author supposes his/her readers to be. There is always the danger of under- or over-reporting. Collins (2008: 14) gives an impressive example: the gun-fight at OK Corral. In reality this can only have lasted 30 seconds, but was extended to seven minutes in the movie. Similarly, the emotion of fear in war can be nearly totally absent in novels that celebrate male heroism, as can be shown by a reading of Ernst Jünger's *Storm of Steel*. It is not only the conscious intentions of the artist that are important, but also the many unconscious traits of the socially shaped person who is the literary author. Above all, the author must have been in a position to understand the milieu he or she is writing about, first hand. In our examples, this *is* the case: Jane Austen writes about her own family; Siegfried Sassoon was an officer serving on the Western Front; and Len Deighton owes his Hollywood insights to the experiences he collected when his books became successful movies in the 1960s (*The Ipcress File, Funeral in Berlin, Billion Dollar Brain*, etc.).

Of course, the sociologist has to accept that genres, formulae, plots, narrative structures, symbols, and metaphors—all kinds of "intertextuality"—must be understood as such, and should not be naively interpreted as properties of an easily observable reality. Jane Austen, for instance, was very much aware of the conventions of the so-called "courtship novel" (Kaplan 1992) and the romanticist discourse of an idealized heroine that accorded with the norm of "genteel domesticity." Her realism can be defined as deliberate deviation from the postulates of this genre. But the use of metaphors, even if they are common currency, can help to describe aspects of emotions—namely, the cultural-cognitive aspect of an emotion that is more complex than simply "joy" or "fear" (proud distance, or courage of the cockfighting kind).

Literary sources: dimensions of evaluation

We can name four aspects, or dimensions, of evaluating literary sources as helpful for understanding the role of emotions in social behavior:

1. That of the pragmatic intention, in which this act of communication took place; and the effect which this intention has on the correctness of self-characterizations and of the perception of the behavior of others, including external, institutional constraints (see Laslett's (1976) empiricist skepticism).
2. That of the value which can be attributed to the author's utterances from the "emic" perspective of his/her everyday view of the world, in the dialectics of "Selbst-" and "Fremdverstehen" according to Schütz (1932) and Schütz and Luckmann (1975).
3. That of the meaning of the new source's evidence, seen and judged from the "etic" perspective from the professional scientist him/herself (who adds theories, and historical and institutional knowledge).
4. That of the innovative, falsifying, or confirming character of the new information: how typical is it for theoretical classification?

Emotions via literature: a comparison of methods

The basic problem of every sociological attempt to acknowledge human feelings is simply to overcome the disbelief of all those who mistrust deeply the possibility of gaining reliable, intersubjective access to a person's inner world of feelings and perceptions. Critical voices can be found among quantitatively oriented social historians, sociologists, source-guarding narrative historians, and behavioral psychologists. Survey methods in sociology can certainly deliver statistical rates of emotions. In the pioneering study, *The American Soldier* (Stouffer *et al.* 1949: 201), a surprising number of soldiers serving in the Pacific theater confessed that they had experienced (at least sometimes) somatic symptoms ranging from "losing control of bowels" (21 percent) to "urinating in one's pants" (10 percent). Some 65 percent of the soldiers surveyed (ibid.: 232) admitted to having experienced—at least once—a state of fear that had made them virtually unable to react "adequately" in battle. But even these indicators do not tell us much about their complex subjective meaning. An Italian author and soldier fighting during World War I paints a much clearer picture of behavior under heavy fire—instead of using his pistol, he threw a stick, an *alpenstock*, at a group of stupefied Austrians, who managed to catch it mid-flight (Lussu 1992: 128). If we believe that male pride seldom allows for confessions such as those reported by Lussu and the American soldiers in the Stouffer *et al.* study, we gain an idea of how often this emotion will be under-reported (even in fiction!); and of what "courage" or "boldness" really means (as a conscious, reflexive action; or as an automatically trained behavior in face of terrible fright).

It is not my intention to contest the value of quantitative methods in principle, but rather to argue for the use of complementary qualitative information, particularly in cases where the former methodology cannot be applied. Among the many qualitative methods that are able to refer to emotions, I would like to compare the use of fiction, as has been demonstrated here, with the text-related "Grounded Theory" of Strauss (1987). Since the interpretation of novels is the legitimate subject of literary studies (Eagleton 1983), I want to outline in a few words what their main differences are when compared to a sociological understanding of literary texts.

Fiction as sociology and Grounded Theory

Open, axial, and selective coding are the well-known steps[1] of a method that aims at linking data to theory—while at the same time trying not to simply confirm preconceived opinions. Since the strategy departs from the individual actor and his or her interactions with others—the conditions of these interactions, strategies, and tactics of the actor, and the consequences of the interaction—and since fiction also provides us with narratives in which natural persons play a central role, there are many elements common to both methods. Emotions can be depicted in descriptions of all channels through which they are mediated: expressions—involuntary or intentional—of affects via mimics, gestures, body language, sounds, smells, and so on. Furthermore, we have descriptions and dialogues referring to "inner states" that can also be rendered in self-reports of the main actors. These expressions and utterances can be classified, according to Grounded Theory, either through natural codes or through sociological codes. In the case of "fiction as sociology," a third component has to be taken into account: the author—who can be treated either as a kind of sociologist him or herself, or as someone who only fabricates a "source." He or she is not a simply "neutral" mirror. Therefore, the method proposed here has to be applied with considerable theoretical care—only then can we decide whether the author's imagination has enriched our sociological understanding or not.

Fiction as sociology and literary criticism

Skepticism about realist text interpretations is nearly as old as literary criticism itself. "Literary Theory" has developed in a powerful way in recent decades under the influence of Marxism, structuralism, hermeneutics, phenomenology, psychoanalysis, post-structuralism, and post-Modernism. At one end of this development, so-called "deconstructionism" (De Man; Derrida) arose, where the claim of representing reality is seen as ridiculous. Of course sociological reality does not equal literal reality: what we aim at is the sociologically typical and not an exact representation of the "real world" of the protagonists in time and space—the weather on Tuesday, October 5, in Prague, 1935, does not really matter. I do not want to deal here with the most radical solipsists but with an attempt to bridge the gap between the various conceptions in a kind of "synthesis." R. Hodge's *Literature as Discourse* (1990) is a work that incorporates the new "theory of signs," and builds on the latter. Authors/speakers meet readers/listeners. These readers and listeners share a kind of knowledge which helps them to understand and to "create" the meaning of what the author says. The relationship between the text and "reality" can never be understood as a simple "mapping" of the world around us. The restricted credibility upon which literary texts can count, is, in Hodge's language, a low degree of "modality." This concept can best be conceived as the truth value of a proposition, or a more complex corpus of knowledge. Between "true" and "semiotic" reality there lies a fractured relation of representation—different genres, "domains," production regimes, and reception regimes imply different values (high or low) of the "modality" of a text. This "modality" (of the detective novel,[2] pornography, poetry, etc.) refers to context and usage, and cannot simply be seen as a relation between the text and reality. Let us look at an example Hodge discusses for a sociological interpretation: Emily Brontë's *Wuthering Heights*, which contains a passage that has been taken by Philippe Ariès (1982) as evidence for the modern tendency to romanticize death (with a slightly necrophilian tendency). Here, Hodge is able to demonstrate that Ariès does not fully understand the genre of the "Gothic Novel" (and at the same time underrates Emily Brontë as an observer of burials). But the focus of the analysis is on text and narrative, and not on the subject—society—itself. At the center of attention is the *detail* and not the comprehensive sociological description and explanation of the area of interest. Decisions about what can be seen as needing an explanation are not taken from the perspective of systematic research interests; but rather due to the caprices and contingencies of the business of literary criticism. The latter tends to ignore or downplay the possibilities of an holistic, contextual interpretation of social reality with the help of literature if the latter really deals with the typical and relevant in society in a way similar to that of sociology itself. Novels or a literary style of documentary representation can come quite close to the complexities of real life; but in that case, we have to take into account the intentions, emotions, and the social position of the author from a sociology-of-knowledge perspective in order to estimate the possible bias of the narrative.

Notes

1 This method aims at securing conceptual openness against a kind of theorizing that only seeks to confirm preconceived ideas about the social reality that is the subject of scrutiny. It proceeds from open coding of concepts found in the qualitative material, originating in notions introduced both by the sociologist and the interviewees themselves; to axial coding along distinct dimensions; and selective coding with the purpose of sociological explanation.

2 To give a simple example: Raymond Chandler's "hard-boiled detective," Marlowe, is a hero in the tradition of Homer's *Ilias* or the Indo-European warrior-gods. But the low likelihood of finding such heroes in the America of the 1930s does not destroy the plausibility of Chandler's portrait of the upper class, *nouveau riche* society of California, complete with their houses, butlers, and psychotherapists.

References

Ariès, P. 1982. *The Hour of Our Death: The Classic History of Western Attitudes Toward Death over the Last One Thousand Years*. New York: Vintage Books.

Austen, J. 1988 [1813]. *Pride and Prejudice*. Oxford: Oxford University Press.

Collins, R. 2008. *Violence: A Micro-Sociological Theory*. Princeton: Princeton University Press.

Deighton, L. 1972. *Close-Up*. London: Jonathan Cape.

Eagleton, T. 1983. *Literary Theory. An Introduction*. Minneapolis: University of Minnesota Press.

Edling, C. and J. Rydgren (eds). 2011. *Sociological Insights of Great Thinkers: Sociology through Literature, Philosophy, and Science.* Santa Barbara: ABC-CLIO, LLC.

Elias, N. 1987. "Human Beings and their Emotions," *Theory, Culture and Society*, 4 (2–3): 339–61.

Hodge, R. 1990. *Literature as Discourse: Textual Strategies in English and History.* Cambridge: Polity.

Kaplan, D. 1992. *Jane Austen Among Women.* Baltimore, London: The Johns Hopkins University Press.

Kuzmics, H. 2006. "The Marketing-Character in Fiction: Len Deighton's *Close-Up* (1972) as a Sociological Description of Post-War Hollywood and the Process of Americanisation," *Irish Journal of Sociology*, 15 (2): 23–40.

Kuzmics, H. 2007. "Ungleicher Rang und stolze Distanz. Gefühlsmanagement in Jane Austens 'Stolz und Vorurteil'" in A. Neumayer (ed.) *Kritik der Gefühle. Feministische Positionen*: 236–53. Wien: Milena Verlag.

Kuzmics, H. and R. Axtmann. 2007. *Authority, State and National Character. The Civilizing Process in Austria and England, 1700–1900.* Aldershot: Ashgate.

Kuzmics, H. and G. Mozetic. 2003. *Literatur als Soziologie. Zum Verhältnis von literarischer und gesellschaftlicher Wirklichkeit.* Konstanz: UVK.

Laslett, P. 1976. "The Wrong Way Through the Telescope: A Note on Literary Evidence in Sociology and Historical Sociology," *British Journal of Sociology*, 27 (3): 319–42.

Lepenies, W. 1985. *Die drei Kulturen. Soziologie zwischen Literatur und Wissenschaft.* Reinbek: Rowohlt.

Lussu, E. 1992. *Ein Jahr auf der Hochebene.* Wien: Europaverlag.

Merton, R. K. and E. Barber. 2006. *The Travels and Adventures of Serendipity: A Study in Sociological Semantics and the Sociology of Science.* Princeton: Princeton University Press.

Northrop Frye, H. 1990. *Anatomy of Criticism. Four Essays.* Princeton: Princeton University Press.

Sassoon, S. 1997 [1930]. *Memoirs of an Infantry Officer.* London: Faber and Faber.

Scheff, T. J. and S. M. Retzinger. 1991. *Emotions and Violence. Shame and Rage in Destructive Conflicts.* Lexington: Lexington Books.

Schütz, A. 1932. *Der sinnhafte Aufbau der sozialen Welt. Eine Einleitung in die verstehende Soziologie.* Wien: Springer.

Schütz, A. and T. Luckmann. 1975. *Strukturen der Lebenswelt.* Neuwied: Luchterhand.

Strauss, A. 1987. *Qualitative Analysis for Social Scientists.* Cambridge, England: Cambridge University Press.

Stone, L. 1977. *The Family, Sex and Marriage in England, 1500–1800.* London: Weidenfeld and Nicolson.

Stouffer, S. A., A. A. Lumsdaine, M. H. Lumsdaine, R. M. Williams, Jr., M. B. Smith, I. L. Janis, S. A. Star and L. S. Cottrell, Jr. 1949: *The American Soldier. Vol. 2. Combat and Its Aftermath.* Princeton: Princeton University Press.

White, H. 1975. *Metahistory. The Historical Imagination in Nineteenth-Century Europe.* Baltimore, London: Johns Hopkins University Press.

Chapter 3

"It's all in the plot"

Narrative explorations of work-related emotions

Yiannis Gabriel and Eda Ulus

This contribution examines how researchers may study work-related emotions in the field by listening carefully and engaging emotionally with stories and narratives that they encounter. The chapter starts with a recognition that emotion (*pathos*) is a crucial element of story (*mythos*), something noted a long time ago by Aristotle. Emotions may seem to surface and subside irregularly in the course of a story, a drama, or a conversation, but they have an inner logic that ties them to various plot-lines, such as tragic, comic, or epic. In particular, we examine how researchers can recreate the emotions of their respondents, as well as their own emotions in the field, by recollecting and re-engaging with significant stories as well as metaphors that punctuate their research material.

"Emergence" or "surfacing" of emotions spontaneously in the field

Emotions, it seems to us, can be observed (as opposed to personally experienced) in three ways—when a person declares that he/she feels a certain way ("I am angry with my boss"); when they act in a certain way (she throws a glass of wine at the boss at the Christmas party when he tells a sexist joke, or she blushes on hearing a particular story); or when they tell a story which gives clues about how they may feel ("Guess what I did to my boss's car..."). In the course of fieldwork, researchers have ample opportunity to observe emotions in situ, as and when they surface in words and actions. At times, people expressly state their feelings, or display emotions through bodily expressions or indirectly through narratives that they spontaneously relate.

Reflecting across numerous interviews or observational sessions, certain recurring emotional patterns may be identified—for instance, anger or resentment towards particular groups or individuals; compassion and sympathy for others; enthusiasm for certain projects; and cynicism for others. Sometimes a particular emotion (anger, bitterness, cynicism, depression, disappointment, and so forth) can suffuse an entire interview; or sometimes an amalgam of emotions (for example, nurses displaying their commitment to patients, their mistrust of managers, and their respect for clinicians) may surface repeatedly. By reflecting on such patterns in our own research, we came to appreciate the importance of nostalgia in organizations—an emotion that can profoundly influence current experiences and sense-making of longer serving employees (Gabriel 1993). Nostalgia was not part of the research agenda, but something "thrown up" by the fieldwork. Having noticed and named this emotion, it was then possible to identify how it surfaced in particular narratives—attaching itself, for instance, to old colleagues or old leaders.

There are times during the course of an interview, a focus group, or an observational session, when a particular emotion surges forward unexpectedly and dramatically to take control of a situation. Yiannis Gabriel had ample opportunity to observe this during recent interviews with unemployed senior professionals in their fifties. During long interviews, many of these professionals maintained an appearance of calm self-assurance in the face of adversity. Then, a seemingly innocent question would throw them off course, opening the floodgates for painful self-expression. To the question "So what advice would you give somebody who has lost his job and been made redundant?" one of the respondents was overwhelmed with rage and became virtually incoherent:

> I would just, oh gosh you wouldn't really want you to hear my words! [laughs exuberantly] you know, I was tempted to say, I'd say to them, forgive me for this, but I'd say to them, f**k the system, f**k them all, get on with it yourself, you know because [breaks down in tears and is quiet for several seconds] I'd say the system doesn't care—people do, so that's what I'd say, you know, whatever is holding you back from getting on just forget it, just get on with it ... [long pause] just—yes, I don't know what more you can say to somebody because you can empathise and sympathise with them but unless you can actually give them re-employment ... sometimes you have ... to say no don't know, haven't you, you know and er, you know you can put your arm around an unemployed person and give them lots of cups of tea but it doesn't necessarily solve the problem ... you know, I don't know how, you know, I haven't thought it out or thought it through, I've just responded emotionally to it, I guess, and that, that's it and just say, you know, system's a system it doesn't care about you, you know [becomes virtually incoherent].
>
> (Peter)

In this narrative, emotion emerges not by being explicitly articulated ("I am desperate"), or by being tied to the experience of the story's protagonist. Instead, it is expressed in the collapse of the narrative itself—the narrative struggle that leaves the researcher in no doubt that an emotional crisis is unfolding in front of his/her eyes.

Eliciting emotions in the field

Such expressions of powerful emotion come, quite unprompted, from patient interviewing, empathetic listening, and careful rephrasing of questions over prolonged periods. Alternatively, researchers may ask more direct questions about their respondents' emotional experiences at work. "Was there ever a time at work where you had some strong emotions but couldn't show them?" Such questions invite the respondent to share significant experiences without placing limits on the kinds of events that may be revealed. They can, however, be seen as intrusive, and may result in perfunctory or defensive answers. A different way of inviting emotion is by asking respondents to think of an incident that sums up their experience in some way. Consider how the question "Can you describe a story or an incident that sums up your experience of being unemployed?" triggered off an overwhelming emotional response in another unemployed professional:

> It's a bit like walking on ice when the water's frozen and you know at some stage that ice could melt and the thing about that is that you know you can swim but don't know where the land is, so it's like a sense of drowning really and because everything is white you lose signs of detail as well but you have to get up every day you have to stay afloat so there is a sense there of trying to do little things each day.
>
> (Robert)

Researchers can seek to draw out emotions more directly—for instance, by tying an emotion to a particular incident. Thus, questions like the following can generate powerful insights:

- Can you think of an incident while working for this organization that made you feel proud/happy/satisfied/etc. of being a member of it?
- Did anything ever happen to you in this organization that made you feel disappointed/upset/angry?
- Can you think of something that happened to someone else that made you feel afraid/concerned/anxious?
- Can you think of an incident in this organization that made you feel embarrassed/stressed?

Such questions are somewhat different from conventional critical incident research (Chell 2004; Gremler 2004); instead of looking for objective departures from routine, they invite respondents to relate experiential landmarks—i.e., moments of emotional significance that have left a mark on them. Instead of probing the causes and consequences of the incident, researchers would explore its symbolism and the emotions it stirred.

Attaching an emotion to an incident is especially useful in a focus group, when the researcher has an opportunity to witness the response of other participants to an emotion-triggering story. In a classroom of graduate students in India, Eda Ulus's questions about emotions at the workplace prompted a variety of powerful stories about struggles against bosses—and occasional triumphs over them. One male respondent told how he openly disobeyed his boss in order to spend more time with his sick, hospitalized baby. His story not only underscored important emotion rules for his organization and its culture, it also elicited strong, sympathetic, and envious reactions to his defiance from among his classmates. These group dynamics facilitated the analysis of the meanings of emotion at individual and at organizational levels.

Another example of the power of storytelling with a wider audience occurred during a focus group conducted by Yiannis Gabriel with junior doctors in a gynecology department. When asked "Can you think of an incident that made you feel good about your work as a doctor in this hospital?" one junior doctor told the following story:

> A pregnant woman came in through A&E [Accident and Emergency]. She was having problems with her pregnancy. I asked the registrar [senior doctor] what to do. They decided that the best thing to do was get the woman scanned to find the problem. However, being a night shift there were no porters to be seen and the scanning units were closed. I felt that the anxious woman could not stay in A&E surrounded by drunks and druggies as it was inappropriate. Instead of calling for porters, which would have taken time, I and the registrar moved the pregnant lady to the maternity ward ourselves where we opened up a scanning unit to find out what was wrong with the lady's pregnancy. I was proud of the leadership that I had received from my registrar; not every registrar would have done this but he solved the problem and delivered good patient care in the process. The problems were resolved within an hour with only skeletal night staff.

This rescue narrative centers on a helpless character saved by the dedication of others. Like most such narratives, it is framed by the emotion of pride ("I was proud of the leadership"), though it surveys other emotions ("anxious woman," "[desperate] drunks and druggies") and delivers moral judgments ("it was inappropriate," "delivered good patient care"). It also suggests some nascent emotions—respect for the registrar, disapproval for the absent porters, and at least indifference towards the plight of the "drunks and druggies." The other participants in the focus group enthusiastically endorsed the story as a good example of patient care and also of the kind of leadership they expected from their seniors.

A story, like the one above, may be further interrogated in the field by asking follow-up questions like:

- is this a common occurrence in this organization?
- how does this type of incident make other people in this organization feel?
- who, in your view, should take the credit/blame for this type of incident?
- is this the type of story that does the rounds in the organization? Why?

It will be noticed that in asking follow-up questions, researchers should generally refrain from questioning the factual accuracy of the story. Such questioning may be appropriate when investigating an accident or a failure, but is entirely inappropriate if establishing the meaning and emotional tone of a narrative. To achieve this, researchers must become "fellow travelers" of the narrative, engaging with the story emotionally and symbolically while displaying interest, empathy, and pleasure in the storytelling process (Gabriel 2000). Researchers risk alienating the storyteller by questioning the narrative and placing him/her under cross-examination; instead they can conspire to detach the narrative from the discourse of facts, guiding it towards free association and fantasy. Contradictions and ambiguities in the narrative are accepted with no embarrassment. Ambiguity lies at the heart of many stories, displaying an individual's ambivalent feelings or partial knowledge or understanding. While the researcher may ask for clarification of particular aspects of the story, the storyteller should feel that such clarification is asked in the interests of increased understanding, communication, and empathy—rather than in the form of pedantic inquiry.

Being a fellow traveler on a story is neither emotionally nor ethically easy, most notably when the story one encounters is upsetting or offensive. Researchers who genuinely wish to explore and understand phenomena that are distasteful to them—which might range from bullying at work, to pedophilia, to racism, and to group violence—must frequently swallow their own convictions and allow the voice of the respondents to be heard, no matter how repugnant their views and emotions may be.

Eliciting stories through metaphors or projective techniques

In organizational research, questions like those above frequently fail to lead to stories for a variety of reasons—respondents may be guarded; they may wish to "stick to the facts"; or they may simply be poor storytellers who find it hard to articulate their emotions or views in narrative forms.

One line of investigation that we have found helpful in such situations is to elicit emotion by inviting respondents to think of their organization in terms of a metaphor. Respondents may be told "People sometimes think of their workplace through an image or a metaphor—here are some examples on a card. Does your organization feel like any of these on the card?" The metaphors on the card can be carefully compiled to reflect culturally significant themes, or issues thrown up by earlier research. They may include:

- a machine
- a family
- a football team
- an episode from a soap opera
- a nest of vipers
- a castle under siege
- a dinosaur
- a conveyor belt
- a prison
- an orchestra
- a pressure cooker
- a rose garden

The researcher slowly reads each line, noticing how respondents react to each metaphor—they may be perplexed about some, amused by others, strongly reject some, or instantly alight to others. It then becomes possible to explore the meanings and emotions raised by the appropriate metaphor through follow-up questions like:

- a machine: Is it a well-oiled one? Is it a creaky one? How often does it break down?
- a family: What kind? A happy one? Who is the father/mother? How do they treat their children?
- a football team: Who are the stars? Who are the opponents?
- a pressure cooker: Where does the pressure come from? How do people let off steam?

A follow-up question may then be asked that frequently elicits a story, revealing the emotional associations of the metaphor: "Can you think of an incident that illustrates how this organization works as a family/pressure cooker/prison, etc.?"

Such lines of investigation draw the respondent into sharing with the investigator more private and intimate emotions than the more direct approaches described earlier. Even these, however, may not be very effective in bringing to the surface emotions that are socially censured or "dangerous"—emotions such as envy, *schadenfreude*, shame, resentment, and contempt. For inquiries into such emotions, less direct approaches may be used. Such approaches still rely on narratives but seek to detach narratives further from what is falsifiable or factual. In such situations, projective and scenario techniques may be used.

In projective techniques we may invite a respondent to reflect, not on whether they have had a particular emotion (such as envy, vanity, or *schadenfreude*); but rather, whether they have ever been the target or victim of such an emotion. Alternatively, they may be invited to reflect on a particular scenario (or even a story related by another participant), with the aim being to draw them into a discussion about how such proscribed emotions might surface in organizational contexts (for more on this, see chapter by Ishan Jalan in this volume).

Emotional disclosures

Using a storytelling approach in research interviews relies on the creation of a safe space in which a respondent feels comfortable sharing their experiences—sometimes in a free associating, unstructured manner that allows the disclosure of emotionally charged fantasies. This space supports the sharing of specific stories that unveil further important emotions. Sharing involves mutuality, something that cannot be achieved so long as the relation between the researcher and the researched is deeply asymmetrical—the former asking questions, the latter disclosing personal, even intimate, emotional experiences. One of the most fruitful approaches that we have found for eliciting emotional disclosure is through a process of leveling the field—i.e., the researcher being willing to share some of his/her own emotional experiences with his/her respondents.

This is especially effective in settings where there may be enhanced resistance as a result of cultural, class, or occupational differences between the interviewer and the interviewee. During an interview conducted in India, Eda Ulus shared a dream in which she is about to deliver a lecture to a class of expectant students, but has forgotten important materials. This disclosure prompted the respondent to share many similar dreams about her own working life by creating a shared space where fantasy and dreams—topics which are sensitive and may be inaccessible through more objective means—can be legitimately discussed. As a result of disclosing this dream, the respondent felt secure enough to share a vivid story about a difficult subordinate whose insolence had caused her sleepless nights by breaching the boundary between personal and work experiences. Emotions shared through this exchange generated crucial insights about the emotion rules of her organization, as well as the emotional effects when such rules are transgressed. Sharing the researcher's own experiences in this instance also helped to bridge cultural divides and minimize the feeling of the researcher as outsider, intruder, or even colonizer.

Self-disclosure should be implemented at appropriate times and with suitable sensitivity during an unfolding interview interaction. Not all settings are conducive to the sharing of emotional experiences, and there are other methods that can encourage the respondent to relate powerful and personal stories. The interviewer can encourage such narratives through the use of extensive emotional investment in the exchange, demonstrated through empathic responses, mirrored statements, and supportive comments. Attempting to put one's self in the place of the interviewee—for example by reflecting on how it might feel to be threatened with redundancy by a bullying boss, or challenged by an unruly subordinate—helps to shape a genuine encounter, opening up the possibility of entering the employee's emotional world.

In the same study, an Indian employee shared a story about her friend's sudden dismissal from work and its devastating emotional effect on her—notably the terror that she would be next in line. When she first started to relate this story the narrative could have been easily broken, or even killed off altogether, through insensitive questioning. To show empathy for this employee's trauma at learning of her friend's dismissal, Eda Ulus responded spontaneously with comments like, "Oh my goodness"—thus placing herself as a fellow traveler in the narrative. When the interviewee disclosed powerful words like "terrified," the interviewer offered in return "I can imagine"—to demonstrate further an appreciation of the intensity of her interviewee's experience. Such explicit emotional responses may appear to breach the convention of interviewer objectivity, or non-interference. However, when the research interest is emotion, it is this very objectivity and non-interference which themselves are the obstacles of the research goal.

Some approaches to studying emotions display similarities with therapeutic approaches. It is critical, however, to underline their differences. In therapeutic interactions, therapists frequently offer interpretations as part of the treatment. Interpretations during a research encounter would be inappropriate. In this context, deploying a storytelling approach entails listening carefully and encouraging the sharing of meanings, but not challenging the experience or offering alternative interpretations. The research space is one of curiosity and interest in learning about emotions—with interpretations by the researcher commencing later, during analysis of audio files and transcripts (Clarke 2006; Kvale 1999).

Counter-transference

Therapeutic consultations and research encounters have fundamentally different aims and require quite different skills on the part of the professional who guides the conversation. Neither set of skills can be formalized and routinized, being highly contingent upon situational factors—timing being of the essence in both. The suitability of a particular approach may change over the course of spontaneous interview exchanges, and it may vary according to the emotional dynamics of the dyad—shaped by cultural and historical factors which individuals bring into the conversation.

One feature that both the therapeutic and the research conversation have in common is transference and counter-transference. Meeting somebody in the contrived environment of a guided conversation can reawaken in a respondent emotions and fantasies associated with significant figures from their past. This is known as transference, and can be positive (generating warm and supportive feelings) or negative (generating fearful, envious, or suspicious feelings). Counter-transference represents the response of the person guiding the conversation—the therapist or the researcher—to the transference of the other. Reflecting on our own emotions during and following an interview—i.e., seeking to analyze our counter-transference—can offer powerful insights into elusive unconscious emotions, and can also help us make sense of the emotional dynamics of the interview situation itself.

Working with our counter-transference may involve taking notes of our immediate reflections after an interview has finished. For example, we may write about feeling claustrophobic, anxious, puzzled, jubilant, or unsettled at specific points. Such emotions can serve as additional resources for interpreting the stories we have heard. We can also revisit audio files or interview transcripts at multiple points in time, and compare our responses to them during that passage of time. Doing so can assist in re-engaging with the emotions of an interview, while maintaining a critical distance from which to analyze the different layers of meaning that emerge from the stories. As noted by Howard F. Stein, who has written extensively on the issue (Stein 1999; 2001), we may also

> write a poem or paint a picture now and then as a way of better understanding the organizations.... Far from distracting you from keen observation, interpretation, and explanation, it will serve as a valuable instrument for all three of these virtues.
>
> (Personal communication with the authors)

A note on ethical awareness, and conclusion

Research on emotions inevitably raises thorny ethical issues. Interesting research tends to focus on individuals who are going through difficult times, transitions, traumas, tribulations. Respect for a person's anguish, grief, and despondency may inhibit researchers from asking direct questions that may unsettle their sibjects, and which may unleash irreversible and potentially damaging feelings that can lead to the breakdown of the research relationship. At the same time, researchers seeking to understand the experiences of such subjects must often penetrate a façade of rehearsed and "safe" answers, wishful thinking, and evasion. During field research, an invisible barrier can come between respondents and researchers, the latter being perceived as having comfortable and safe jobs with secure salaries. This can be offset through extensive familiarization, informal conversations, a genuine desire to learn from the respondents' experiences, and, as noted above, self-disclosures which confirm that researchers themselves are not immune from troubles.

Researching organizational emotions in the field is certainly not easy; all the same, we are of the opinion that it is a craft that can be acquired and developed. It is a craft that may not come naturally to those researchers more accustomed to highly abstract academic reasoning, or who may feel an inherent aversion to emotion as something that contaminates the data or the analysis. As scholars of organization, however, we believe that the time has come to view emotions (including the researcher's own) not as contaminants, but rather as resources.

References

Chell, E. 2004. "Critical Incident Technique" in C. Cassell and G. Symon (eds) *Essential Guide to Qualitative Methods in Organizational Research*: 45–60 London: Sage.

Clarke, S. 2006. "Theory and Practice: Psychoanalytic Sociology as Psycho-Social Studies," *Sociology—the Journal of the British Sociological Association*, 40 (6): 1153–69.

Gabriel, Y. 1993. "Organizational Nostalgia: Reflections on the Golden Age" in S. Fineman (ed.) *Emotion in Organizations*: 118–41. London: Sage.

Gabriel, Y. 2000. *Storytelling in Organizations: Facts, Fictions, Fantasies*. Oxford: Oxford University Press.

Gremler, D. D. 2004. "The Critical Incident Technique in Service Research," *Journal of Service Research*, 7 (1): 65–89.

Kvale, S. 1999. "The Psychoanalytic Interview as Qualitative Research," *Qualitative Inquiry*, 5 (1): 87–113.

Stein, H. F. 1999. "Countertransference and Understanding Workplace Cataclysm: Intersubjective Knowledge and Interdisciplinary Applied Anthropology," *High Plains Applied Anthropologist*, 19 (1): 10–20.

Stein, H. F. 2001. *Nothing Personal, Just Business: A Guided Journey Into Organizational Darkness*. Westport, CT: Quorum Books.

Chapter 4

"Studying up"

Emotions and finance decisions

Jocelyn Pixley

Starting out

Money is a totally uncertain, conflict-ridden institution; an interrelation of trust and fear among creditors, debtors, and governments. This statement may seem obvious since the 2007 financial crisis, when trust in banks collapsed, and corporate betrayal of trust is depressingly evident. But when I started research on money in 1997, trust was the unspoken because, to the finance sector, uncertainty was of no concern and money was apparently "future-proof."

How can one investigate the unspoken? Why did I even suggest trust? Many people think up research questions through "abduction": it is a third mode of inference between deduction (the top-down approach from "theory") and induction (gathering "facts" from the bottom up). "Abduction" is immanent or resides in the observer: it infers hidden causes, and new ideas emerge in formulating hypotheses. Optimism, arrogance, trepidation, or empathy may motivate a hypothesis and drive one to find out if it is convincing, or to change one's views. I was hopeful about whatever might be found and disbelief prompted my hypothesis: these emotional aspects are common, and switch. Emotions move from a sense of futility or shame at the banality of feeble ideas, to exhilaration with inspiring new leads.

I tried new combinations of ideas. Keynes emphasized uncertainty and why emotions are unavoidable—necessary for facing unknowable economic futures. Keynesians stress that animal spirits inspire executive decisions—confidence helps to press ahead, whereas depression brings listless inactivity. To me this stress was logical, but its psychology—often of CEOs' personal traits—seemed a problem. Back then, banks claimed money was "risk-free." Under uncertainty, these corporations—which do not "feel"—seemed untrustworthy. Sociological research on impersonal trust was more credible, I thought, than psychology.

Many in the sociological trust area studied how and which social groups respond with trust or faith in coping with huge corporations (see Pixley

2004: Chapter 2). In contrast, economists explained crises and booms as the fault of crowds, of manias, not of financial organizations. But money is a power relation: banks were surely as relevant to study as "crowds."

Money, a promise, is totally future-oriented and, unlike most jobs, financiers' primary (impossible) task is to guess the future "well." They deal with predictions by the minute, and their decisions can create massive losses; populations are always vulnerable to the outcomes of bankers' decisions. I decided I should "study up"—as Smart and Higley (1977) said of their research on elites: "why not ask them?"

Did they really believe the future is predictable? How did they decide? I wanted "on-the-record" interviews: probably because I hoped my data with their famous names might have an effect. Laughable though that proved, it was undeniable that I was a total outsider, armed for the dotcom boom of that time only with long university experience of the internet. To me, IT was a useful but hardly "revolutionary" reason for this financial selling game. My aim was to seek confirmation, disagreement, or elaboration of my case that specific emotions might be involved in the uncertainties of finance. The idea had instant problems. The main one was that orthodoxy could not tolerate trust. Decisions were rational—predictive in the anti-Keynesian literature. Emotions were irrational—they only influenced the masses, the herds. How dare I ask elites?

The related problem was that it was unlikely financiers would admit their job is difficult. Why would a major public figure want to tell me they created money on guesswork and trust? Imagine the outcry if the Governor of the Bank of England, or the CEO of Deutsche Bank, came out of a meeting and announced to the press: "Hey, we flipped a coin!" or "Guess what? We are bedazzled by a huge hedge fund."[1] Nobel prizes are awarded to people who "prove" that money is risk-free. To ask if this were possible might be impertinent. I would be nervous. Asking about trust would call in question their brilliance; it might suggest mendacity. If there were no dangers to banks, states, or populations, there was "therefore" no need to study emotions. Emotions were dogmatically taboo under the dotcom boom.

If officials were most likely to simply repeat this hegemonic line, whom could I ask? The answer was easy. I would ask seasoned experts who had left their star status even if still active in the finance sector. I needed to learn, and those who had experienced a few booms and busts, those no longer having to inspire confidence in public, might reflect.

Plan of action: method

Disbelief or irritation can lead to selective investigations that confirm prejudices: poor scholarship at the least. My own understanding of the process of making decisions under ever-present uncertainty was limited. In my imagination, taking momentous decisions was a terrifying job description. How could they do it? Why? Surely some emotions are involved. How many could I interview, and what were the justifications for my method? Finance journalists sympathetic to my theme discussed the best way for me to proceed. Real constraints of time and funding were less a factor than the nature of my questions. I never aimed to select a representative sample. It did not need to be statistically generalizable data because, as Mario Small argues about "sequential interviewing," qualitative work that asks "how and why" questions aims for empathetic understanding, a type of *verstehen* (Small 2009).[2] Small says it follows the "case study logic" because each case builds the understanding of the researcher, whereas a "sampling logic" would not achieve that (2009: 21–3).

If I tried to sample one whole elite, say bankers, some might stonewall, or never admit to uncertainty. They would close the door and waste my time and pathetic funding by regarding their time as so much more valuable. Some "pre-research" interviews were like that; but one former IMF official (Washington DC 1998) said "I do regret my advice to Sweden" even though it prolonged that country's banking crisis. Eureka. My written requests specified my interest in impersonal trust, which by definition ruled out true believers of the then hegemonic message. I merely wanted to find out if countervailing practices, even minor worries, exist, and why they might do so; these were further reasons that retired people in various parts of the finance sector might be more forthcoming, and ideally tell me about specific emotions.

The answers did not confirm my prejudices; rather, I discovered new things. As case study "logic" suggests, some were central bankers, some bankers, others finance journalists and PR people. Some were American, British, Swiss, and Australian (later also Japanese, French, and German). Most were very senior; a few were not; a few were women. Although I interviewed an impressive number, many of the later ones were not telling me anything new or surprising, just as Mario Small said (2009: 21–3). In fact, explanations were so sensational in a scholarly sense I could hardly keep up. I had "saturation" in my understanding and ability to make logical inferences. My comparative case study was no more "biased" than random sampling, which has built-in bias from the fact of non-response rates (often 80 percent). The group presented "empirical cases" (and how) but not from which to generalize, because they were a minority and, as they said, completely ineffectual in publicly counteracting the shameless or brazen claims.

Why answer my questions? Strategies

It is all very well to decide on the method, but how or why would even retired financiers talk about trust? One cannot ask how people feel, or remember how they felt, let alone do so relentlessly. It is invasive (brazen), a problem often ignored in studying "down" where the powerless are asked thousands of intrusive questions. Journalists do this in their practice of "door stopping"—putting a foot in the door. They ask people how they feel now their whole family has just been lost to calamity; they want crying, anger, anything for a headline. In studying up, in contrast, one faces gatekeepers. In studying up, the ethical conduct of research is built into these people's inner sanctums so that they can prevent intrusions. They have taken thousands of press conferences; they talk on and off the record at the drop of a hat. Even so, I would miss my research aim, I believed, unless they were able to correct their transcripts and change their responses to being anonymous and off the record.

Since I interviewed in order to learn, not to put them off talking, it seemed important to depersonalize and ask about the duties of office. I found a fabulous "process" diagram on decisions and animal spirits by a Post-Keynesian economist, David Dequech (1999). As a sociologist I disagreed with some of it. Turning to Theodore Kemper's discussion (1978) of anticipatory emotions and the later attributions (e.g., blame) from social psychology (Weiner 1986), I worked up my diagram of decision-making. I could depersonalize, and just show the people I interviewed these alternatives—and ask if either was at all accurate.

Another factor was that this is a huge sector of banks and central banks, which taken together cannot be said to have "feelings." Emotion-rules

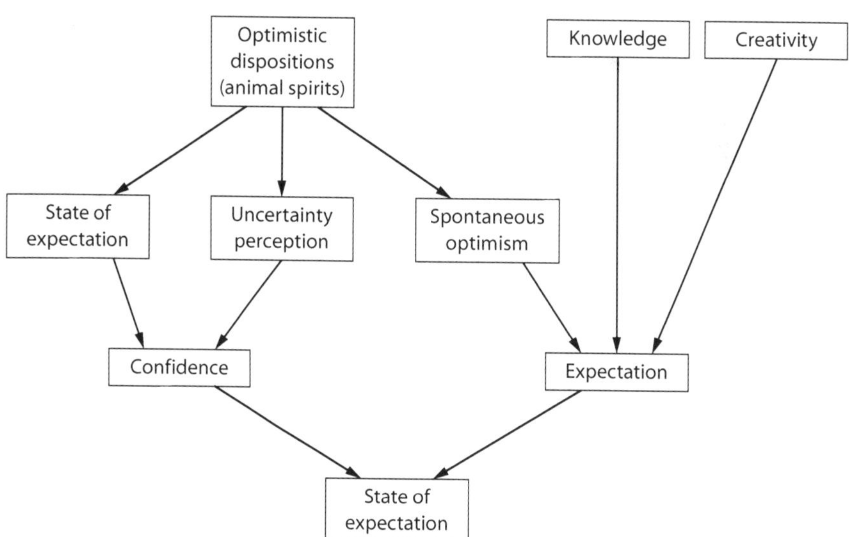

Figure 4.1 Post-Keynesian economics—determinants of the state of expectation (source: adapted from the diagram by D. Dequech (1999: 418), reproduced with permission, in Pixley (2004: 69)).

Table 4.1 Pixley's sociological model—the role of emotions in expectations and decision-making (adapting Kemper 1978: 74–5, and others)

	Projection of results of past decisions and their outcomes	*Projection of present situation*	*Into the future; "unknown" expectation*	*Result; later outcome; "the future"*
Expectations/emotions about the future; at least six permutations of anticipations and interaction rituals about past and present	Optimism/pessimism about decision outcomes, attributions of outcomes, etc. Retrospective old decisions whether success of failure	Confidence/lack of confidence about positive or negative macro situation surveys, forecasts, data, profit, and loss, rumor, etc. Todays "news"	Sum of emotions Feelings of past and present Convention Imagination equals expectation decision via trust/fear/distrust	New situation, new emotional states New interpretation of past and present data Attribution struggles start here!

Source: Pixley (2004: 70).

(Hochschild 1983; Flam 1993) seemed one way out of this impasse of moving between individual emotions and organization rules. I could then ask those involved in high-level decisions about typical procedures, the interactive rituals, and the cognitive rules—how they faced the future.

Interviews started with two set questions. First, I offered the two diagrams of possible decision procedures—the Keynesian description and my sociological one.[3] Participants assessed both, adding and subtracting various factors—emotion-rules were "OK" to some; often we had expansive discussions of emotions. Second, I questioned them about different parts of the finance sector—banks, stockbrokers, accountancy and credit-rating firms, central banks, and the finance press—and asked which they trusted from most to least. This they loved. Trust was my "entry point" emotion. For those with lengthy experience, I asked about changes from personal to impersonal trust, and historical changes in formal rules and social relations. This theoretically led preparation was crucial. Given that emotions were taboo, my abstract questions referring to their jobs— and not to vague "feelings"—were a good way to move into more taboo aspects: anxiety, guesswork, distrust, anger, and sycophancy. Some proffered stories of groveling and fear.

As I started to understand things, I became more comparative. I would say that so-and-so had spoken of *entscheidungsfreudige* bosses, and did they agree or not;[4] or what did they think about Enron's corruption? Everyone knew they were on the record, so all sides felt better once I had built up a repertoire of stories from others. There were a few unpleasant and (interestingly) uninformative interviews (which were unused), but on the whole most participants were thoughtful. They never merely "agreed" with me, and although I felt I was an incredibly slow learner it was a riveting, if slightly intimidating, time.

By 1999 my seasoned journalists[5] were extremely worried about the illicit side of the US dotcom boom; the opposite of "countervailing" practices. But only the police and regulators have formal powers to investigate illegal activities. At first I felt they were too alarmist, maybe just gossipmongers. Talk about naive. I had actually found that distrust prevailed *before* the bust. Soon into my main interviews, court judgments made my research easier. Reports of hearings and government inquiries of financiers required to answer under oath were publicly available. There were also the accounts of the whistleblowers of the 1980s with their personal "memoirs" of Wall Street banks, and insiders going public against prevailing World Bank and IMF policies. The Enron scandal broke in 2002 while I was completing the first interviews. At last I felt their distrust and pessimism.

Today, in 2014, there is an overwhelming empirical literature from government inquiries and the transcripts of heated exchanges in the US Senate—with data that none of us mere academics could ever have obtained before, or use, without risking a libel suit. The existence of this dark side of finance had mounting evidence—the charges were investigated minutely, the ugly emails appeared in headlines. This dark side had entailed much corruption during the "boom"—the so-called "normal" time that is only revealed as such during the corresponding "crash." Rigging the interbank lending rate had been going on, apparently, since 1991; but we only heard about it in 2012. The legitimacy and the social benefits that the sector claimed for itself had long been dubious, and legal evidence supported my research. Whereas many social science textbooks advise against research in "unusual" times, the financial sector is never "usual."

What all this meant was that I could draw on the publicly available dark evidence to discuss with my group—whom I eventually called "informed skeptics" (some of us talked it over). This was an important point because they were facing ridicule about being "bearish"—pessimistically gloomy about prices, as opposed to optimistic and "bullish." They thought the boom was damaging, illicit, or dubious: some were scathing, sarcastic, angry, or anxious about an approaching crash that was likely to hurt so many. Some did not see "arbitrage" serving a public purpose. They did not see "the market" as having the capacity to think or to feel. The market comprised traders working for big banks with leverage to "move" markets. Many grumbled about market "noise"—meaningless, but zero-sum, buy/sell trades; profitable for banks, but not for society.

One further method was fairly easy. Social sciences use comparison because "universals" (deductions) may not be valid. Culture, national policies, and moral economies "matter" against individualistic accounts and excuses like "human nature." I could expand my conclusions by asking if centers varied. Was Wall Street different from the City of London? Did European financiers draw on different processes? My interviews started in 1998 when Wall Street seemed particularly "aggressive," even to City bankers. Frankfurt or Zurich still emphasized "relationship banking" and trust. I was surprised at the number of complaints about the "one best way" that Europeans saw as being imposed by "Washington-Wall Street." So contrasts were useful: European experts were happy to lift the curtain on this hidden, supposedly monolithic world.

Along with theories of money and emotions, I had steeped myself in the economic uncertainty that was so strongly emphasized by Keynes, Knight, and Minsky, who wrote magically about the "tranquility of success." Although well prepared, finance was a foreign world: it frightened me. Anyone who mentioned discount windows, bid/ask spreads, or short selling had to correct their transcripts. This was all pretty embarrassing; a former Governor of the Reserve Bank of Australia seemed relieved that I had learned a bit more by my second interview. And my tape recorder had not worked for his first one: I kept that secret.

Finding my willing and skeptical group

My own (often feeble) self-confidence about asking for interviews was boosted by the public justifications for looking behind the scenes. The "on-stage" officials wield vast influence; indeed they can create recessions. For the sake of a more decent society (my hope, maybe a far-fetched one), it seems appropriate that the public should be able to assess how financiers and statesmen make decisions. Also, the civil servants in central banks needed to be questioned. Since the 1970s the common model central banks drew on for reaching decisions was driven by an assumption that if inflation was "accelerating," then that could only be because "too many" workers had jobs. The cure was to raise unemployment levels. This was cynical—how could they come to such decisions? But they surely would not tell me if I attacked them.

Through snowballing and writing polite letters, I did find many public-spirited experts. My informed skeptics were like a "social network" group (Small 2009): the benefits of snowballing are many. Recommendations helped to gain their trust. A former US Federal Reserve vice chairman personally knew a former governor of the RBA. A former editor of two major Australian newspapers knew that governor—and a former editor of *Barrons*, the Dow Jones weekly. A former London banker/stockbroker also knew two senior Bank of England officials (retired); another knew the bankers I met in Zurich. They let me use their names for the purpose of making more contacts and raising questions.

A sense of duty pervaded their agreement that these procedures should see the light of day. Perhaps because many began their careers when Keynesian policies and history were still fashionable, they were not impressed by the new jargon. But it was nerve-wracking to ask potentially embarrassing questions that could ruin an interview: a tightrope between groveling and challenging. Many probably thought sociologist meant socialist—although one advantage was that I was not a journalist, so they knew my results would be confined to an esoteric academic book rather than being splashed on the evening TV News. I doubt whether my being from an obscure and faraway country helped: every researcher is a stranger.[6] They were impressed, however, that I was so well prepared. (This is incredibly important.) Some thanked me for this.

Results written up

The fairest conclusions—yet nevertheless new knowledge—were that under uncertainty, emotions, mainly of impersonal trust, distrust and suspicion completely predominate. They insisted decisions were guesswork, and talked about a widespread "financial peep show." Their professionalism led them to dismiss the psychology in the first, Keynesian, diagram, because confidence in finance is not a trait, but a judgment about the current situation. The future might suggest great confidence about bleak *or* rosy conditions, but "mixed signals" (part bleak/part rosy) destroyed any confidence to act. Some assumptions remained taboo. Most central bankers defended rising unemployment levels and *caveat emptor*—people *should* lose on the market. They diligently corrected what were, (even to them, let alone me), embarrassing transcripts full of "rambling." Some marked certain points as off the record. One former British central banker grumbled that "emotions" and "interaction rituals" were not fashionable terms in his profession. Instead, economists had "prognostications" about the future. Am I being fair in concluding that this expresses an emotion-rule that denies emotions?

And yet I do not agree that qualitative methods are the only avenue. The basic difference is that statistical work only permits correlation, with not even a gesture at causation. With surveys we can ask about facts and attitudes, but have to guess about the "meaning" of responses, despite significant demographic data and high response rates. To back up my hypothesis about uncertainty and emotions, I did place my questions in high quality, representative population attitude surveys in both the UK and Australia. A response rate of nearly 50 percent, with some survey questions being answered by 2,000 respondents, and others by as many as 4,000+, ensured that my argument was neither circular nor notably biased. If populations accept uncertainty against the claims of high finance, then my "informed skeptics" were not unusual, and neither did they present themselves as freak geniuses. As one expert put it: "anyone with half a brain" knew there was uncertainty.

The extent to which those I surveyed accepted uncertainty and "worry a lot about their financial future" varied. In Australia, in 2005, 48 percent "worry a lot." Australians expressed the least confidence in financial institutions (in 2003, 75 percent) and the most in institutions like the national broadcaster. In Britain, more people trusted banks—only 37 percent "worry a lot," even in 2007 after the run on the English bank, Northern Rock. So, Australians were more cynical.[7] But for what reasons?

My conversations with so many experts turned into a mutual construction of new knowledge. They were intrigued about the "necessity of trust" as an unusual idea (back during the dotcom), and we joked that maybe some of our ideas were half-baked. Some of us keep still keep in touch, even now. Many are brilliant "all-rounders," such as one central banker's quote from David Hume that "passion drives reason", or a financier talking about Dickens and his capitalist characters. As for "bias," most are modestly pro-capitalist and, just as importantly, implicit sociologists.

My "informed skeptics" never accepted that uncertainty could be used as an "excuse" for major failures, or a lack of precautionary measures to protect against it. The hegemonic message is that uncertainty is a "surprise" caused by an outside "event"—but this is inadmissible to skeptics. They know any projection from the past to the future can fail at any time, and most argue that this narrow rationality, and emotions and morality, are all we have for making any decision.

"Studying up" by interviews is a difficult method—it requires funding, an incredible amount of work, and is frightening, but is great fun. I have not revisited many of the transcripts (paid for by UNSW), something I must do: one can be overwhelmed by saturation. I never carried out N-Vivo coding on people's corrected transcripts.[8] Since they are now historical records, more research is waiting. We must remember that "rational man" was meant to tame his lusts and passions, but this instrumental rationality is based on self-interest and worse. If money stirs up inevitable emotions, trying to study money's specific emotions—or emotions of any topic really—seems to involve a kind of emotional reason that tempers and inspires.

Acknowledgments

Many thanks to Helena Flam, Jochen Kleres, and Sam Dawson for their inspired comments—which greatly improved an essay that remains entirely my responsibility.

Notes

1 In a Federal Open Market Committee (FOMC) of the US Central Bank, Alan Greenspan said "bedazzled" about the gullibility of banks in lending copious amounts of money to Long Term Capital Management (LTCM) right up to its collapse in 1998. He said this with hindsight of the Fed-engineered bailout—see the FOMC transcript of the meeting of September 29, 1998 (www.federalreserve.gov/fomc/#calendars). Each debate at FOMC meetings is taped, transcribed, and released five years later. It is like being a fly on the wall; I also asked Fed participants about their interpretations of these meetings (see, for example, Blinder in Pixley 2012).

2 Although this useful article was published long after I carried out my main interviews, I was fairly experienced and think I learned a lot from senior journalists who specialize in exactly this type of interview research.

3 Mine was put more simply than the one in Pixley (2004).

4 This joy in decisions is a performance or interaction ritual, one that calls into question—again—positivist rationality.

5 I must mention that I have friends/colleagues who are senior journalists. Without their recommendations to top editors, to finance journalists working for the BBC, *The Economist*, the *Guardian*, *Australian Financial Review*, *Barrons*, *Time* and other Wall Street journalists, and on to financiers, I do not think my snowballing method would have been feasible.

6 Howard Becker (1998: 12–13): "we start with images and end with them ... we learn a little (maybe a lot)." But in starting, we use pre-established images, often "unwittingly." All I can say is that few Australians liked being interviewed by an Australian, but those who did were highly informed and critical. For second

interviews preparation is even more important; one must delve further into their earlier points, and raise new questions.

7 Australian Survey of Social Attitudes, run from the ANU; BSA's Omnibus Survey, and Ipsos-Mori in the UK; Pixley (2007); Pixley and Whimster (2010). We could not correlate the results with prior economic training (!), but PhD level respondents tended to trust banks and enjoy taking "risks" the most.

8 Coding picks patterns one might miss, but analysis is better. My best personal story involves being joined by my son—who was in his twenties and "tall, dark, and handsome" (subject to parental bias, of course)—to interview in Chicago and New York City. This gave me the "legitimacy" of having a "so-called" (though qualified) research assistant—we have different surnames and I felt this was none of their business. My impression management failed instantly. My son took notes while I acted as "the leader." He said our first effort had been going really well until I said to him: "Pass me the pencil, darling." The man we were interviewing nearly fell off his chair, apparently. We gave up the pretence that I can act, and left, giggling, to analyze the material together.

References

Becker, H. 1998. *Tricks of the Trade.* Chicago: Chicago University Press.

Dequech, D. 1999. "Expectations and Confidence under Uncertainty," *Journal of Post Keynesian Economics*, 21 (3): 415–30.

Flam, H. 1993. "Fear, Loyalty and Greedy Organizations" in S. Fincman (ed.) *Emotion in Organizations.* London: Sage.

Hochschild, A. 1983. *The Managed Heart.* Berkeley: University of California Press.

Kemper, T. D. 1978. *A Social Interactional Theory of Emotions.* New York: John Wiley & Sons.

Pixley, J. F. 2004. *Emotions in Finance: Distrust and Uncertainty in Global Markets.* Cambridge: Cambridge University Press.

Pixley, J. F. 2007. "How do Australians Feel About Financial Investment?" in D. Denemark, G. Meagher, S. Wilson, M. Western, and T. Phillips (eds) *Australian Social Attitudes 2.* Sydney: UNSW Press.

Pixley, J. F. 2012. *Emotions in Finance: Booms, Busts and Uncertainty.* 2nd edition. Cambridge: Cambridge University Press.

Pixley J. F. and S. Whimster. 2010. *Anxieties About Financial Risk in the UK and Australia.* Unpublished paper at European Sociological Association, Emotion Network Meeting, Graz: October.

Small, M. 2009. "How Many Cases Do I Need?" *Ethnography*, 10: 5–38.

Smart, D. and J. Higley. 1977. "Why Not Ask Them? Interviewing Australian Elites About National Power Structure," *Australian and New Zealand Journal of Sociology*, 13 (3): 248–53.

Weiner, B. 1986. *An Attributional Theory of Motivation and Emotion.* New York: Springer-Verlag.

Chapter 5

Exploring emotion discourse

Tamar Katriel

In their introduction to an early edited collection of anthropological articles that challenged the primacy of philosophical and psychological perspectives in the study of emotion, Lutz and Abu-Lughud (1990) argued for the value of a socio-cultural approach that foregrounds the role of discourse in shaping emotional experience. The distinctiveness of their approach lay in "its focus on the constitution of emotion, and even the domain of emotion itself, in discourse or situated speech practices." They thus proposed an understanding of emotion "as about social life rather than internal states" (Lutz and Abu-Lughud 1990: 1–2); that is, as intimately linked to the interactional management of social relations. Within this constructivist approach to emotions, they pointed out that the discourse pertaining to the realm of emotions in Western societies presents a complex picture. Emotions are at once "physiological forces, located within individuals, that bolster our sense of uniqueness and are taken to provide access to some kind of inner truth about the self" (Lutz and Abu-Lughud 1990: 6), but they are also linked to morality and sociality. Indeed, as Foucault put it, in the Western socio-cultural context "the part of ourselves which is most relevant to morality, is our feeling" (Foucault 1984: 352).

Taking the anthropological perspective on language and emotion promoted by Lutz and Abu-Lughud as my point of departure, I explore some of the ways in which the study of emotion discourse can be approached in studying emotionally laden discourses.[1] In so doing, I draw on Lutz and Abu-Lughud's distinction between two general kinds of emotion discourses that they have identified. The first category is that of discourses on emotion, which are associated with self-distance and reflexivity as well as the capacity to note and interpret the emotional displays of others. This type of explicit attention to emotion is associated in particular with the ethos of modernism and the therapeutic culture to which it gave rise (Giddens 1991; Cameron 2000), and involves linguistic practices of naming emotions, reporting on their presence and force, accounting for their emergence, and narrating about emotion-laden events.[2] The second category is that of emotional discourses. It relates to the expressivity of discourse, i.e., to the "language of affect" (Ochs and Schieffelin 1989)—that is to say, the verbal and non-verbal ways through which people display their emotionality, and its specific nature and force through the act of enunciation. These emotional cues, which form an intrinsic part of all communicational processes, are reified, interpreted, and responded to by interlocutors. At times they give rise to discourses on emotions, as, for example, in the exchange of personal experience stories or in gossip relating to the interpersonal life of others.

Interestingly, this categorization omits another dimension of the link between emotions and discourse, one that has been recognized since antiquity as central to human communication by students of rhetoric—the role of discourse as a strategic tool in evoking audiences' emotional responses in the act of persuasion (Kennedy 1991). Thus, for example, in seeking the consent of their listeners, speakers use language in particular ways to generate trust in their good intentions, or to evoke fear of an impending disaster, and so on. I refer to this third kind of link as involving emotion-evocative discourse. While all discourse is both emotionally colored by the speaker's stance, and calls forth some kind of emotional response—including indifference—on the part of listeners, I reserve this label for language used to bring forth particular emotions so as to affect listeners' attitudes and actions.

In analyzing discourses of emotion, therefore, we may attend to either one, two, or all three of these categories—and explore how emotions are discussed, how they are expressed, and/or how they are evoked. Thus, a person who admits to his or her fear, and discusses the reasons for it, employs a discourse on emotion; a person's emotional discourse may involve expressions of fear indicated by halting speech, the trembling of vocal chords, or stories about dangerous encounters. Finally, the use of veiled threats, forceful admonitions, and premonitions of disaster to arouse listeners' fears and affect their positioning on an issue are examples of an emotion-evoking discourse. While analytically distinct, these categories are variously interrelated in actual social encounters. For example, a discourse on emotions may be highly expressive as well as evocative—as in a sermon on "hope" in a religious setting—or it may be self-distancing and emotionally neutral as in analytic discussions of relational life in the social sciences. Heightened expressivity may itself be evocative, making persuasive appeals by eliciting emotional responses through identification. Studying the language of emotion in given social settings is one way of illuminating the ways in which specific emotional configurations inform the discursive construction and negotiation of self-identities, social relationships, and moral sensibilities.

Videotaped testimonies as a data set

In what follows, I try to demonstrate the workings of these categories in relation to particular cultural texts included in an ongoing study of the testimonial rhetoric of Israeli dissident veteran-activists (Katriel 2009; Katriel and Shavit 2013). Organizing under the name "Breaking the Silence" (hence, BTS) as a "witnessing organization" (Frosh 2006) in 2004, this group set out to collect, disseminate, and archive veterans' testimonies relating to their experiences as enforcers of the Israeli occupation regime in the occupied Palestinian territories. These testimonies are animated by a sense of personal rupture as these young men and women look back on their military service. They include segments that involve explicit discourses on emotions, as well as emotional displays that attend these acts of remembering and witnessing. They are explicitly addressed to the Israeli public at large, making a moral and emotional appeal in mobilizing its support for the politically controversial message they seek to promote. Presenting a voice that mainstream Israeli society and its official discourses studiously ignore, these testimonies capitalize on the authenticity of the veterans as first-hand witnesses. The archive consists of over 900 full-length videotaped interviews conducted, transcribed, and archived by BTS activists—themselves veterans who had volunteered their testimonies in the past. They are conducted one-on-one, usually in the interviewee's domestic setting. The witnesses are casually seated facing the camera, wearing civilian clothing, with the upper body made visible in the camera frame.[3] They are then thematically analyzed by BTS members according to categories that reflect dominant types of human rights violations or military activities—assassinations, bribery, checkpoints, curfews, house incursions, settler violence, rules of engagement, among others. Dozens of such thematically organized segments—typically up to five minutes long—are posted in the video section of the group's website,[4] the English version of which contains English subtitles; and, as indicated by a note on the Hebrew website, new ones are added daily as the testimonial project expands.[5] The same segment may be cross-listed under more than one theme.

Selecting a data segment

Having immersed myself in these materials, I note that in reminiscing about their daily military missions, these soldiers of the occupation regime testify to many incidents of encounters with Palestinian civilians that are emotionally laden in various ways. Given the nature of the situations described, the particular emotions that figure most prominently in these segments are fear, humiliation, and shame. My first step is to choose a set of testimonial segments that address these encounters—all of which were considered memorable enough by soldier-witnesses to be included in their testimonies—but which also have the potential of becoming memorable to viewers through the heightened sense of emotionality they convey. Depending on my particular interest, I can choose to include in my corpus all the segments posted pertaining to one particular soldier-witness, all the segments pertaining to one particular category of military action or human rights infringement, or I can choose to build a corpus that includes a segment pertaining to a blend of such categories. Given the fact that the segments are dated and the soldiers' military placement indicated, I can choose segments relating to a particular period or a particular military unit, and so on.

Whatever selection I make, depending on the specific research question that propels my analysis my goal will be to analyze the different ways in which the emotional landscape associated with this testimonial project is laid out in these accounts. This landscape of emotion is double-layered: it relates to the soldiers' emotional responses during their military service (i.e., in the past), as well as at the time of narration (i.e., in the present). Past-tense emotions associated with military service are identified, narrated, reflected upon and, at times, relived and expressed in the act of telling. Present-tense emotions are those that attend the act of witnessing, of revisiting the past—including the emotional experiences that have shaped the soldier-witnesses' memory-work at the time of the interview. These two layers of emotion discourse play a central role in the soldiers' witnessing. They weave together self-reflexive reports about the soldiers' own emotional responses at the time of the events (e.g., "I was ashamed when I realized I was enjoying the sense of power," *Hebron Booklet*: 10); of memories of events constructed in emotional terms ("The first image that I remember from the attack on the prayer route is a horrid picture of frustration, tears and anger, the bodies of terrorists," *Booklet #1*: 6); of comments concerning the emotional impact their actions were designed to have on the Palestinians under their control (e.g., "We talked to one of the wanted persons that sat in the middle and we sat the dogs next to him, two on each side. We photographed him deathly afraid and asked him, 'What? Are you afraid?'" *Booklet #1*: 41); the observed emotional effects of repressive acts (e.g., "He was a 16-year-old boy who started to cry in jail, just like a girl. And because he was so panicked, he fainted in front of his parents," *Booklet #1*: 14); reports of emotional awakening after the discharge from active duty (e.g., "It takes time to realize that for three years we were not human beings. We were sort of Zombies, not making our own decisions, carrying things out without a second's thought," *Booklet #1*: 24); or imagined emotions that are self-reflexively entertained at the time of narration (e.g., "I think if this happened the other way around, I don't know what I'd do. Really. I'd go crazy if my home would be entered like that. I tried to imagine my parents, my family, what would they actually do if people with guns would enter a home with small children, 4–5 years old, point weapons at them and say 'OK, everybody move!'" *Hebron Booklet*: 4). While foregrounding discourses on emotion, and giving voice to emotional discourses, these testimonies are also designed to elicit identification or empathy—mobilizing hearers to help combat Israel's occupation policies. In other words, they also play the role of emotion-evoking discourses.

Types of discourses on emotion—some examples

I begin my search by attending to the discourses on emotions interspersed in the soldiers' testimonials as they reconstruct emotion-laden moments of their military service by self-reflexively naming and describing particular emotional responses—their own as well as those they ascribe to the people they encountered. I note two different elements that make up discourses on emotions included in soldiers' descriptions of encounters with Palestinian civilians as part of the everyday life of the occupation:

1 references to the intensity of emotional responses, and
2 references to specifically named emotional responses.

Let me give some examples of each. At various points in their accounts the soldiers' testimonies indicate their ongoing preoccupation with the intensity of feelings, and their regulation. Soldiers' accounts of emotional intensity range from the emotional overflow associated with baffling or tantalizing moments in which soldiers are faced with the brutal reality of military action; through to the studiously cultivated detachment that comes with the habituated following of military orders.

The emotionally tantalizing moments are often associated with the experience of "moral shock" (Jasper 1997) that attends the soldiers' realization of the meaning and human consequences of the use they make of the absolute power placed in their hands, or of the shamefulness of the situations they find themselves in. The soldiers' overflowing feeling of power may become a need, an addiction. In one case a soldier describes his elation when manning a checkpoint that controlled the Palestinians' movement, putting it in a way that brings out the paradox of power when it is riddled with a sense of dependency:

> You start playing with them, as if playing a computer game. You come here, you go there.... It's a mighty feeling. It's something you don't experience elsewhere. You know it's because you have a weapon ... but it's addictive. When I realized this ... it was a big bubble that burst.
>
> (*Hebron Booklet*: 10)

In another case a soldier describes an incident in which a Palestinian funeral procession—including the dignified figure of a Palestinian patriarch followed by his clan—is driven away, during curfew, from the graveyard by a unit to which he belonged. As in other, unexpected cases of moral shock, the old man's emotional response overwhelms the soldier and the event becomes etched in his memory, filling him with a sense of self-loathing:

> ... and I see his eyes filled with tears, and he says something in Arabic, turns around, and goes.... I'm not exactly sure why this particular incident is engraved in my memory ... but there was something so noble about him, and I felt like the scum of the earth.
>
> (*Hebron Booklet*: 40)

It is often the overpowering impact of such incidents of moral shock that combine intensity of feeling and a reflexive moment of self-awareness which lead witnesses to discuss and/or label their emotions, as in "I was ashamed of myself the day I realized that I simply enjoy the feeling of power" (*Hebron Booklet*: 10); in describing a fear-stricken Palestinian youth captured by soldiers, who had already wet his pants, a soldier-witness says "this was one of the most humiliating incidents I've ever witnessed" (*Hebron Booklet*: 26); or in describing his reaction to the breach in social code the occupier role forced on him, "A soldier like me felt embarrassed in situations in which I was confronted with adults, old people" (*Hebron Booklet*: 12).

At the other end of the emotional intensity scale, some of these soldier-witnesses describe their encounters with the Palestinian civilian population as involving emotional detachment. As one of them reflected in retrospect: "It's hard to describe the enormous sea of indifference you're swimming in while you're there [Hebron]" (*Hebron Booklet*: 17). Another witness conceded that this state of detachment led to a lack of understanding and empathy for the plight of the Palestinians under military control:

> The thing I managed to understand only later, honestly because that place makes you emotionally detached and you aren't really able to figure out what goes on there.... I understood how inhumane it was. How evil it is to do this to people.
>
> (*Hebron Booklet*: 13)

All of these witness accounts refer not only to emotional intensity, but also to explicitly named and *particular* emotions. These may include the enjoyment of power ("It's a mighty feeling. It's something you don't experience elsewhere," *Hebron Booklet*: 10); or of the quality of one's military performance ("I really enjoyed it.... And we acted flawlessly. We performed superbly," *Booklet #2*: 2); or the trigger-happy quest for shooting targets ("all of us were happy that we got to shoot at streetlights and cars, because there's nothing so cool," Hebron Booklet: 25). Mostly, however, the discourse on emotions in the soldiers' testimonies involves references to negative emotions that imply a moral judgment of their conduct. Thus, frequent mention is made of the Palestinians' fear and victimhood, but also of the soldiers' own sense of helplessness ("I had nothing to say to him. Nothing. I went completely blank," *Hebron Booklet*: 17). Soldier-witnesses describe the humiliation the Palestinians face, and sometimes express their embarrassment and shame at their complicity in inflicting it. At times they voice their outrage at the emotional displays of some of their peers or commanders, as in:

> ... and there were really more than a hundred people who watched this scene of an officer dispersing with such hatred. And through this hatred and insistence on dispersing the funeral, I could really see that he didn't consider them equal human beings.
>
> (*Hebron Booklet*: 11)

Their own, their peers', and the Palestinians' emotional responses are named and described from a retrospective and/or outsider's point of view.

These soldier-witnesses' discourses on emotion are spoken performances that give voice to their emotions at the time of telling. That is, the act of witnessing is partly constituted out of emotional discourses that give expression to the soldiers' state of feeling as they reminisce about—and relive their experience during—their military service. In many cases these emotional discourses involve a self-distancing move as witnesses highlight the distance between the emotional and moral matrix that dominated their lives during their military experience; and their states of feeling and judgment in the present. As in the foregoing examples, some of these emotional discourses come in the form of explicit verbal references to feelings, as also in: "The most striking thing I remember from operation 'Rainbow' ... was the feeling of lack of restraint. I don't have a milder description for it: an indiscriminate use of force" (*Booklet #2*: 15); or in "What disturbs me most, and what bothers me most is the lack of value of human life in the occupied territories" (*Booklet #2*: 23). Such accounts of emotional difficulty are rarely accompanied by emotive cues—such as a choking voice, or halting speech. Mostly, these segments present smoothly flowing accounts of events the speakers witnessed, with their facial expressions and hand movements often included in the frame as they remember and relive reportable incidents from their military past. A detailed analysis of the non-verbal dimensions of the emotional displays accompanying the autobiographical moments captured on film is beyond the confines of this paper. Let me just note that even those witnesses who stated that they were recounting their military experiences for the first time presented animated yet measured accounts of what they saw, did, and felt—preferring to verbalize their emotions rather than being flooded by them. At times, their tone of voice appears dulled, or they employ self-distancing, ironical comments—both of these being strategies that convey an effort to contain the emotions associated with their acts of remembering.

Finally, it is clear that these soldiers' testimonies have an emotion-evocative dimension, attempting to create identification among their audiences by claiming affinity with them as "run-of-the-mill Israelis," or by triggering their sense of outrage through stories of abrasive conduct. Yet their main thrust lies in the first-hand, authentic information they provide, and in the moral stance they project. Their main goal is to attain a new public understanding—and acknowledgment—of the situation in the occupied territories; and the evocative force of their emotional appeal is mobilized towards that goal. At the same time, in stories about the occupation, emotion-evoking discourse was also mobilized as part of the arsenal of control acts designed to subjugate the Palestinian population—shouting, ridicule, and intimidation were some of the army's methods of evoking fear and confusion, with the aim of generating obedience; alongside bodily practices such as street patrols, house incursions, shootings, obstruction of movement, and so forth (e.g., "he hit the man's face with the handle of his rifle, kicked him in the groin, spat on him, cursed him—simply went berserk. In front of the man's little boy. He just humiliated him" (*Booklet #1*: 39).

In this essay I have built on Lutz and Abu-Lughud's insight concerning the need to distinguish different categories of emotion discourse based on different uses of language in conjunction with emotion. In so doing I added another category—that of emotion-evoking discourse that is designed to capture the concern with the way language is used to affect the emotional responses of audiences, a long-time concern of the art of rhetoric. Using examples of testimonial discourse elicited, disseminated, and archived by the Israeli veteran group BTS, I have tried to show how this categorization can serve as a heuristic in navigating our way when exploring the emotional contours of a particular discursive corpus. In different social contexts these categories of emotion discourse may combine to generate a particular configuration of emotionality, with one category taking precedence over the others (or not). In the context of BTS discourse, the discourse on emotions is dominant, reflecting the situation of self-reflexive reminiscing and expressive restraint that characterizes the interview situation in which it is anchored, as witnesses both remember and discuss their past and current emotional responses. This analytic distinction between categories of emotion discourse can help us to recognize the different ways and different degrees to which emotion discourses can serve as tools of self-reflexivity, expressivity, and evocativeness in social settings; and thus guide our inquiry into the social life of emotions.

Notes

1 Reddy (1997, 1999) critiques the constructionist approach in the study of emotion, including the line of research advanced by Lutz and Abu-Lughud. I find their mild version of constructivism helpful, and do not find that it prevents us from acknowledging the role of agency and politics in this kind of inquiry. Indeed, the case study of soldiers' witnessing, discussed below, focuses on the expression of personal emotions that go against the normative order in the context of military engagements, whose very articulations are political acts.

2 Discourses on emotions involve constative utterances, which can be identified as true or false. Reddy proposes the concept of "emotives" as utterances involving "first-person present-tense emotion claims [that] have a descriptive appearance in the sense that emotion words are used in predicates that apply to personal states" (Reddy 1999: 268). These claims, however, cannot be verified. They are, moreover, relationally grounded, and involve "self-exploring and self-altering effects" (Reddy 1999). Given this particular configuration, he suggests that emotives constitute a distinctive category of utterances—neither constatives, nor performatives. As we shall see, most of the examples of emotion talk in my data involve "first-person past-tense" claims, which Reddy also—but tangentially—includes in the concept of "emotives" as they indirectly affect present emotional states.

3 See Breaking the Silence website, available at: www.breakingthesilence.org.il/testimonies/videos (last accessed December 9, 2014).

4 The organization has also published several testimonial booklets, including *Testimonial Booklet #1* (2004)—what I call the *Hebron Booklet* (2004), originally entitled *Breaking the Silence: Soldiers Speak Out About their Service in Hebron* (2004)—and *Testimonial Booklet #2* (2005). Both are used here, as well as a full-length book published in 2012. The group also conducts tours in Hebron, holds traveling photography exhibitions, numerous lecture tours, and other public encounters (all of which are listed on their website).

5 I use the terms "soldier" and "veteran" interchangeably. These young men's situation is indeed ambiguous. While most of the witnesses testified after completing their three-year mandatory military service, some of them continue to be called up for reserve duty for up to one month per year, never quite leaving the army behind.

References

BTS (Breaking the Silence). 2012. *Our Harsh Logic: Israeli Soldiers' Testimonies from the Occupied Territories 2000–2010.* New York: Henry Holt & Co.

Cameron, D. 2000. *Good to Talk?* London: Sage Publications.

Foucault, M. 1984. "On the genealogy of ethics: An overview of work in progress" in P. Rabinow (ed.) *The Foucault Reader.* London: Penguin.

Frosh, P. 2006. "Telling Presences: Witnessing, Mass Media, and the Imagined Lives of Strangers," *Critical Studies in Media Communication,* 23 (4): 265–84.

Giddens, A. 1991. *Modernity and Self-Identity: Self and Society in the Late Modern Age.* Cambridge: Polity.

Jasper, J. 1997. *The Art of Moral Protest: Culture, Biography, and Creativity in Social Movements*. Chicago: The University of Chicago Press.

Katriel, T. 2009. "Inscribing Narratives of Occupation in Israeli Popular Memory" in M. Keren and H. Herwig (eds) *War Memory and Popular Culture: Essays on Modes of Remembrance and Commemoration*: 150–65. Jefferson, NC: McFarland Publishers.

Katriel, T. and N. Shavit. 2013. "Speaking Out: Testimonial Rhetoric in Israeli Soldiers' Dissent," *Versus: Quaderni di Studi Semiotici*, 116: 81–105.

Kennedy, G. A. (trans./ed.). 1991. *Aristotle 'On Rhetoric': A Theory of Civic Discourse*. New York, Oxford: Oxford University Press.

Lutz, C. and L. Abu-Lughud. 1990. "Introduction: Emotion, Discourse, and the Politics of Everyday Life" in C. Lutz and L. Abu-Lughud (eds) *Language and the Politics of Emotion*. Cambridge: Cambridge University Press.

Ochs, E. and B. Schieffelin. 1989. "Language Has a Heart," *Text*, 9:7–25.

Reddy, W. M. 1997. "Against Constructionism: The Historical Ethnography of Emotions," *Current Anthropology*, 38 (3): 327–51.

Reddy, W. M. 1999. "Emotional Liberty: Politics and History in the Anthropology of Emotions," *Cultural Anthropology*, 14 (2): 256–88.

Chapter 6

The rhetoric of emotions

Barbara Czarniawska

The traps of emotion studies

Psychologists worry that people will lie, or report incorrectly, if they are asked to describe their emotions, and so they have turned to neuropsychology for help (see, e.g., Borod 2000). Yet, as Rorty (1980) noted, no matter how successful the neuropsychologists are in locating the physiological equivalents of psychological states, they will not explain the events of social life. In brief, "the inside of people and quasi-people is to be explained by what goes on outside (and, in particular, by their place in our community) rather than conversely" (Rorty 1980: 191).

But even if one abandons the ambition of establishing what goes on "inside of people" (or leaving such matters to psychologists), how is one to establish "what goes on outside?" Traditional methodologies offer two pathways: to ask people to describe their emotions, or to deduce their emotions from their observable behavior (including their speech acts). Both approaches are fraught with peril. In the case of accounts, what if the only result of such a study was the discovery of the rhetoric of emotions—i.e., a way of speaking about emotions that certain people at certain times and in certain places consider to be legitimate? In the case of observations, how can one know that deductions reached about other people's emotions are correct? The external signs of emotions differ across cultures and between individuals, as Camus dramatically illustrated in *L'Etranger* [The Stranger]. In what follows, I agree with the critique of the observational approach and defend the approach of asking for accounts.

The question of incorrect or downright false accounts of emotions becomes irrelevant if the Rortian idea of abandoning the ambition of "mirroring nature" is accepted. As Rorty wrote, "the notion of psychological states as inner representations is unobjectionable but fairly uninteresting" (Rorty 1980: 242). Rather, the starting point could be another of his propositions—namely, that "[t]here is nothing to people except what has been socialized into them—their ability to use language, and thereby to exchange beliefs and desires with other people" (Rorty 1989: 177). Consequently, people's accounts of emotions are all there is, and the very fact that these accounts differ among persons, cultures, and circumstances should be of central interest to researchers. To paraphrase Burke (1950), I plead for studies of the "rhetoric of emotions," because this is all there is and this is what needs to be known—i.e., how people speak about their own and others' emotions in different times and places. In what follows I present two approaches to such studies: an analysis of existing literature, and the eliciting of narratives.

Emotions from high and low

Not all psychologists turned to neuropsychology to study emotions. Stanley Milgram's pupils—John Sabini and Maury Silver (1998a)—contrasted two perspectives on emotions. First they looked at William James's idea that emotions are like the act of sneezing—an outward manifestation of a bodily change but one which is almost uncontrollable to the individual doing the sneezing. That is to say, emotional responses can be triggered beyond an individual's own cognition. The other perspective Sabini and Silver looked at was the social constructivist stance taken by Harré and Gillett (1994), who believed that emotions are elements of conversation equivalent to judgments, and that their relationship to bodily states is an epiphenomenon of Anglo-American culture. Sabini and Silver came to the conclusion that emotions are like both sneezes and judgments—i.e., they are at the same time like bodily states *and* social constructions.

> [W]e argue that what makes an experience an authentic experience of an emotion is that the experience is [...] beyond the will. To ask whether an emotional reaction is a genuine experience of anger, say, is not to ask whether it is an expression of anger, but to ask whether the person experiencing it could do other than experience it. Faked expressions of emotions are just as thoroughly expressions of judgments, i.e., are of the appropriate form to convey the judgments underlying love, or anger etc., as are real experiences of emotion.
>
> (Sabini and Silver 1998a: 226)

One should not assume, however, that bodily experience is necessary for emotional experience. Obsessive thoughts, or an inability to concentrate, are also beyond someone's will, and, as such, can give rise to emotions ("any facet of experience that shows a lack of control will do" (Sabini and Silver 1998a: 226)). Furthermore, "Pleasure and pain are beyond the will and central to emotions.... [O]ne cannot simply decide to feel pain about an aspect of oneself, or to take pleasure in it; the pleasure and the pain come despite one's desires" (ibid.: 227). Even the act of hurting oneself may bring about pain *or* pleasure, no matter what the original intentions were.

Sabini and Silver pointed out that Harré and Gillett had not differentiated between the *expression* of emotion and the *experience* of emotion, and had thereby failed to take note of the importance of unintentional bodily signals and that "[bodily] expressions of emotions are more powerful than verbal glosses because they are taken to be involuntary and for that reason taken to be authentic and sincere" (ibid.: 232).

Indeed (at least in the cultures that I have experienced), it is assumed that the body "betrays" the mind, despite the learned behavior of giving off "appropriate" body signals. But while I would agree that the separation of the expression of an emotion and the experience of an emotion makes a great deal of sense, I do not see how the relationship between the two can be examined by anything other than speculative means. After all, many combinations are possible: a person can, for example, hide an experience by faking the expression (poker face); express an experience incorrectly (by unintelligible signals); or fake a non-experience by faking the expression (politeness). So, perhaps on one point Harré and Gillett were correct: expressions of emotions lead to judgments of experience by the observers.

In their 1982 book Sabini and Silver signaled their departure from the experimentalist tradition of social psychology, and moved towards work descriptions, ideal types, and discourse analyses:

> (1) we arrive at the nature of phenomena through linguistic analysis, and (2) we use "ideal type" explanations.... [W]e agree with Austin that the proper starting point of analysis is ordinary language, and that ordinary language is likely to provide the important distinctions that are necessary to understand the social life.... [A] second method we use [is] akin to the method of ideal types. This method is addressed in part to causal questions.... And here, no doubt, is where we look most like we are speculating—and we do, a bit.
>
> (Sabini and Silver 1982: 7, 9)

And this is precisely what they did in their book on the relationship between emotion, character, and responsibility. They analyzed Kant's view of emotion and responsibility, and contrasted it with Aristotle's. They constructed a great many hypothetical examples (e.g., "Imagine my being insulted by my boss," Sabini and Silver 1998b: 37). They examined texts written by philosophers and social scientists, but also those penned by authors including Rousseau, Joyce, and Camus. In other words, their work was purely speculative. They concluded that emotions are connected to passions, and that an element of disruption—of goal-directed activities and reveries—connects emotions to one another. Yet emotions are significant "because they have empirical connection to authentic desire. Those authentic desires are important per se, the emotions aren't" (ibid.: 160).

Both the discussion and the conclusions are noteworthy, but they cannot be reached by way of speculation alone. How, then, could one study emotions in practice, without recourse to experiment? In the next section I present two such attempts, both of them related to Sabini and Silver's perspective.

Studying humiliation

One work that had its origins in Sabini and Silver's perspective on emotions was the Silver *et al.* (1986) study of humiliation. The theoretical framework of the paper is the same as in other Sabini and Silver writings, and the article contains many fascinating speculations—but also a novelty. It analyzes a case of humiliation enforced by guards upon prisoners of German labor camps during World War II. Silver *et al.* used secondhand material—accounts of camp survivors collected by Terence Des Pres (1976). They quoted Des Pres's analysis, but also entered into a polemic with his interpretations and offered some interpretations of their own, bolstering their speculations with corroborating examples from the movies (Lina Wertmueller's *Seven Beauties*), The Bible (Matthew 27: 21–31), and novels (Orwell's *Nineteen Eighty-Four*).

My own interest in humiliation arose from a study of another phenomenon: the exercise of power in organizations. My colleagues and I asked students in seven European countries (Sweden, Norway, Finland, Italy, Poland, Germany, and England) to write short stories illustrating the phenomenon of power in work organizations (Czarniawska-Joerges and Kranas 1991; Czarniawska-Joerges 1994).

The procedure employed in the project was influenced by Egon Bittner's suggestion that one ought to study the concept of organization as a commonsense construct (Bittner 1965). Replacing the concept of "organization" with that of "power," one can say that if one isolates the concept of power from the world of everyday life, it becomes empty—in the sense that it is impossible to establish the facts to which it relates or how it relates to them. "Without knowing the structure of this relationship of reference, the meaning of the concept and its terms cannot be determined" (Bittner 1965: 247).

In order to tackle this difficulty the researcher can use one of three procedures. The first involves making assumptions for the purposes of the study in hand, i.e., that "the unexplicated commonsense meanings of the terms are adequate definitions" (ibid.). Thus, one might construct a questionnaire comprising questions about power distribution, power structures, and power allocation—on the assumption that the potential respondents know what "power" is, and that their knowledge and understanding of it is identical to that of the researcher.

The second procedure requires the construction of an operational definition. This requires those being surveyed to temporarily abandon their *own* definitions in favor of those of the researchers. This approach, at least, limits the possibility of the researcher and those being studied talking at cross-purposes.

The third procedure is to study "how the terms of [the researcher's] discourse are assigned to real objects and events by normally competent persons in ordinary situations" (ibid.). I have used this procedure myself, albeit in a variation adapted to the circumstances of my own study. True, I did not observe actual organizing, but I knew from many previous field studies that "normally competent persons" in work organizations talked about power, and that they used the concept to interpret the significance of their own and other people's actions. It might be questioned whether the students I studied could be considered "normally competent persons," but these were MBA, business administration, and organizational psychology students who had either professional experience in organizing, or at least some familiarity with the reality of work organizations gained via various placements, apprenticeships, and study projects.[1]

About 5 percent of the stories in this study described how people in power humiliated their subordinates. I might not have paid special attention to these stories were it not for the intensity of their comments. But the young people who wrote them saw such events as repugnant, and intended to change things when given the opportunity to do so.

I was reminded of these stories during a later study of big city firm management that included my shadowing officials in the Municipality of Warsaw (Czarniawska 2002). Here is an excerpt from my field notes: a meeting of about ten people, including the Deputy Mayor and a female manager (in the field notes referred to as "Woman Top Professional") who held the highest staff position in her specialty.

> The meeting cannot begin because a quorum is lacking. Woman Top Professional (age about 60) is standing at the table opposite to Deputy Mayor, listening to his complaints about lack of punctuality, and smiling at him. I would call it a gracious and understanding smile. "Will you erase that stupid smile from your face, madam," says he. Her smile fades. She tries to explain: "Nothing of the kind, I was smiling with understanding . . ." Deputy Mayor: "There is nothing funny in this situation."
>
> Woman Top Professional returns to her chair like a scolded girl. Her chin shakes; I am sitting opposite her and can see tears in her eyes.
>
> (Czarniawska 2008: 1035)

To me, it was a clear case of publicly inflicted humiliation. Later, however, I began to wonder. Did it feel like humiliation to her? Does it matter whether she and I perceived it in the same way? And, in the face of Sabini and Silver's quest for authenticity, and the difference between experience and expression, did she want to show sympathy or did she *intend* to irritate Deputy Mayor? Did he misread her smile on purpose, or merely because he lacked sensitivity? I am showing how such a chain of unanswerable questions can be spun practically *ad infinitum*; and the only way out, therefore, is to stop asking them and take the expressions of emotions at their face value—literally.

These excerpts from different field materials piqued my interest in the issue of humiliation in the context of organization, partly because generating humiliation seemed to be in such contrast to the apparently rational *raison d'être* of work organizations. Thus I decided to conduct my own study of humiliation, specifically humiliation related to work situations.

Constructing a theory of humiliation in workplaces

My study and my construction of a theory of workplace humiliation comprised five steps.

Step 1

I entered "humiliation" into AltaVista (my browser at the time), which revealed more than 250,000 entries. More than half were focused on sexual acts, and of the rest more than half referred to religious matters. Within the still-shrinking bulk of entries, many were connected to war and the humiliation of a conquered enemy. Finally, I concentrated on two types of entry: actual materials from work organizations, and social science works on the issue of humiliation.

Step 2

The great variety of entries made me aware that there are different views of humiliation as an experience. It was time, therefore, to reach for social science studies of the phenomenon. I located one text relating to humiliation in organizational settings (Dennis Smith 2002), but it was again a speculative piece: using Norbert Elias's framework, the author introduced a typology of humiliation mechanisms. I therefore remained with Silver *et al.* (1986), having decided to test their conclusions against my material.

Whether humiliation is a positive or a negative emotion depends on its cognitive component. According to Silver *et al.*, the feeling of humiliation is related to an assessment of a person's socially relevant capacities or powers. Feeling humiliated means feeling powerless—not of one's own choice (emotions are beyond the will). Thus, a person who willingly participates in sexual activities that are considered humiliating by non-participants is actually arranging a social act of humiliation as a play—and there is no reason for this person to feel humiliated. As for the observers, they may perceive such an act as "evil" or "alien." Therefore, "what separates 'humiliation' from 'the evil,' 'the alien' is choice and power" (ibid.: 274). The power to choose saves a person from feeling humiliated, no matter what observers may think. The observers' negative opinions may be grounded in different standards or norms of expected behavior, be they be moral, aesthetic, or simply those of appropriateness.

Similarly, a person who chooses to submit to humiliation while being able to withdraw from it, does not feel humiliated. The Pope washes the feet of the poor, and whereas this action is commonly recognized as potentially humiliating, its context and the standards set for it by a particular community do not make it so. "[A] flaw measured against the standard of one group may be a reason for celebration when seen against the standards of another" (ibid.: 277).

Silver *et al.* (1986) also claimed that although humiliation is often public, it does not need to be so. It is possible to feel humiliated when alone, or when the only witness is the person doing the humiliating. Public humiliation is the most strongly felt, however: "Knowing that a public knows your humiliation makes the story harder to reinterpret or forget" (ibid.: 279). In sum, "humiliation involves not having the powers that we believe members of a group should have and this in turn involves standards of what is appropriate" (ibid.: 277).

For the rest of my study I decided to follow Latour's (1986) plea to search for performative definitions (which is equivalent to Bittner's (1965) third procedure), and therefore limited my attention to social acts and situations that are labeled by actors or observers (including myself) as "humiliation." A performative definition that can be rendered in a text (rather than observed when performed in practice) would therefore collect commonalities in the descriptions of such situations. Intentions, motives, and feelings can be represented only in utterances—ascriptions or descriptions. Thus equipped, I turned to my own field material (as different from that provided to me by the AltaVista search).

Step 3

I went back to the power stories written by the students, looking for stories that described social acts perceived as humiliating by an observer (including self-observation, i.e., introspection); or by the reader (my co-author and myself). We found seven such stories, all of which reported events that fit the definition of humiliation suggested by Silver *et al.* (1986): that humiliation is the perceived inability to exhibit a socially expected reaction to a situation in which a person is deprived of his or her dignity—as defined by a given community. In the stories written by the students, people in power took away from their subordinates the rights that are taken for granted in societies in which the described situations occurred. The humiliated persons felt powerless to resist such a withdrawal of rights. A new question then arose: "Why did the observers not oppose the humiliation?"

Step 4

My field notes provided me with material to help me to answer this question (I could not ask the students for further explanations). This material, and the speculations grounded in its re-reading, led me to formulate three tentative answers. The first was that the reason was yet another emotion—the embarrassment felt by the observers (but possibly also by the victims). Silver *et al.* (1987: 48) suggested that embarrassment "is a flustering caused by the perception of a fumbled or botched performance."[2]

The second answer—perhaps the most obvious one—has been clearly visible in the analysis of labor camps: fear. Observers (and victims) do not react because they fear further humiliation or some other retaliation.

The third answer is that, in some organizational contexts, humiliation is perceived as "natural"—its occurrence does not cause surprise. An female Italian politician, telling the story of her career to the participants of a workshop on "Gender as Social Practice" (in Trento, Italy, November 28, 2003), said: "It wasn't that bad.... I wasn't constantly humiliated."

Thus, my grounded theory of humiliation in work organizations was that it is, in fact, a standard organizational product. I needed a further test of my emerging theory. What I then knew was that people other than myself had observed humiliation in work organizations, and understood it by the same term. Thus encouraged, I moved to the final step in my study.

Step 5

I elicited narratives of humiliation by asking organizational practitioners to whom I had access (friends or acquaintances) if they had experienced humiliation in their professional lives. If the answer was positive, I asked for a detailed description. I also extracted narratives from earlier interviews with practitioners in which they themselves mentioned feeling humiliated.

The results of my analyses can be read in full in Czarniawska (2008). In brief, my summarizing concept "standard product" was not meant to suggest that incidents of humiliation always look alike, but that they are "normal, typical, usual, ordinary, regular, customary, everyday" (*Encarta World English Dictionary*). The question was, however, if it was also "prevailing," which is another synonym for "standard." In other words, one could ask how pervasive is the phenomenon of humiliation in work organizations?

It has been generally agreed that bullying in workplaces, marginal as it is, deserves the most serious attention. My humiliation stories can be clearly seen as illustrating a type of bullying. According to Ellis (1997), humiliation is the second most frequent type of bullying—after aggressive shouting. In his questionnaire-based study of the British retail industry, 56.6 percent of respondents recounted cases of bullying—70.6 percent of which were cases of "public humiliation of the victim."

Remarkably, it is not always subordinates who are humiliated; people in middle management can also be humiliated by their subordinates. Women in Denise Salin's (2003) study revealed that they were often bullied by their subordinates, and David Sims's (2003) vignettes show that junior officers are especially vulnerable. In such cases, humiliation is a by-product of power, which the middle managers do not have enough of. Humiliation, I concluded, may not be a mass-produced product, but it is certainly manufactured in work organizations.

Methodological comments

Studying the ways in which people judge (and misjudge) the authenticity of expressions of emotions by others is of great interest, not least when it is applied across cultures. It is not an easy task from the point of view of field methodology, but I think one solution is to apply the same approach that I recommend for all sensitive issues, including gender discrimination (Czarniawska 2006).

This approach grew from the observation that studying sensitive issues in organizations, especially negative phenomena, is always problematic because methods and techniques that are commonly used are not suitable here. To begin with, events such as gender discrimination, which create negative emotions, are rarely, if ever, revealed in interview—unless the fact of discrimination is the reason for the interview. Interviews with victims of discrimination have little credibility on the somewhat paradoxical grounds that the participant must be biased because they have been wronged (on silencing female voices in interviews, see Reinharz and Chase 2002). Furthermore, an interview with a traumatized person requires both courage and therapeutic skills that few organization scholars possess.

It seems to follow that an empirical study of emotions in the workplace should require prolonged direct observation. Even this method, however, is not without its complications. For one thing, the observer's interpretations may differ drastically from the interpretations of those who are observed. I have quoted some examples—actual and hypothetical—but a much more dramatic example is Barbara Ehrenreich's (2001) remarkable participant-observation study of low-wage US workers. Her worker colleagues firmly opposed the suggestion that they were being exploited, and explained to her that they were fully satisfied with both their work and their work conditions. Resorting to the "false consciousness" hypothesis in such cases can be seen as both condescending and defensive, as Reinharz and Chase (2002) rightly observed.

Thus, whereas participant and direct observation—difficult as they are—may remain ideal ways of undertaking field research, I find that an analysis of narratives describing emotional states—observed or experienced—is to be recommended. Such narratives can be extracted from fiction—literature and film, like Silver *et al.* (1986) did—or as I did studying gender discrimination (Czarniawska 2006). But narratives collected in one way or another (from documents, from interviews, from field notes) provide useful field material, especially when the focus of the work of fiction, or the field study, lies elsewhere. In fiction, works focused on a certain social problem usually contain the author's theory of that problem (for example, all Sara Paretsky's books can be seen as a series of sociological treatises on the various ailments of US society; Czarniawska 1999). In such cases the social scientist competes with the original author of the work of fiction in their attempts to theorize—a difficult task, as we all know from conducting interviews with interlocutors who are prone to theorizing. The authors of fiction, however, usually cover a marginal topic with care for the reason of veracity—they try to avoid marginal mistakes that may detract the reader (or the viewer) from the main plot.

Similarly, narratives either from interviews or elicited, as in my study of power, may be more informative on the issue of emotions if their main topic is different. For my study of humiliation, described in this paper, I elicited narratives concerning humiliating events only once I had obtained a great deal of material documenting the existence of the phenomenon in other contexts. In this way, "artificial" enunciations—such as interview answers or "commissioned" stories—come closer to the "natural discourse" so cherished by ethnomethodologists. Under the microscope, emotions may become too dark or too bright. Seen from a corner of the eye, however, they look ordinary. In such a way, researchers can learn more about "what has been socialized into people"—as far as expressing emotions and speaking about them is concerned.

Notes

1 The instruction ran as follows: "Power is one of the phenomena that always interested social scientists, whether they are philosophers or organization theorists. Nevertheless, we do not really know what power looks like in concrete, contemporary organizations. Please think for a moment about an incident involving organizational power that you recently observed. Take some time now, before reading further, to remember the details of that incident. [Next page] Now please describe, as fully as possible, the details of that incident, explaining the situation that led to the incident, the people involved, what was said and done by whom, and the consequences of the incident. Take as many additional pages

as you wish [Blank page]. Why have you chosen this particular incident? Could you comment on organizational power as you see it and as it is described in your incident? Thank you very much for your cooperation!"

2 And again, importantly: "a bad performance of a character is not the same as the performance of a bad character" (Silver *et al.* 1987: 47). Embarrassment may result from bad performance. Observers may feel embarrassed by someone else's botched performance (Silver *et al.* (1987), called this "secondary embarrassment")—in this case, of the *victim* (who should have acted as a proper organizational citizen and protested), not of the bully (who is playing a bad character well).

References

Bittner, E. 1965. "The Concept of Organization," *Social Research*, 31: 240–55.

Borod, J. C. 2000. *The Neuropsychology of Emotions.* New York: Oxford University Press.

Burke, K. 1950. *A Rhetoric of Motives.* Upper Saddle River, NJ: Prentice-Hall.

Czarniawska, B. 1999. *Writing Management. Organization Theory as a Literary Genre.* Oxford, UK: Oxford University Press.

Czarniawska, B. 2002. *A Tale of Three Cities, or the Glocalization of City Management.* Oxford, UK: Oxford University Press.

Czarniawska, B. 2003. "Social Constructionism in Organization Studies" in S. Clegg and R. Westwood (eds) *Debating Organizations. Point-Counterpoint in Organization Studies*: 128–134. Oxford, UK: Blackwell.

Czarniawska, B. 2006. "Doing Gender Onto the Other: Fiction as a Mode of Studying Gender Discrimination in Organizations," *Gender, Work and Organization*, 13 (3): 234–53.

Czarniawska, B. 2008. "Humiliation: A Standard Organizational Product?" *Critical Perspectives on Accounting*, 19: 1034–53.

Czarniawska-Joerges, B. 1994. "Gender, Power, Organizations: An Interruptive Interpretation" in J. Hassard and M. Parker (eds) in *Towards a New Theory of Organizations*: 227–47. London: Routledge.

Czarniawska-Joerges, B. and G. Kranas. 1991. "Power in the Eyes of the Innocent (Students Talk on Power in Organizations)," *Scandinavian Journal of Management*, 7 (1): 41–60.

Des Pres, T. 1976. *The Survivors: An Anatomy of the Death Camps.* New York: Oxford University Press.

Ellis, A. 1997. *Workplace Bullying.* Online resource, available at: www.worktrauma.org/research/research02.htm, last accessed July 17, 2011.

Ehrenreich, B. 2001. *Nickel and Dimed. Undercover in Low-Wage USA.* London: Granta.

Harré, R. and G. Gillett. 1994. *The Discursive Mind.* London: Sage.

Latour, Bruno (1986) "The Powers of Association" in J. Law (ed.) *Power, Action and Belief*: 261–77. London: Routledge and Kegan Paul.

Reinharz, S. and S. E. Chase. 2002. "Interviewing Women" in J. F. Gubrium, and J. A. Holstein (eds) *Handbook of Interview Research. Context and Method*: 221–38. Thousands Oaks, CA: Sage.

Rorty, R. 1980. *Philosophy and the Mirror of Nature.* Oxford, UK: Basil Blackwell.

Rorty, R. 1989. *Contingency, Irony and Solidarity.* New York: Cambridge University Press.

Sabini, J. and M. Silver. 1982. *Moralities of Everyday Life.* New York: Oxford University Press.

Sabini, J. and M. Silver. 1998a. "The Not Altogether Social Construction of Emotions: A Critique of Harré and Gillett," *Journal for the Theory of Social Behaviour*, 28 (3): 223–35.

Sabini, J. and M. Silver. 1998b. *Emotion, Character and Responsibility.* New York: Oxford University Press.

Salin, D. 2003. "The Significance of Gender in the Prevalence, Forms and Perceptions of Workplace Bullying," *Nordiske Organisasjonsstudier*, 3: 30–50.

Silver, M., R. Conte, M. Miceli, and I. Poggi. 1986. "Humiliation: Feeling, Social Control and the Construction of Identity," *Journal for the Theory of Social Behaviour*, 16 (3): 269–83.

Silver, M., J. Sabini, and W. G. Parrott. 1987. "Embarrassment: A Dramaturgic Account," *Journal for the Theory of Social Behaviour*, 17 (1): 47–61.

Sims, D. 2001. "Organizations and Humiliation: Looking Beyond Elias," *Organization*, 8 (3): 537–60.

Sims, D. 2003. "Between the Millstones: A Narrative Account of the Vulnerability of Middle Managers' Storying," *Human Relations*, 56 (10): 1195–1211.

Smith, Dennis. 2002. "The humiliating organization: The functions and dysfunctions of degradation" in A. van Iterson, W. Mastenbrœk, T. Newton, and D. Smith (eds) *The Civilized Organization. Norbert Elias and the Future of Organization Studies*: 41-57. Amsterdam: John Benjamins.

Part II

Eliciting emotions through interviews

Chapter 7

Researching dark emotions

Eliciting stories of envy

Ishan Jalan

Humans are emotional beings, and bound to project, internalize, share, and manifest their desires, thoughts, and feelings in the social environment. Through social constructions and the sharing of common cultural norms, individuals learn from childhood various ways to express and suppress emotions. This often influences the way that they manifest a particular feeling (like disgust), learn where and when it is appropriate to express such an emotion, and ways to act and react when confronted with such emotions (Hochschild 1979; Shott 1979). This process of social and cultural structuring of emotions often allows for some emotions (joy, sadness) to be publicly acceptable and to be openly shared, whereas others (jealousy, revenge) are taught as necessary to hide as they project aspects of the self that are not socially accepted—and in some cultures may even be frowned upon. Other emotions, such as envy and *schadenfreude*, are perceived as being too toxic to even consider within oneself. These emotions are seen as being socially reprehensible, and hence often considered as social and cultural taboos. In some cases, such emotions are hidden and repressed to the extent that even the individuals themselves may not be fully aware of their presence. Leaning on Freud we can say that this act of repression, or the process through which the subject attempts to repel or confine to the unconscious various ideas, thoughts, memories, and, in particular, emotions that they find unpleasant or even traumatic, is a defense mechanism through which the self defends itself from narcissistic wounds, such as feelings of inferiority, shame, or guilt. It is important to explore the potency of these hidden, taboo emotions, and the effects they may have—not only on one's own identity, but also on social relations and everyday life. What happens, then, when a repressed and hidden taboo emotion, such as envy, surfaces? What havoc might it cause?

Gabriel (2008: 108) writes, "feelings are no simple side effects of mental life, no performances staged for the sake of audiences, no instruments of interpersonal manipulation." When we consider the terrain of hidden, proscribed, or taboo emotions, the task of surfacing them and exploring them within an interview context becomes challenging. In this text I will address some of the methodological challenges that hidden, proscribed, and taboo emotions pose, due to their unacknowledged qualities. Gabriel (ibid.) further observes that human beings are not merely emotional; they are also desiring, passionate, beings. This element of desire is important in researching dark emotions as it offers that crucial window into the individual's subjectivity. Feelings such as lust, greed, and hope all represent different forms of desire oriented towards different states or objects—and proscribed dark emotions, like envy, are no exception. Both desires and feelings have a remarkable ability to mutate and transform themselves, and it is this mutational and transformational quality that poses a serious difficulty and a methodological challenge—especially when specific feelings are considered taboo and are thus hidden. I will focus upon the emotion of envy—a *primus inter pares* amongst them since it is often repressed and largely remains unconscious— to illustrate some plausible methods of surfacing and studying taboo emotions.

Envy

As a morbid, dark, and malicious emotion, envy has been a social and religious taboo for over two millennia. It is the only emotion that results in pain as a result of others' happiness. Envy is the emotion experienced when the self observes the envied person to possess something that they desire for themselves, but is unable to obtain. Envy is usually seen as the pain caused by the good fortune of others. It combines with severe anxiety, and feelings of insecurity, that often lead to the envious destruction of the envied object or person. When dealing with such hidden and potentially dangerous emotions we encounter many questions and challenges. Experiences of envy, and similar proscribed emotions, go to the heart of people's identities, influencing who they believe they are, and what they have failed to become. This makes studying such emotions crucial within the social sciences. Yet a consideration of envy is often very painful, and even frightening. Further, the shaming experiences that are associated with such emotions and feelings pose an obstacle to revealing or facing them. The researcher must be extra vigilant in such situations—they must be careful not to stir up deep-seated anxieties, fears, or feelings of vulnerability by using questions that may be seen as too intrusive or perhaps immediately expose the respondents' well-guarded secrets.

In my research exploring the dynamics of envy, I often found that approaching the topic directly would immediately generate defensive reactions, sometimes leading to very strong expressions of hatred or simple denial. Such responses are very informative. For example, one of my colleagues was sharing a story in which she was the victim of intense envy. I remarked that her story would be ideal for my research, at which point she immediately clammed up. I realized that my remark had made her feel exposed and vulnerable, so I changed the topic to make her feel at ease. Later, when she continued her story, I listened with empathy and it slowly emerged that she was in fact equally envious of the other person, which in turn caused her to see all his actions as being envy-driven. This is one of the classic traits of envy: it burns the envier and the envied, and thus is not likely to be a casual conversation item. Keeping in mind such concerns and obstacles, researching dark emotions seems to benefit most from research techniques which draw from psychoanalytic theory. It enables us to understand and use fantasy as a research tool.

Using fantasy

Psychoanalytic theory primarily deals with unconscious mental processes and their conscious manifestations. As Gabriel (2008: 306) observes, "unconscious elements cannot be brought to consciousness at will and may only be studied through their conscious manifestations which include symptoms, symbols, dreams, fantasies, slips, jokes, emotional outbursts, cultural artefacts, and so on." This view justifies the use of both of psychoanalytic lenses, and of narrative methods such as storytelling, in research. Vidaillet (2007) highlights the ability of psychoanalysis to bring unconscious phenomena to consciousness by lifting the repression that buried them. She further says that this approach helps to closely examine not only how envious people experience this emotion, but also how they perceive the person they envy as well as making it possible to gain access to the subjectivity of the envious person through enabling them to freely express the feelings, ideas, and fantasies associated with their envy—which would otherwise remain repressed. This approach brings to the surface various experiences in our lives which also, unknown to us, have left deep marks on our personality. It tries to access the psychic foundations of envy or other proscribed emotions, and addresses the level of emotional intensity attached to such emotions. Narrative interview techniques help to break the ice and gradually broach difficult and often painful questions about experiences which, at worst, were corrosive or traumatic. Surfacing emotions refers to a process of revealing a dark emotion or bringing it out of its hidden realm. There are different ways of doing this and each method can posit its own challenges and obstacles. Here I show how to combine relying on fantasy and storytelling as interview tools to access individuals' subjectivities without raising defenses. This approach relies on providing scenarios to elicit proscribed emotions.

The element of fantasy is important since it allows the individual to create a hypothetical scene, while simultaneously allowing a researcher to study the emotions on which this scene is based. As Gabriel (2008: 105) writes, "exhilaration, anger, love, disgust, awe, shock, nostalgia, hope, despair, and nearly every powerful emotion can be triggered by fantasy."

Fantasy can be seen as a product of the imagination which expresses an idea or a desire in one or more scenes (for example: winning the lottery, or driving around in a new BMW car). It may manifest itself in the form of day-dreaming, or in the construction of different scenarios. Fantasy is like an experiment where the effects of desire and their emotional yield are imagined.

What is of importance to us in the context of researching dark emotions is the notion of unconscious fantasies or desires that are partly or fully excluded from one's consciousness, because they are either too painful (e.g., fantasizing of speaking to a deceased loved one) or socially unacceptable (e.g., destroying or killing a rival). Often, such unconscious or hidden fantasies are the outcome of desires that are distorted by the presence of defense mechanisms (e.g., the feeling of hatred towards one's father is met with the defense of "denial," since it is morally reprehensible to hate one's father). The original feeling may become distorted and expressed, instead, in contrasting fantasies that weaken their original emotional thrust—such as visualizing one's father as a martyr in a war, or fantasizing about destroying his favorite watch. In such situations the individual will not consciously be aware of her/his repressed anger or hatred towards her/his father, and will instead act upon fantasies—giving vent to her/his underlying hidden feelings. Such fantasies often assume "a clandestine existence, mostly censored by the forces of rationality, efficiency, and order and occasionally may surface through gossip, jokes or stories" (Gabriel 2008: 106).

Herein lies the crucial link between a storytelling approach, and fantasy as a research tool—one of the primary achievements of stories lies in their ability to express experience rather than emphasize factual details. Stories tend to give a legitimate vent to fantasy by privileging wish fulfilment over verifiable fact. It is thus no surprise that some of the most important stories we share are, in fact, stories about ourselves—stories of victories and defeats, achievements and mistakes, good and bad luck, love, loss, and longing—which sustain those tangled webs of truths, half-truths, and wishful fantasies that make up our identities (Gabriel 2008: 106). Furthermore, these narratives, whether they are individual stories, symbolic myths, organizational rituals, cultural artifacts, stories from one's memory, or even manifestations of shared belief systems, provide material for in-depth interpretations, observations, and surfacing of the hidden emotional dynamics. Through the use of stories it becomes possible to engage in a dialog, and surface emotions, without specifically acknowledging them. This will help elicit some of the more undesired qualities of the self, such as envy.

Using stories it may be possible to see how the envious person constructs her/his imagery of the envied, and what elements she/he uses to draw the picture. Stories further uncover the means in which the envious perceives the envied, and, most importantly, the fantasies of destroying her/him. There is also a third, theatrical, or cinematic, aspect which endows fantasy scripts propelled by a desire or a strong emotion. Of relevance here is the idea of fantasy as a space where the self can freely interact with the object of fantasy. This is very important, since it implies that the individual can act upon his or her object of fantasy—in our case, act upon objects or people whom she/he wants to punish or harm in an uninhibited way. Fantasy, then, is a space of imagined enjoyment in which individuals can act upon their true feelings and unleash their innermost wishes and desires.

Scenarios versus vignettes

The philosophy behind developing the scenario construction is that when individuals narrate their stories, they often project their "unspoken" emotions and experiences onto the created story character—thus, in effect, unconsciously recognizing and acknowledging these. When a respondent authors a character's identity in the story, this respondent—through projection or transference—reveals a part of his/her own identity that is hidden or suppressed. Fantasy helps to bypass defenses and counteract denials.

Scenarios differ from the vignettes sometimes used in qualitative research. Vignettes are questions about hypothetical people in a given situation that the respondent is expected to analyze and evaluate. For example, research on delinquency might entail vignettes describing teenagers with different types of delinquency; while research on romantic love might entail vignettes on more-or-less romantic first encounters. Respondents across different social or cultural groups are presented with the same vignettes, so that their evaluations can be compared within and across social or cultural groups. This is not the case when working with scenarios.

Scenarios are only *sometimes* about hypothetical people in a given situation that has already been decided by the researcher. Instead, they are suggestive thoughts similar to guided imagery, not tied to a particular person or place. A scenario allows the respondent to interpret it as he or she wishes, wherein the interpretation itself provides data for analysis since it reveals emotions, belief systems, and possible defenses. The scenario is a simulated imagery, or an imaginary scene within which the individual is to place himself or herself—and relies on fantasy for its development. The individual is asked what she/he might do or feel if a particular situation, scene, or scenario were to happen. When analyzing or examining a situation in fantasy, the defenses are eased, allowing the respondent to introspect in a less inhibited manner. The aim is to bring hidden emotions to the surface and access stories that reveal elements of dark emotions that are not often discussed or talked about openly. The story's protagonist—

whether angry victim, proud survivor, or troubled sufferer—allows the narrator to give "voice" to the unspoken realities within herself, and allow them to become part of her self-identity.

Examples

The following excerpt is from one of the interviews I conducted as part of my research on envy, and illustrates how scenarios work. For about an hour of the interview the respondent had comfortably stayed away from revealing any personal experiences with envy. At this point I introduced a scenario to see if it might open a window I was looking for. The scenario that I gave was: "If you were ever asked to be a part of a duel, what role do you see yourself more in—the victim or the aggressor? What would you do to the other person, if need arises? Why?" The respondent was quite surprised by this scenario, and it was easy to see that he was both amused while at the same time introspecting deeply. The image of an arena, and the context of a duel, made him slightly edgy. I could see that for the first time in the interview he felt vulnerable, and he immediately replied saying he would be the victim because he believed in peace and that because he did not have issues with anyone in particular he could not imagine the opposite aggressor situation being the case. However, a few moments later his face turned grim and he confessed that what he had said was what he had wanted me to hear. He took a long breath, paused, and said he saw himself as the aggressor; if given the chance he would destroy his professional rival—the person he was envious of—and in a manner that would not be limited to professional or even personal harm. He wished to destroy the very identity of his opponent. As he was revealing his innermost thoughts, it felt like he was visualizing the situation in his mind—his body language was stiff, and he seemed to have forgotten he was being interviewed. While disclosing this desire and imagining the situation in fantasy, he seemed to let loose the thoughts that he had been harboring for some considerable time. Following this revelation he seemed to relax and went on to share another hour-and-a-half of stories and experiences that, needless to say, were far from superficial.

As you can see, the above scenario was successful in breaking the ice during this interview. Through the scenario my subject fantasized and projected his deep envy and resentment against the other person, and by narrating it to me via fantasy he was able not only to achieve a degree of catharsis for himself, but also reveal in the process a considerable depth of material about a feeling that was both dangerous and harmful. The scenario was loose enough to allow for personal interpretation, but succinct enough to not digress entirely. It well illustrates how to incorporate guided imagery and fantasy, along with storytelling tools that facilitate transference. Posing scenarios as a way of asking questions invites respondents to share details and experiences related to their innermost and most intensely felt emotions.

Another example to illustrate how a scenario may help in making unconscious motives surface comes from research on resentment. The scenario presented was this: "A failing artist suddenly does very well and becomes an overnight success. Your thoughts?" The respondent replied, "publicly I'm really happy for the guy, he's worked hard for many years and it has finally happened. But privately I might have a sense of, 'Well I've been slugging away too.'" Although the scenario is succinct and actually asks for thoughts rather than for emotions, it is extremely effective. The respondent went on: "Publicly I'd make a really good show of congratulating. I'm pretty self-aware. I'd make such a show of showing that I was fine. Deep down I'd go home and feel terribly depressed."

The respondent revealed not only his feelings of resentment and depression about somebody else's success—emotions normally not demonstrated in public—but also how he would play-act, put on a show of well-wishing, to hide such feelings. Through the scenario, the defense mechanism of reaction formation, which is clearly at work here, comes to the surface.

Constructing scenarios

Constructing a scenario is not always easy or straightforward. First, the key emotion or emotions that one wishes to study has to be recognized. Then, one needs to think of different real-life contexts in which such emotions are most likely to be felt or experienced. Being reflexive about one's own experiences is very fruitful at this stage. Letting fiction and movies speak intensifies creativity (see Czarniawska, this volume).

The scenarios can be used at any time during interview, but I would suggest that they are best reserved for engaging with the more nuanced questions. The first few questions in an interview are meant to allow the respondent to relax, ease into a dialog, and gradually set the tone for the interview. The first few questions, when exploring or dealing with such topics as hidden emotions, should always aim for generalized objects so as to avoid engaging with or raising any defenses early on. At the point when the interviewer realizes that most of the "superficial" questions have been covered, the "general turf" has been explored, and that enough information has been gathered about specific points of interest, it is time to turn to scenarios to explore more deeply. Throwing a scenario in invites the respondent to engage with their more private experiences, thoughts, and feelings. Scenarios, conversely, can also be used in an interview when the interviewer feels the conversation has become "stuck"—in order to move ahead in the interview. Sometimes the respondent does not have much to share, or does not want to share. In such instances scenarios can help by circumnavigating defensiveness or initial reluctance. The responses to such scenarios can then be analyzed either by using psychoanalytic tools or other theoretical lenses.

When analyzing scenarios I feel that having awareness of basic psychoanalytic theories—such as of repression, or of unconscious and defense mechanisms—helps to unpack unconscious motives and thoughts better than the alternatives. The simplest way to go forward then would be to apply a hermeneutical approach, one that combines the reflexivity of the interviewer with the basic tools of interpretivism. To take an example: if we consider the above statement ("publicly I'm really happy for the guy, he's worked hard for many years and it is finally happened. But privately, I might have a sense of, 'Well I've been slugging away too'"), we can clearly see an underlying emotional tension. The element of one's own sense of failure comes in in the words "I have been struggling too." They touch immediately upon the respondent's own pain, as well as possible resentment that he might feel as a result of seeing someone else succeed where he failed. His subsequent statement confirms and qualifies the initial analysis because it associates resentment with sadness—both of which are covered up in public: "[P]ublicly I'd make such a show of showing that I was fine. Deep down I'd go home and feel terribly depressed."

Scenarios in themselves are not a definitive point of reference or interpretation. Scenarios are windows that help us to "see beyond," and to allow for possible hidden emotions, thoughts, and feelings to surface. Approaching hidden emotions hermeneutically entails looking for and detecting possible patterns of similar surfacing emotions, thematic coding of these emotions, and identifying shared themes. When such themes emerge, their analysis and interpretation can begin.

Words of caution

When dealing with dark emotions such as envy, one must take into consideration that other elements of communication—such as symbolic gestures, facial expressions, long pauses, and, most important, words, experiences, or stories that are stressed more than others—can reveal much more than what the respondent is actually saying in their plain speaking. Similarly, the self- and other-characterization within the fantasy scenarios allows the hidden emotions to get anchored to tangible plots that can then be questioned more directly, or gently probed for further insight. In this light, the scenarios serve the purpose of providing an arena in which various metaphors that are often absent in straight conversations might emerge or surface.

Nonetheless, the use of stories, fantasies, and scenarios has its limitations. One of the greatest is to assume all shared elements as facts, and thus lose the symbolic quality of the interpretations—misquoting the respondent. Another failing is to become part of the story itself, either by getting carried away or through counter-transference. Furthermore, during the course of analysis the stories and scenarios need to be interpreted after time and personal distance has been gained. The researcher has been an active audience to the storyteller's performance, and it is important that he or she does not become biased or make inferences while still under the subject's influence.

References

Gabriel, Y. 2008. *Organizing Words: A Critical Thesaurus for Social and Organization Studies.* New York: Oxford University Press.

Hochschild, A. R. 1979. "Emotion Work, Feeling Rules, and Social Structure," *American Journal of Sociology,* 85 (3): 551–75.

Jalan, I. 2013. *Envy as a Defence Against Lack: A Psychoanalytic Inquiry Into Destructive Workplace Emotions.* Unpublished PhD dissertation, University of Bath, UK.

Shott, S. 1979. "Emotion and Social Life: A Symbolic Interactionist Analysis," *American Journal of Sociology,* 84 (6): 1317–34.

Vidaillet, B. 2007. "Lacanian Theory's Contribution to the Study of Workplace Envy," *Human Relations,* 60 (11): 1669–1700.

Chapter 8

Emotional expertise

Emotions and the expert interview

Jochen Kleres

Introduction

Expert interviews have a long history in empirical research. They have been frequently used without much methodological reflection—hence their status as something of a quick and tainted method. This has changed since the 1990s when a focused methodological debate set in (see Bogner *et al.* 2009).[1] The appeal of expert interviews is that they promise a fast(er) route to outcomes—especially when resources are limited, other research strategies impracticable, and direct field access difficult. Little has been said to date about applying expert interviews to emotion research: this will be explored here for both interviewing and analysis. For this purpose I will reflect on different research projects in which I relied on expert interviews (Kleres 2005, 2007, 2009).

Experts

The basic idea of expert interviews is to gather information from people who are in a position to have a privileged and/or socially formative knowledge about some sphere of social life that is of interest to the researcher. Possession of privileged knowledge implies possessing power, *inter alia*, to shape the field—in particular, the interacting actors, organizations, or entire organizational fields within which they interact. Rather than gathering data directly from all these actors or organizations, expert interviews require identifying and interviewing people with expert knowledge about the field.

The central methodological issue is how to conceptualize the expert and thus the criteria for identifying and choosing them. Who qualifies as an expert in a given field of interest? Experts are not of interest as "entire persons," but rather through and in their function as experts, their expertise being a function of their specific position within—and knowledge about—a concrete institutional-organizational context (Meuser and Nagel 1991: 442–5). Exactly who counts as an expert is to be determined by their location within their respective field. Typically they are those in a decision-making position, or with unique access to information. Experts must be in a position which enables them to witness and interact with social groups of focal interest to the researcher.

Of immediate relevance here is the cognitive bias in the debates about who an expert is. Bogner and Menz (2009), for example, differentiate experts according to the relevant knowledge they possess: technical knowledge, process knowledge, and interpretive knowledge. This focus on knowledge in much of the methodological debate is indicative of its hitherto cognitive outlook. My concern is to show that expert interviews can be extended to focus also on emotions. I will show how we can conceptualize emotional experts.

The expert interview offers at least two principal options for learning something about emotions. Experts can provide information about emotions in an empirical field, or about their own emotions as experts—since they, as experts, are actors with formative power not only over cognitive constructions of reality but also over emotions and feeling rules that operate in their field. Power, knowledge, and power to shape feeling rules, often overlap. An expert, then, is a person in the field who has (co-)shaped it—or a person who was subject to, or a witness of, the exercise of power, knowledge, and the operation of feeling rules. This places the "expert" in a position to reflect on their intertwining dynamics; they are persons who, in one way or another, participated not just in practices that are of interest, but also in the emotional processes at stake. This is likely to put them in a position to be able to talk about the emotion of others which they have witnessed, as well as about their own emotions.

One consideration in deciding who counts as an expert on emotional issues, therefore, is that they need to be—or have been witness to—emotions experienced by actors operating in the field of activity that is of interest. This could apply to central organizers in social movements who regularly interact with a broad range of other activists or actors outside the movement; and who engage with them in emotion-laden exchanges (Kleres 2005). In this sense, experts would be actors sharing in emotional processes as peers. However, witnessing or partaking in others' emotional processes may also be a matter of professional practice—as is often the case with social workers, for whom dealing with others' emotions is part of the job (Kleres 2009; Terpe and Paierl 2010). Professional skills and professional rules may provide conceptual bases for discerning and interpreting others' emotions in specific ways.[2] Professional practice entails particular forms of institutionalized interactions that allow for witnessing and talking about others' emotions. In the case of volunteer organizations, for instance, internal group meetings and supervision are key for emotion management facilitated by social workers (Kleres 2009). To be sure, dealing with others' emotions may not be an explicit part of a professional's workload but it may constitute an important element of it, nevertheless (see, for example, Sieben and Wettergren 2010).

The second consideration in deciding whether the potential interview partners are suitable as experts on emotion is their ability to talk about emotions just as about actors, rules, procedures or typical interaction patterns. They should possess a degree of emotional reflexivity—emotional expertise, as it were. This assumption may be more plausible for some than others. Ultimately, this will emerge only during the interview itself.

In principle, any level of analysis is possible with expert interviews. Pragmatic approaches take experts' information at face value, focusing on what experts make explicit. Ambitious methodological approaches aim at unearthing latent structures of expert knowledge (Bogner and Menz 2009). In the same vein, one could look for latent knowledge on emotions in expert interview texts, but this would require refining analytical tools, so that these help to identify an entire array of linguistic emotion markers (for an example pertaining to autobiographic, narrative interviews, see Kleres 2011; Jahr 2000 focuses specifically on texts of scientific expertise).

Performing emotional expertise

The existing literature has considered in some depth the *interactional* dynamics during expert interviews, but its emotional dimension has only remained implicit in methodological debates. I would like to offer some thoughts about how to tease out emotions to generate better research.

The literature lists possible role configurations during the interview, and describes the corresponding response styles of interviewees (Bogner and Menz 2009; Vogel 1995). Central to these conceptualizations of interview dynamics are perceptions of social difference, especially with respect to status and power. Experts may see an interviewer in the following ways: as a *co-expert*, and thus engage with them in a kind of horizontal communication between equals; as an *expert in a different field* of knowledge, a situation which can evoke curiosity but also provoke insecurity or a slightly patronizing style; as a *lay person*, leading to lengthy, lecturing monologues; or, conversely, as a *superior authority or evaluator*, resulting in an over-positive self-presentation; as a potential *partisan critic*, translating into a defensive attitude; or finally as an *accomplice*, which can lead to openness but also reduced explicitness and detail. These mutual ascriptions of status are continuously negotiated, produced, and reproduced during the interview and even before it. Interviewers are advised to be prudent and reflexive about these negotiative positions, and to consider the different heuristic potentials of each (Meuser and Nagel 1991; Bogner and Menz 2009).

What is crucial for present purposes is that these dynamics be reconstructed in, or translated into, emotion terms. Status and power differentials can be seen as central aspects of emotions (Kemper 1978; Neckel

1991, 1996). From this perspective we could ascribe different emotional modes to each of the just-listed interviewer-interviewee constellations. The first two dynamics—co-expert, and expert in a different field—are characterized by the lack of status/power differences. Both actors acknowledge the other's expertise. This leads to an atmosphere of mutual respect. What is more, expertise grants a prestigious and powerful social position that allows its incumbents to derive a sense of honor and pride from it. This remains intact, and is mutually recognized—in principle—throughout the interview. Qualitative differences in the "expert in a different field" scenario can, additionally, make for an element of mutual curiosity—but there is always the potential for the situation to veer towards emotional modes of superiority and inferiority.

This possibility of an inferiority/superiority dynamic is, in fact, constitutive of three of the other role configurations: lay person, evaluator, and critic. The differences between these relate to the attributions of inferiority and superiority by the expert and the interviewer respectively. In the first of these three dynamics the proud position of the expert remains unquestioned and is powerfully asserted over the "lay" interviewer, who is seen as not being up to the expert's level of knowledge. The expert uses the interviewer to interactively construct her or his own proud position as "expert" by treating the interviewer with condescension. The status of the proud expert is in danger when the interviewer is cast in the role of "evaluator" or "critic." In the case of "evaluator" the informant accepts the superiority of the interviewer, assuming a shameful position of submitting to authority. But the expert aspires to prove him/herself to the "interviewer-as-evaluator." While there is always the fear of not passing as an expert, there is also the aspiration of having one's proud expert status recognized. Alternatively, this may result in a kind of "closing up" during the interview. In the "critic" scenario the expert rejects the perceived superiority of the interviewer—and this is expressed in an angry and defensive stance.

In the last scenario, where the interviewer is seen as "accomplice," a shared opposition to outside actors is constructed during the interview wherein the interviewer is seen as siding with the expert. Positing a shared, outside enemy usually engenders strong emotional bonds of solidarity with the interviewer, and creates an emotional atmosphere of confidence.

Theorizing these dynamics in emotional terms highlights the emotional dynamics that accompany claims to, and various types of, (non-)recognition of expertise. It questions expertise as the property of a particular person, as well as the claim to emotion-free rationality and objectivity that expertise is allegedly founded on. Beyond this principal point, the focus on the emotional dynamics of expert interviews allows us to analyze the specifics of how this emotionality of expertise is constituted, especially in cases of unequal interview dynamics. Essentially, this calls for asking how

Table 8.1 Emotional dynamics of expert interviews

Interviewer seen as	*Status/power difference*	*Resulting emotions*
Co-expert	None	Mutual respect, honor/ pride about expertise
Expert in different fields	None, only qualitative difference in expertise	Mutual respect, honor/ pride, curiosity, but more fragile
Lay person	Expert in superior position	Pride/honor for the expert, condescension towards the interviewer
Authority/evaluator	Superior interviewer	Fear/shameful submission, ashamed retreat or ascent to pride
Critic	Superior interviewer	Angry rejection of shameful submission
Accomplice	None, external difference	Solidarity, confidence

feelings of superiority and inferiority are constituted. While the literature on expert interviews explains these dynamics with generic factors—differences in gender, age, education, etc.—realistic analysis should focus on the constitutive specifics of the emotional dynamics of expert interviews and how they relate to concrete instances and contexts in which claims to expertise are made. For this it may be fruitful to analyze the argumentative parts of expert interviews—to systematically scrutinize throughout the transcribed interview or its relevant parts to discover what methods the "experts" have used to legitimize themselves and lay claim to the superiority of their own knowledge. Of specific interest, then, is how such "experts" deal with emotions while they are engaged in the process of legitimizing their expertise, and making their superiority claims.

Interviewing about emotions

Expert interviews are typically conducted to an interview guideline; that is, in the same way as semi-structured interviews. The guideline lists the different topics of interest and their specific aspects. The list should be handled flexibly to allow for an open exploration that follows the conversational turns and allows for unforeseen aspects to come to the fore. This procedure is opposed to wielding a "guideline bureaucracy" (Hopf 1978). As for the questions that are raised during the interview, a number of general rules for qualitative interviewing apply. For example, neutral, clear, and simple questions are recommended (see Gläser and Laudel 2004: 131–8).

With respect to emotions, there are a number of principal strategies. One option is to address emotions directly—either in a general fashion ("How did it feel?"), or to focus on specific emotions ("When was there fear? What role did guilt play?") These are questions of experience. Other questions may focus on tapping into experts' emotion knowledge by asking about, for example, how to deal with feelings of fear in certain situations or settings? "Why is it important to do it that way?"

Asking about emotions touches upon another general problem with expert interviewing: the pragmatic argument of taking expert information at face value may not always produce valid results. For instance, in a project on institutional discrimination, some experts described instances that were clearly about discrimination (e.g., racist bullying in school; teachers' relegating students to dead-end classes only for those same students to later prove themselves gifted and move to better schools). Yet they failed to criticize or frame such occurrences *as* discrimination. Instead they constructed the discriminated persons as being responsible for their own situation, or blamed migrantic[3] parents for their children's initial poor performance (Kleres 2007; Flam and Kleres 2008). In my research into volunteers carrying out a particular kind of AIDS-related work (Kleres 2009), I asked a social work coordinator whether feelings of guilt (such as survivors' guilt, see Odets 1995) played any role among volunteers. He denied that it did. However, some of the volunteers from his team, in their interviews, talked about feeling guilt related to not helping more in people's situations of need—a feeling that had indeed given them an urge to do something concrete about it. How can we deal with this kind of problem within the framework of expert interviews? One possibility is systematic and broad comparison. In the case of the AIDS volunteers this was a matter of talking to a wide range of experts and comparing their statements. In turn, this requires sampling strategies that result in capturing diverging forms of expertise. Looking for internal cracks in the interview text—such as that provided by the experts on migrants talking about the actual practices of discrimination while at the same time denying that it existed—is another possibility. Reading the interview transcript against other available data, or in the light of theoretical concepts, would be a third option. In the case of "experts on migrants," comparative knowledge about forms of discrimination and discourses across a spectrum of European countries helped to sensitize researchers to the possibility that individual national discourses and feeling rules about migrants give specific twists to "expert" knowledge. A final strategy is to also include narrative questions; that is, questions which stimulate the production of a shorter story.[4] While stories are not the primary form of expert interviews—too strong a focus on narration could lead to digression and limit the thematic depth of the interview—shorter narrative sections in the interview are immensely valuable for exploring new thematic terrains, especially if direct questions fail to yield detailed answers. This is particularly relevant for unearthing emotions—especially those that experts are otherwise reluctant to talk about.

Analysis

Moving on to how to analyze such interviews, let me note that contradictory findings are of particular analytical interest. With respect to emotions, contradictions and incoherencies make it necessary to always reflect the extent to which feeling rules may impede or skew the expression of certain emotions while encouraging that of others. In the case of the migration experts mentioned above, interviewees were arguably influenced by the dominant German migration discourses. These discourses construct migrantic denizens as uneducated, unmotivated, dirty, negligent, etc., and rely on these characteristics to enable the attribution of the difficulties they face as being their own fault. These discourses express and encourage feelings of indifference or antipathy towards migrantic denizens (Flam and Kleres 2008). Teachers who tried to sympathize with their students found no ready-made words or phrases with which to do so. The stories they told about the discriminated against and victimized—but in the end victorious—pupils, were told hesitantly and in a language of personalized, disconnected anecdotes submerged in a larger migrant-blaming discourse. The stories made the disparities between the lived experience and the national discourse painfully palpable, even though the experts failed to articulate this pain.

However, other possible interpretations need to be considered. Failure to address emotions overtly may also be a matter of a lack of emotional reflexivity. What is more, not all knowledge of one's experience is available to the self, reflexively. To a considerable extent this knowledge has a narrative form (Schütze 1987). People know how things have come about in their own experience, and they can communicate this knowledge only in its narrative form—by telling the story of "what happened." To some extent this goes for experts as well.

With emotions taking on a narrative dimension (Kleres 2011), even direct questions in an expert interview may yield pieces of narrative that leave the emotions in question, implicit. When I interviewed activists (Kleres 2005), asking explicit questions about what they felt in certain situations, they would often not spell out their feelings. Instead, my questions triggered further narratives and descriptions of what happened at the time (see, for example, Sarbin 1989). In this case, Scheff's (1988) markers of shame helped me to analyze some of the emotional dimensions. Even the very fact that interview partners failed to respond in a straightforward manner to a direct question may be indicative of their emotions—shame, and the recursive quality (Scheff 1988) that makes it shameful to be ashamed, a situation that discourages acknowledging it in the first place. Beyond that, of course, the entire gamut of linguistic manifestations concerning emotional expression can be used for analytic purposes (Kleres 2011). For example irony, diminutives, genre, and tempo speak about the narrated emotions.

The standard way of analyzing expert interviews involves some kind of coding technique, either a variant of grounded theory (Meuser and Nagel 1991) or a qualitative content analysis (Gläser and Laudel 2004). This requires making assumptions about how to apply emotion codes to parts of the interview transcript. Again, this is relatively unproblematic as long as emotions are explicitly spelled out. Where this is not the case, the abductive,[5] increasingly abstracting, grounded theory-inspired procedures (Meuser and Nagel 1991) can provide a basis for the interpretation of emotions: interviews are generally transcribed as paraphrase with only the important parts transcribed verbatim. This is a process of data reduction, and thus needs to be carried out with an eye to detail that is suited to emotions analysis. Analysis starts by categorizing—applying labels or codes to segments of the interview. At this point the wording of applied codes remains close to the interview transcript, but should capture the emotional significance of what transpired (e.g., "pissed [off] with boss"). In the second step the transcript's chronology is ignored as the text is taken apart: similarly coded segments are juxtaposed, compared, and summarized, more abstract categories ("frustration") can be created. This may lead to a regrouping of text segments and/or further differentiation ("frustration with superiors/colleagues/clients"). In the third step, similarly coded segments from different interviews are juxtaposed and compared. Emotion labels may now be further refined or changed, and single segments regrouped accordingly. Groups of segments now receive more abstract codes. In the last step, codes are related to theoretical constructs and categories.

Conclusion

Perhaps even more than is the case for other qualitative methods, because of its focus on "experts" the "expert interview" has been conceived as extremely cognitive in orientation. Yet, as I have showed in this text, it can be fruitfully extended to enable research on emotions. Upon closer inspection the expert interview itself turns out to be co-structured—not just by knowledge and power differentials, but also by its emotional dynamics. As is the case with many other domains of seemingly unshakable rationality and objectivity—such as finance and economics (Pixley 2012a, 2012b, this volume; Barbalet 1998), or science (Jahr 2000; Barbalet 2009)—there is an essential emotional dimension to expertise which has the potential, if explored, to generate additional heuristic value. Furthermore, as I have made an effort to show, it is not only possible but also very promising to analyze expert interview texts looking for explicit and implicit expressions of emotions. In the text I have pinpointed some of the problems raised by such analyses, as well as describing the analytical steps required to do so. In summary, expert interviews present a pragmatic approach to empirical emotion research that can nevertheless yield tremendous insights. Its full potential for this remains to be explored through further application, reflection, and methodological debate.

Acknowledgments

I would like to thank Helena Flam for her valuable comments on earlier versions of this chapter.

Notes

1 Much of the literature on this is in German and will not be listed here.
2 Such professional practice will not be necessarily devoid of emotions, but professional feeling rules may keep immediate personal emotional involvement at bay and instead highlight other emotions such as feelings of rationality or of professional pride (Kleres 2012). For a text on how to handle one's own and one's clients' emotions, see Terpe and Paicrl (2010).
3 I use this term to refer to those who would be commonly identified in society, and/or identify themselves, as having a migration background—even though they may have been born and raised in Germany and their families may have lived there for a number of generations.
4 The dynamics of narrative production constitute forces that lead narrators to reveal a certain degree of detail. Schütze's (1987) theory of narration describes how narrators are compelled to provide enough detail to make the overall story plausible, and to complete a narrative figure once they have begun it. Conversely, they also need to make a selection choice about which details of their own experience are essential to the narrative.
5 Kelle (2005) has argued that an abductive logic in grounded theory can balance the contradictory requirements of openness and preconception understood as sensitizing theoretical concepts.

References

Barbalet, J. M. 1998. *Emotion, Social Theory, and Social Structure: A Macrosociological Approach*. Cambridge, New York, Melbourne, Madrid, Cape Town, Singapore, Sao Paulo: Cambridge University Press.

Barbalet, J. M. 2009. "Consciousness, Emotions, and Science" in D. R. Hopkins, J. Kleres, H. Flam, and H. Kuzmics (eds) *Theorizing Emotions: Sociological Explorations and Applications*: 39–71. Frankfurt am Main, New York: Campus.

Bogner, A., B. Littig, and W. Menz (eds). 2009. *Interviewing Experts*. Basingstoke, New York: Palgrave Macmillan.

Bogner, A. and W. Menz. 2009. "The Theory-Generating Expert Interview: Epistemological Interest, Forms of Knowledge, Interaction," in A. Bogner, B. Littig, and W. Menz (eds) *Interviewing Experts*: 43–80. Basingstoke, New York: Palgrave Macmillan.

Flam, H. and J. Kleres. 2008. "Ungleichheit und Vorurteil. Deutsche SozialwissenschaftlerInnen als ProduzentInnen von Gefühlsregeln," *Österreichische Zeitschrift für Soziologie*, 33 (2): 63–81.

Gläser, J. and G. Laudel. 2004. *Experteninterviews und qualitative Inhaltsanalyse.* Wiesbaden: VS Verlag für Sozialwissenschaften/UTB.

Hopf, C. 1978. "Die Pseudo-Exploration – Überlegungen zur Technik qualitativer Interviews in der Sozialforschung," *Zeitschrift für Soziologie*, 7 (2): 97–115.

Jahr, S. 2000. *Emotionen und Emotionsstrukturen in Sachtexten.* Berlin, New York: de Gruyter.

Kelle, U. 2005. " 'Emergence' vs. 'Forcing' of Empirical Data? A Crucial Problem of 'Grounded Theory' Reconsidered," *Forum: Qualitative Social Research*, 6 (2). Available at: www.qualitative-research.net/index.php/fqs/article/view/467, (last accessed June 13, 2014).

Kemper, T. D. 1978. "Toward a Sociology of Emotions: Some Problems and Some Solutions," *American Sociologist*, 13 (1): 30–41.

Kleres, J. 2005. "The Entanglements of Shame: An Emotion Perspective on Social Movement Demobilization" in H. Flam and D. King (eds) *Emotions and Social Movements*: 170–88. London, New York: Routledge.

Kleres, J. 2007. "Experteninterviews: Die Methode und ihre Durchführung im Projekt XENOPHOB" in H. Flam, B. Carius, B. Dietrich, U. Froböse, J. Kleres and A. Philipps (eds) *Migranten in Deutschland. Statistiken – Fakten – Diskurse*: 282–92. Konstanz: UVK Verlagsgesellschaft.

Kleres, J. 2009. "Just Being There: Buddies and the Emotionality of Volunteerism" in D. R. Hopkins, J. Kleres, H. Flam, and H. Kuzmics (eds) *Theorizing Emotions: Sociological Explorations and Applications*: 291–314. Frankfurt am Main, New York: Campus.

Kleres, J. 2011. "Emotions and Narrative Analysis: A Methodological Approach," *Journal for the Theory of Social Behaviour*, 41 (2): 182–202.

Kleres, J. 2012. *AIDS Organizations as Civil Society Actors.* PhD thesis, Leipzig: University of Leipzig.

Meuser, M. and U. Nagel. 1991. "ExpertInneninterviews – vielfach erprobt, wenig bedacht. Ein Beitrag zur Methodendiskussion" in D. Garz and K. Kraimer (eds) *Qualitativ-empirische Sozialforschung: Konzepte, Methoden, Analysen*: 441–71 Opladen: Westdeutscher Verlag.

Neckel, S. 1991. *Status und Scham. Zur symbolischen Reproduktion sozialer Ungleichheit.* Frankfurt am Main, New York: Campus Verlag.

Neckel, S. 1996. "Inferiority: From Collective Status to Deficient Individuality," *Sociological Review*, 44 (1): 17–34.

Odets, W. 1995. *In the Shadow of the Epidemic: Being HIV-Negative in the Age of AIDS.* Durham: Duke University Press.

Pixley, J. 2012a. *Emotions in Finance: Booms, Busts and Uncertainty.* Cambridge: Cambridge University Press.

Pixley, J. (ed.). 2012b. *New Perspectives on Emotions in Finance. The Sociology of Confidence, Fear and Betrayal.* New York: Routledge.

Sarbin, T. R. 1989. "Emotions as Narrative Emplotments" in M. J. Packer and R. B. Addison (eds) *Entering the Circle: Hermeneutic Investigation in Psychology*: 85–201. Albany: State University of New York Press.

Scheff, T. J. 1988. "Shame and Conformity: The Deference-Emotion System," *American Sociological Review*, 53 (3): 395–406.

Schütze, F. 1987. *Das Narrative Interview in Interaktionsfeldstudien I.* Hagen: Fernuniversität.

Sieben, B. and Å. Wettergren (eds). 2010. *Emotionalizing Organizations and Organizing Emotions.* Basingstoke: Palgrave Macmillan.

Terpe, S. and S. Paierl. 2010. "From Bureaucratic Agencies to Modern Service Providers: The Emotional Consequences of the Reformation of Labour Administration in Germany" in B. Sieben, and Å. Wettergren (eds) *Emotionalizing Organizations and Organizing Emotions*: 209–29 Basingstoke: Palgrave Macmillan.

Vogel, B. 1995. "'Wenn der Eisberg zu schmelzen beginnt…' Einige Reflexionen über den Stellenwert und die Probleme des Experteninterviews in der Praxis der empirischen Sozialforschung" in C. Brinkmann, A. Deeke, and B. Völkel (eds) *Experteninterviews in der Arbeitsmarktforschung. Diskussionsbeiträge zu methodischen Fragen und praktischen Erfahrungen*: 73–83. Nürnberg: Institut für Arbeitsmarkt und Berufsforschung der Bundesanstalt für Arbeit.

Chapter 9

Dialogic introspection

A method for exploring emotions in everyday life and experimental contexts

Thomas Burkart and Jenny Weggen

Up until the 1930s, psychologists relied on introspection to explore individual experience and thus also feelings. Introspection was the standard method used in classical philosophical psychology by Franz Brentano (1838–1917) and Edmund Husserl (1859–1938); in the experimental psychology of Wilhelm Wundt (1832–1920) and Edward B. Titchener (1867–1927); in the thought experiments performed by the Würzburg School of Oswald Külpe (1862–1915) and Karl Bühler (1879–1962); and in the psychoanalysis of Sigmund Freud (1856–1939) (Witt 2010). The method drew much criticism and was subsequently banished from empirical research when behaviorism, introduced by John B. Watson in 1913, rose to a dominant position during the post-war period. Behaviorist theorists have argued that only observable behavior can be subject to scientifically oriented objective psychology. Until recently, feelings and other internal phenomena have remained unattractive and neglected as objects of study.

The Hamburger Forschungswerkstatt, an interdisciplinary and informal research group of psychologists and social scientists at the University of Hamburg, established in 1996, recently rediscovered the method of "introspective observations."[1] The researchers developed the method further by, for example, applying it in a group context and by systematizing and formalizing it. "Introspection" refers to the psychological method of introspection, but since a dialogic element was added it was named "dialogic introspection" (Burkart *et al.* 2010). The method calls for a deep self-observation (introspection) of one's own concurrent, remembered, or imagined experience.[2] All studies using dialogic introspection produce emotion data, even when the objects of research are allegedly "rational" inner processes such as "considering" (Burkart 2008).

The method presented here thus revives a former standard research method in psychology. By adding a distinctly dialogic element, it upgrades the method of introspection to a group-based experiment, thereby increasing its applicability and efficiency. Dialogic introspection can be recommended as a good instrument for eliciting individual emotions experienced in specific situations.[3] We describe various strategies that can be employed for gathering emotion data using this method. We also compare its benefits and disadvantages to focus groups and qualitative interviews.

The method of dialogic introspection

Everything associated with individual experience is a suitable topic for the method. A trained supervisor is responsible for taking a group of 4–12 participants through 2–3 rounds of reporting on their recollected, concurrent, or imagined individual experiences. The supervisor at first asks participants to engage in topical self-observation, and to take notes. The participants are granted a specified time to explore their past or current experiences silently and in depth. Usually this takes around 10–15 minutes. Afterwards, they are each asked to report as much as they wish to the group, with and without a time limit.[4] After hearing each other's reports, the participants are free to expand on their initial reports in light of what they heard. Those who wish to add to their initial statements may do so in a second and final round. A concluding third discussion is not necessary but may be included if desired by the participants. The sessions are recorded and transcribed. By their very design, the generated data have a subjective content. The researcher can, for example, instruct the group as follows:

> Our topic today is XXX. Please recall your own experiences regarding XXX. You may have perceptions, thoughts, fantasies, desires, and feelings about it. Keep in mind that introspections are neither right nor wrong. Please take notes. Your notes will be your own and it is for you to decide what you would like to share with the group.

The group setting facilitates the emergence of inner recollections in response to others: the individual can pick up on others' reports and relate them to his or her own personal experience. In this dialogical manner, individual self-observations may become more specific and rounded off.

The instructor should guide the interaction of the group in accordance with four key principles. These are meant to reduce conformity; that is, statements formulated for the sake of social desirability, on the one hand, and hostile group dynamics and conflicts within the group, on the other. These four principles are:

1 critical contributions or judgmental comments are unwanted;
2 everyone is encouraged to present as many self-observations as he or she wants; in extreme cases, none;

3 disrupting other people's reports for inquiries or discussion is not permitted;
4 additional self-observations, which emerge during the first round, can be communicated in the second round.

The intention is to produce a prejudice-free atmosphere that minimizes negative group dynamic processes and encourages participants to open up about their experiences.

Strategies for explicating and collecting emotions

Dialogic introspection has great potential for explicating emotions in all their multifarious richness. It offers different strategies that may be distinguished according to their

- time distance to the situation in which the emotions arise—either self-observation of one's own concurrent experiences (that is, direct reporting in the situation itself); or self-observation of one's own remembered experiences (that is, recalling a situation);
- substantive openness—engaging in introspection in response to thematically open or focused instructions;
- extent of situational authenticity—self-observations in a "natural," experimental, or imaginary situation.

Each research question combines three of these features. "Please recall the birth of your child and the emotions that you experienced at the time" is a good example of a question that calls for past experience, is substantively open, and is close to being "natural."

Each strategy, sketched out in this way, is linked to certain advantages and disadvantages that can be minimized by combining different strategies:

Direct and indirect strategies

To survey emotions directly one asks straightforwardly for specific emotional experiences. For example: "Please think of two situations at work when you were happy about a colleague and recall your experience." The procedure would be indirect if one asked for and about non-specific emotions. In such a case emotions are recollected as if they occurred incidentally. The instruction "Please think of experiences with co-workers and recall these" does not specify any emotions.

When one asks for recollections without specifying the emotions that one is interested in, the risk that emotions will not be mentioned explicitly is high. Specifying emotions of interest might cause an overemphasis on the emotion(s) to the disadvantage of clarifying the context and conditions in which it/they emerged. To prevent this situation arising, supplementary instructions may be given, such as: "Please try to remember as exactly as possible why and how your feelings emerged."

Experimental versus ethnographic survey of feelings

The experimental strategy tries to establish a "survey situation," which usually triggers emotions. In one experiment at the Hamburger Forschungswerkstatt an alarm clock rang during a university seminar with the purpose of startling the participants. Directly afterwards the participants were asked how they experienced the situation (see Kleining and Witt 2010). They expressed emotions of confusion, fright, and fear.

Alternatively, it is possible to ask participants to conduct a thought experiment, instructing them as follows: "Imagine that your boss criticizes you because of your work. Visualize this situation in your head, watching your internal processes, your thoughts, and your feelings." Triggering emotions experimentally—such as in the case of the alarm clock unexpectedly going off—can have ethical implications. Participants might find the stimulus, the experience, or its repercussions, problematic. The thought experiment bypasses this problem.

The "collection" of emotions is ethnographic when individuals observe their emotional processes in specific situations in their everyday life and communicate their emotions at a later point in time in the group situation. The instructions could be: "During the next week, please observe your internal processes, your feelings and thoughts in a situation where someone criticizes you. If possible, record what you observed as soon as possible afterwards."

Concurrent versus past experience

A survey of recalled past experiences may ask for emotions directly—as in "Please recall a situation at work in which you were happy/upset and recall how you experienced it"—or indirectly, as in "Please recall an important conversation with your boss and remember how you experienced it."

One may also ask for details of concurrent and burgeoning inner experiences observed by the subject at the exact moment when they are formed. This is the case in experimental or ethnographic situations. The focus on present-time versus past experience once again addresses the question of immediacy. Remembering past events has a built-in bias: it is always selective and has possibly been influenced by newer experiences.

Thematically open versus narrow "survey of emotions"

A "collection" of all emotions is thematically open, while thematically specific instructions focus on specific emotions such as anger or joy. Here we encounter a problem similar to that of the direct versus indirect strategy: asking to focus on certain feelings excludes, *a priori*, other feelings that might also be relevant. If the instructions are open, we may not find out anything about the emotions of interest.

Examples: direct versus indirect survey of feelings

Two studies relying on dialogic introspection aimed at capturing the multifaceted and detailed emotional processes. However, they differ with regard to the data access method. In a broader heuristic study on feeling (Burkart 2005), emotions were collected directly and ethnographically via contemporaneous experiences. The subjects were asked to register and write down the inner processes related to a feeling of anger, as well as a second emotion of any kind experienced in their everyday life. A few days later they came together and compared notes on their feeling processes during a group session that followed the rules of dialogic introspection.

Focal to the second study was the recollection of a "special encounter"—an experience understood as an intense emotional process. The emotions were addressed indirectly in two survey situations using the method of dialogic introspection.[5] We instructed the groups to recall an experience of a special encounter that took place in their everyday life, not explicitly asking for the experienced emotions. The question asked was direct, thematically open, and data collection was based on past experiences.

The results have the character of an explorative study. Because of the limited amount of data, they cannot be seen as typical for all human encounters and emotions experienced in similar contexts. Nonetheless, these results suggest that encounters have a specific structure characterized by strong involvement and profound emotional intensity. As our research shows, encounters are associated with a wide range of different emotions: anger, rage, hatred, annoyance, defense, frustration, horror, humiliation, disappointment, hopelessness, fatigue, anxiety, alienation, stress, shock, confusion, amazement, surprise, relief, empathy, pity, sympathy, admiration, pride, confidence, contentment, calmness, gratitude, joy, happiness, and love.

The feelings vary in their intensity. Frequently, ambivalent and contradictory emotions—such as excitement and concern—are experienced simultaneously, or rapidly alternate. Furthermore, emotions are embodied and accompanied by physiological reactions. In the following excerpt, a woman in her thirties depicts a random encounter with her former boss—an encounter that she experienced as unpleasant. She considers whether to confront him. The excerpt first reports manifestations of fear—this emotion is physically expressed by sweating and a racing heart—followed by feelings of relief and calmness that are closely related to other emotions.

> And I was just overwhelmed. Sort of like a blood rush. And it was. I didn't know what to do, and then I actually felt really relieved and I thought I would actually like to go and see this person.... But at the same time, my heart was racing and I was sweating and you know. And then I wanted to avoid the situation.... And I went up and I shook his hand and I said: "How are you?".... And I felt great; I felt relieved and I felt calmed and I felt, you know, that's been put to bed. So it brought up a lot of different emotions throughout the different encounters.

The situational circumstances or the chance interaction with the other person triggers the emotions. This happens either unintentionally or intentionally, when one interaction partner purposely tries to provoke certain emotions in his/her counterpart. Emotion work also takes place: one adjusts one's own feelings to the situation. The emotional relationship to the person changes during the encounter, with intense emotions promoting a strong bond. The emotional state can take a sudden turn, accompanied by a moment of inner or outer change—as is the case in another excerpt in which a man describes his encounter with a drunkard on a harbor ferry:

> I realized that I was shocked at first.... And then ... I saw that he had a pretty badly treated harelip.... And then I thought that I was extremely lucky with my own cleft palate.... And what happened next, happened within a few seconds, or even just a fraction of a second. My own childhood feelings came up, this feeling of utter alienation.... And I saw him more as a human being with his true tragedy. And I also felt compassion.

The irritating man in the encounter is experienced as disruptive—he is drunk and loud. The encounter sets in motion an internal process in the man describing the incident—in the disruptive man he discovers physical parallels to himself and thinks of his own childhood isolation, at which point the initial feeling of anger changes abruptly to compassion and sympathy.

Comparative advantages and disadvantages of the method of dialogic introspection

The examples presented above show the diversity of emotions and physical and mental processes that the method of dialogic introspection helps to explicate. The method is able to achieve all this because it entails intense self-observation with dialogic sharing within a group. The data generated by the group-based dialogic introspection is very rich. Getting participants to look inwardly and focus on their experiences enables the understanding of both the significance of contexts in which emotions arise, as well as the effects of emotions in social contexts. Mutual sharing of personally meaningful and engaging data usually results in an intimate atmosphere, thereby promoting participants' openness.

The method of dialogic introspection is open-ended and contrasts with several forms of prestructured interviews in which questions—often reflecting the researcher's state of knowledge and prejudice—restrict and distort the responses. Table 9.1 compares three instruments of data collection. It presents the advantages of explicating emotions by relying on the method of dialogic introspection in comparison with the two most common data collection instruments: focus groups and qualitative interviews. The table shows that focus groups are less appropriate for studying emotions since they allow for less depth as a result of the limited time allowed for individual reflection. The structure of focus groups also promotes strong group dynamics that can lead participants to support a consensus opinion, or lead to the polarization of opinions—rather than reporting one's own emotional experience.

The qualitative interview, on the other hand, seems to be more appropriate for explicating emotion data since it is easier for interview partners to open up in a one-on-one situation with a non-judgmental interviewer than it might be in a consensual or conflict-ridden focus group. The exploration of one's own experience is not, however, stimulated by the reports of others as it is in a group situation.

All three methods, however, depend upon language. It is assumed that the respondents can express their emotions verbally. This is their shared limitation (for a counter-argument, see Terpe in this volume).

Every data collection method has its advantages and disadvantages; the group-based dialogic introspection is no exception. It is always advisable to combine different instruments to illuminate all facets of the investigation object, as defined by the concept of triangulation. When emotions are the object of analysis it is useful to mix the group-based dialogic introspection with other qualitative instruments for data collection—such as interviews with a few open and unhurried questions. Dialogic introspection can be recommended since it calls for such a variation of methods: its subordinate methodology of qualitative heuristics follows the principle of a maximal structural variation of perspectives, meaning the use of different survey settings and methods for achieving a complete representation of the object of research or a complete answer of the research question.

Table 9.1 Advantages and disadvantages of the method of dialogic introspection in comparison to focus groups and interviews

	Advantages	*Disadvantages*
Dialogic introspection	*Dialogic group setting*: stimulates the emotional experience of the participants *Minimization of undesirable group dynamics*: the group rules create a situation for free expression of emotional experience *Non-hierarchical interactions*: the group rules provide equal opportunities to self-report one's emotional experiences *Practical advantages*: the method produces dense and rich data within a short period of time *Explorative*: the method ensures that the theoretical preconceptions of the researcher have little impact on what the participants report *Equivalence of reports*: all reports are included equivalently in the analysis	*Risk of inconsistency*: asking questions is inadmissible, vagueness can occur—it is possible, however, to add a discussion for clarification *Social desirability*: there is the risk that participants keep personal emotions to themselves because they think they are not desirable; or report emotions that they do not actually feel for the same reason
Focus group	*Control of content*: group-centered, thematic control is possible *Causal condensing*: the situation allows key messages to be stressed during the discussion	*Group dynamics*: the participants feel obliged to defend their emotional experience and therefore adjust their emotional display to the group. An undesirable consensus formation within the group might arise *Distortion of the data*: it is likely that single participants will dominate the discussion *Lack of analytical depth*: it is hardly possible to reflect emotional experience in an in-depth manner

Single structured interview (with preset guiding questions)[1]	*Reactive ad hoc consistency*: the researcher can ask clarifying questions if something is not understood *Deepening*: the researcher can be empathic, and guide the interviewee to recall more about present-time or past emotional experiences *Intimate interview situation*: the interview is private and held in an atmosphere of trust that can encourage the explication of emotions	*A lot of effort*: one interview produces data for only one person *High risk of interviewer bias*: the interviewer influences the interviewee consciously or unconsciously because of his/her theoretical pre-assumptions or attitudes *Sequence of question and answer*: there is little time to reflect, in-depth, upon one's own emotional experience; the questions may disrupt one's thought processes

Sources: Burkart et al. (2010); Weggen (2012).

Note

1 Interviews with just one opening question—such as autobiographic-narrative interviews—are not considered at this point.

Conclusion

Dialogic introspection reveals emotions, via research, of past or present-time experiences and imagined scenarios. This essay has demonstrated that the method provides excellent tools for explicating emotions. It has been applied to a multitude of different contents of experience (Burkart *et al.* 2010); as well as in cross-cultural surveys, comparative studies of different cultures (Schweickhardt 2011), and in interculturally mixed groups (see the survey at the University of Queensland in 2011, see endnote 5). The design of the interview situation—a supervisor guiding two open rounds of individual reporting in group situations—is key to creating an atmosphere suitable for deep self-exploration; one that allows for conclusions to be reached about the phenomenology of emotions, their contexts, and impacts. Intersubjective structures surface because of the dialogic character of the method.

Notes

1 See www.introspektion-hamburg.net/html/introenglish.html.
2 Retrospection—in our comprehension—means remembering past experiences. Introspection is therefore the broader concept, including both current and past experiences.
3 Dialogic introspection is based on "qualitative heuristic methodology," a general methodology of discovery developed for psychology and the social sciences by Gerhard Kleining (1994; see also Kleining and Witt 2000). The method can also be used in other methodological settings, such as grounded theory. See www.heuristik-hamburg.net.
4 If one participant is reporting so much that it threatens the time allocated to the whole survey, the supervisor can ask that participant to finish his/her report within the next two minutes. In our experience, this has never happened.
5 Both surveys took place in 2011. The first was at a meeting of the Hamburger Forschungswerkstatt; the second at a workshop at the University of Queensland in Brisbane, Australia.

References

Burkart, T., G. Kleining, and H. Witt (eds). 2010. *Dialogische Introspektion. Ein gruppengestütztes Verfahren zur Erforschung des Erlebens.* Wiesbaden: VS Verlag für Sozialwissenschaften.

Burkart, T. 2005. "Towards a Dialectic Theory of Feeling" in L. Gürtler, M. Kiegelmann, and G. L. Huber (eds) *Areas of Qualitative Psychology – Special Focus on Design*: 39–62. Tübingen: Ingeborg Huber Verlag.

Burkart, T. (2008): "Introspektion als empirischer Zugang zum Erwägen" in G. Jüttemann (ed.) *Suchprozesse der Seele. Die Psychologie des Erwägens*: 121–34. Göttingen: Vandenhoeck & Ruprecht.

Kleining, G. 1994. *Qualitativ-heuristische Sozialforschung. Schriften zu Theorie und Praxis.* Hamburg-Harvestehude: Fechner.

Kleining, G. and H. Witt. 2000. "The Qualitative Heuristic Approach: A Methodology for Discovery in Psychology and the Social Sciences. Rediscovering the Method of Introspection as an Example," *Forum: Qualitative Social Research*, 1 (1).

Kleining, G. and H. Witt. 2010. "Erleben eines Schreckens" in T. Burkart, G. Kleining, and H. Witt (eds) *Dialogische Introspektion. Ein gruppengestütztes Verfahren zur Erforschung des Erlebens*: 107–14. Wiesbaden: VS Verlag für Sozialwissenschaften.

Schweickhardt, A. 2011. "The Inside Journey. Dialogic Introspection in Market Research," *P&A international market research, Magazine for Market Research and Marketing* 2011 (2): 45–7.

Weggen, J. 2012. "Dialogische Introspektion: Eine Erweiterung des empirischen Methodenspektrums durch die Wiederentdeckung von Introspektionsverfahren" (Review Essay), *Forum: Qualitative Social Research*, 13 (1).

Witt, H. 2010. "Introspektion" in G. Mey and K. Mruck (eds) *Handbuch Qualitative Forschung in der Psychologie*: 491–505. Wiesbaden: VS Verlag für Sozialwissenschaften.

Part III

Observing emotions in self and others

Chapter 10

How do we know what they feel?

Åsa Wettergren

Introduction

Approaching emotions in the empirical setting is a challenge—partly because they were long considered irrelevant to social scientists, partly because lay people also tend to consider them irrelevant outside their private spheres. Asking about emotions tends to put the interviewee on guard, as if s/he was expected to reveal private secrets. Even when people are willing to talk, they associate emotions with "emotional situations," or clear "emotional expressions" (e.g., crying), or emotion words ("I am sad"). But these are only the tip of the iceberg. Underneath the (out) spoken, the world of emotional communication and exchange is vast and complicated; it is where body and society intersect; where emotion, reason, and cognition blend; it is the partly conscious, partly unconscious source of motivation and action.

Consequently, emotions tend to be concealed in the data. The analysis has to backtrack from the action to the emotion; or to shift focus from the action that is described to the emotion that accompanies it. Similarly, when undertaking observations, the question arises how to record the atmosphere of a room, or the fact that the observed persons exchange emotions. It is very hard to "see" these things. As both researchers and lay people, we do know a lot about the emotions of others, and we constantly act upon this knowledge, routinely managing both our own and others' emotions. But *how* do we know it?

In the following section I will discuss an excerpt from my field notes concerning a project about interactions between frontline workers (employees working with migrants) and migrants in the reception of asylum seekers in an Italian region. I used shadowing as a technique (Czarniawska 2007), meaning that I followed employees on the job. I also conducted loosely structured interviews. Using this excerpt I will discuss two valuable tools for doing emotion analysis: (1) emotional participation, and (2) backtracking emotion by using the excerpt as an emotional narrative. The second part also discusses the important use of theory.

Emotional participation at an Italian accommodation for asylum seekers

While carrying out fieldwork on the rehearsals for a theater play, Bergman Blix (2010; 2009) began to reflect on what she called emotional participation. She found herself becoming engaged in the emotions that the actors evoked and worked with—feeling, for instance, the anger or sadness of a particular role:

> There was an all-embracing focus on the actors. If I were to lose my focus on them, it would have disturbed their work; I had to participate in the sense that I was emotionally participative, even though I did not say anything. At first, emotional participation was a tool that I used not to disturb the others, but gradually I started to use my own emotions as a methodological tool, generating reflections and insights relative to the situations and the persons that were the object of observation.
>
> (Bergman Blix 2010: 61)

On the one hand, the concept of emotional participation makes explicit what the ethnographically inspired researcher always strives to do—to blend with the site in order to avoid disturbance. It tells us that passing as one among the others—to the degree that this is possible for a researcher—is to a very large extent a matter of emotion management. On the other hand, thanks to emotional participation as a tool—i.e., reflecting on how one participates and the difference between the researcher's emotion and the participants'—Bergman Blix began to understand the acquired skill of an actor's emotion management, a skill that she herself was not a master of. Unlike them, she could not "snap" in and out of a genuinely felt emotion, for instance.

The way to be emotionally participative depends on the site and object of investigation. Let me give an example. In the excerpt from my field notes below I describe an event that occurred when I was shadowing Giovanni, who was employed at an accommodation center for undocumented migrants and asylum seekers (see Wettergren 2012a). Leaving the accommodation ("the Villa"), we had picked up Ben in Giovanni's car. Ben was a migrant who was late for his obligatory Italian class. This event took place some days after I had witnessed another frontliner yelling at the residents of a different accommodation for having had visitors stay over for the night. The migrants had offered shelter to friends who were homeless—which was forbidden.

> The Italian class was in a suburb center (in a Casa del Popolo), in a small room. There was only one more student in the room, a female

teacher and a man whose function I did not understand. I thought that having a small class like this, two hours, three times a week, should be quite a good way to learn Italian. Alfons [migrant] was supposed to have been here too but Giovanni told the teacher that "he escaped" before we left with the car. Probably he had gone to his room and the frontliners do not want to interfere with the migrant residents' privacy (it seems to be a general rule). However, Giovanni now spent some time telling the students off, because "the reason he took Ben in his car to the class was that Ben would otherwise have missed it, since he didn't leave the Villa in time to get here by bus." "This," he explained, backed up by the teacher, is your Italian class, it is important. You must learn Italian if you want to find a job. And also it is job training, it is like a job appointment. You must be on time. This is your job appointment. If you don't keep it, you lose your job. Do you understand?! When you know you have to be here at ten you must leave the Villa in time. You cannot sleep late … it is as important as a job appointment. Why do you think that we have located the class here, in town, and not at the Villa? Because it is a job appointment, and to teach you how to make plans to get here in time! Do you understand?!"

The two Somali men nodded slightly and said they did understand, but their faces were blank.

I was thinking that something is wrong here, you cannot talk to grown up people that way (Giovanni's tone was not really angry, it was more upset and annoyed, like a parent who corrects his children)—or can you? Do the frontliners know something I don't? I would interpret their [the migrants'] blank faces and stiff bodies, where they sat on the chairs on the other side of the narrow table in the small room (they could not move out of there if they wanted without asking the other Italian guy to stand up), as hurt pride/shame/withheld anger. I thought that maybe they like Giovanni and the teacher and all these people who really try to help them out—that's why they are so polite and do not react angrily; but they don't like to be talked to this way, like children. It reminded me of when [another frontliner] corrected the resident in [a different accommodation] for having a guest, and him saying afterwards that "It is OK, but to say that it is OK I first have to show that I am angry because otherwise they don't get it (that they are, in fact, not supposed to have guests but that it is OK as an exception once in a while)."

(Field notes 1: 4)

During this event I obviously displayed neither emotional participation in the anger of the frontliner, nor in the (assumed) shame of the migrants. I tried to stay in the background, and to keep a neutral face. Revealing the slightest sympathy with either the frontliners or the migrants would have endangered my ability to build trustful relationships with any of them. In this case, and contrary to the case of Bergman Blix, displaying emotional participation would have disturbed the field.

Yet I did experience and participate in the emotions of the field, in the sense that sometimes I identified with the frontliners, and sometimes with the migrants. In general, I registered my tendency to feel much more sympathetic towards the migrants, but I had to keep that feeling to myself in order not to upset my relationship with the frontliners. The frontliners were always on the go, always busy, and eager to perform efficiently. The strongest emotion they displayed to me, with regard to the migrants, was frustration and resentment—in particular with the fact that they skipped their Italian classes, and also in other ways used their time-limited (six months) stay at the Villa to break the rules of an integration program that had been set up for their benefit. For instance, they would skip job training placements in order to do illicit work. I had been observing meetings with newly arrived residents at which the frontliners would tell them about the rules and about the program, and the migrants generally consented to everything. In spite of this, out of around 50 residents in total, only two or three showed up in class each time—the others apparently preferring to use the time to take illicit jobs. So, it was easy for me to track the source of the frontliners' frustration. I could use this understanding to express empathy with the frontliners in my interviews with them, thus building an atmosphere of mutual respect and understanding between us.

But this understanding did not change the fact that I felt extremely uncomfortable with what seemed to be the condescending, controlling, and sometimes arrogant way that frontliners treated the migrant residents. Trying to empathize with the frontliners, however, I had to reconsider my emotional alignment with the situation of the migrants. I had entered the field with sympathy for, and a readiness to pick up on, what the migrants felt. But now I had to ask myself if the migrants were really worthy of this sympathy—whether they were responsible for making things worse for themselves, as the frontliners argued. Moreover, was not the type of compassion I felt in itself condescending and belittling of the migrants? My emotional disposition made me look for—and therefore construct—a suffering subject: a victim. Reflecting upon my emotions—which were prejudiced in favor of the migrants—and trying to achieve emotional participation with both the migrants *and* the frontliners, put me on the track of the emotional careers embedded in the structure of an integration/reception program that suffered from absurd expectations. This structure also shaped the interaction between frontliner and migrant (Wettergren 2012b).

As I talked to and interviewed the migrants, I realized that many of them had been in a low-status position as receivers of help (from different helping agents) for a very long time, sometimes years. Their fates kept touching me, and I felt that I could be any one of these migrants. I could easily have been the man in his early twenties who had been constantly moving and tossed back and forth between Somalia, Kenya, Egypt, Libya, Italy, and the UK for all his teenage years; and who, in spite of his best efforts to start anew and build a normal life at every new place, found himself back at square one. I could be the young mother who had suffered a recent miscarriage and who had a three-year-old epileptic son born soon after arriving by boat to Lampedusa, and who had been a homeless squatter living in a mix of lodging houses and train stations ever since. I could be the father who was still appalled by the fact that he had survived the horrific journey from Somalia to Italy, but was unable to rejoice in this achievement because he was tormented by anxiety for the one-year old son he had left behind. All of them said that it was a tough life, but that they had to "keep going."

Interviewing migrants, I also realized that the anger I felt was not theirs. The sadness and grief that they felt was expressed in the interviews, but it was not articulated unless I asked directly. They wept during the interviews; they displayed resentment, fear, pride, and shame—but they talked very little, or not at all, about their emotions, even when I tried to ask directly. This absence of emotional reflexivity puzzled me and forced me to dig deeper into my imagination of what *I* would have felt in a similar situation. Then I slowly understood that they were, in fact, coping with strong emotions by avoiding reflecting upon them. Talking about what you feel is a privilege, because emotion talk enhances the emotions. Thus, talking about the feelings of sadness, grief, and shame might easily have interfered with the migrants' determination to get on. So the emotions were there, but they were also not there—as if the feeling subject was not fully aware of them. I realized that my own accessible feelings of sympathetic anger and grief were a very clear indication that I was not one of them.

Interviewing the frontliners, I learned that they shielded themselves away from the situation of the migrants. I had no problem understanding why. At some point I had to make a break in my daily trips to the Villa, since meeting with the migrants made me feel guilty and ashamed of my own privileged position—guilty and ashamed of my research, which implicitly profited from their suffering but could not alleviate it; and of my freedom to move between worlds (a stimulating academic work life, the life of a tourist, a family life with healthy children), and between countries (as a Swedish citizen I could travel freely). My position was similar to that of the frontliners. Like me, they met and interacted with the migrants—but this was their job, so directly or indirectly they were profiting from the existence and the situation of these people. Just like me, they had been overwhelmed by sympathy and guilt when they had first come into contact with the migrants they were looking after (the frontliners all contrasted their feelings towards the migrants in the beginning with those of the present). Like me, they had learned that migrants are not just victims; they are also agents who make their own choices from a range that are available. But like me, they saw that these choices seemed only to entrench the migrants deeper into misery and social exclusion. Unlike me, however, they could not simply exit the field and recover from this painful emotional turmoil. They could leave the Villa and go home to a different world, but they had to come back every day. They were locked into their positions as helpers, just as the migrants were locked into their positions as receivers of help. The frontliners could not distance themselves physically, and so, just like the migrants, they had to achieve this distancing *emotionally*; and they did it through a process they called "being professional" (cf. Wettergren 2010).

I began to understand that being locked in a subordinate position—as a receiver of help— does not lead to a life without choice. However, the choices available tend to break the rules set by the privileged; they tend to be illegal or semi-legal. We all make choices; it is an essential part of asserting ourselves and our own agency. The difference between the privileged and the deprived is that the privileged, to a much greater extent, decide for themselves the terms of the choices. This, however, was obviously not something the frontliners were aware of. They realized that the designated "integration trajectory" that they were offering to the migrants was unlikely to be successful, but they resented them for not following this designated pathway. After all, had not the migrants themselves consented to the imposed integration rules? As for the rest, they tried to avoid thinking too much about the meaning of the job they were doing. They were grateful if the migrants did not blame them, personally, for failing to help; they were grateful if the migrants understood that the help that *was* on offer was strictly limited in terms of the resources provided by the state and by the municipality.

Emotional participation had helped me to understand the "emotional career" of the frontliners as moving from past sympathy to present resentment; and the "emotional career" of the migrants as one in which emotions become sealed off and cast to one side. Part of this was tied in with the fact that the migrants' mental timescale took them far beyond the present and what was going on in the here and now; as part of a process of striving to sustain the emotional energy needed to move forward they would see themselves somewhere in a distant future, leading a normal life. This goal would justify any available means. Sealing their emotions off in the meantime helped them endure repeated instances of humiliation, shaming, and blaming. The frontliners, as professionals, however, had the six month-long "integration trajectory" as their timescale. Their goal was to ensure that the migrants learn to follow the rules within this more limited timeframe.

The emotion work enacted by frontliners and migrants was conducive to their respective goals. Both parties protected themselves from painful emotions, and engaged instead in surface-acting. Frontliners avoided the guilt of privilege, or any sort of empathetic grief or anxiety about the migrants' plight, by instead displaying anger at their "rule-breaking," "lazy" nature (as they saw it). Migrants avoided the shame and humiliation of subordination, as well as any grief and anxiety about their precarious situation, by displaying gratitude and acquiescence. Both migrants and frontliners managed their emotions as a way of coping with their interlocking and asymmetrical positions; as receivers of help, on the one hand, and as professional "givers of help," on the other.

My own emotions did not simply reflect the emotions of the field, they were crucial in helping me to understand and interpret emotions and emotion management in the field. I could not display emotional participation in situations that involved both migrants *and* frontliners. In this situation I had a surface-act of my own to play: the neutral observer. But my emotions *could* be displayed in the interviews, enabling me to establish trust with my subjects. Most crucially, in the migrant interviews, emotional participation freed me from my prejudiced feelings of grief and compassion, enabling me instead to feel their need to keep suffering at a distance. During such interviews there was a lot of crying, but also a lot of laughing.

To sum up, as argued by Bergman Blix, the researcher's emotions contain information that provide clues about the emotional processes relevant to the field. They encourage the researcher to dig deeper in order to resolve breakdowns in previous understandings, and to reach new coherences (Agar 1986). Emotional participation is a necessary tool of the ethnographer generally, but even more so when the purpose is to analyze emotional processes. We will now move on to the second part of this paper and complement these insights with a narrative perspective on emotion, and the use of theory.

Backtracking emotion

Let us reread the excerpt from my field notes quoted above. The observant reader may have noticed that there are actually scarce explicit references to emotions. I frame the whole event as an expression of anger, based largely on describing what Giovanni says, and the context of his talk. There are no notes of his physical expressions. Instead, I describe what I think the objects of anger feel, and their expressions. I reflect on the display of anger by trying to remember the tone of voice, and by comparing to a similar angry event. Despite not being mentioned explicitly, the excerpt clearly conveys my point: the humiliation and shaming of the migrants, and the (contemptuous) reduction of their adult status to one of a child. I describe my own discomfort not by emotion words, but by conveying my thoughts ("I was thinking that something is wrong here"). There is a degree of emotional ambivalence in my description—my own, but also something I pick up from the migrants: I notice that the small class seems to be an efficient way to learn Italian, and I ponder the possibility that the migrants accept humiliating treatment because they are grateful for the assistance and feel sympathy for the frontliners, expressed in the excerpt as "they like the people who try to help" (I got this from migrant interviews).

I have argued that emotion tends to be concealed in the data, and field notes are no exception. But texts—no matter whether spoken, written, or drawn—cannot help but communicate emotions, as argued by Kleres (2011). Narrative conveys emotion, and emotion is narrative in its character: "The crucial idea to be taken from this is that the narrative elements of a story together configure emotional experience. The *gestalt* of actors, events, conditions, thoughts, feelings, etc. constitutes an emotion" (Kleres 2011: 185). The story of my emotional participation is everywhere in my field notes, but it is rarely direct and explicit. The field notes, often descriptive and present-oriented, can be seen as "moment-in-time stories" (Kleres 2011), conveying emotions by their narrative structure and by the way they describe positions, actions, and interactions between people.

This perspective sheds light on why we tend to describe situations rather than, or alongside, emotions in order to evoke emotional responses in the other. It is situations that evoke an emotion, not the emotion *per se*. We also recognize emotions in actions. In turn, we know something about the way events will unfold when we know what they feel like. If I see someone hugging another person, and the recipient is responding with a warm hug also, I assume they like each other. I share this tacit knowledge with others, and I use it to get my everyday life rolling without much reflection (Collins 1981). But in order to meet the criteria for scientific viability, researchers must ask "how do we know what others feel, and what does it mean?" Part of this question has been answered already: we conduct interviews. Through interviews we validate some of the observational results. But to support an interpretation beyond interviewees' sometimes-very-limited reflections upon their emotions, we need theory. My story of emotional participation may *seem* fairly descriptive, but it is already loaded with theoretical assumptions.

I was never in any doubt about having observed an angry display. Speaking with a loud and angry voice, using accusatory words intended to shame and blame, framing a situation of failure as the other's responsibility—these are all actions pertaining to an expression of anger (Kleres 2011; Retzinger 1991) Anger is theoretically conceived of as an emotion of threatened status, therefore it reveals the position of the angry subject (Barbalet 1998; Kemper 2006). According to the literature it is also a place-claiming emotion (Clark 1990) and thus threatens the integrity of the object of anger. The angry subject claims a position above the anger object, who may as a result feel afraid or ashamed. Thus, Giovanni's anger communicated that he was the powerful one in the relationship, but his authority was challenged. I knew that he felt challenged by the migrants' failure to follow the rules. Exactly how angry he was, however, was an open question. I was told that displays of anger were sometimes "necessary" in relation to the migrants. Since Giovanni quickly calmed down, and did not enact his right to expel misbehaving migrants from the accommodation, I concluded that his display of anger was part of his work role (whether surface- or deep-acting). It was meant to intimidate the migrants, to shame them into conformity. We often do this with children, so my description of the event in these terms conveys my point about humiliation.

The scolded migrants, however, did not display the expected emotions of shame and fear. Their faces were blank and they were silent. In fact, it made me think of the face of my own son when he has done something wrong—which I associate with shame-rejection. Previous research and theory suggest that shame is painful to the self and therefore often bypassed and angrily rejected (Scheff 1997, 1990). Hence, it might be that the migrants strongly resented the outburst and therefore would become even less inclined to follow the rules. As I followed the Italian classes over the course of a few weeks, I observed that attendance levels remained low, and that migrants tended to drop in only when they had nothing better to do. The blank faces, however, inspired my emerging theory of the migrants' coping with strong emotions. This occasion was likely just one in a series of humiliation experiences that they managed to shake off and repress (cf. Smith 2001).

Conclusion

In this chapter I have used a field note excerpt to discuss: (1) the use and function of emotional participation for scientific discovery, and (2) how an "emotion as narrative" perspective enables us to understand that field notes or interview transcriptions need not *articulate* emotion (words) in order to *communicate* emotion, and (3) how the use of theory as an analytical toolkit can back up and develop the emotion analysis, and help in constructing scientifically robust texts.

It follows from the above that there is no such thing as a non-emotional text or narrative, but the recording technique may of course strive to refine the empirical basis. Interviews also convey emotions through linguistic markers, the construction of sentences, the choice of words, or prosody (cf. Bloch 1996; Kleres 2011). During observations we may record peoples' body postures, facial expressions, or gestures. But nowhere in the analysis of emotions can the emotions of the researcher be overlooked. Not using them as clues and sensitizing devices will make for a poor analysis. Not critically reflecting upon them will make for a superficial and subjective analysis.

References

Agar, M. 1986. *Speaking of Ethnography*. London: Sage.

Barbalet, J. M. 1998. *Emotion, Social Theory, and Social Structure – A Macrosociological Approach*. Cambridge: Cambridge University Press.

Bergman Blix, S. 2009. "Emotional Participation: The Use of the Observer's Emotions as a Methodological Tool When Studying Professional Stage Actors Rehearsing a Role for the Stage," *Nordic Theatre Studies*, 21: 29–38.

Bergman Blix, S. 2010. *Rehearsing Emotion*. PhD thesis, Stockholm University.

Bloch, C. 1996. "Emotions and Discourse," *Text*, 16 (3): 323–41.

Clark, C. 1990. "Emotions and Micropolitics in Everyday Life: Some Patterns and Paradoxes of 'Place' " in T. D. Kemper (ed.) *Research Agendas in the Sociology of Emotions*: 305–33. New York: State University of New York Press.

Collins, R. 1981. "On the Microfoundations of Macrosociology," *The American Journal of Sociology*, 86 (5): 984–1014.

Czarniawska, B. 2007. *Shadowing and Other Techniques for Doing Fieldwork in Modern Societies*. Malmö: Liber.

Kemper, T. D. 2006. "Power and Status and the Power-Status Theory of Emotions" in J. E. Stets and J. H. Turner (eds) *Handbook of the Sociology of Emotions*. New York: Springer.

Kleres, J. 2011. "Emotions and Narrative Analysis: A Methodological Approach," *Journal for the Theory of Social Behaviour*, 41 (2): 182–202.

Retzinger, S. M. 1991. *Violent Emotions: Shame and Rage in Marital Quarrels*. Newbury Park: Sage Publications.

Scheff, T. 1990. *Microsociology. Discourse, Emotion, and Social Structure*. Chicago: The University of Chicago Press.

Scheff, T. 1997. *Emotions, the Social Bond, and Human Reality. Part/Whole Analysis*. Cambridge: Cambridge University Press.

Smith, D. 2001. "Organizations and Humiliation: Looking Beyond Elias," *Organization*, 8 (3): 537–60.

Wettergren, Å. 2010. "Managing Unlawful Feelings: the Emotional Regime of the Swedish Migration Board," *International Journal of Work Organization and Emotion*, 3 (4): 400–19.

Wettergren, Å. 2012a. *A Normal Life. The Reception of Asylum Seekers Into Italy and Sweden*. Göteborg: University of Gothenburg.

Wettergren, Å. 2012b. *Sympathy, Humiliation and Shaming of Institutionalized Helper Interactions*. Gothenburg: Department of Sociology, University of Gothenburg.

Chapter 11

Emotional insights in the field

Stina Bergman Blix

> To be able to trust yet be skeptical of your own experience, I have come to believe, is one mark of the mature workman.
>
> (Mills 2000 [1959]: 197)

Introduction

In line with Mills's statement, this chapter investigates the importance of continuously reflecting on the researcher's emotional experiences during fieldwork. The rehearsal phase of a professional theater production is normally closed. When I carried out my study of stage actors' work with emotions during rehearsals (Bergman Blix 2010), the reason I was granted access was because I had previously worked as an assistant director, so the directors could be confident that I knew how to behave in order not to disturb the fragile climate of actors trying out new characters in a play. The trick that applies to all supporting personnel at a rehearsal (from prompter, to dramaturge, to stage manager) is to be silent but intently focused on the actors working on the stage. If I were to lose my focus on them it would have disturbed their work. When I was working as an assistant director I had practical tasks to attend to; but this time my focus was on emotions. I wrote down the minutiae of details behind the building of a scene: the actors' discussions of what the scene was about, and its relationship with present society and their own personal experiences. Then, moving to the stage, how the actors moved, their gestures, their tone of voice, the changing of the physical distance between the characters, as well as my reflections on how these building blocks generated emotional experiences and expressions.

Being co-present during the actors' emotion work involved "emotional participation" (Bergman Blix 2009). I cried silently when a character cried, I laughed when they laughed, and I sometimes found myself pursing my lips in unison with a character who was pursing her lips at her father on stage. As long as my emotions—although toned down in expression—

were congruent with the expressions on stage, they were invisible; that is to say, they were in line with the emotional climate of the room.

To understand dancing you have to hear the music

As early as 1838 Harriet Martineau argued that a researcher needed the ability to feel sympathy; a researcher who could not emotionally understand the people and situations she observed was "like one who, without hearing the music, sees a room full of people begin to dance" (in Lengermann and Niebrugge-Brantley 1998: 48). This also implies that methodologies in fieldwork need to be somewhat open-ended, leaving space to adapt to the specificities of a particular field. In Goffman's poignant words: "[Y]ou should feel you could settle down and forget about being a sociologist" (1989: 129).

The most vivid discussions about the use of emotions as a methodological tool in fieldwork come, not surprisingly, from anthropology. Within the anthropological discipline the often-long periods of fieldwork in secluded areas of the world makes the researcher's involvement an unavoidable issue. In an edited book, *Emotions in the Field* (Davies and Spencer 2010), the authors propose the use of "radical empiricism," implying (1) the focus on relations (rather than isolated persons or things) between people, between people and method, and between people and materiality (the environment), and (2) the critical importance of fieldwork experiences when relaxing our research persona and "our personality or posture, so to speak, bends itself back to its habitual form" (2010: 23). Observations that are made during a long period spent in the field, and involve close participation, entail anxiety and doubt, especially in faraway cultures. They probably prevail in a "lighter" form in most fieldwork, but the analysis of these emotions connects in particular to the study of "the imperatives of existence" (Jackson 2010), involving personal change and political action. My focus here is different: using emotions as analytical tools. This involves using the discrepancy between the field participants' habitual emotions, and the visiting researcher's non-habitual emotions, as an analytical clue.

A common skepticism regarding actually using one's own emotions, concerns validation. Attunement with, or, as Geertz puts it, "inner correspondence of spirit with" (1984: 125) your informants, runs the risk of projecting the researcher's own emotions on the subject of study.[1] However, the classic call for scientific distance is built on the assumption that emotion and reason are opposites, that neutrality generates good results, and that the researcher can be emotionally neutral—assumptions that modern research has challenged. In fact, emotions shape creative ideas, manage skepticism (Parker and Hackett 2012), and are vital to analytical research processes (Barbalet 2011).

Emotional participation furthers our ability to sense emotional shifts in the field and focus on emotions that we are observing. It is vital to be aware of our emotions, since a lack of awareness of them often results in bias (Blumer 1969: 86); and the effort to suppress them takes energy and focus from our work (Kleinman and Copp 1993: 33). Experience in itself is "the intersubjective medium of social transaction" (Kleinman and Kleinman 1991: 277), experience being both universally shared and culturally specific. The researcher can thus gain access to emotional understandings in the field, but, in contrast to the people under observation, also benefits from culturally specific experiences from her own field that create an interpretative space, a distance with room for reflection. In line with the focus on shared experiences, Hastrup argues for the importance of being open to "raw moments" (2010: 204)—emotional experiences that in short, sudden instances nail the researcher to the field.

This also involves awareness of our own emotional proclivites (Luhrmann 2010), both in general and in relation to the topic under study. We tend to pick research topics that catch our interest and might further our ability to understand the field; but even so, our previous experiences, as well as our personalities, can be more-or-less attuned to different settings. Even though it is difficult to change our emotional proclivities, awareness of them in relation to a certain topic can help us disentangle our perception of the field.

How to make notes

The bottom line of stage actors' work is to bring life and emotions into a story. At least three elements are important to understand and study emotions in the theater. A well-written play, from the actors' perspective, has space for emotions. "The narrative elements of a story together configure emotional experience" (Kleres 2011: 185), so the story and how it is told suggest emotions. Actors also work with their voice, both to find the character's specific way of expressing herself and as a way of interacting with the other characters on stage. An actor I observed found her character by starting to talk fast, as if afraid of being interrupted; this way of talking, in itself, generated emotions. To study the building up of emotions is to a large extent about how bodies come closer and move away from each other during rehearsals. Consequently, some hands-on tips on what to focus on when observing emotions are: to note the vocal dimensions of emotional expressions (e.g., how loud and fast a person talks); to note changes in the voice; and to note expressions that are not part of the dialog itself, like sighing (Bloch 1996). One should also note narrative elements, focusing on how a story is told, what parts matter to the narrator, and how they matter (Kleres 2011); and to note the closeness and openness, or looseness and tenseness of, and distance and proximity between, the actors telling the story.

However, field observations often last for a long period and involve the interactions of many people—making the research field much messier than it is in the neat and ordinary one-to-one interview. The observer needs to constantly decide what to focus on, and decide which of the apparently trivial things to pay attention to; and to spark up the energy to notice and write down all the details of what is going on.

The researcher's emotions are crucial at this point. When I started to go through my field notes I soon realized that emotion-rich, or emotion-shifting episodes were recorded in more detail than other episodes. This was natural since my object of study was emotions, but they were often accompanied by descriptions of how my own feelings changed,[2] since I was supposed to stay engaged:

> The rehearsals are in their third week and one of the actors is falling behind. She cannot understand her character; why her lines are so mundane and why she is so cruel to her daughter. She displays her distance towards her character both verbally and bodily. When the other actors or the director says that they can understand her character, she always opposes, and she sits with her arms crossed during readings and talks, rarely smiles or responds to other people's efforts to cheer her up. "I feel no sympathy at all for this person, it is really hard to see how she treats her daughter," she says with a firm voice at one rehearsal. She is evidently stuck. One day, after lunch, something happens. They are rehearsing a key scene where she, the mother, meets and reproaches her desperate daughter whom she has not seen for several years. They have been doing this scene for almost three weeks and they have been yelling and raving, but I have not felt it; the mother is so distanced. My notes are all about how they change the blocking,[3] over and over. This time, they scream at each other like they usually do, but then the actor playing the daughter suddenly becomes still; she pleads with her mother while looking down, begging quietly with a trembling voice; she looks vulnerable. The mother is clearly moved by the daughter's emotions. I also become moved; it suddenly becomes persuasive, even though they say the same things with similar emphasis and gestures. The director continuously comments on their acting and says that it is clear that they are being moved by the interaction, and the actor playing the mother replies: "Yes, I don't mean that they do not feel anything, just that feelings are fatal." Afterwards, when they talk about the scene, her body is all different. She leans forward towards the others with her hands folded in her knees. The director says: "If you give birth to a child you meet yourself, and this mother cannot do that." The actor playing the mother replies: "I was terrified before I had my child. I understood that afterwards; that I was so afraid of repeating my relationship with

> my own mother." At the next rehearsal there is a huge change in the mother's body movements and also in her character: her fear is now evident. She is stressed, she talks too fast, her body jerks, she changes position, she sits with her foot moving up and down, straightens her jacket, fixes her purse. The character is suddenly there. Before, she was tense as an actor and just appeared distant; now she is looser, as an actor, but appears tense as a character. When the director and I walk out after that day's rehearsals he comments: "She couldn't do it until she understood that she is scared." "Yes," I replied: "It was a huge difference. Suddenly she had a body."

The episode described above was useful, both in a methodological and in an analytical way. I will start with the methodological aspects. My emotional engagement helped me to select what to look for. Being "moved" intensified my presence as an observer and I started to note small details in the actors' expressions that I had not seen before. Whether or not my emotions corresponded in detail to the actors' emotions, the fluctuation in emotional intensity could be felt. It helped me understand the process they were going through and how their discussions during rehearsals were affected by their level of emotional engagement.

The episode also gave me a clue about the instigation of emotions in a professional setting, and how these on-stage emotions relate to private ones. The mother did not start with a private memory; the emotional experience came from the situation on stage. Her co-actor reached an intense emotional experience and expression during an interaction that involved a clear distance from the mother's side. Her lines, the physical distance between them, her being seated while her daughter was standing up, etc., made the daughter's vulnerability palpable and the mother's lines and physical positioning made the fear of answering her daughter, evident. This interaction, and the director's comment, opened up a private memory that validated the interpretation—being afraid of motherhood could be a useful rationale for her character in the play. The emotion of fear made sense when the actor used her private experience, but the lines and the blocking reshaped the expressions of fear and eventually "settled them" in a professional setting. I could disentangle the complexity of the interface between professional and private emotions through this episode.

The usefulness of feeling too much

The episode above shows two interfaces that came to the fore during my study of stage actors: the private and the professional; and the experience and expression of emotions. These two interfaces were related; the emotional experience was associated with private life, and expressing appropriate emotions during rehearsals and on stage was associated with professional life. Actors evidently need to express their characters' emotions—but as professionals they interpret these emotions for the audience, not for themselves. However, in order to present credible emotional expressions on stage, underlying private experiences are drawn into the professional setting.

> I am sitting in the circle with the actors and the director. The prompter sits farther away. I can see a lot and I can feel a lot, but I cannot take notes when they are this close—and they talk so openly about episodes from their own lives. If I move closer to the prompter I might be able to take notes, but then I will miss the nuances and feelings. I choose to stay close and miss some notes, and to be closer when they start working on the floor. One of the actors, Maria, tells the story of when her close friend died. A very tragic event. I become overwhelmed, being this close, and start crying. Conversations about death can be hard on me. I think about leaving, but that would shift the focus to me. For a few moments I feel that I can't handle it. I am too afflicted. I try to keep the tears from falling, but occasionally have to wipe away a stray tear from my cheek. I wonder whether the others can see my emotional state. I look at them. To avoid feeling too much I turn all my focus to the actors. They look at me, do they see? No one shows it. No one else seems close to tears; they are earnest, but not overwhelmed. More like the story being a relevant example for the play; the truth can be kept at a distance, when unbearable. Maria does not seem to lose it either. She has a steady voice.
>
> I keep thinking about the interface between private and professional. If they talk professionally about things that many people would consider private, what is then private to them? What differentiates the things they talk about during rehearsals from the things they don't talk about? Does it ever become too emotional, or cross through a private boundary—like it did for me just now? Another curious thing is how they didn't react to my expressions, which must have been visible. What does that say about the situation? How do they separate between what is private and what is professional, when their own body, experiences, and emotions are their working tools?

My emotional reaction made the professional versus private aspect obvious and it helped me formulate specific research questions. It also made me notice the actors' handling of emotions at work. The in-character crying during rehearsals sometimes spilled over into the sessions between scenes; the actor concerned would talk with a stilted voice, dry her eyes, blow her nose—but no-one ever offered comfort. The situation was work, not private life. Even though the source of the tears might be private, the emotion that drove such tears was a tool, not a state that required comfort. If they were to comfort the actor concerned, or indeed offer it to me, it would turn private. Sometimes, actors "doing" strong emotions said that they would "play it dry" during a rehearsal, an acknowledgment of the fact that emotion work is draining. But they never related to a character's emotions when talking out of character.

Hage (2009) also addresses the issue of feeling more than the actual participants in the field. His feeling of hatred towards Israel after its bombing of Lebanon in 2006 was far stronger than the hatred expressed by the relatives of the actual Palestinian victims. The unexpected mismatch in these "political feelings" made him notice that anger and sadness were associated with a lack of resources to fight back. Identifying with the power to act, the power to hit back, toned down emotions towards the other party; Hage's own intense feelings made him aware of more subtle complexities of feelings in the Lebanese group he was studying.

Hage made a conscious effort to feel what his respondents felt; likewise I tried "to be present" in a professional situation, but became overwhelmed. We both tried to experience the situation like our respondents. That effort offered clues about how our feelings differed from theirs. It was our identification with the situation, of being involved emotionally, that made us notice the great mismatch between our involvement and theirs. Keeping emotional distance, trying to be "objective," runs the risk of either missing the emotional complexity of the situation, or attributing our emotions to the participants we are studying.

Time out

Emotional participation is demanding work. Sometimes I had to physically force myself to remain silent at rehearsals. After all, I was interested in *their* process, not mine; but taking part in theirs made me tick as well. Seeing and feeling many strong emotions during rehearsals—actors crying, yelling, being desperate, flirting, falling in love, etc.—I co-experienced, but could not express fully. To better deal with these emotional experiences I began to walk the half hour it took to reach the theater as a way of purging my own excess emotions—tears running down my cheek. I was not really sad, just full of experiences and in need of venting them before entering the field again. Lorimer (2010), who studied patients being treated for depression at a psychiatric hospital, spent half her day at the hospital talking with people, and the other half taking long walks. She became involved in a struggle to keep hold of a sense of self—a well-known issue for people who are committed to institutionalized care, but one that also affected her as a researcher.

Being co-present in the field of theater rehearsals involved "emotional participation." In hindsight, I can see how my emotional involvement affected my notes right from the start, but it only became apparent as a methodological tool when my emotions evidently clashed with those of the actors. My reflections on my *own* emotions during rehearsals enabled me to understand the phenomena under investigation, but also to find new ways to describe the field, and to begin conceptual work.

Notes

1 An issue that is well known within the psychotherapeutic encounter, is counter-transference—i.e., the therapist's emotional reaction to the patient and how that can be of therapeutic value. The use of counter-transference in social anthropological studies has been discussed by Crapanzano (1994) and Davidson (1986). This issue, however, is beyond the scope of this chapter.
2 Writing "notes-on-notes" (Kleinman and Copp 1993) is a way to continuously describe your emotions in the field so that you can reflect on them in relation to what you observed and if/how they can be analytically relevant.
3 Movements and gestures on stage.

References

Barbalet, J. 2011. "Emotions Beyond Regulation: Backgrounded Emotions in Science and Trust," *Emotion Review*, 3: 36–43.

Bergman Blix, S. 2009. "Emotional Participation – The Use of the Observer's Emotions as a Methodological Tool when Studying Professional Stage Actors Rehearsing a Role for the Stage," *Nordic Theatre Studies*, 21: 29–38.

Bergman Blix, S. 2010. *Rehearsing Emotions: The Process of Creating a Role for the Stage.* Stockholm Studies in Sociology, NS 45. Stockholm: Acta Universitatis Stockholmensis.

Bloch, C. 1996. "Emotions and Discourse," *Text*, 16: 323–41.

Blumer, H. 1969. *Symbolic Interactionism: Perspective and Method.* Berkeley: University of California Press.

Crapanzano, V. 1994. "Kevin: On the Transfer of Emotions," *American Anthropologist*, 96: 866–85.

Davidson, R. H. 1986. "Transference and Countertransference Phenomena: The Problem of The Observer in the Behavioral Sciences," *The Journal of Psychoanalytical Anthropology*, 9: 269–83.

Davies, J. and D. Spencer. 2010. *Emotions in the Field: The Psychology and Anthropology of Fieldwork Experience.* Stanford: Stanford University Press.

Geertz, C. 1984. "From the Native's Point of View: On the Nature of Anthropological Understanding" in R. A. Shweder and R. A. LeVine (eds) *Culture and Theory: Essays on Mind, Self, and Emotion*: 123–36. Cambridge: Cambridge University Press.

Goffman, E. 1989. "On Fieldwork," *Journal of Contemporary Ethnography*, 18: 123–32.

Hage, G. 2009. "Hating Israel in the Field: On Ethnography and Political Emotions," *Anthropological Theory*, 9: 59–79.

Hastrup, K. 2010. "Emotional Topographies: The Sense of Place in the Far North" in J. Davies, and D. Spencer (eds) *Emotions in the Field: The Psychology and Anthropology of Fieldwork Experience.* Stanford: Stanford University Press.

Jackson, M. 2010. "From Anxiety to Method in Anthropological Fieldwork" in J. Davies and D. Spencer (eds) *Emotions in the Field: The Psychology and Anthropology of Fieldwork Experience.* Stanford: Stanford University Press.

Kleinman, A. and J. Kleinman. 1991. "Suffering and its Professional Transformation: Toward an Ethnography of Interpersonal Experience," *Culture, Medicine and Psychiatry,* 15: 275–301.

Kleinman, S. and M. A. Copp. 1993. *Emotions and Fieldwork.* Newbury Park, London, New Delhi: Sage.

Kleres, J. 2011. "Emotions and Narrative Analysis: A Methodological Approach," *Journal for the Theory of Social Behaviour,* 41: 182–202.

Lengermann, P. M. and J. Niebrugge-Brantley (eds). 1998. *The Women Founders: Sociology and Social Theory, 1830–1930.* New York: McGraw-Hill.

Lorimer, F. 2010. "Using Emotions as a Form of Knowledge in a Psychiatric Fieldwork Setting" in J. Davies and D. Spencer (eds) *Emotions in the Field: The Psychology and Anthropology of Fieldwork Experience.* Stanford: Stanford University Press.

Luhrmann, T. 2010. "What Counts as Data?" in J. Davies and D. Spencer (eds) *Emotions in the Field: The Psychology and Anthropology of Fieldwork Experience.* Stanford: Stanford University Press.

Mills, C. W. 2000 [1959]. *The Sociological Imagination.* New York: Oxford University Press.

Parker, J. N. and E. J. Hackett. 2012. "Hot Spots and Hot Moments in Scientific Collaborations and Social Movements," *American Sociological Review,* 77: 21–44.

Chapter 12

Emotions

The discovery of an object and the development of a method

Denise Van Dam and Jean Nizet

In this contribution we will focus on the construction of emotions as one of our research objects, and on the development of our methodology to study this object. For the past few years we have conducted interdisciplinary research on organic farmers in several French and two Belgian regions. We interviewed some 50 organic farmers—using in-depth interviews—about various themes such as their life histories, their training and learning, their networks, their values, and their commitment to collective action. The interviews were mostly carried out before the visit to the farm, and they continued (in a more informal way, without recordings being made) during the visit to the farm.

The study of emotions in the framework of our research was a somewhat surprising outcome. Indeed, in the beginning our project did not include the study of emotions at all. But the empirical evidence of their importance to our project was so overwhelming that we ended up deciding to devote part of our research to them. For instance, a lot of farmers began their interviews by expressing anger at agro-business and the use of pesticides. Some told us they felt deeply ashamed before their conversion to organic farming methods: "I had the feeling of doing a very foolish thing when I used pesticides.... Most of us had a feeling of culpability because we knew we were doing something wrong by using the pesticides." Most of them expressed fears about their own health, the health of their familes and about humanity as a whole: "Today such a lot of farmers have cancer that medicine cannot explain. All those pesticides and chemicals we use, our health has taken whack." Those negative emotions contrasted sharply with their joy at talking about their "new job" as organic farmers: "That's it, I finally have found my way!"; "I really feel in harmony again with nature." Some talked with tenderness about their cattle: "Taking time to take care of the calves doesn't mean wasting time. On the contrary, one gains time. For people it's the same." Others talked with wonder about the way the environment of their farms has changed since the conversion to organics. Some wine-growers talked in detail, and with a lot of tenderness, about the earthworms that are so important for the health of the soil; and about the small flowers and vegetation that has re-emerged since the conversion of their farms.

Strong emotions were not only expressed by farmers—they were also felt by us during the interviews. So we also felt anger about the inflicted injustices; and we too were overwhelmed with feelings of tenderness when listening to the story of the special relationship between the farmer and his cattle. We decided to pay heed to emotions also because our field research experience was underscored by the regained interest in emotions in both the sociology of social movements and in the psychology of work. For a long time both had undervalued emotions, mainly because of rationalist paradigms. Following the abduction method (Pierce 1995; Van Maanen *et al.* 2007) we started to look for those theories that were relevant to the framework of our research about organic farming.

Methodology to study emotions

The study of emotions demands a particular approach, especially when the emotions of the interviewee and interviewer converge. This was the case in our research where one of the interviewers is herself involved in the social movement of organic farming. This research situation offers both advantages and disadvantages.

The most important advantage of the sharing of emotions between the interviewee and the interviewer consists of the creation of a "warm climate" which wipes out inhibitions and stimulates the gathering of profound and rich information through verbal and non-verbal expressions. Many interviewees answered our questions in depth and talked about their very personal feelings towards organic farming. The length of some of the interviews, the "off the record" conversations once the interview was finished, and various invitations to share a meal and visit the farm, testify to the successful mutual construction of a sense of trust. The interviewers, too, went beyond the call of duty—for instance, by buying some goods in the shop of the farmer.

The disadvantages of this proximity have already been underlined by scholars who investigated the new social movements that have emerged since the 1970s—such as the anti-nuclear, peace, women's, and civil rights movements; and more recently the anti-globalization movement (Touraine 1978; Kriesi *et al.* 1995). If the proximity creates a climate of trust that helps to secure the interviewed persons, it might also give rise to "socially desirable" answers (Edwards 1957).

Most scholars underline the phenomenon of the proximity of values. In our research it is evident that values go hand-in-hand with emotions. In order to reduce the influence of the proximity of values/emotions, we decided to do most of our interviews in a team of two—a female researcher who was involved in the organic movement, and a male researcher (either the sociologist or the anthropologist) who was not. One of the interviewers would lead the interview. The other one, taking a more retired position, would note non-verbal emotional expressions by means of a grid inspired by the emotions work of Argyle (Argyle 1975, cited in Fiske 1990: 68–70; see Table A12.1 in the Appendix at the end of this chapter). Argyle distinguishes ten non-verbal indicators of emotions: physical contact, physical proximity, body orientation, appearance (hairstyle, make-up, clothes, etc.), nods, facial expressions, gestures, postures, eye movements, and finally non-verbal aspects of language (volume, intonation, speed, language errors, etc.). This means that two types of indicators—verbal (the transcript of the interview) and non-verbal (the observations by means of the grid)—can be used, to varying degrees, to analyze different variables. Verbal expressions allow us to grasp more specifically the nature and valence of emotions, whereas non-verbal expressions reveal their intensity.

The interviewers were debriefed a few hours after the interviews took place about the emotions of the interviewee, and about their own feelings. The interviews were fully transcribed and were, as a rule, analyzed by the team of all three researchers.

Conducting the interviews in this way enabled us to distinguish two axes of personal proximity/distance in the interview situation:

1 the sharing (or not sharing) of the values (which occurred when the researcher involved in the movement was co-interviewing), and
2 the emergence or not of shared emotions.

However, the analyses of the interviews did not show any difference for any of the two axes.

Typology of emotions

Most scholars (Sander and Scherer 2009; Garcia-Prieto *et al.* 2009) conceptualize emotions as a multicomponent phenomenon that includes a cognitive appraisal (e.g., the interpretation of a situation), emotional feeling (e.g., happiness, shame, anger), visual expression (e.g., smiling, frowning, eye movements), reactions of the autonomous nervous system (e.g., quickening of the heart), and action trends (e.g., preparing oneself to run away). Thus, emotions are considered as an indispensable component of the capacity of subjects to assess events, make decisions and undertake actions.

We borrowed, at first, a classification of emotions from social-cognitive psychology (Garcia-Prieto *et al.* 2009: 195–222):

- emotions of accomplishment: pride, excitement, joy, and satisfaction
- emotions of approach: relief, hope, interest, and surprise

- emotions of resignation: sadness, fear, shame, and guilt
- emotions of conflict: envy, disgust, contempt, anger.

But our empirical findings were so rich that we had to complete this classification by adding two other categories: emotions of "flow" or "optimal experience," on the one hand; and sensory emotions (smell, touch, visual feelings), on the other.

The feelings of accomplishment do not adequately capture the emotion of "deep happiness" that the interviewees feel at specific times in their work as organic farmers and in their involvement in collective action. To understand this particular emotion we refer to the "psychology of happiness" developed by Seligman (1998, 2002) and Csikszentmihalyi (2004). The experience of "flow," or mental fluidity, occurs when the subject engages freely in order to achieve a personal goal, is fully focused on his/her own activities, and mobilizes all the skills required. This "optimal experience" is consistent with the feeling of "deep happiness." The emotional power with which the interviewees expressed their commitment enables us to categorize some of the practices as real "optimal experiences" that immerse the subject in the state of "flow." In addition, the presence of a real "challenge" is one of the major characteristics of the optimal experience. Indeed, we found that giving oneself a "challenge" was of central importance among our interviewees. Therefore we extended the class of feelings of accomplishment with those of deep feeling of happiness, or "flow."

The typology does not report the emotions of bedazzlement, wonder, and tenderness that were felt about biodiversity. These emotions are expressed with great intensity and frequency: through words, facial expressions, tonality of voice, small hand gestures, touch, and smell. We, too, observed these emotions during visits to the farm, when tasting the products, or when the farmers showed us pictures. As a consequence, we included another new category: the sensory emotions to reflect sight, taste, touch, smell, and hearing. This extension implies the introduction of the sensorial appraisal besides the cognitive one. This, then, became our typology of emotions:

- emotions of accomplishment: pride, excitement, joy, and satisfaction
- emotions of flow: optimal experience
- emotions of approach: relief, hope, interest, and surprise
- sensory emotions: sight, taste, touch, smell, hearing
- emotions of resignation: sadness, fear, shame, and guilt
- emotions of conflict: envy (jealousy), disgust, contempt, anger.

In the following paragraphs we present the results of our research on emotions in two areas:

1 the transition to organic farming
2 organic farming as a social movement.

The role of emotions in the transition to organic farming

In our research about the transition process from conventional farming to organic farming (Van Dam *et al.* 2010) we mobilized the theories of cognitive dissonance (Festinger 1957; Harmon-Jones and Mills 2006) and social psychology of emotions (Garcia-Prieto *et al.* 2009). We showed how emotions and cognitions evolve together during the three stages of transition:

1 withdrawing from conventional farming
2 approaching organic farming, and
3 "staying in" organic farming.

The divestment from conventional agriculture is characterized by a strong cognitive dissonance and the presence of distancing emotions (anger, shame, guilt). The farmer, or his relatives, have a lot of negative experiences (intoxication by pesticides, or discovery of the disappearance of flowers in the fields) which produce a state of dissonance between two cognitions: "I am a farmer" and "this profession is harmful to health." At that moment, the subject experiences resignation and emotions of conflict: anxiety, anger, shame, culpability. "We have to become aware that we have arrived at a point where it becomes dangerous for humanity;" "I don't accept any more that one is poisoning people and betraying the harmony with nature." Faced with this cognitive and emotional conflict, the farmer adopts the strategy of cognitive rationalization: he tries to reduce the dissonance by arguing with himself that it is possible to solve the problem *within* the system—for instance, by adopting some or other ecological measures. But at a certain moment this strategy of "changing *within* the system" is not sufficient any more. The strategy of cognitive rationalization shows its limits.

In the second stage, behavioral rationalization pushes the farmer towards the act of conversion. The farmer becomes curious and engages in a process of discovery, both on a cognitive and a social level: reading books, brochures, and reviews; participating in conferences; meeting with organic farmers and their organizations, etc. This new situation provokes emotions of approach such as hope, interest, and relief. They open the period of emotional attraction towards organic farming.

In the third stage ("staying in organics"), when the farmer has converted to organic farming, emotions of accomplishment, flow, and sensory emotions tell the farmer that his choice to convert to organic farming was right. Profound harmony exists between the subject and his environment through the presence of a challenge. Some talk about the feeling of having finally found their way; about the rediscovery of working with the soil; about the pleasure of taking care of their animals. One farmer recalled being a child, sleeping in a room surrounded by barns and being able to smell the cows and hear their breathing. The pleasure of taste was particularly prevalent among the winegrowers and the arboriculturists—reinforced by the thought that the apples were "non-stressed." Others talked about a new serenity, ethics, some kind of mission, creativity, liberty: "We feel free because we just use things that are simple. We are much less dependent." And then there is the pride: "a farmer proudness." Very few farmers evoked negative emotions, though we can suppose that they must have been present. This surplus of positive emotions can also be explained by the theory of cognitive dissonance. Once the farmer has effectively converted his farm, he is pushed towards a convergence between this actions and his emotions. Negative emotions would tend to question his new behavior and thus create a cognitive-emotional dissonance.

The role of emotions in organic farming as a social movement

We consider organic farming as a "new social-economic movement" (Gendron and Turcotte 2006; Gendron *et al.* 2010). Since its origins, organic agriculture profiles itself as both a protest movement and as an alternative production method. In our research about the role of emotions in bridging collective action and professional activity in the area of organic farming (Van Dam *et al.* 2012) we demonstrate that emotions are a key factor for the unity of the movement.

Recasting Touraine (1978) to make room for emotions, we found that when the interviewees talked about the stakes, the opposition, and the identity of their movement, they talked simultaneously about the challenges, the conflicts, and the belonging of their "work as a farmer." All the time emotions are present. The convergence of emotions in both components of the organic farming movement (protest and production) bears witness to the unity of the movement.

Stakes full of hope and excitement, challenges of passion, and "flow experiences"

Following Touraine, the stake is the first central component of each social movement. The fundamental stakes of organic farming belong to the fields of the environment, public health, and freedom/professional autonomy: the interviewees considered organic farming as a privileged way of building a world without the pollution, health problems, and dependencies that usually accompany the agro-food industry. Positively formulated, organic farming contributes to a "green" world in which people eat healthily and in which the farmer can blossom. The word "dream" was used by several interviewees. These farmers talked with great emotional force about universal values such as freedom and responsibility, which they strongly believe need to be implemented in the agricultural sector. When they talk about the challenges of their daily work as farmers, they talk mostly about their personal blossoming and the biodiversity of their farms.

The emotions expressed are frequent and strong, and express themselves in the tonality of voice, eye expressions, and in the rapidity of speech. One of the challenges concerns their quest for coherence between the universal values they defend and their professional practices. This quest permeates into their private lives: organic meals, sustainable housing, use of soft medicine, etc. The realization of this coherence generates profound emotions of well-being: "I feel good in my shoes," "I feel really happy," "I feel in harmony with myself and the world." When they talk about biodiversity in their farms, the key words are not "challenge" or "action" but "letting go," "wondering," "facing the beauty and diversity of nature." Here we are in the field of sensory emotions. We also witnessed emotions of deep happiness or "flow," which are characteristic of an optimal experience.

Opposition and conflict against the system

Touraine (1978) highlights the importance of the designation of an "historic" opponent for the existence of a movement. In our research, the principal opponent is, above all, the "system"—and not individual people. Very few farmers expressed hatred or anger towards conventional farmers; rather, this was directed at the agro-food industry, the crop protection industry, the government, the education system, and scientific research. These were all subjected to much criticism and negative emotion, with anger and rebellion (emotions of conflict) predominating. These two emotions have a powerful action power.

Identity: shared joy, conviviality and excitement about social action. Belonging: warmth, friendliness, joy in the professional exchanges

Following Touraine (1978), the identity question is the third central component of social movements. The identity question goes back to the origins of the organic farming movement. Since the beginning it has had a very open design, and includes farmers, environmentalists, and consumers. It has never had a strong identity, referring instead to a vast network (Michelsen 2001). Shared joy and excitement are considered by its members as a necessary condition for organizing social action—which is often stressful and time consuming. Members talk about "activism in conviviality and coziness," "warmth," "charm," and even "adventure."

The interviewees talked a lot, and very deeply, about their relationships with other farmers, their customers, and the local community. The sharing of emotions of joy, enthusiasm, and passion constitutes a motivational factor. Many farmers highlight the difficulties of organic farming, the necessary investment of time, and the technical problems. But the pleasure felt in attending training courses, visits to the field, or attending exhibitions or tasting events, constitute real compensation for the problems they face. The farmers insist on the absence of feelings such as conflict or envy. A lot of them rediscover themselves as teachers, and take time to show off their farms, their vineyards, etc. They are very proud of it.

Conclusion

The question of emotions has led us to investigate new objects: the role of emotions in the transition from conventional farming to organic farming; and the role of emotions in organic agriculture as a social movement. This emotional component of organic farming has been neglected in previous research. We showed that emotions, considered as a complex phenomenon, are a necessary tool for understanding the progressive transition towards organic farming, on the one hand, and the unity of the organic movement, on the other.

Appendix

Table A12.1 Grid of the non-verbal emotional expressions—example of a Walloon organic farmer

	Physical contact	*Physical proximity*	*Body orientation*	*Appearance*	*Nods*	*Facial expressions*	*Gestures*	*Postures*	*Eye movements*	*Non-verbal aspects of language*
Sequence 1 Non-verbal expressions at the beginning of the interview	No	The other side of the table	Approaches us	"Normally" clothed	Shakes his head up and down	Smiling	"Embraces" the animal	Leaning towards us	Fixed on us	Gentle, with confidence
Summary of the verbal content linked to the first non-verbal changes	The farmer is talking about the little calves he cares for, the time he spends generally with his animals, and the importance of his tenderness towards the animals. He also talks about the importance of having a dog at the farm. He says that the time a farmer spends with his animals is never "wasted" time, but always "good" time.									
Sequence 2 First non-verbal changes	No	The other side of the table	Turns to the side	"Normally" clothed	Shakes his head from right to left	Contraction	Finger pointing	Sitting, pressed against the back of the chair	Avoiding	Nervous, aggressive
Summary of the verbal content linked to the first non-verbal changes	He is talking about the massive problems he had with a governmental public health agency, and the unfair treatment he received from it. He said that all this would have tipped the farm into bankruptcy had not been for the support of his custumers and of the organic farmers union.									
Sequence 3 Second non-verbal changes	No	Variable, visiting the store	Goes ahead and then follows us	"Normally" clothed	Orients his head to the products he shows us	Smiling	Shows and takes products in his hands	Standing	Regards us and the products	Enthusiasm
Summary of the verbal content linked to the second non-verbal changes	He talks about the store on the farm, and the way it was created with his wife; he talks about his relations with his customers. He talks about the importance of the time spent with his customers in the same way that he talked about the importance of the time spent with his animals. He talks about the human, social, and health quality of his products.									

References

Argyle, M. 1975. *Bodily Communication.* London: Methuen.

Csikszentmihalyi, M. 2004. *Vivre. La Psychologie du Bonheur.* Paris: Editions Robert Laffont.

Delobbe, N., O. Herbach, D. Lacaze, and K. Mignonac (eds). 2009. *Comportement Organisationnel.* Brussels: De Boeck.

Edwards, A. L. 1957. *The Social Desirability Variable in Personality Assessment and Research.* Ft Worth, TX: Dryden Press.

Festinger, L. 1957. *A Theory of Cognitive Dissonance.* Stanford: Stanford University Press.

Fiske, J. 1990. *Introduction to Communication Studies,* 2nd Edition. London, New York: Routledge.

Garcia-Prieto, G., V. Tran and T. Wranik. 2009. "Les Théories de l'Evaluation Cognitive et de la Différenciation des Emotions: Une Clé Pour Comprendre le Vécu Emotionnel au Travail" in N. Delobbe. O. Herbach, D. Lacaze, and K. Mignonac (eds) *Comportement Organisationnel*: 195–222. Brussels: De Boeck.

Gendron, C. and M.-F. Turcotte. 2006. "Les Nouveaux Mouvements Sociaux Economiques au Cœur d'une Nouvelle Gouvernance," *Organisations et Territoires,* 16 (1): 23–32.

Gendron, C., J.-G. Vaillancourt, and R. Audet. 2010. *Développement Durable et Responsabilité Sociale. De la Mobilisation à l'Institutionnalisation.* Quebec: Presses Inernationales Polytechnique.

Harmon-Jones, E. and J. Mills (eds). 2006. *Cognitive Dissonance. Progress on a Pivotal Theory in Social Psychology.* Washington DC: American Psychological Association.

Michelsen, J. 2001. "Recent Development and Political Acceptance of Organic Farming in Europe," *Sociologia Ruralis,* 41 (1): 3–20.

Kriesi H., R. Koopmans, J.-W. Duyvendack, and M. Giugni. 1995. *New Social Movements in Western Europe.* London: UCL.

Pierce, C. S. 1995. *From Pragmatism to Pragmaticism.* New York: Humanity Books.

Sander, D. and K. Scherer. 2009. *Traité de Psychologie des Emotions.* Paris: Dunod.

Seligman, M. 1998. *Learned Optimism.* New York: Simon and Schuster.

Seligman, M. 2002. *Authentic Happiness: Using the New Positive Psychology to Realize your Potential for Lasting Fulfillment.* New York: Free Press.

Touraine, A. 1978. *La Voix et le Regard.* Paris: Seuil.

Van Dam, D., J. Nizet, and M. Dejardin. 2010. "La Transition des Agriculteurs Conventionnels Vers le Bio: Une Dynamique Cognitive et Emotionnelle," *Les Cahiers Internationaux de Psychologie Sociale,* 85: 159–81.

Van Dam D., J. Nizet, and M. Streith. 2012. "Les Emotions Comme Lien Entre l'Action Collective et l'Activité Professionnelle," *Natures Sciences Société,* 20 (3): 318–30.

Van Maanen, J., J. Sorensen, and T. Mitchell. 2007. "The Interplay Between Theory and Method," *Academy of Management Review,* 32 (4): 1145–54.

Chapter 13

Emotional alliances in bureaucratic encounters

Alberto Martín Pérez

Based on research on face-to-face encounters in bureaucratic organizations, this chapter explores paths to unearthing emotions and their role in formal interactions. I studied different public offices in Spain at two points in time. In 2004–5 I focused on several immigration offices and a police station. In 2009–10 I did research on the encounters between clients and civil servants in social security offices. In the following text I retrace the moment I noticed that emotions were circulating between individuals engaged in bureaucratic encounters. I realized that emotion management was a key issue for the understanding of interactions as they were strongly embedded in emotions. This insight—once I engaged reflexivity to notice and interpret my own emotions, since these presented themselves during the scenes I observed—generated a plethora of novel observations during my fieldwork. This contribution recounts some key points of this process.

Reflexivity and the discovery of emotions

When starting a project that includes ethnographic fieldwork, we usually feel attracted by the unknown, yet at the same time anxious about what we are going to explore. We wonder about the interactions we are going to establish, and we care about how to manage our first steps in a new environment. Without being particularly conscious of it, we are already producing some reflexivity that is strongly embedded in emotions; although normally we are still not aware of their importance. Social scientists are taught about the virtue of neutrality in research, and it is difficult to leave aside that idea when emotions such as fear or anxiety block us when we make the first steps in the field. For example, when I first arrived at social security offices in 2009 I was more worried about the impression I was making on the office director and the civil servants I was going to work with than about my purpose of collecting objective interaction data. I was confronted with the contradiction of pursuing neutrality and objectivity, while feeling the emotion of anxiety at the same time.

Ethnographers usually write daily field reports and there is consensus on their usefulness for gathering precise information. Although our awareness of the emotional implications of fieldwork may not be evident at the time we make our initial notes, it is quite common to note down jumbled feelings alongside first observations. Beaud and Weber (2003) argue that this happens because the discovery of the unknown at the beginning of our research leads us to unearth what is unknown within our own feelings. The reflection on the manner in which we approach the people involved in the setting under study, or the way we intend to observe them, results in some sort of introspection. In order to improve our approach to fieldwork this introspection should be examined—traced back through revision of our past field notes. In my own case, when looking back at the notes I took during past research projects, I still find it surprising that my first field notes were always filled with emotions. Most of these field notes included comments about how I was feeling as I started to observe the different settings, and after meeting my initial informants.

Emotions in initial field notes

My first notes, taken as I waited in line in front of the police station and the immigration office in 2004–5 (Martín Pérez 2006), were full of rhetorical questions that demonstrated my own fear, panic, and a strong feeling of anxiety: "What am I doing here?; How should I approach these people?; What would happen if I say 'hello, do you have some time for ...?'; I'm not sure this is going to work" (February 2005). At the same time, there was hope in my writings after each new observation session, and excitement about the discovery of the details I was gradually perceiving: "I realized today that I already know a little bit about these waiting lines.... OK, the most important thing is to keep on coming here!" (February 2005). Years later, when I started fieldwork in the social security offices, all these emotions reappeared: "I am happy about how this project is starting. I think I am going to do quite well" (June 2009).

Introspection when approaching the field is not spontaneous. In my case, it depended on my previous experience, and more specifically on my readings about qualitative methods and the strategies and tricks presented in the manuals; when I became conscious of the quality of my first field notes, I realized that I was focusing on trying to do methodologically "proper" observations, rather than observing what was really happening. This made me feel still more anxious than I already was.

A particular concern about our own emotional reactions is the way we deal with the people we observe. Instead of discovering, step-by-step, the lives being played out in the scenes I was looking at, I started to become obsessed about the *roles* played by those present in these scenes. In front of the immigration offices I was more worried about the national-foreigner divide than about the observation of actual interactions between migrants and the authorities; at the social security offices, the existing internal hierarchies of officials and their various roles, and those resulting from the daily life of the office's dealings with its clients, absorbed my attention—leading me to overlook other possible issues for exploration.

Role-playing as participant observers

In an article on the experience of doing qualitative research with migrants (Martín Pérez 2006), I analyzed the role played by the personal characteristics of the participant observer in the interactions he observes when there are clear social boundaries between him (a native Spanish citizen) and the people involved (immigrants lining up for their documents in front of a police station). This is a good example of how to go beyond suspicion and fear of rejection. At the beginning of my fieldwork I was worried about immigrants' refusal to talk to me. Based on *my* perception of socio-cultural cleavages, I thought I would be obligated to justify my presence:

> Why has somebody like me—middle-class, university-educated, with parents who are both civil servants, and who has travelled abroad freely and voluntarily—decided to get to know immigrants' life stories; as if I were "going to help them?" Apart from a strong commitment to democracy and human rights—which can paradoxically be traced back to my secure status as a content, bourgeois, or even paternalist middle-class citizen—which elements of the social position and the biographic trajectory of the researcher determine the choice of such a topic? How does this position affect the making of this research?
>
> (Martín Pérez 2006: para. 9)

At the end of the article I show how I managed to overcome the emotions (fear and anxiety) that were blocking the development of my research, and how this strategy made me feel both surprised and satisfied:

> I tried to intervene in migrants' encounters with officialdom by using the publicly accessible space of the queue. I did this through: words of support; "innocent" questions; and, answering the doubts raised by migrants. In doing this, I never hid the fact that I was a researcher; I simply preferred to be open and use this honesty as a basis for establishing confidence. Once confidence was established I then used "banal" conversations ..., perhaps followed by an invitation to take a cup of coffee, and was on the whole very surprised by how few people rejected my offer.
>
> (Martín Pérez 2006: para. 21)

Focusing on emotions

At the very beginning, the research project I developed at the social security offices had little or no connection with the study of emotions. It was commissioned by the government, and its main focus was to study how welfare was being implemented through daily practices carried out in public offices. The authorities never thought of a project in which emotions had any role to play; consequently, I did not have the intention of exploring, in any shape or form, the role of emotion management in the implementation of social policy by front desk civil servants.

My observation sessions consisted of spending entire work days with individual officials who were serving in the office at that time. The purpose was to have spent, by the end of my fieldwork, at least one session with every civil servant. After being introduced by the office director to all of the office workers, I usually spent my first session with the "kindest" one—although this categorization was made by the office director himself. Talking to civil servants who were initially uncomfortable about the idea of having their job performance and role observed by a stranger helped me overcome their reluctance to be involved.

I would spend the whole day shadowing the chosen civil servant, including during break times. I decided I would sit directly next to him or her, rather than sitting next to clients who they happened to be meeting, or keeping a certain distance away from their desk. I was soon aware of the effects of this decision on the clients' perception of me—I was going to be seen as another civil servant. But I soon realized that this perception was, in fact, useful: though I was not exactly taken for an official by most clients, but rather for a relatively young trainee.

Clients are received by following a sort of ritual. They arrive at the office, are assigned a turn number, and wait to be called. Once their number is shown on the screen in the waiting area, they walk to the desk and introduce themselves to the public servant, and in this case also to the supposed trainee (me). Clients would then have a chance to relate their case. They usually give details about different aspects of their lives which they thought might have an important bearing upon social security office decisions. Officials would listen to these stories selectively—paying interest in information that was considered useful for administrative purposes, and interrupting clients' narratives when they were adjudged less relevant.

These routine activities, although defined by most officials as monotonous, are strongly embedded in emotions. Clients' stories demonstrated confidence, pain, or resignation; while the clients themselves displayed pride, fear, shame, anxiety, or even anger. The listening officials' interaction management is also deeply connected to emotions: their clients' stories awake in them self-confidence, emotional proximity or distance, stress, anxiety, and sometimes also anger.

As a participant observer I was aware of the emotions circulating around the desk: despite being framed by routine, the "presentation of the self" by each individual displayed some kind of emotional dramatization relevant to the resolution of each particular case. This was a project about welfare implementation through bureaucratic practices; but when I started to study the interactions between officials and clients more closely, emotions arose "naturally." Such emotions were a challenge that needed addressing if I was to complete the map traced out by the research problem initially defined by the government. But how?

Which emotions to focus on?

Given awareness that emotions play an important role in the understanding of the interactions I was observing, the next step was to identify those relevant for my purposes. Since Hochschild's (1983) seminal research on emotion work in organizations, two processes have become identified as crucial: (1) emotion management as a fundamental activity of public service, and more precisely of serving clients, and (2) the way rules (administrative proceedings, legal prescriptions, and work organization) are felt by every actor intervening in the bureaucratic encounter (Bolton 2005).

Feeling rules on both sides of the front desk, together with the ongoing emotion management—specifically on the part of the civil servant—set the framework for our observations. In my case, without any knowledge of relevant literature at that time, I was only able to perceive "positive" and "negative" emotional reactions. I only had the capacity to see supportive attitudes in officials in reaction to clients' positive narratives, and rejection in response to negatively perceived stories.

Reaching a deeper understanding of emotion management, however, occurred quite quickly. Civil servants are trained in communication skills and emotion management. From the very first observation sessions, and probably in order to prove to me their capacities, they told me about their skills in silence management. I had the opportunity to see them put these into practice when they met with particularly whingey clients. These clients' complaints helped me unearth the first emotion that appeared quite clearly: anger. This discovery gave rise to the disclosure of a long series of emotional reactions: the compassion of civil servants when listening to an especially painful story, or the fear and shame of hesitant clients who felt inferior in relation to a public service office perceived as a dominant institution; but also confidence and pride on both sides of the front desk when the middle and upper class clients—who perform well in institutional environments—were present; or anxiety on the part of public servants when they experienced institutional constraints. These emotions that were circulating around made me understand the front desk as a social-emotional world, to use Scheff's (2011) words: emotions were not a collateral issue within bureaucratic encounters, but a constitutive feature of social policy implementation at the front desk.

Emotionalized stories

The discovery of the role of emotions and emotion management was linked to some particularly painful and miserable stories. In the beginning I took them as anecdotes within the routine of "normal" stories, but in fact they were extremely influential in the construction of the office routine. Let us look at two excerpts from my field notes:

> June 25, 2010: This is the case of a woman who is applying for permanent incapacity, who has obtained a confirmational medical report. Her company wants her to return to work until the final administrative decision is made. She was clearly incapable of remaining standing at the reception desk of the hotel she was working in, and is asking for a quick resolution of her case. She suffers pain whether standing or sitting, and the official does not know how to react. Another official takes care of the case and starts the application process for the woman so that she will not need to go back to work. This case evokes compassion in civil servants, as well as anger against inhuman and unfeeling companies.

> July 23, 2010: This is the story of an elderly couple. The man is applying for a retirement pension, as he was previously pre-retired from a company that has closed down. There is a problem, however. He was receiving, simultaneously, a part-payment from his pre-retirement as well as his unemployment benefits. The official consults the office director and it takes quite a long time before they reach a solution: unfortunately, the man will be penalized and will see his pension reduced. The couple are left speechless. The woman starts crying, and they both confess that this situation compounds their suffering the recent death of their daughter. This very personal story shocks the official, and a strong feeling of compassion overcomes the two of us.

Emotional alliances and the understanding of interactions

After discovering different emotion sequences, the next step is to link them to the way interactions are produced. I realized that in fact the three individuals involved in the encounter (the client, the official, and myself) were concerned about each other's emotional reactions. Emotions were circulating among us and were attributing to each actor clearly defined roles. For the understanding of this circulation I seized upon the notion of "emotional alliances" (not far from Randall Collins's idea of "interaction ritual chains"—see Collins 2004) to capture how the three of us ally, under different circumstances, with one or another actor by joining his or her emotional expressions. For instance, if I thought that the official was in the right, I tended to support him by implicitly approving his or her emotional reactions. On the contrary, if I felt the story told by the client was unfair and believed that he or she was being mistreated, I allied with the client. If the client wanted support for his or her story, he or she usually tried to set up an alliance with me in order to convince the official about the fairness of his or her demand. Certainly, there were many other combinations and variations.

The important task while observing these alliances was to unearth the emotions mobilized by each actor, and the meaning attributed by the rest. For example, the shame expressed by most clients when approaching the public servant's desk indicated an understanding of bureaucracy as an instrument of domination. This could only be offset by (unexpectedly) finding in the public servant, and the observer, associates rather than opponents. The client's fear would change to self-confidence if he or she found reciprocity in the other actors' emotional expressions—experiencing proximity rather than distancing during the encounter. The shift from shame to self-confidence would then reflect a successful adaptation of public institutions to citizens' demands. In a more extreme case, the client's anger against the official (due to a perceived unfair situation or decision) could only have the effect of altering the resolution of the case if the client succeeded in allying with another actor—such as the observer, or other civil servants or clients. Anger could thus involve the possibility of opposing official policy through an alliance with others—a kind of subversion.

How to preserve neutrality?

Although our involvement in these "emotional alliances" necessarily has an effect on our observations, neutrality is sometimes an ideal "happy medium" for the completion of our research. Reflexivity plays here, once again, a critical role. We become aware of our influence on interactions, but at the same time we need to avoid extreme positions, particularly in view of conflicts between clients and officials, or between the latter. That happened to me in different situations at the social security offices when aggressive clients tested the patience of civil servants', who in turn became aggressive. Those were cases in which emotion and silence management were replaced by visible conflict. In such situations it is very challenging to position ourselves in favor of one or other actor, and our best option seems to remain neutral. But other civil servants usually put pressure on us to reveal our sympathies for one of the contenders, since they tend to support their colleagues regardless of "right" or "wrong." In doing so they are implicitly asking us to do the same. In such cases, I managed to remain discreet (most of the time); thus avoiding the need to take a stance in favor of the "wrong" contender. I then realized that in order to conclude fieldwork satisfactorily I needed to balance involvement in observations, good relations with officials, and neutrality in conflicts.

At the end of fieldwork, and once aware of the meaning of these alliances, we must be able to analyze their social implications. We now have abundant empirical evidence about the role of emotions, and have informed ourselves about the methodological issues these raise. We are now ready to answer questions about our influence on our own observations, and we can argue in favor of our methodological decision to study emotions, emotion management, and emotional alliances, after having been careful about—and succeeding in—maintaining a more-or-less neutral position. We can do so because we are at this moment apt to understand the entire emotional map of the bureaucratic encounter. We are finally ready to see that the emotions we have explored and disclosed are associated with different social roles that explain how the policy implementation process works at the front desk. This is a map made of power relations that define bureaucratic routines—resignation, passivity and clients' ignorance of administrative proceedings—but also their mobilization of knowledge and capacities in search of more equal treatment; some possibilities for the empowering of clients by transforming public services in an opportunity for new learning about their entitlements; as well as for the promotion of active citizenship.

Concluding remarks

Emotions are constitutive features of human interaction. Frontline bureaucratic practices only make sense through the encounter between officials and their clients in a formal interaction ritual. However, those social scientists who not expert in the study of emotions usually neglect emotions in the study of face-to-face encounters, favoring instead supposedly stronger perspectives on organization and policy analysis. This is a weakness, as my chapter shows: emotion management has now become a crucial feature of public service, and a consensus prevails that bureaucratic interactions are connected with the way rules, social norms, or even legal prescriptions, are felt, experienced, and interpreted by individuals and groups.

I have summarized my own experience in discovering the importance of emotions and the way they circulate among participants in formal interactions. Gaining an understanding of the social-emotional world of a public office has provided me with tools for a better understanding of the problems of work organization, policy implementation, and the role of bureaucracies and citizens in relation to these institutions. My particular experience at the public offices I studied differs, maybe, from that of other social scientists—but its strength lies in the way it addresses surprises, the role of reflexivity in turning them into research tools, and the unexpected paths fieldwork takes as a result.

References

Beaud, S. and F. Weber. 2003. *Guide de l'Enquête de Terrain*. Paris: La Découverte.

Bolton, S. 2005. *Emotion Management in the Workplace*. New York: Palgrave.

Collins, R. 2004. *Interaction Ritual Chains*. Princeton: Princeton University Press.

Hochschild, A. 1983. *The Managed Heart: Commercialization of Human Feeling*. Berkeley, CA: University of California Press.

Martín Pérez, A. 2006. "Doing Qualitative Research with Migrants as a Native Citizen: Reflections from Spain," [34 paragraphs], *Forum: Qualitative Social Research*, 7 (3): Art. 1. Available at: www.qualitative-research.net/index.php/fqs/article/view/135 (last accessed 13 December, 2014).

Scheff, T. 2011. "Social-Emotional World: Mapping a Continent," *Current Sociology*, 59 (3): 347–61.

Chapter 14

Can you feel your research results?

How to deal with and gain insights from emotions generated during oral history interviews

Benno Gammerl

If emotion is inseparable from cognition, then the researcher's feelings cannot be disconnected from the analytical process. This holds true for every kind of research, but it is particularly obvious when emotions themselves are the phenomenon under consideration (Probyn 2011; Bondi 2005). On the one hand, pretending to proceed in a completely objectivist fashion fails to acknowledge the effects emotions have on knowledge production, and thus renders them non-transparent. On the other hand, interpretations based on intuitive empathy and the assumption that researchers and research subjects share the same understanding of emotional phenomena can be equally misleading.[1] Such a supposedly direct approach is particularly problematic in the history of emotions, which presumes that emotional patterns and practices change across time. Thus it is necessary, for example when interpreting oral history interviews, to differentiate between the reported emotion and the emotions that accompany the report. Simultaneously, one has to be aware of the interrelations between the feelings pertinent to the period under research and the emotions generated during the research process. These are intertwined by the intricate dynamics of memory, as well as by the (re)constructive historiographical endeavor itself. Thus, past and present emotions are distinct, yet not clearly separable from each other (Gammerl 2009).[2] Instead of pushing aside these entanglements, or empathetically reducing their complexity, researchers should, rather, reflect upon them.

In the following pages I will demonstrate the analytical potential of such contemplations by discussing three examples taken from my current research about homosexuality and emotional life in rural West Germany between 1960 and 1990. This oral history project is primarily interested in the change of emotional patterns and practices accompanying the gradual emancipation of lesbians and gays, or the growing normalization of homosexualities since the 1970s.[3] By focusing, first, on emotional interactions between interviewee and interviewer; second, on the bodily display of feelings during the conversation; and third, on clashes between diverging emotional styles, I will show how fresh methodological perspectives on the emotions generated during the research process enable empirical insights that would otherwise have remained unexplored.[4]

In the notes I took after the first interview with Ms. Opitz, born 1955, I characterized her as an anxious person who was carefully avoiding names of places and persons that would allow readers to identify the published narrative as hers. Furthermore, I noted that she was permanently afraid of getting lost within her own life story and that she repeatedly doubted the correctness of her recollections. In light of these impressions it is quite plausible to assume that these anxieties were intensified or caused by the challenging interview situation with its intimidating asymmetries between researcher and research subject. The interpretation of the narrative needs to take these circumstances into account, if it wants to avoid depicting Ms. Opitz wrongly as a generally very fearful and insecure person.

At first sight, the narrative contains a number of passages that support this supposition. Ms. Opitz talked about her "highly complex" family constellation, her dropping out of high school, her "limited love life with men" which—together with her "helper's syndrome"—she made responsible for her somewhat involuntarily "sliding into" her first lesbian relationship. In short, she highlighted the deficits in her life and did not tell it as a success story. Additionally, Ms. Opitz exhibited insecurities about the interview situation itself. She was not sure whether the fact that she was an adopted child was relevant. And she doubted her ability to adequately describe her bygone feelings. Thus, her narrative and her performance seem to befit a contained and not very self-assured person.

That this assumption is at least partly mistaken can be inferred from a more thoroughgoing analysis of the emotional interaction within the interview.[5] This analysis takes Ms. Opitz's cautious skepticism as a point of departure which she already voiced in her very first words that were tape recorded. Replying to my introductory remark about the "bits of information" she had received in advance of the interview, she said: "Very little bits, yes." Ms. Opitz put forward this critique of my preparation of the interview more explicitly at the end of the second interview, making suggestions for amending the procedures. Yet at the outset I did not take her remark as useful advice, perceiving it rather as a threat to my authority and pushing it aside in a slightly brusque manner. Later on, similar interactions occurred twice when Ms. Opitz critiqued my questions that aimed at her emotional life: "Well, I always find this question somewhat problematic, because it is hardly concrete. Feeling is so many things." This critique hit the point, because I had formulated a question that was indeed hard to answer. In addition, I violated basic rules of good interviewing practice by asking the interviewee one of my research questions about emotional differences between rural and urban spaces:

> and now in a more narrow sense in regard of feelings, so would it be possible to say something like, feelings [...] develop more slowly, more cozily it is (pause) [...] well, that is to say the, the, the [...] velocity [...] is different [...] one could say, there were maybe also diverging dynamics, well, it's a question.

This short excerpt demonstrates that Ms. Opitz was not the only one performing helplessness and insecurity. The notes I took after the first conversation mention Ms. Opitz's anxieties, but also my own "fear" of disrupting the narrative flow by allowing for too long pauses. These doubts about my interviewing capabilities surface even more clearly in the notes about the second conversation: "I did not always manage to control my features and my smile to the extent that I would have wished for." It is interesting to contrast this with my description of Ms. Opitz's behavior in the first interview: "She often looked into my eyes, performed calm gestures with her hands and seemed generally rather controlled."

The interpretation of the emotional interactions has turned full swing by now: from emphasizing Ms. Opitz's insecurity—potentially amplified by the situational asymmetries—to asserting an inversion of this power disequilibrium. Ms. Opitz hinted at this reversal towards the end of the first session: "Well, I'm not here to pose questions. It's actually a pity." This inversion brings the interviewee in control and makes the interviewer feel insecure. Both interpretations are viable. Their combination probably describes best the emotional interaction as a row of mutually enforcing feedback cycles raising anxieties about not meeting the requirements of the situation on both sides of the table. The following passage exemplifies this logic, with the several laughs indicating the exchange of insecurities:

NARRATOR: [...] sorry, now I said something that I maybe shouldn't have said here. (laughs)
INTERVIEWER: no, well, as I said, that's no problem. (laughs)
NARRATOR: no, well. (laughs)

This analysis allows for a more nuanced understanding of how Ms. Opitz told her life story. Furthermore, it also bears on the overall interpretation of her narrative, as it uncovers a notion of personal strength behind the contradictive emphasis on deficits. Ms. Opitz repeatedly depicted herself as energetic and strong: "I'm not the kind of person who accepts things as they are without questioning them." This self-assertiveness seems to be at odds with her insecurity. Ms. Opitz's narrative is shaped by the contradiction between these two dimensions.

Yet to push the argument one last step further, one can also discern different notions of insecurity being at play here—insecurity as weakness, and insecurity as strength. I started speaking about "insecurity" and introduced the first notion. After her telling me that she did not consider her first lesbian relationship a life-long commitment, I suggested that this implied a certain degree of insecurity. Thereby I wanted to hint at her undecidedness that—in my interpretation—resulted from the fact that she had not yet developed a firm homosexual identity. Thus, I pushed her to consider her non-commitment as a deficit. Ms. Opitz accepted the word "insecurity," but immediately reinterpreted it as "a certain movement between closeness and distance" that should guard herself as well as her partner against false expectations.

In this understanding, insecurity is a strength that honestly confronts the unpredictable future without taking resort to illusionary hopes for enduring stability. Later on, Ms. Opitz, in a similar vein, critiqued the gay and lesbian community as well as the general public for their inability to cope with persons who cease to identify as homosexuals after having spent some years in same-sex relationships. This inability, one might claim, results from the fact that most people cling to a potentially deceptive sense of security by fetishizing gay and lesbian identity. Only people strong enough to do without such false stability can admit: "After 20 years of being lesbian, nope, now I found out, it's still maybe not ..." I might have perceived of Ms. Opitz as an insecure person not because she displayed anxieties, but because I was intimidated by her daringly challenging notions of a stable homosexual identity.

So far I have been examining rather subtle and non-obvious emotional interactions. Yet while doing qualitative research one also encounters more graspable and manifest emotions. Sometimes the interviewee starts crying. These are particularly awkward moments. It is next to impossible to navigate such situations in a satisfactory way. A very wise rule of thumb recommends asking one's conversation partner whether she or he wants to have a break, whether one should switch off the tape recorder, or whether one should leave the room. Nevertheless, when analyzing the text one has to interpret these moments in which the interviewee non-verbally displayed strong feelings. It is tempting to assume that such displays mark episodes of particular emotional importance. Thus, crying would accompany eminently sad episodes; and laughter, joyful ones. Yet such interpretations rely on potentially misleading presuppositions. Thus, one should rather avoid such simple interpretations and instead attend to the ambiguous character of non-verbal displays.[6]

My interview with Mr. Melling, born 1949, illustrates this point. Mr. Melling had, for a long time, lived a double life as a husband and father on the one hand, and as a regular visitor of gay cruising areas on the other. At age 37, when his wife was pregnant with their third child, he was tested positive for HIV. After telling me about the moment when he got the bad news, Mr. Melling described in detail how he tried to cope with his fear of death, his self-accusations, and his grief during long lonesome walks in the forest. He was most troubled by the thought of the hardships his family would encounter after his death. He reported his attempts to get his wife's and his new-born son's blood secretly tested for HIV, and his relief when he learned that they were not infected. For years to come he hid his homosexuality and his HIV infection from his family. One of the very few situations where he could openly talk about his problems was a self-help group of gay fathers with HIV that he joined after some time:

NARRATOR: these were wonderful hours [...] it is the honesty, (.) the openness, (pause) the openness in talking to each other. While, when facing death, then one doesn't need to pretend. (pause) There everybody just behaved as he is. (pause) Here I get to very, (pause) very deep feelings. (sobs)
INTERVIEWER: Shall we have a break?
NARRATOR: Yes, briefly.

In this passage Mr. Melling was doubtlessly talking about a very sad and distressing experience. Actually his crying and my switching off the recorder mark the end of this episode. At first glance it seems strange that he brought back these dreadful memories for almost 30 minutes in a rather composed manner, and only then started to display bodily signs of grief, just when mentioning the "wonderful hours" he spent with the group of gay fathers.

There are at least five possible explanations for this. The first refers to the fact that HIV is still incurable. Thus, Mr. Melling might have cried because his death was still more imminent than he could bear. Second, his tears possibly indicate his mourning the fate of the other group members, almost all of whom have—as he mentions just after the break—passed away since. Third, and in a completely different vein, his tears might hint at his relief about having managed to narrate this challenging episode. A fourth interpretation assumes that the bodily display lagged behind the narration of the grief-stricken story. This is supported by closely listening to the original recording. When Mr. Melling talked about waiting for the result of the HIV test for which he had secretly obtained blood from his then pregnant wife, he took a deep breath and cleared his throat with a characteristic noise before saying: "This was the worst week of my life." The impression that his breathing and harrumphing at this moment indicate his efforts to avoid crying is confirmed by the fact that he made very similar noises towards the end of the episode, just before he started crying. Thus, his tears might actually mark an emotionally most relevant part of his story. Yet it is not the part he narrated when his eyes filled with tears, but an earlier one instead. Maybe he held back his tears at first only to let them flow when he finished the complete episode.

The fifth interpretation, finally, links his tears to the open display of emotions that characterized the gay self-help group:

> this HIV-group [...] where one, at least for me it felt that way, well so truthfully. I have not experienced that before that people interact with each other so truthfully, so openly, that one could talk about everything that occupied one's mind. [...] I think that was the energy that was vested in me there.

In this group Mr. Melling learned to handle his emotions in a way completely new to him. Within his family, his religious community, and his workplace, a reserved emotionality had been predominant. In a way, he performed the transition from hiding his feelings to openly displaying them within the interview. While reporting how he successfully concealed his infection, his grief, and his fears from his family, he held back his tears. But as soon as he talked about the self-help group where he was encouraged to "talk about everything that occupied [his] mind," he started crying. Thus, his crying hints at the particular emotional style he acquired within the therapeutic self-help setting, and is not simply a spontaneous expression of feelings. His sobbing might mark a decisive turning point in his emotional biography, when he came out as HIV-positive within the group of gay fathers and simultaneously supplemented his previous emphasis on reservation with an emotional mode highlighting openness and expressivity.

Mr. Melling's narrative thus supports my hypothesis that a change in emotional patterns and practices has accompanied the emancipation or normalization of homosexualities since the 1970s. Another respondent, though, explicitly objected to such assumptions about the malleability of emotions. Mr. Schumann, born 1935, repeatedly emphasized that feelings did not change. When I wanted him to talk about the differences between the emotional modes prevalent in the 1950s and in the 1980s, he declined to accept the emancipation narrative about the increasing emotional openness of men who loved other men. Instead, he held that humans were at all times capable of voicing their feelings in the same manner. The only relevant question was whether people were strong and autonomous enough to "listen to their heart," which he implicitly claimed to have been doing throughout his life. Thus, Mr. Schumann conceived of emotions in a sentimentalist fashion as an unchanging inner truth. This concept resembles his understanding of homosexuality as an innate disposition, which is quite typical for homosexuals who came of age in the 1950s or earlier. The claim that same-sex desire was inborn and God-given was then a forceful argument against the criminalization of male-to-male intercourse.

Against this background it is not surprising that Mr. Schumann rejected my assumptions about the changeability of emotions. The more intriguing question concerns my own conduct. I doubt most descriptions of homosexuality in the 1950s as being totally closeted. And I know that one should not maneuver interviewees into certain directions. But still I persistently tried to counter my conversation partner's arguments and challenge his self-image as someone who was always true to his feelings. Why?

Obviously, my constructivist notion of emotions as something malleable does not suffice to explain my efforts. A more likely reason is that I disliked Mr. Schumann's heroic self-portrayal. As I noted after the first interview, he often seemed to stage himself in too-coherent a fashion and in too-positive a light. In order to disrupt this self-display I pointed out to him that he abandoned his homosexual love life, got married, and founded a family in the 1970s—while the gay movement was just under way. More confrontational was my following, rather unmotivated, intervention:

NARRATOR: [...] I like being gay. Yes.
INTERVIEWER: Now, you have mentioned your depressions twice [...]

This aggressive change of topics indicates a further reason for my conducting the interview in an adversarial fashion: to a certain extent I personally disliked Mr. Schumann. I was convinced that he hid behind what I held to be an emotional façade. When he played some—as I noted afterwards—"cheesy" songs to me that were connected to his different lovers, he half closed his eyes in a gesture of inward joy, and grief, and memory, but not without—I assumed—simultaneously trying to secretly ascertain whether I was duly appreciating his emotional performance.

If my skepticism merely resulted from antipathy, considering it more closely would not enhance the analysis. But there was more at stake. I offended my conversation partner, because I, born 1976, thought that he tried to disavow—not just on an analytical, but also on a personal level—my understanding of emotions as shaped by socio-cultural rules. With several insinuations he critiqued my feelings as flawed. His notion of emotional intensity entailed a devaluation of my alleged preference for cognitive reflections. When I—again trying to unsettle his self-display—asked him whether he had continuously held that one should not resist, but indulge in one's inner feelings, he replied: "This doesn't change, once you will surely experience that personally as well, there are things that happen to you. And this is independent of age, of status, of intelligence, of intellectualism, completely." Within this opposition between emotional and intellectual dimensions Mr. Schumann clearly favored the former as the essential origins of authenticity, truthfulness, and experiential intensity over the latter's hollowness. As I represented the scientific stance—trying to scrutinize, as it were, the inexplicable—I took his remarks as referring to my own over-intellectualized understanding of feelings. This perception engendered a line of thought that increased my uneasiness and explains my defensiveness: did my personal emotional life lack intensity? And did Mr. Schumann treat me like one of the young men who regularly sought his advice, and whom he mentioned repeatedly?

The assumption that Mr. Schumann tried to help me to improve my own emotional life also explains his frequent questions about my love experiences. Thus, his sentimentalist understanding of feeling as inner truth concerned not only my theoretical assumptions, but also my personal ways of dealing with emotions. These are, rather, informed by notions of work, and ambivalence, and thus directly contradict Mr. Schumann's emphasis on immediacy and self-assuredness. This clash of diverging concepts best explains my attempts at unsettling his account.

The re-examination of the confrontational interaction between Mr. Schumann and me finally hints at opposing emotional styles which are typical for the different generations of gay men each of us belongs to.[7] Researchers are not situated outside of, but rather within the field they scrutinize. They also lead quotidian emotional lives. Once one acknowledges this, paying attention to conflicting emotional styles within an interview can yield fruitful insights. Here it results, first, in identifying generationally specific emotional modes and, second, in modifying my impression that Mr. Schumann's emotional performance was inauthentic.

To push the argument a bit further: When the assumption that feelings are variable across time relies itself on a historically specific emotion concept, is it then at all possible to disprove—on an analytical level—Mr. Schumann's claim that humans were at all times able to voice their feelings in the same manner? Of course it is. But the question reminds researchers of how cautiously they should handle universal claims—even their own ones. And it triggers important reflections about how specific histories are shaped by the particular constellations from which they emerge.

These exemplary interpretations of emotional interactions, bodily displays of feelings, and clashes between diverging emotional styles within interview situations illustrate two important points: thoroughly scrutinizing these phenomena, first, enhances methodological rigor. It enables us to understand how feelings contribute to the production of certain results. Second, such analyses can—if carried out with appropriate caution—enable insights that other interpretative means would fail to reveal. Thus, it could easily escape attention how vital Ms. Opitz's understanding of insecurity as a strength is for her biographical narrative, or how crucial the self-help group is for Mr. Melling's emotional trajectory. Paying attention to feelings generated during the research process does therefore form a viable, legitimate, and sometimes even a particularly rewarding route of enquiry.

Notes

1 Kathleen Gilbert (2001: 11), in my view, overemphasizes "empathy" and the "comparability of experience," when recommending to use "the researcher [as] research instrument." Simultaneously, she underestimates the potential of difference and strangeness.
2 For psychological perspectives on the relations between "emotional content of memory," "emotional state at encoding," and "emotional state at retrieval," see Parrott and Spackman (2000: 478), who recommend context-sensitive approaches.
3 I conducted two interviews with every respondent, a biographic-narrative and a semi-structured one of about three hours each. The following is based on these conversations and the research notes I took afterwards. I quote my own translations.
4 In this vein, Janet Holland (2007: 195) claims that "emotions are important in the production of knowledge and add power in understanding, analysis and interpretation."
5 On how such analyses of emotional interactions in general can produce valuable insights, see Joanna Bornat (2010: 51); on mutually amplifying anxieties between interviewer and interviewee see Michael Roper (2003: 24–6).
6 Theodore Sarbin (2001: 220–1) emphasizes the need to interpret crying with reference to social and narrative context, and asks "what impression [the crying person] is trying to manage."
7 For another example of distinct emotional styles clashing within an interview situation see Celia Hughes (2013: 80–2); on emotional styles in general see Gammerl (2012). The example illustrates that conflictive questions valued by researchers who highlight the political dimensions of oral history (Niethammer 1985: 410–2, 431) often yield more fruitful insights than empathic interviewing modes favored by researchers interested in emotions (Gilbert 2001: 11).

References

Bondi, L. 2005. "The Place of Emotions in Research: From Partitioning Emotions and Reason to the Emotional Dynamics of Research Relationships" in J. Davidson, L. Bondi, and M. Smith (eds) *Emotional Geographies*: 231–46 Aldershot: Ashgate.

Bornat, J. 2010. "Remembering and Reworking Emotions: The Reanalysis of Emotion in an Interview," *The Journal of the Oral History Society*, 38 (2): 43–52.

Gammerl, B. 2009. "Erinnerte Liebe: Was kann eine Oral History zur Geschichte der Gefühle und der Homosexualitäten beitragen?" *Geschichte und Gesellschaft*, 35 (2): 314–45.

Gammerl, B. 2012. "Emotional Styles – Concepts and Challenges," *Rethinking History*, 16 (2):161–75.

Gilbert, K. R. 2001. "Why Are We Interested in Emotions?" in K. R. Gilbert (ed.) *The Emotional Nature of Qualitative Research*: 3–15. Boca Raton: CRC Press.

Holland, J. 2007. "Emotions and Research," *International Journal for Social Research Methodology*, 10 (3): 195–209.

Hughes, C. 2013. "Negotiating Ungovernable Spaces Between the Personal and the Political: Oral History and the Left in Post-War Britain," *Memory Studies*, 6 (1): 70–90.

Niethammer, L. 1985. "Fragen – Antworten – Fragen. Methodische Erfahrungen und Erwägungen zur Oral History" in L. Niethammer and A. v. Plato (eds) *"Wir kriegen jetzt andere Zeiten." Auf der Suche nach der Erfahrung des Volkes in nachfaschistischen Ländern*: 392–445. Bonn: Dietz Verlag J. H. W. Nachfahren.

Parrott, W. G. and M. P. Spackman. 2000. "Emotion and Memory" in M. Lewis and J. M. Haviland-Jones (eds) *Handbook of Emotions*: 476–90. New York: Guilford Press.

Probyn, E. 2011. "Glass Selves. Emotions, Subjectivity and the Research Process" in Shaun Gallagher (ed.) *Oxford Handbook of the Self*: 681–95. Oxford: Oxford University Press.

Roper, M. 2003. "Analysing the Analysed: Transference and Counter-Transference in the Oral History Encounter," *Oral History*, 31 (2): 20–32.

Sarbin, T. R. 2001. "Embodiment and the Narrative Structure of Emotional Life," *Narrative Inquiry*, 11 (1): 217–25.

Chapter 15

When your data make you cry[1]

Deborah Gould

Even as we live in a time when scholars have punctured a once pervasive dualism pitting emotion against reason, and debunked the idea of the dispassionate, objective observer, it can be unsettling to be moved by your research. In this essay, I discuss how researchers' feelings can strengthen their analyses. Drawing from a research experience in which I moved from "participant" to "observer," I argue that feelings are a potential source of knowledge that can help defamiliarize one's common sense, especially if one approaches feelings in a historical, psychoanalytic, and affective manner.

My research project focused on the direct action AIDS activist movement, ACT UP.[2] I was intimately involved in ACT UP for six years, and only later decided to take it up as an object of study. I began the project in the fall of 1996, about two years after my home chapter—ACT UP/Chicago—held its final meeting and disbanded. My initial intent was to explain the origins, development, and decline of the movement, and that goal, indeed, established the narrative arc of the book. But the project took a number of twists and turns that I had not anticipated when I began. Most of all, I had not expected to be moved by my research. That may sound surprising given the endless deaths from AIDS-related complications that occurred from among ACT UP's membership—as well as in gay communities across the country, more generally—through the mid-1990s. While I was participating in the movement, I felt mainly anger, or better, fury, that both state and society regarded queers as "better off dead." I approached my research with that emotional orientation intact.

But as I sorted through ACT UP's archives, and thousands of news articles about AIDS activism, I repeatedly found myself dissolving into tears—overwhelmed by the enormity of all those deaths, by what participants in ACT UP had been through, and by what we had been trying to achieve. I was overcome by the intensity of participating in a movement in which so many members had been sick and dying, in which so many were experiencing such immense loss—a movement that tried to fend off death but was manifestly unable to do so and instead was surrounded by it. While reading through my growing archive of ACT UP material, I would suddenly start weeping uncontrollably. Or I would find myself astonished, in jaw-dropping disbelief at the sheer number of deaths experienced within the movement. I would sit in an affect-flooded stupor, transported to a temporally disjunctive state, experiencing, virtually for the first time, the horrors of a recent past that I had lived through but on some affective level had refused. I began to catalog the material that moved me to tears.

- A remembrance by lesbian AIDS activist Jane Rosett of her close friend David Summers, an early AIDS activist, who died in 1986. David's lover, Sal Licata, had invited Jane and a few other close friends to David and Sal's seventh anniversary celebration, to, as Sal put it, "hang out in bed and hold David while he pukes." Jane wrote,

  > Who could resist? It was a party. David held court and stressed how honored he was to have lured a lesbian into his king-size bed. Sal joked that David always did entertain best in bed. Vito Russo, Don Knudson, and I relayed the latest PWA dish. "More people are in love than in the hospital!" David cheered. Within a few days, David was dead, and within a few years, everyone else in David's bed that day—except me—was also dead.
  >
  > (Rosett 1997: 40)

- A tribute to Danny Sotomayor, a charismatic member of ACT UP/Chicago who was well known, widely loved, and controversial, both within ACT UP and within the broader lesbian and gay community. Chicago gay journalist Rex Wockner wrote about his visit to Danny four days before he died:

  > He weighed 75 pounds, was bald from radiation treatment, couldn't talk because of a brain lymphoma, and was covered with tubes. "Can you hear me? Do you know who I am?" I asked.... I sat down and found a tubeless place to touch him.
  >
  > (Wockner 1992: 28–9)

- A column about a lesbian and gay anti-violence march in Chicago in April 1992 where Mayor Daley showed up and was booed by the marchers. *Windy City Times* columnist Jon-Henri Damski found himself pointing at the mayor and echoing chants of "Shame, shame, shame!":

  > Voices came from everywhere, like a disorganized chorus without a director. It was a flood of emotion coming from the deep tunnels of our grief. [Alderman Helen] Shiller was stunned, speechless for a moment, then said: "This is something different, it's deeper than anger." I agree.... Out of every corner of my eye,

> when I am at this kind of randomly attended queer gathering, I see the faces of people I have lost, and hug the bony bodies of guys who soon may be gone. The loss, the tears, the grief, the fear, the human terror and disbelief is constant.
>
> (Damski 1992: 15)

- ACT UP/NY member and cultural theorist Douglas Crimp's recollection about what a younger gay man in ACT UP had said to him after seeing an early 1970s gay film:

  > [He] was very excited about what seemed to me a pretty ordinary sex scene in the film; but then he said, "I'd give anything to know what cum tastes like, somebody else's that is." That broke my heart, for two different reasons: for him because he didn't know, for me because I do.
  >
  > (Crimp 1989: 10–11)

- A first-person account of ACT UP/New York's first political funeral, held in October 1992, where activists hurled the ashes of people with AIDS over the White House fence. On the day of the march, a small group of people who would lead the funeral procession met together. Arthur Gursch, from Chicago, held up a worn sack that contained the ashes of his lover, who had been a member of ACT UP/NY and later ACT UP/Chicago. "This is Ortez" (Finkelstein 1992: 10).

What do you do when your data make you cry? As a way into that question, I consider a methodological difficulty I encountered that derived from studying something in which I had been intimately involved. I'll call it the issue of "familiarity," and let me venture that it is an issue that can confront any ethnographer. A central goal of ethnography and participant observation, of course, is precisely to become familiar with the social group you are studying. The researcher is trying to ascertain people's understandings of what they are doing, to make sense of their beliefs, values, norms, and actions from their perspective, in their own terms. In what sense, then, might familiarity pose methodological problems?

The difficulty I faced was that through six years of involvement in the movement, ACT UP's self-understanding and perspective on the AIDS crisis—its commonsensical beliefs, values, and norms—had become my own. Common sense has a background quality to it that makes it hard to notice; we take it for granted to such an extent that it fails to rise to the level of conscious recognition, and is even less likely to impress itself upon one as being worthy of investigation in its own right. Through my involvement in the movement, ACT UP's understandings of itself and of the AIDS crisis—I'm thinking here of the beliefs and values held by nearly everyone in the movement, internal conflicts notwithstanding—had come to seem natural, axiomatic, and unremarkable to me. Those understandings were so pervasive within the movement—and so obvious to participants—that initially I failed to see them as socially constituted and historically contingent, and therefore phenomena ripe for inquiry and explication. The methodological challenge, then, was to get outside of ACT UP's—and my own—common sense enough to notice it and then denaturalize and inquire into it. I needed to turn what seemed to be a nondescript, unremarkable, background, given, into something that was an oddity—a puzzle that invited investigation.

To be sure, my intimate knowledge of ACT UP's common sense aided my research. Some of my key questions concerned ACT UP's emergence and sustainability: I wanted to understand why lesbians, gay men, and other sexual and gender outlaws had taken to the streets in 1986–7; and how this relatively militant movement had sustained itself into the early 1990s. One of ACT UP's main self-understandings was that the movement had turned to confrontational, direct action tactics because its members were angry about the government's genocidal negligence and punitive handling of the AIDS crisis, and because we sensed that more conventional activist responses had been ineffective in exerting pressure. Along with sharing that understanding, I also knew from direct experience that anger suffused ACT UP. Beyond stating ACT UP's motto at the start of every general meeting—"we are united in anger to fight the AIDS crisis"—participants regularly enacted and embodied anger. A member of ACT UP/NY describes how this anger, displayed by ACT UP's contingent in a New York Gay and Lesbian Pride Parade, drew him to the movement:

> When ACT UP passed ... I took one look and said, "I am going to go to the next meeting of that organization." There was a sense of power, a sense of action. It didn't appear to be about pity or shame or sadness or guilt. It seemed to be about anger and action.
>
> (G'dali Braverman, quoted in Shepard 1997: 113)

My familiarity with ACT UP's common sense, then, directed me to look at the role anger played in the movement's emergence and growth.

However, while correct in many ways, my initial supposition about the importance of gay anger problematically naturalized that anger and suggested that ACT UP participants' feelings were always and only uncomplicated, non-contradictory, and remarkably coherent and rational—given both the state and society's responses to the AIDS crisis, of course we were angry, period. The grief I experienced while doing research—when the loss of friends, comrades, and queer worlds overtook and devastated me—helped to unravel that commonsensical supposition, inciting me toward a more historical, psychoanalytic, and affective understanding of gay anger and, indeed, of feelings in general.[3]

In what follows, I will explain what I mean—but first consider that that deluge of grief occurred *not* while I was in the heat of the movement, with the urgency and intensity and death swirling all around, but years *after* the decline of ACT UP, while reading media accounts and activists' recollections of demonstrations and other events; looking at photographs and watching video footage of ACT UP actions; amid interviews with members of ACT UP/Chicago and ACT UP/NY; and going through my folder of obituaries. To be sure, I experienced profound sadness during my years in ACT UP, but as I noted earlier, I mostly remember feeling anger about the AIDS crisis. The experience of grief while doing research, then, was jarring and, perhaps counterintuitively, a source of knowledge in that it prompted a line of questioning about feelings and activism that fundamentally shaped the project.

I wondered in particular about the seeming absence of grief in the movement, at least in the early years. During ACT UP's heyday we only had space for anger, for a sense of urgency, for action. I am not critical of ACT UP's emotional habitus that elevated anger above all other feelings; there was every reason to be furious and, unquestionably, that fury helped drive our very effective activism. But the flood of grief that overcame me amid my research suggested an earlier denial that I wanted to consider. What had I done with my grief? Indeed, what had *we* done with our grief? It's not that grief was entirely absent from the movement. At the many memorial services held to honor ACT UP's dead, participants experienced the movement's losses. And we were constantly aware of the deaths that were devastating our lesbian, gay, queer communities. Still, as a movement, ACT UP did not dwell on grief, and we certainly were not overwhelmed by it—at least not consciously, in the early years. In the tumult of the time we had little chance to reflect upon what we were going through; we thought we only had time to *act*. Many of us viewed mourning as cutting into this precious action time, which was already in short supply. Indeed, just as an earlier generation of activists had advised "Don't mourn, organize,"[4] ACT UP's common sense approach was to "turn grief into anger."[5]

And, indeed, we did turn our grief into anger and confrontational action. But how, by what mechanism, and to what extent did such transformations in feelings "work?" In the face of my delayed grief, I realized that instead of naturalizing and simplifying participants', and my own, feelings, I needed to explore how unconscious processes affected people's relation to painful feelings like grief; how various feeling states emerged and circulated within the movement; how some feelings became normative while others were *verboten*; how participants embodied and reproduced ACT UP's prevailing emotional habitus; and how those emotional navigations, and shifts therein over time, affected the movement.

In addition to forcing questions about psychic responses to painful feelings, and about ACT UP's emotional habitus (especially our emotion norms), my experience of grief prompted a slew of other questions that similarly historicized ACT UP's, and my own, common sense: why did we understand the AIDS crisis in the manner that we did? Why did we blame the government for what could be construed as simply a health problem? Why did we use a rhetoric of genocide, and why did such an extreme characterization of the crisis resonate with us and our supporters? What about earlier in the crisis, before ACT UP came on the scene—what feelings circulated in lesbian and gay communities then? Were people angry? If not, why not, and what prompted anger to emerge? If they were angry earlier, what did people do with that anger? Why was it not tethered to confrontational activism in those early years, as it was during the ACT UP years? And what about when the movement declined in the early 1990s when the AIDS crisis was still exploding and people were still dying all around us, from among us—did the anger disappear, did it change? What happened to that once-dominant feeling state that had defined a queer generation? My project increasingly became an ethnography of a shifting emotional habitus and an exploration of how different constellations of affects and feelings decisively shaped the trajectory of lesbian and gay, and eventually queer, political responses to AIDS.

The grief that overcame me amid my research, then, became a source of knowledge. Its jarring, disjunctive quality confronted me with the inadequacy of presuming that gay anger was an uncomplicated and solo emotion that had sparked the movement; the experience raised new questions that I had to explore in order to understand the trajectory of AIDS activism and the place of anger and other feelings in that history. My grief, in short, helped to upend and defamiliarize my common sense enough to allow me to see its contingency and that it could be, and indeed needed to be, interrogated, rather than taken as unquestioned truth.

Familiarity potentially poses a problem for any ethnographer in the sense that growing knowledge of a social collectivity's common sense can impede other ways of understanding what is happening. A way through this difficulty, I am suggesting, is for the researcher to attune to her own feelings, a practice that can incite a more interrogatory relation to that common sense and thereby allow the researcher to hold multiple understandings simultaneously. Introspective, emotional self-knowledge allows one to observe and read in a manner that can pick up the unspoken, the repressed, the less-than-fully conscious, the inarticulable. Consider, for example, a researcher studying a social movement who encounters participants who are reluctant "to admit their emotions," not wanting "to be labeled 'soft-hearted' when that is dismissively opposed to 'hard-headed'" (Goodwin *et al.* 2001: 15; see also Groves 1995); they consequently might understand themselves and self-represent in a solely cognitive, rationalist manner. A researcher who is attuned to social norms that typically privilege reason over emotion, and who is aware of how such norms affect her relation to her *own* feelings, can approach participants' rationalist self-representations in a respectfully interrogatory manner—taking them seriously while simultaneously considering the silences and erasures such self-representations perform. In other words, the researcher's attunement to her own feelings and ways of navigating them equips her with a useful way to discern the different realities that might exist in a given context. Her task, then, is to consider and work with all of those realities, rather than defaulting to the one that reigns as common sense.

My point is not to disparage common sense, or to suggest that it is "wrong" or "false." Returning to what I said earlier about my initial naturalization of gay anger regarding the AIDS crisis, I do not believe that my delayed grief was somehow "truer" or more significant than my own and other ACT UP participants' anger. But, like any form of knowledge, common sense is partial and it can obscure the multiple realities at play in a given context. In this case, because we represented ourselves as angry, and experienced ourselves as such, it was easy to overlook other feelings in the mix—like grief. My own grief while doing research helped me to defamiliarize and denaturalize ACT UP's anger, but that didn't make this grief truer than my earlier (and, incidentally, ongoing) anger.[6] Instead of viewing feelings as telling the truth of our selves, and the truth of a situation, I am arguing that researchers need to approach feelings—our own and others'—historically, psychoanalytically, and affectively. *Historically*: feelings are context-bound, meaning their sources, objects, and effects are contingent, unpredetermined, and variable; rather than naturalizing, therefore, we need to consider the range of feeling states that might be in the mix and the effects they might have, given specific historical conditions. *Psychoanalytically*: in the face of painful and difficult feelings, humans ward off, repress, deny, and disavow—and as a result our emotional life is more complex, conflictual, contradictory, and opaque than we usually realize; in the face of our non-transparency to ourselves, it is important to listen for the painful, the anxiety-producing, the ambivalent, the discordant, the forbidden, and other emotion-ridden silences that might lead us to richer, more multifaceted analyses. *Affectively*: our emotional responses to the worlds we encounter are often amorphous, emergent, a sensing of something rather than a fully formed, known, defined, or even definable emotion; while perhaps more difficult to discern, greater attunement to those inchoate but nevertheless forceful aspects of feelings can provide a more nuanced picture of social life that explores what it is like to be a relational being affected by the world around oneself and affecting it in turn.

Approached in this manner, through a historical, psychoanalytic, and affective lens, feelings become a source of knowledge. When we as researchers hold a curious, inquisitive relation toward feelings—our own and feelings in general—when we understand them as an incitement toward questioning rather than an indication of some static truth of the self or of the place one is studying, they become tools for deepening and enriching our analyses.

Notes

1 This essay builds on material from Gould (2009, Introduction).
2 ACT UP emerged in New York City in 1987 and eventually consisted of more than 80 chapters across the United States, and more than 30 internationally. The movement intervened in every aspect of the AIDS crisis during the late 1980s and early 1990s, and many credit the movement's confrontational activism and political savvy with changing the course of the epidemic and saving millions of people's lives. For a history of the movement see Gould (2009). Although most ACT UP chapters disappeared in the early and mid-1990s, some persisted, and in 2012, 25 years after ACT UP/NY's emergence, a few chapters revived.
3 My attunement to my grief increased as I got further into my research, as evidenced by the greater emphasis I put on grief in my book (Gould 2009) than in an earlier essay (Gould 2001). Thank you to Helena Flam for pointing this out to me.
4 Joe Hill, labor activist and member of the Industrial Workers of the World, is credited with this phrase.
5 With great empathy, but also out of concern, Crimp observed that mourning became militancy within the movement (Crimp 1989: 9).
6 Stuart Hall's article, "The Problem of Ideology: Marxism Without Guarantees" (1983), importantly and lucidly distinguishes between "false consciousness," on the one hand, and, on the other, a partial or distorted understanding that focuses on one aspect or moment of a phenomenon to the neglect of other aspects or moments.

References

Crimp, D. 1989. "Mourning and Militancy," *October*, 51 (Winter): 3–18.

Damski, J.-H. 1992. "Mad Gaiety and the Political Carnival," *Windy City Times*, April 23: 15.

Finkelstein, A. 1992. "The Other Quilt," *QW*, October 25: 10.

Goodwin, J., J. Jasper, and F. Polletta. 2001. "Introduction: Why Emotions Matter" in J. Goodwin, J. Jasper, and F. Polletta (eds) *Passionate Politics: Emotions and Social Movements*: 1–24 Chicago: University of Chicago Press.

Gould, D. 2001. "Rock the Boat, Don't Rock the Boat, Baby: Ambivalence and the Emergence of Militant AIDS Activism" in J. Goodwin, J. M. Jasper, and F. Polletta (eds) *Passionate Politics: Emotions and Social Movements*: 135–57 Chicago: University of Chicago Press.

Gould, D. 2009. *Moving Politics: Emotion and ACT UP's Fight Against AIDS*. Chicago: University of Chicago Press.

Groves, J. M. 1995. "Learning to Feel: The Neglected Sociology of Social Movements," *Sociological Review*, 43 (3): 435–61.

Hall, S. 1983. "The Problem of Ideology: Marxism Without Guarantees" in B. Matthews (ed.) *Marx: 100 Years On*: 57–85 London: Lawrence & Wishart.

Rosett, J. 1997. "The Buddy Line: A Love Song for a Fallen Fighter," *POZ*, March: 40.

Shepard, B. H. 1997. *White Nights and Ascending Shadows: An Oral History of the San Francisco AIDS Epidemic.* London: Cassell.

Wockner, R. 1992. "The AIDS Activist the Mayor Feared," *Nightlines*, February 12: 28–9.

Chapter 16

Funerary emotions

Categorizing data from a fieldwork diary

Julien Bernard

Introduction: emotions in funerals

This contribution is an analytical reflection of the work experience as a pall-bearer in two French funeral firms in 2003 and 2006 which led to a PhD dissertation about "emotions and rituals in an undertaker's job."[1] This analytical reflection relied to a great extent on a fieldwork diary. During the observation and writing stages, I chose to focus on emotions, professional actions linked to the ritual sequences,[2] interactions, and locations.

I would like to propose here that fieldwork diaries can be analyzed for the study of emotions just as interviews or other types of documentation can. A content analysis can throw light both upon the position of the sociologist (or anthropologist) as he/she faces her/his subject, and on the attitudes or behaviors that are observed in situ.[3] To demonstrate this, I will discuss the following points: (1) the selection of emotional sequences in situ, and in the diary, (2) the analysis of the selected data, and (3) the identification of the advantages and limits of this method.

Selecting the emotional sequences

Actor perspectives

Selecting the emotional sequences depends on the field actors the researcher focuses on. I have distinguished three actor perspectives:

1 the researcher who focuses on his own emotions: these can be categorized as "first person" emotions
2 the researcher who observes others' emotions': these can be categorized as "second person" emotions
3 the researcher who collects discourses about others' emotions from other "neutral" participants—in this case funerary professionals, members of the clergy, etc.): these can be categorized as "third person" emotions.

Each of these implies specific methodological issues and problems: "first person" emotions may differ from one researcher to another; a researcher may misinterpret behaviors associated with "second person" emotions; and in the third perspective, the focus is more on the way third party actors *analyze* emotions than on real feelings. Nevertheless, these distinctions allow us to organize the bulk of data.[4]

Markers of emotion

Selecting and recording the emotional sequences depends also—even if I tried to entertain no preconceptions about what I was going to witness—on a subjective interpretation of what we see as "emotions." I identified and analyzed my own emotions based on what I sensed/interpreted I was doing and feeling. I also analyzed the emotions of others based on the conduct, attitudes, and bodily expressions that I witnessed. Funerary professionals seem to use the same method. Here are some excerpts from my diary showing the three perspectives I adopted while observing funerals:

> Then the family who kept watching over the dead child had to kiss him for the last time.... The mother shouted, the father cried.... People in the crowd outside, especially young women, howled at the sight of the coffin. I had a sort of twitch (my cheek quivered nervously) and I screwed up my eyes.
>
> (Observation No. 6, first and second person emotion)

> We had to close the coffin.... The widow appeared with drawn features.... She started to weep and to stagger. She came close to the coffin, had a glance at her husband and almost collapsed on him. I was very near.
>
> (Observation No. 22, second person emotion)

> A 49-year-old woman passed away, leaving a son (who seemed to be about 18 years old). The cemetery keeper told me later that the boy might need to be watched over because during the ceremony he seemed totally confused, "at a loss."
>
> (Observation No. 13, third person emotion)

During the funerary process most mourners express their emotions without clearly verbalizing them. However, people sometimes talk about what they feel, and these comments can shed light on their emotions:

> When the body was placed in the coffin, I noticed that the son-in-law said [talking to the manager]: "this moment is very hard emotionally." I thought: especially the closing.
>
> (Observation No. 2)

> At the end of the ceremony, before the benediction, the son and the daughter of the deceased made their speeches.... The daughter expressed contradictory feelings: regret on one side, for not having done/talked more with her father; and a sense of fatality on the other, understanding he was old, that the time had come for him to be relieved from his suffering and to join all those who had left before him. His death was a normal thing, even if a chapter of life was closed with sorrow.
> (Observation No. 26)

Analyzing the selected emotional sequences

The emotional sequences selected—based on bodily markers and verbal expressions—can be analyzed, on the one hand, depending on the perspective (first, second, or third person) and emotional categories. They can also be analyzed according to other supposedly independent variables, such as: tasks undertaken by professionals, age of the deceased, number of funeral attendants, location, the size of the funeral procession, etc., in order to see whether these explain bodily expressed emotions.

Categorizing emotions from the actor perspective

Sorting out field records according to emotional categories and perspectives unravels different affective patterns depending on the selected field actor.

From my point of view, "first person" emotions fell into four main categories:

1 compassion, sadness: feeling sad about the death of children or youngsters, or families in conflict experiencing a blend of compassion and "affective" solidarity while participating in a funeral—funerals can, in this sense, have a "touching beauty"
2 discomfort, embarrassment, shame: feeling ashamed about mishaps that occur during rituals—such as being late for the ceremony, or being clumsy while carrying the coffin in front of the family; distressing mourners by being unable to say anything; or feeling embarrassment when facing mourners' strong emotional displays; feeling the burden of having to engage in the unpleasant "realization of the reality"
3 pleasant times with colleagues—always in the background
4 disgust—felt rarely when facing a corpse.

The analysis of "second person" emotions observed in mourners revealed another affective cluster which is here listed in order of its occurrence:

1 sorrow, sadness, heartbreak: these emotions can be read from the swollen eyes, crying and sobbing

2 disarray, confusion: these were read from the blind staring/blank looks, introversion or bewilderment
3 inner prayers or collective communion conducted with composure, dignity, and respect: these were interpreted based on restraint, the distancing from strong emotional displays, looking down, and words and gestures of compassion towards others
4 strong composure or disregard: this case it is the most difficult to be accurate about in determining the underlying emotion
5 relief: read as a positive feeling
6 gladness, comfort in meeting with people unseen for a long time: emotions potentially linked to other categories.

Moving from (1) to (6) one can see a continuum of emotions starting with sadness and ending with gladness.

From the "third person" perspective, the records of emotions often mentioned:

1 the intensity of sorrow or the state of disarray of certain mourners
2 the judgments pronounced by the funerary professionals about whether or not these were adequate and/or corresponded to the habitual behavioral patterns, and
3 the invitation to overcome pain and find solace in faith and hope expressed by the officiating clergymen.

In search of explanations

The classification of these emotional categories and affective patterns according to field actors and perspectives can be cross-referenced with some parameters of the action's frame, which can potentially influence the mourners' affective dispositions.[5] The emotional sequences can be coded according to their link(s) with locations, intercourses, ritual steps or professional actions, or other circumstances—such as the age of the deceased or the number of funeral attendants, etc.

The analysis of my own emotions—ranging from compassion/sadness to discomfort/embarrassment—showed that they often occurred in the most painful moments of the funeral ceremonies, possibly as an effect of an emotional contagion; and that they were mainly linked to professional tasks, and/or distant observation of the mourners' attitudes (as opposed to direct interaction with the mourners). For instance:

> I had a look at the mother, she seemed completely lost and confused and it appeared that she still didn't understand what was going on. I felt some compassion and a bit of pity.
>
> (Observation No. 24)

> His sister was totally distressed (overwhelmed); she shouted, sobbed, and wept very loudly. I felt embarrassed. She said "I don't want him to go!… My brother!… Don't leave me alone!… What am I going to do now?… Now that you're gone! … Why did you go?… Why have you forsaken me!…" and so on.… I couldn't help but think "Please calm down."
>
> (Observation No. 25)

> I was standing near the condolence book; mourners were passing by to express their sympathy to the deceased, and to sign it.… Everyone was upset and the atmosphere started to weigh heavy on my shoulders. At one point, a father and his young son [around eight years old] appeared. The father started to write something and told his son to do so. The boy wrote "kiss and good bye" which upset me. I said: "Very well done boy," and smiled at his father, before taking a deep breath and letting out a sigh, with cheeks as plump as a trumpeter.
>
> (Observation No. 17)

Mourners' emotions are often linked to the actions taken by professionals as they move through the burial steps—placing the deceased in the coffin, closing the lid, then loading it into the hearse, etc. Each step evokes different emotions in mourners.[6]

> When I came in with the coffin lid, the room became silent. When I gently installed it on the frame, a woman wept and the others sobbed.
>
> (Observation No. 5)

> The daughter, who was about 15 years old, appeared tough, but she heaved as we removed the coffin from the hearse.
>
> (Observation No. 4)

> The sister instinctively moaned when the coffin disappeared from her sight [for burial].
>
> (Observation No. 25)

It seems that the interactions between mourners and funeral professionals influence the modifications of emotional expression, when these interactions help to channel or to activate emotions:

> I touched her arm and showed her a chair, in case she wanted to sit down.… [M]y gesture seemed to calm her down at first, and then, becoming more aware of the situation, putting her body up, I showed her the chair again and she sat. She took a handkerchief and breathed. We closed the coffin, screwed in the bolts and put the caps.
>
> (Observation No. 22)

> In front of the church, on the square, the participants in the funeral procession became silent. The priest appeared and said some words to the family. As the coffin was in front of him, he poured holy water drops on the child's forehead. He was baptized. It was suddenly a real relief, especially for the grandma; the appeasement spread in the group and the cries stopped.
>
> (Observation No. 6)

My field notes also revealed that while some funerals had been very emotional, others had a more moderate affective tonality. Especially in the case of the funerals of old or isolated people, affective tonality during the funeral ceremony itself was very low:

> Today, we're in charge of an old lady who died in a geriatric hospital. She has been receiving medical assistance for weeks, so the family was, in a way, prepared for her death. Nonetheless, only the family was there.... People were not dispirited. It seemed that they had not had much contact with the deceased.... Some of them came from far away, [for them] it was a chance to meet with people unseen for a long time.
>
> (Observation No. 7)

> The family seemed to share three feelings: the sadness of mourning, the satisfaction of finishing the funeral, and the curiosity of seeing familiar faces [after a long time apart].
>
> (Observation No. 10)

> Aged person. The persons attending the funeral discussed—and seemed to share—social links; even if they didn't know each other (for instance, the family didn't know the neighbors). Even so, people had lively conversations in groups (the ceremony wasn't sad).
>
> (Observation No. 11)

Advantages and limits of the diary analysis

The analysis of the diary content has many advantages, including: (1) helping us analyze our own feelings and points of view, (2) making explicit the observed bodily and facial emotional markers, and (3) allowing an analysis of the emotional category combinations, producing affective patterns according to the perspective (first, second, and third persons) in a specific interaction situation and/or in a particular location.

Looking for patterns and categories helps us take first steps towards explanations. Examining the emotional categories can, for example, unearth tensions and contradictions between different emotions. For example, the mourners' emotions oscillate between silent disorientation and the expression of sadness. These tensions raise a question about emotion work: in which circumstances, and for what reason, do some emotion patterns seem more "active" than others? Are there specific "display rules" for different situations—such as, for example, being less sad during the condolences than during the ceremony itself?

As professionals, we can also see tension. For example, mourners waver between compassion and embarrassment when they face the deceased, carry out tasks, or become party to the emotions of others at the funeral party. Diary notes reveal that they have a strong sense of the kind of standard display of grief that they judge to be "appropriate."

One of the major issues is the classification of certain emotional sequences using the distinction between the "first person," "second person," and "third person" perspectives. It sometimes seems that the whole situation is emotional. We can see a circulation of emotion, as in this case—which involved the death of a teenager:

> And then the father came in with his two remaining sons. We stood discreetly in the room [we had just brought the body back home to lay him on his bed]; they silently looked at the body for about two seconds; the father quivered and the two brothers started sobbing. One of them said "My little bro'," a tremolo stressing the last syllable. He embraced his brother and we left the room promptly [to leave them alone and because of the emotion], we caught our breath and walked along for a little while. The father left the room a few minutes later; it seemed he took it all in his stride. He told us that it was hard but that he wanted to stay close to his son for the last moments.
>
> (Observation No. 12)

But interpreting certain feelings can be problematic when trying to match a facial or bodily expression to an underlying feeling. The researcher can make errors here—for example, analyzing a numb face as a sign of indifference, when in fact it may result from an intense emotion, or even from the effects of taking a tranquillizer. This raises the issue of the inapproachability of some emotions:

> When it came to closing the coffin, the family managed to keep their composure, or didn't seem affected much. Respect prevented me from passing judgment about them; I just noticed the scarcity of common emotional signs: no shivers, loss of balance, or even tears. What may have been strong composure appeared to me as clear detachment. I cannot say they didn't feel anything, and to be honest, I think they did, but I felt like they put aside all their affect in a rather

> "cold" fashion. Habitual emotive expressions are "warm," this one was awkwardly "cold."
>
> (Observation No. 16)

Finally, many factors can trigger an emotional surge (for example, the sight of the corpse/hearse, thinking about the past), so it would be necessary to analyze the emotional variations over time during the funeral process. That would require further categorization work, which would probably show that certain action sequences are more emotional than others, and that people feel differently as they go through various states of mind that are themselves linked to the various ritual steps.

Conclusion

The diary content analysis presented here is based on four main filters. First, the emotional sequences selection itself—based on expressive, physical, or verbal markers. These sequences can be developed from the chosen perspective (first, second, or third person), and by field actor. We can then build affective fields according to recurring emotional categories and subjects; before finally looking for the environmental factors that are likely to influence emotional patterns.

This method helps to unearth tendencies and regularities in the expression of specific emotions, and identifies some of the external factors involved in these expressions (interactions, professional actions, ritual steps, number of persons in the funeral party, age of the deceased, etc.). This allows comparisons to be made between sequences: cross-referencing the "mourners' emotions" with the various "professional actions" carried out during a funeral, shows, for instance, that emotionality intensifies during the ritual of the closing of the coffin.

The nature of the subject—a ritual with repetitive steps/phases which exhibit strong regularities—facilitated this making of observations and comparisons. But the method should still be useful even in less standardized situations. First and second person perspectives show how the researcher attributes emotions to himself and to others, making clear his/her reflexivity when the identification of third party emotions by the various people involved lead to identify the "framing rules" (Hochschild, 1979: 566) of the situation. By comparison of the case's frequencies, it allows building sociological hypothesis about the external factors of emotional rise, while paying attention to the inner dynamic of emotional situations.

Acknowledgments

Many thanks to Julien Venault, Jacques Séjournant, and Helena Flam for their help in translating this article from French into English.

Notes

1 The main part of my PhD dissertation has been published in Bernard (2009).
2 Most actions of the funerary professional concern "phase transitions" in the ritual—either they initiate a phase (placing the deceased in the coffin, placing the coffin in the church); or they close it (closing the coffin, leaving the church for the cemetery, sealing the grave).
3 In this contribution, I used my reports from 27 funerals—from which 60 text sequences concerning emotions have been extracted (personal descriptions or reflections about emotions, or forms of discourses about emotions heard in situ).
4 For more details see Bernard (2007).
5 Generally, these parameters, factors, and variables are *not* at the origin of emotions, which probably lie in mourner's life experiences, and in the relationship they had with the deceased. But they can inflect or modulate the emotional displays.
6 According to Livet (2002), the emotion in this case only presents itself when the confirmed reality (the deceased is gone) differs from what the affected people would have liked (that the deceased were still alive).

References

Bernard, J. 2007. "Objectiver les Emotions Dans l'Enquête de Terrain" in O. Leservoisier and L. Vidal (eds) *L'Anthropologie Face à ses Objets. Nouveaux Contextes Ethnographiques*. Paris: Archives contemporaines.

Bernard, J. 2009. *Croquemort. Une Anthropologie des Emotions*. Paris: Métailié, Traversées.

Hochschild, Arlie R. 1979. "Emotion Work, Feeling Rules, and Social Structure." *The American Journal of Sociology*, 85 (3): 551–75.

Livet, P. 2002. *Emotions et Rationalité Morale*. Paris: Presses Universitaires de France.

Chapter 17

Researching "emotional geographies" in schools

The value of critical ethnography

Michalinos Zembylas

Empirical attention to emotion in education has grown in recent years; emotion is now recognized as an important feature of school life (Schutz and Zembylas 2009). However, little attention has been given to emotion, methodologically—that is, how emotion might be investigated in schools, what methodological problems arise, and how to overcome them. Needless to say, the issue of doing empirical research in schools also draws attention to more general methodological, theoretical, and political concerns on how emotion is defined and in what ways it should to be investigated—and the solutions are highly contested.

The position adopted here is broad. Following Burkitt (2005), emotions are understood as multidimensional (thinking, feeling, acting) "complexes" which are both cultural and embodied, and arise in power relationships. This means that emotions are part of the relations and interactions between humans rather than an individual or internal phenomenon; thus, power works through social relations "as a structure of actions that aims to affect a field of possible actions" (Burkitt 2005: 683). Therefore, emotions need to be understood in terms of their socio-spatial dynamics of movements and social relations. Specifically, the study of emotional geographies (Davidson *et al.* 2005) suggests that there are different emotion repertoires that arise in particular locations. This idea emphasizes again that emotions are understood—experientially and conceptually—in terms of how they are socio-spatially determined and articulated, rather than as entirely interiorized subjective mental states.

The present chapter is organized in the following manner. First, the notion of "emotional geographies" is briefly introduced to show that this concept facilitates the analysis of emotions in schools. Next, methodological issues are highlighted with particular attention to critical ethnography—which is particularly appropriate for capturing the political aspects of emotions; that is, for showing how emotions arise in power relations. To illustrate how this methodology is implemented in data collection and data analysis, I use brief anecdotes from my own ethnographic research on the emotions of racism and nationalism in a Greek-Cypriot school (Zembylas

2011). Finally, some implications for future investigations of emotions in schools are discussed.

Emotional geographies and emotion analysis in schools

As Good (2004: 529) argues, the links between emotion and space need to be investigated "in contemporary settings of globalized economic crisis, state violence, exploited migrant communities, and hegemonic gender politics of post-colonial states." These settings might include locations, such as workplaces in which migrants are exploited; conflict areas around the world in which an oppressive regime limits the freedom of its people; or contexts in which women are victims of trafficking. Similarly, scholars in the recently emerged field of emotional geographies (Davidson *et al.* 2005) seek to understand emotions in particular spatial contexts. They argue that understanding the spatiality of emotions can only be gained through a careful study of the location of emotion in places such as schools, hospitals, or workplaces. The notion of emotional geographies draws attention both to the relationality, and to the spatiality, of emotions—highlighting the complex range of emotions that emerge as a consequence of movement, that is, the circulation of emotions through individual and collective bodies, shaping social relations, and challenging taken-for-granted boundaries of the self (Ahmed 2004); and, the strong links between emotion and space/place, that is, the emotionally dynamic spatiality of belonging and subjectivity (Good 2004). My research casts the school as a setting in which symbolic and discursive violence employed by the nation state to stake out its symbolic borders translates into daily practices of exclusion and hurt for the ethnic or migrant "other."

In my home country, Cyprus, previous research has highlighted the prevalence of nationalist and racist attitudes, and perceptions of Greek-Cypriot people—including children—towards the Turks, whom they consider responsible for past trauma as well as the ongoing occupation of their homes and land in north Cyprus (Zembylas 2008). Discourses at the nation and state level do not differ much compared to school discourses, although they are not always expressed in primitive-racist or nationalist terms. Discourses of race, ethnicity, class, etc., become reflected in the ways in which majoritized and minoritized children position themselves in school (Troyna and Hatcher 1992). In fact, these discourses provide inclusion/exclusion criteria which shape how majoritized children behave toward minoritized children. Through the processes of racialization and ethnicization, "sameness" and "otherness" are both reified and assume a naturalized form in schools (Connolly 1998).

An important question arises, then, within the theoretical frame of emotional geographies in schools: how exactly are teachers' and students' emotional practices and discourses "racialized" and "ethnicized?" Emotional geographies focus on the ways through which power relations shaping constructions of race and ethnicity produce (and are produced by) particular emotional practices and discourses that include some students and exclude others. My study of the socio-spatial dynamics of racism and nationalism focuses on students and teachers talking and moving in school space. It shows how racialized and ethnicized exclusion manifests itself in emotions and emotion-laden talk generating embodied ostracism.

If larger social/political forces and discourses influence school practices of exclusion and inclusion, it is crucial to show how these practices understood as transactional processes take place, and what consequences they have. These processes connect some bodies to other bodies; they involve seeking proximity between bodies which are perceived as similar, while asserting distance to other bodies which are considered dissimilar. If so, the processes of inclusion and exclusion can be traced by following the ways in which individuals—here the schoolchildren and their teachers—construct and implement inclusion/exclusion criteria through their emotional discourses and bodily movements that diminish or increase distance between specific categories of bodies. If we accept this conceptual framework, the next question which has to be posed is: which research methodologies are suitable for the investigation of emotional geographies in schools?

Critical ethnography and the study of emotion in schools

In terms of research methodologies that can adequately investigate emotional geographies in schools, ethnography in general (Denzin 1997) draws attention to the dynamic and interactive nature of verbal and nonverbal expressions of emotions through the study of social interactions over time (Sturdy 2003). Critical ethnography (Carspecken and Walford 2001) pushes the investigation a step further. Since it is committed to a critical exploration of existing power hierarchies, it focuses on the exclusionary and inclusionary emotional geographies in school. Ethnographic field research entails all-encompassing data collection—of photographs, documents, field notes, videotapes, interviews, and observations—all of which reveal different dimensions of participants' emotional expressions. The collection of the data calls for staying in the field for a considerable amount of time. Usually a few weeks to several months are necessary to collect empirical evidence at the micro level, which is entangled with exclusionary socio-political discourses and practices at the macro level. The discussion below is divided into two parts—data collection methods and data analysis processes—and includes brief excerpts from my interviews and observations stemming from my larger study of the emotional geographies of racism and nationalism at one particular school.

Data collection methods

One of the first challenges that ethnographers face is how to observe and document verbal and non-verbal expressions of emotion. An important step toward the rich description of the socio-spatial dynamics of emotions is to conduct participant observations of the classroom, and school life, over time. Participant observations draw attention, as Sturdy (2003: 87) explains, "to the varying persistence of feelings from the transient to the enduring and to their conditions and consequences." Observations can have a broad or narrow focus depending on the research questions; yet the most important thing is arguably to document feelings, their transformations, and their consequences, in as much detail as possible.

For example, my two-months-long ethnographic observations on the emotional geographies of racism and nationalism in one primary school in Cyprus (Zembylas 2011), focused broadly on the interactions between majoritized and minoritized students, the teachers' actions and words, and the nature of the teachers' responses to minoritized students. These observations were documented in detailed field notes and described the ways in which emotions manifested themselves in the school's organizational structures and spaces. An example of field notes—which were fully transcribed and enriched as soon as possible after each observation so that all possible details were included—is provided in the excerpt below:

> The lesson is over and the students are waiting for the bell to ring. A Turkish-speaking [minoritized] girl, Emine—who usually sits alone in the back row—makes a move to join a group of Greek-Cypriot [majoritized] girls who are getting ready to read together a Greek children's journal. The Greek-Cypriot girls are laughing and joking and seem to enjoy what they are reading. The teacher is writing something in a notebook and seems absorbed in what she is doing. Emine moves slowly toward the group of Greek-Cypriot girls. As soon as one of the girls notices the presence of Emine her look becomes angry and she yells at her: "You, leave us right now!" Emine turns back, her face looks very sad, and she goes back to her seat. I slowly approach the Greek-Cypriot girls' table. They whisper among themselves. "Can you imagine? That stinky Turkish-girl coming to our table?" said one girl, and another responded: "We told her a thousand times, we don't want her to sit with us! She's stupid! She doesn't understand!"

These field notes capture how the feeling of "disgust" affects the interaction and the location of the majoritized and minoritized students in this classroom. "Disgust" involves not just corporeal intensities, but also discourses that make majoritized students "pull away from" and "send away" their minoritized classmates. These discourses—evident through other data sources, as shown below—are also found in the everyday rhetoric of community leaders, parents, and teachers. In the above example the label "stinky" is attached to a girl who comes from the "unwanted" community; this emotion-laden label in turn affects majoritized students and colors their perceptions of the "other."

To make this claim stronger, however, it is necessary to engage in a multi-pronged approach that captures emotionality and its transformations over a long period of time. The combination (or triangulation, as it is known in ethnographic research methodology, see Denzin 1997) of data from observations (this example) and interviews with those involved in the interactions (next example) adds something that would otherwise not have become evident. The interviews help to confirm or to reject the observer's interpretation of the interactions. Interviews give participants a chance to provide their own accounts of these interactions. Particularly, when the feelings of participants and their transformation over time is focal, it is valuable to document in detail how participants report what they feel at various points in time using a variety of data sources.

For example, in the following interview, a teacher explains how negative emotions toward minoritized students become manifested in everyday school life. The researcher has already observed that the majoritized students expressed their emotions in ways that clearly excluded minoritized students; this observation becomes confirmed by the interview, in which the researcher asks teachers for their "reading" of the situation.

RESEARCHER: How do Greek-Cypriot students express their emotions about their Turkish-speaking classmates? Can you provide an example?
TEACHER: They often say "I don't want to be with them."
RESEARCHER: In front of those children?
TEACHER: Yes.
RESEARCHER: That cynical?
TEACHER: Yes. They may not always say it in this manner but their body movement and facial expressions show disgust or complete apathy towards them.

This teacher's perception is then further "tested" by bringing in evidence about the feelings of the majoritized students. These are focal in the following excerpt, taken from a conversation between two second-graders and the researcher:

RESEARCHER: Do you have children from different countries in your school?
CHILD 1: We have Blacks [*mavrous*]
RESEARCHER: Who are these children? I don't understand.

CHILD 2: The Blacks, miss, the Turks.

RESEARCHER: You mean the Turks are Black?

CHILD 2: Yes, they are not like us.

RESEARCHER: What do you mean they are not like you?

CHILD 1: They are not our friends. I don't like them, because they are black.

CHILD 2: They beat us all the time, we don't like to play with them. They often stink, they are not clean.

This interview strengthens evidence derived from observations and other interviews which shows that majoritized students in all school classes express feelings of intense dislike toward minoritized students. These feelings, their movements, and their various effects—expressions of dislike and rejection captured in a command by the majoritized children for the minoritized ones to increase their distance; and the shy, cautious, attempts by the minoritized children to reduce that distance, or challenge the boundaries of it by resorting to violence against the majoritized children—are examples of situated, embodied, expressed emotions moving bodies in space. They show how majoritized children attempt to marginalize the minoritized children, and also how they, in turn, resist these attempts.

In general, critical ethnography as a methodology draws attention to emotion as embodied, socially constructed, political, and localized. The combination of critical ethnography as methodology, and emotional geographies as a conceptual framework, allows researchers to identify the entanglements between localized marginalizations of minoritized students and manifestations of racism and nationalism at the macro level; what this means is that emotional geographies of racism and nationalism are scaled down to the micro level of the school (Zembylas 2011). A critical discourse analysis of the speech repertoires applied to migrants and "ethnic" others at the national level shows great similarity to those utilized by the students at the school where I made the observations and conducted the interviews reported here. At both macro and micro level, migrants are "filthy," and Turks are "evil." The use of critical ethnography helps to show that emotions become politicized and attached to particular objects or persons, and sheds light on how they become important components of practices of exclusion in schools.

Data analysis processes

There are three main types of "texts" to be analyzed from data collection methods: spoken, written, and visual (Keats 2009). Spoken texts may include transcribed interviews and informal conversations, and discussions with participants. Written texts may include reflexive journals, letters, emails, and other texts. Finally, visual texts can include drawings, pieces of art, artefacts, photographs, videotapes, and other image-based texts. The "triangulation" (Denzin 1997) of different types of texts is very helpful for validating purposes—especially when some data, for example non-verbal, make the recording of emotions difficult. By analyzing these different data types the researcher gains a multifaceted understanding of how emotional geographies are manifest in the researched field—in this case, a school. For example, my research showed that the feeling of "disgust" is not expressed in the same way by the majoritized children of different grade levels, nor does it imply the same kind of exclusion for minoritized children across different grade levels; in the cited excerpt from my field notes, exclusion has multiple dimensions (linguistic, racial, ethnic), while in the conversation with the two second-graders, exclusion is primarily racial. All these manifestations of emotions amount collectively to the emotional geographies of racism and nationalism. The methodological challenge of analysis is to go through a process of interpreting all these complex and diverse manifestations of emotions, while taking into consideration the larger socio-political context and its implications in interpreting the data collected.

There are different ways of analyzing written, visual, and spoken texts with regard to: (1) how to select passages or images that help highlight emotions, and (2) how to analyze these particular passages or images. Following Lieblich *et al.* (1998), there are generally two types of interpretive model that help to make sense of the collected texts: holistic analysis, and categorical analysis. In this chapter I only discuss the holistic approach because this is the one used in the analysis of data collected in my ethnographic research.[1] In a holistic type of analysis all the texts (field notes from observations, interview excerpts) are considered holistically: the researcher looks for explicit or implicit evidence of participants' shared emotions and their interrelations. In this type of analysis the focus is on the major themes emerging from the texts as a whole, and thus attention is given to the interrelated manifestations of emotions. An important aspect of this type of analysis is the contextual development of emotional geographies over time—both in terms of content and form/level.

For example, one of the topics that has emerged from my ethnographic research on the emotional geographies of racism and nationalism at a school is the segregation and emotional distance between majoritized and minoritized students, and how these are played out in everyday school life. A researcher following a holistic type of analysis will not necessarily search for particular words expressing emotions of dislike for minoritized students, but rather the emphasis will be on finding explicit and implicit evidence of feelings related to segregation and emotional distance. Thus, in the data from observations and interviews cited earlier, there is evidence showing how majoritized students feel that they are at a "distance" from minoritized students.

However, to capture holistically the various elements of this emotional distance, it is also important to include evidence about how minoritized students feel. The data which reveals how minoritized students talk about their feelings— for example, mentioning their fear of, or sadness about, being excluded—shows the emotional effects of marginalization. The boundary-making between majoritized and minoritized children at this school provides specific indications about the toxic implications of emotional geographies for minoritized children. When we asked, for example, a minoritized girl to describe how she felt at her school, she said: "Not so good. Greek-Cypriots [majoritized] tease us all the time. They don't play with us. They call us 'Blacks' and 'filthy Turks.'" This piece of evidence, in conjunction with the following dialog with two other minoritized girls, is indicative of the overall emotional impact that this toxic environment has on the minoritized children:

RESEARCHER: Can you tell me how you feel about being at this school? Are you OK? Is there something you don't like?
CHILD 9: I don't like Greek-Cypriots.
RESEARCHER: Why is that?
CHILD 9: They don't like us.
RESEARCHER: Why don't they like you?
CHILD 9: They kick us, they call us bad names. They don't want us.
CHILD 10: Once I was kicked so hard by a Greek-Cypriot student, it hurt a lot.
RESEARCHER: Did you complain to anyone, to the principal?
CHILD 10: No.
RESEARCHER: Why not?
CHILD 10: Because they will say [we are] traitors.
RESEARCHER: How does this make you feel?
CHILD 10: Not happy. Very sad.
RESEARCHER: You? (turning to Student 9)
CHILD 9: Scared.
RESEARCHER: Why scared?
CHILD9: [long pause] They can beat us.

This conversation shows the emotional pain expressed by minoritized children when speaking about their relations with their majoritized classmates. The emotional geographies of exclusion highlight the hardship and marginalization caused by the socio-spatial dynamics of racialization and ethnicization processes at this school.

The next level of analysis is to discuss how these geographies of exclusion are embedded in the power relations evident in the flows of toxic emotions between "us" and "them" (Ahmed 2004). It is at this point that localized analysis becomes more broadly politicized, when the researcher takes into consideration how larger political forces of racism and nationalism may be reflected in the emotional geographies of everyday school life; that is, how emotional events at the micro level are reflections of macro-level discourses and practices involving interactions between majoritized and minoritized groups. An important clarification that has to be made here is that this type of analysis does not look for any theoretically predetermined categories; themes emerge from the micro-level analysis, and often turn out to show similarity with macro-level discourses and practices. Schools do not exist in a social or political vacuum.

Conclusion

Altogether, the methodology of critical ethnography illustrated in this chapter constitutes an "interpretivist" approach that is deeply descriptive and aims at bringing emotional experiences "alive" (Denzin 1997). This description pays attention to capturing "emotion in process"; that is, showing how emotional geographies come alive in schools. The major advantage of critical ethnography is that it offers a promising avenue through which to recognize the workings of insidious power and tenacity in certain manifestations of emotions in schools. The important intersection of emotion and race/ethnicity is seen in the constitutive role politicized emotions play in the formation and maintenance of particular racialization and ethnicization processes. As was shown in the text, schoolchildren express emotions that establish or strengthen particular exclusions and inclusions in the school. Attending to the ways in which students' emotions are variously manifested in everyday school practices is essential if we are to understand how emotions are part of power relations and interactions, rather than just being an individual or internal phenomenon. As was indicated earlier, macro-level power relations are scaled down to the classroom and to school life through the creation of toxic and politically charged emotional geographies. Critical ethnography is helpful in showing what emotional practices do, and how emotional geographies of inclusion and exclusion are created in schools. Developing theoretical and methodological frameworks and practices that affirm an in-depth look at teachers' and students' lives provides new ways of exploring the practices and discourses through which emotions are constituted and have consequences in school spheres.

Note

1 Contrary to holistic analysis, categorical analysis looks for specific segments of evidence which are counted and categorized by the researcher on the basis of certain criteria that are relevant to language use—e.g., at the lexical level (words), the syntactical level (sentences), and prosody (rhythm, stress, intonation, etc.) (see Kleres 2011).

References

Ahmed, S. 2004. *The Cultural Politics of Emotion.* Edinburgh: Edinburgh University Press.

Burkitt, I. 2005. "Powerful Emotions: Power, Government and Opposition in the 'War on Terror,'" *Sociology,* 39 (4): 679–95.

Carspecken, P. F. and G. Walford (eds). 2001. *Critical Ethnography and Education.* New York: Routledge.

Connolly, P. 1998. *Racism, Gender Identities and Young Children.* London: Routledge.

Davidson, J., L. Bondi, and M. Smith. 2005. *Emotional Geographies.* Aldershot: Ashgate.

Denzin, N. 1997. *Interpretive Ethnography: Ethnographic Practices for the 21st Century.* Thousand Oaks, CA: Sage.

Good, B. 2004. "Rethinking 'Emotions' in Southeast Asia." *Ethnos* 69(4): 529–533.

Keats, P. 2009. "Multiple Text Analysis in Narrative Research: Visual, Written, and Spoken Stories of Experience," *Qualitative Research,* 9 (2): 181–95.

Kleres, J. 2011. "Emotions and Narrative Analysis: A Methodological Approach," *Journal for the Theory of Social Behaviour,* 41 (2): 182–202.

Lieblich, A., R. Tuval-Mashiach, and T. Zilber. 1998. *Narrative Research: Reading, Analysis and Interpretation.* Newbury Park, CA: Sage.

Schutz, P. and M. Zembylas (eds). 2009. *Advances in Teacher Emotion Research: The Impact on Teachers' Lives.* Springer: Dordrecht, The Netherlands.

Sturdy, A. 2003. "Knowing the Unknowable? A Discussion of Methodological and Theoretical Issues in Emotion Research and Organizational Studies," *Organization,* 10 (1): 81–105.

Troyna, B. and R. Hatcher. 1992. *Racism in Children's Lives: A Study of Mainly-White Primary Schools.* London: Routledge.

Zembylas, M. 2008. *The Politics of Trauma in Education.* New York: Palgrave, Macmillan.

Zembylas, M. 2011. "Investigating the Emotional Geographies of Exclusion in a Multicultural School," *Emotion, Space and Society,* 4 (3): 151–9.

Part IV

Speaking emotions

Chapter 18

Indexing anger and aggression

From language ideologies to linguistic affect

H. Julia Eksner

Introduction

How are emotions encoded in linguistic practices, and how can we study them? Drawing on the field of linguistic anthropology, this chapter introduces language ideologies as site for research on emotions. Anthropological research on language acquisition, poetics, and performance has shown the numerous ways in which language and emotion displays are linked to each other. Linguistic displays of emotion serve important semiotic functions in the negotiation of relationships between social groups in stratified societies, such as class identification and ethno-cultural identification. Language users strategically exploit the different meanings and values attached to various affective keys in this negotiation. Emotion displays in language may be employed as tools of hegemony by dominant groups and state institutions, and as vehicles of resistance by non-dominant groups (Gal 1995; Woolard 1985). As such, the study of linguistic practices as site in which the relationship between emotion and social structure is enacted, presents an important methodological avenue for emotion researchers.

This chapter addresses the methodological challenge of studying emotions as invoked and implied through language. It presents a case study of the linguistic displays of anger among the "36 Boys," a local peer group of German Turkish working class youths in Berlin-Kreuzberg. The case study demonstrates, up close, how cultural ideas about speakers become transformed into ideas about language and into speech style characteristics that index speakers' anger and aggression. It aims to demonstrate how ideologies about languages and their speakers become laden affectively, and how affective identities come to be enacted in language use. Language ideologies and the indexing of affect through linguistic practices are thus explored as a promising field of inquiry at the intersection of emotions and linguistic practices.

Language ideologies

Ideologies about language and their speakers

Language ideologies refer to what speakers know, imply, and say about language and its speakers (Kroskrity 1999). Research on language ideologies investigates the relevance of power relations for language as cultural practice, and asks how essential meanings about language are socially produced as effective and powerful. Ideologies are present both in everyday language use (i.e., linguistic practice), and in explicit talk about language (i.e., meta-linguistics or meta-pragmatic discourse). Thus, research on language ideologies considers pragmatics, i.e., the meanings that sentences have in particular contexts in which they are uttered; and meta-pragmatics, i.e., the language users' reflexive awareness of this meaning. As my use of the plural already indicates, language ideologies are always multiple and contesting (Gal 1998). There is not one dominant ideology; rather we find dialogic and heteroglot ideologies about languages. As a cultural system of ideas about social and linguistic relationships, language ideologies have been shown to be loaded both morally and politically (Irvine 1989: 53); and, as this chapter will show, language ideologies are also heavy with affective meaning.

One of the key semiotic processes through which we are able to study ideologies of language is the process of iconization. Iconization describes a process in which language is seen as indexical for its user. Indexes are signs that indicate "connection, co-existence, or causality" (Urciuoli 1998: 7).[1] Linguistic indexes are words, sounds, or grammatical characteristics that are perceived to carry information about a speaker. Thus, someone may be said to "sound" upper class or working class. Indexes often transform social relationships to various kinds of iconic relations, i.e., linguistic forms "look" like icons. Thus, nasal pronunciation of Standard English may become an iconic trait for upper class membership. Conversely, iconization also implies that speakers perceive an inherent relationship between speakers and linguistic forms. This inherent relationship may be described as linguistic "essentialism", i.e., certain linguistic traits are taken for granted in certain speakers. Thus, a working class laborer is socially expected, and iconic for, the use of a particular social register dubbed "working class speech."

Of the many characteristics of people which language invokes and implies, some may be affective. Affective indexes similarly conjure culturally constructed categories in which affective characteristics are linked to speakers' positioning in the social world. Different speech genres, speech-act types, and performance styles may become iconic for different kinds of affect. For example, the dialect spoken at home and with the family may carry connotations of love and empathy, which may contrast with standard language registers spoken at school or work. Informal speech may carry connotations of connection and friendship, while science jargon assumes a neutral or "non-affective" stance. By implication, switching between different codes allows speakers to exploit the different affective connotations of these codes.

The case study presented here describes a performance genre called "tough talk" that was employed as "emotion sign" by the "36"—a peer group of working class, German Turkish boys—in order to indicate anger and aggression. Psychological research shows that anger and aggression are intimately linked, with aggression being the behavioral expression of anger. Aggression is generally considered to occur when anger is not controlled, i.e., when there is a failure or neglect to self-regulate. Thus, when people display aggression, they typically indicate (or, index) that they are angry.[2] The following case study engages the nexus between anger and its behavioral expression, a nexus at which speakers employ linguistic displays of anger as emotion sign which invokes the speaker characteristic of aggression.

Finding emotions in talk

Field site, methodology and data analysis

The data presented here were collected in an ethnographic study with the "36 Boys," a group of working class youths from the Turkish community in Berlin-Kreuzberg. In 2000 I conducted eight months of participant observation on their contestational forms of language use in and around a neighborhood youth center in Berlin-Kreuzberg. The youths were predominantly male teenagers aged 14–18 years (thus in mid-adolescence), generally second and third generation immigrants, and long-term regulars at the local youth center in which I conducted my study. They were of low social, economic, and educational status, had few expectations for stable employment in the future, and shared an awareness of their precarious social status.

The data set analyzed for this chapter consisted of field notes, interaction transcripts, qualitative interviews on youths ideologies about different linguistic codes and their speakers, as well as data collected with an adapted version of the *Inferred Personality Characteristics Test* (Lambert 1960; Urciuoli 1998) with which explicit ideologies about speakers were elicited. While listening to speech samples on tape, informants were asked to comment on how people talk, their accents, and describe the speaker in images of personality or social categories.

Data analysis focused on youths' ideas about language, speakers, and the conditions that govern the use of the different available codes. After transcribing youths' recorded exchanges, as well as interviews, the transcripts were coded by employing both open (grounded) and theory-driven coding. My unit of analysis was the phrase level, i.e., semantically bounded units that are possibly smaller than the sentence level. I first coded the data to identify important local cultural domains, and then focused on youths' ideas about the different social groups in their life world. Affect and emotions were not initially a focus of my analyses, and yet they emerged in the process of open coding. In a second round of analyses, I added prosodic markers to some of the transcripts, and then analyzed more closely discourse characteristics, interaction patterns, contextualization cues, as well as prosodic markers of speech. My final coding scheme incorporated pragmatics and contextual information, on the one hand, and discourse characteristics (including contextualization cues (Gumperz 1982)) on the other. In this way I was able to situate the smaller level of analysis of discourse characteristics within my larger theoretical framework.

The case study: indexing anger and aggression among the "36 Boys"

Level 1: Ethnography and discourse analysis—language ideologies

The "36 Boys," regulars at a neigborhood youth center in Berlin-Kreuzberg, were the self-described successors of a local youth gang (the "36"). They were a speech community—defined by a shared set of social practices—which had several linguistic codes at their availability, including colloquial Turkish and German, Standard German, and a contestational speech style called "tough talk." During the 1990s, and after, discourse portraying immigrant youth as aggressive, antisocial, and violent saturated public discourse in Germany (Toelken 1985; Ewing 2008). It portrayed immigrant youths, including German Turkish youths, as violent, disobedient, antisocial, and aggressive (Eksner 2006). This discourse arose as early as the 1970s when the German newspaper *Der Spiegel* (1973) warned of "Ghettos in Germany: One Million Turks" and conjured the image of Turkish male underclass workers who were characterized by "violent, uncivilized, and battering" behavior (cited in Stehle 2006: 54). Picking up on hegemonic discourse—but also reappropriating it in creative ways (Eksner 2006), the "Boys" utilized different tropes as "gang" or "ghetto" to describe themselves and construe a dichotomized difference between "Turks" and "Germans"—the most salient social categories in their lives. In the interviews most of the "Boys" described "Turkish" youths—i.e., German-Turkish youths growing up in Berlin—as more aggressive and tougher than "German" youths. It was in fact through this trait that the main opposition to "Germans" was constructed. For instance, 17-year-old

Kara, when talking about Turkish youths in his Berlin-Kreuzberg neighborhood, said:

> Let's say it like this, that foreigners have more ... hmmm, how should I say this, among the youths in any case, have more say, you know? Aah, not all, naturally, but most of the Germans are rather fearful and look at us as being stronger, and so, because we are so ... you know ... because we maybe are a little bit more aggressive and stuff, you know.

Similarly, 17-year-old Murat depicted local Turkish youths through an imagery of aggression and violence:

> Well, sure, that ... many Turks maybe beat [the Germans], I could imagine. Here we have this *situation*, where ... more Turkish confront Germans. You know, not confront on them, but always *beat* them, and stuff. That happens a lot.

The "Boys" thus appropriated a discourse of (physical) strength, aggression, and violence and constructed a dichotomy around two dominant cultural themes: "being a victim" (*Opfer sein*) and "being aggressive" (*aggressiv sein*) which were conflated with "being German" and "being Turkish/'foreigner.'" The "Boys" assigned aggressiveness as a trait to Turks, while Germans were depicted as fearful. Aggressiveness was one of several ideological oppositions surrounding the construction of identity among the "Boys." Other intricately connected dichotomies included class positioning, traits of being active or passive, and masculinity or femininity. Importantly, they constructed an iconic relationship between "being Turkish" and being "aggressive."

Just as the boys were perceived, and perceived themselves, to be "more tough" and "more aggressive" than German youths, they also believed that their "toughness" and "aggressiveness" was also reflected in how they spoke both German and Turkish. Iconization thus existed in the "36 Boys'" talk about their social world and its inhabitants, but it was also present in their reflexive awareness of language. When talking about their own ways of speaking, and the codes at their disposal, the boys drew on traits such as toughness, masculinity, and aggressiveness that were seen as iconic for "Turks." They described their own speech as harder and as filled with more swear words than the speech of "Germans." This perception was shared by patrons and staff at the youth center as well. The boys' speech, in particular in Turkish, was characterized as having "hard," "chaotic," and "fast" traits. Magbule, a 21-year old intern at the center, herself bilingual, captured these locally shared ideas about how the boys' Turkish might be perceived by "Germans":

> Well, I don't mean that [boys who speak in Turkish] talk serious or use bad words, just. .. you perceive it that way as a. .. hmmm. .. sound, I don't know. It really is a little bit like that, if I for example wouldn't know Turkish, and it would sound pretty tough to me. Chaotic and fast, and somehow, somehow ... hard and strange, you know.

Among the youths of both genders, "Turkish" men were believed to use more swear words than German men, and women generally. Also, young "Turkish" women were believed to speak better German than young "Turkish" men. For the "Boys," speaking standard or "good German" was connected to softness and femininity, while their own code, swearwords, and the code of the street indexed "masculinity."[3] "Hardness" of talk was also seen as connected to lower class status and illiteracy. While illiterate and lower class "Turks" thus were said to talk "hard," literate upper class "Turks" spoke "softly." The boys thus indexically linked their language to their social position and the way that they perceived themselves to be socially situated within German society. Thus, to Murat, the "36 Boys" way of speaking Turkish was "more tough, yea... (*laughing*). That's right. There are a couple of words, that ... sound tough, you know."

The ideological alignment of the "Boys" ideas about languages and their speakers ordered as follows: Turkish:: German; male:: female; loud:: silent; rapid talk:: slow talk; swear words:: polite language; incorrect speech:: correct speech; accent:: native speaker. Just as dominant discourse ascribed lower class status to them, they reflected this positioning in their own iconized understanding of speech. Thus, cultural ideas were translated into ideas about language and their users. In the youths' ideologies about language, accented or incorrect speech, rapid and loud talk, as well as swear words thus come to index Turkishness, lower class status, masculinity, violence, and aggression. The content of the youths' language ideologies mirrored hegemonic ideologies of toughness, masculinity, and aggressiveness as they constructed an iconic relationship between forms of elaboration and forms of social life. As a result, the speech-style characteristics of the "36 Boys" came to be iconic for "toughness" and "hardness" in the social world of Berlin-Kreuzberg.

Level 2: Prosody in language—indexing anger in "tough talk"

Let us now move from analyzing affect in talk about language (i.e., language ideologies) to the analysis of how affect was indexed in everyday language use. Affect-encoding mechanisms in language are manifold and they include code choice (e.g., English, German), switching between codes, word meaning (e.g., the phrase "I don't care"), the connotation of words and phrases (e.g., "I couldn't care less"), ideophones (i.e., words whose phonological structure encodes meanings), and onomatopoeias, diminutives, exclamations, expletives, insults, prosody, and intonation (e.g., higher pitch to indicate arousal states, such as anger); all these mechanisms are affectively charged. Importantly, there is no inherent affective meaning tied to any linguistic sign. Affect-encoding mechanisms can only be interpreted in relation to their users and context, which implies that affective meaning of particular features can vary according to who uses them and in which contexts they are used.

Based on hegemonic discourses about immigrant youths in Germany and their own local ideologies about language and its speakers, the "36 Boys" employed a "foreignized" German with Turkish paralinguistic features, its properties closely modeled on the discourses that gave rise to linguistic indexes of Turkishness, including loud, rapid, and accented speech. The "Boys" consciously enacted "tough talk" through speech style characteristics, which in this particular cultural context had come to be seen as indexical for aggression. In specific situations of conflict they switched pitch, style, speed, and rhythm to create "tough talk." "Accent" was increased or performed, also by speakers who normally spoke without or with little accent. The performance of accent was then not a natural "echo" of youths' accented German. Rather, it was a newly created situational code whose properties drew on the dichotomous characteristics of "Germans" and "Turks" outlined above.

In the following excerpt, Murat describes and re-enacts the use of "tough talk" in interactions in which power was negotiated with out-group members. This excerpt is not presented for its semantic content, but as an example for the prosody of "tough talk."[4] (See the Appendix at the end of this chapter for a reference guide to the symbols used in the text below.)

JE: Are there any situations, in which you talk harder than you talk now with me?

M: Naturally there are, yes. For example if I **see** a guy here, who, let's say, is getting on my **nerves** or something, or who wants to **confront me**, or something like that, then I'll talk a little bit harder. (.) While now ... now I'm giving an **interview**, let's say, I'm still talking more friendly. Now I'm still talking friendly, you know. (.) Then, let's say, another one comes, like this [*Murat's voice rises to higher pitch, and gets louder. Facial expression and body language more tense*] **He::y** (0.2) >**What's up, why'ya staring at me** < (0.3.) [*lowered voice and pitch again*] **naturally** I'll talk hard with him, that's automatic. Not (0.2) [*lowered voice*] **ye::s ah::ah::**, [*and back to original pattern*] I won't talk like **that**, because then he thinks **softballs**. (.) What's up.

Rahman gave a similar demonstration:

> It depends who's in front of you. (.) Let's say, if you talk tough and the man says, (.)⇓ > oh, ok (.) this guy's tough, I better not get in his way. (0.5) < And, if you talk tough again and someone says ⇑> **AH>> Why does he talk tough, lan? > What's⇑up?** < (1) ⇓ and then he's on your back.

Rahman, when re-enacting "tough talk" for me, had difficulty describing what exactly he was doing differently at the word or code level in situations of conflict. As he enacted the same pattern of pitch, stress, and style as Murat, his emphasis was on the prosodic characteristics of his performance, which he described "like Turkish-German, somehow. All different," and in which he made intentional use of "such a strange accent."

The paralinguistic dimension is of crucial importance here: "Tough talk" is defined by a prosodic overlay that—tied to the local meaning outlined above—is highly laden affectively. With this, "tough talk," which evokes images of aggression, then comes to sound "angry" in the context of Berlin-Kreuzberg.[5] Having previously identified the "Boys'" ideologies about different groups of people in their social world, and how they are thought to speak, we are able to understand the sound symbolism[6] which they employ as culturally specific and tied to the local discursive context.

Level 3: Linguistic practices—enacting affect

The boys understood utterances in "tough talk" as acts in an interactive continuum. Displays of aggression via "tough talk" which indexed anger were used in particular contexts, with particular interlocutors, and in interactional closures. All of the "36 Boys" described how they switched into and out of "tough talk" in appropriate situations, thus indicating something akin to the situational switching of affective registers, or affective switching. Rahman referred to this when he asserted that by using "tough talk" and by saying "*Lan siktir* [Tk., fuck off]" he made sure that his German interlocutor would "take him seriously ... because you come across tough somehow."

By using "tough talk," the "Boys" thus invoked the authority of hegemonic language ideology, which ascribed the properties of toughness and aggressiveness to male Turkish youth.[7] In appropriating and using German "images of fear and aggression," i.e., in linguistically playing on discursive tropes, the boys gained situational power in situations of conflict in the surroundings of the neighborhood center with out-group members such as German youths. While German public discourse constructs displays of anger as expressions of innate aggressiveness and incitability, the "36 Boys" saw them as adaptive performance. The "Boys" "waved" emotion signs at their interlocutors and consciously performed displays of anger and aggression in pursuit of their goals and in order to negotiate interactional closures with "Germans." When they code switched into "tough talk," they intentionally indexed hostility, anger, aggressiveness, and ethnicized boundaries of the in-group versus the out-group in order. This raises implications for our understanding of emotion as-experienced versus as-enacted, and whether their social efficaciousness even depends on experiencing (Besnier 1990).

Theorizing emotions through the lens of linguistic anthropology

The case study investigated emotion in language at three levels: first, by analyzing discursive portrayals of "Turks" in Germany and by conducting ethnographic fieldwork on local language ideologies in Berlin-Kreuzberg, it explored the conditions of possibility that gave rise to an iconic representation of "Turks" as aggressive and, in turn, a local variant of Turkish that become iconic for the trait of aggressiveness. Second, by studying *prosodic markers* of "tough talk" up close, the analyses tied the local meaning ascribed to these markers to the ideologies about language that had been identified before. The case study revealed that local language ideologies and the iconization of "Turkish" speech shaped the "Boys" linguistic enactments of anger through "tough talk." Third, by studying the "Boys" everyday *linguistic practices*, the study unveiled how the "36 Boys" came to agentively and strategically exploit the different social and affective meanings attached to their speech. "Tough talk" was shown to become socially efficacious because it drew on these iconic relations that were expressed by prosodic markers. By "talking tough" they efficaciously managed affect in and of their surroundings in order to "define contexts, social structures, and their relationship to discourse" (Besnier 1990).

The case study adds to the existing literature that shows that Turkish boys' ritualized insults, boasts and other genres of competitive verbal play have complex affective functions (Besnier 1990; Dundes 1972; Eksner 2006). It further shows that displays of anger in language—which on the surface mirrored hegemonic discourse—were employed as a vehicle of resistance. The relational construction of affect between "Turks" and "Germans" was reified by the "Boys" themselves: they reflected them in affective self-stereotypes and affective identities. The "Boys' " use of momentary affective switching into and out of "tough talk" to gain situational power also shows, however, how dominant themes can become turned around and recoded without actually changing their symbolic form. Centrally, the "Boys'" linguistic practices emerged as site in which the power-laden relationship between affect and social positioning was enacted and contested.

Appendix

Transcription symbols

(0.2)	pause, measurable length indicated in seconds and tenths of seconds
((smiles))	action, gestures, smiling, etc.
[well	
[no	two people speaking at one
if you can =	latching; someone starts speaking immediately after another has finished, or
= I don't agree	interrupts
[-]	indecipherable
may-	a word has not been finished
eno:::rmous	a word is stretched out
↑	intonation; rising pattern
↓	intonation; falling pattern
rea::lly	a rise in pitch
the people	something was emphasized
he DOESN'T	increase in volume
no, _not really_	decrease in volume, whispered
> really, really<	spoken fast

Notes

1 For Peirce, an index is "a sign, or representation, which refers to its objects ... because it is in dynamical (including spatial) connection both with the individual object, on the one hand, and with the senses of memory of the person for whom it serves as a sign, on the other hand." (Peirce 1985 [1931]: 12f.). Interpreting indexes, however, depends on the interpreter's perspective. For example, right or left cannot be distinguished by general description, but need a reference point (Peirce 1985 [1931]: 16).

2 In Western societies, the failure to control anger and its expression is a social taboo (Steffgen and Gollwitzer 2007; Underwood *et al.* 1992). Aggression displays that occur after early childhood are thus seen as non-normative and are associated with a range of negative developmental outcomes such as conduct disorder, depression, anxiety, and academic problems.

3 Social class is itself gendered: several kinds of masculinity are iconically grouped according to class. For instance, the hegemonic form of masculinity is linked with working class. Standard speaking in the middle class is seen as closer to women. Thus, men are assumed to speak standard less, and femininity is linked to upward class mobility. This male-female opposition is one form of the "civility v. toughness" discourse, which was an imagery of the nineteenth century.

4 A note on data collection: I observed interactions of anger displays, but I didn't record many. The ones I did record are not a good fit for the objective of this methodological paper. The data presented here thus is limited to interview data in which youths talked about their practices or reenacted it.

5 While the final interpretation of prosody and speech style characteristics depends on both context and speaker, the paralinguistic characteristics of "tough talk" in this case happen to match the paralinguistic cues for displays of anger in German (Retzinger 1995). They include high pitch, heavy stress (volume and emphasis), style (fast, staccato), and a rhythmic and repeated pattern of pitch and stress. While the prosodic properties of "tough talk" are closely modeled on the indexes of Turkishness in Germany, at the same time they correspond to cues for anger in German more generally.

6 Research on sound symbolism explores the relationship between particular sounds and cultural concepts (such as [i] and "smallness"). Though research is looking for universal correlates in sound symbolism, the affective meaning of sounds appears to a large extent to be tied to particular languages. Thus, the interpretation of utterances based on intonational cues appears to be highly context dependent (Besnier 1990; Bolinger 1978).

7 There is a striking incongruity between the experience of social exclusion from mainstream society and the youths' own ideologies of power. It is therefore important to add that "tough talk" and ideologies of power are reserved to (safe) territory and reversed power relations in interactions with out-group members on the youths' own territory (Eksner 2006). Linguistic repairs which I have witnessed when "tough talk" was employed in other settings indicate that there are in fact right and wrong times to employ "tough talk."

References

Besnier, Niko. 1990. "Language and Affect," *Annual Review of Anthropology*, 19: 419–51.

Bolinger, D. 1978. "Intonation across languages" in J. H. Greenberg (ed.) *Universals of Human Language*, Vol. 2: 471–524. Stanford: Stanford University Press.

Gumperz, John J. 1982. *Discourse Strategies*. Cambridge: Cambridge University Press.

Der Spiegel. 1973. "Ghettos in Germany: One Million Turks." Issue 31. Available at: www.spiegel.de/spiegel/print/d-21112684.html.

Dundes, Alan, J. W. Leach, and B. Ozok. 1972. "The Strategy of Turkish Boys' Verbal Dueling Rhymes" in J. Gumperz and D. Hymes (eds) *Directions in Sociolinguistics. The Ethnography of Communication*. New York: Holt, Rinehart and Winston, Inc.

Eksner, H. Julia. 2006. "Ghetto Ideologies, Youth Identity and Stylized Turkish German. German Turks in Berlin-Kreuzberg." *Spektrum. Berliner Reihe zu Gesellschaft, Wirtschaft und Politik in Entwicklungslaendern*, 91. Hamburg: LIT Publishing House.

Ewing, Katherine Pratt. 2008. *Stolen Honor. Stigmatizing Muslim Men in Berlin*. Stanford University Press.

Gal, Susan. 1995. "Language and the 'Art of Resistance.'<th" *Cultural Anthropology*, 10 (3): 407–24.

Gal, Susan. 1998. "Multiplicity and Contention among Language Ideologies: A Commentary" in B. B. Schieffelin, Woolward K. A., and Kroskrity, P. V. (eds) *Language Ideologies. Practice and Theory*: 317–32. New York, Oxford: Oxford University Press.

Gumperz, J. J. (1982). "Social Network and Language Shift" in J. J. Gumperz (ed.), *Discourse Strategies*. Cambridge: Cambridge University Press.

Irvine, J. T. and S. Gal. 1999. "Language Ideology and Linguistic Differentiation" in P. V. Kroskrity (ed.), *Regimes of Language. Ideologies, Politics, and Identities*: 35–84. Santa Fe, New Mexico: School of American Research Press.

Kroskrity, Paul V. 1999. "Regimenting Languages: Language Ideological Perspectives" in P. V. Kroskrity (ed.) *Regimes of Language. Ideologies, Politics, and Identities*: 1–34. Santa Fe, New Mexico: School of American Research Press.

Kulick, D. 1992. *Language Shift and Cultural Reproduction: Socialization, Self and Syncretism in a Papua New Guinean Village*. Cambridge: Cambridge University Press.

Labov, William and D. Fanshel. 1977. *Therapeutic Discourse: Psychotherapy as Conversation*. Orlando: Academic.

Lambert, W. E. (1960). "Evaluational Reactions to Spoken Languages." *Journal of Abnormal and Social Psychology*, 66 (1), 44–51.

Peirce, Charles S. 1985 (1931). "Logic as Semiotic: The Theory of Signs" in R. E. Innis (ed.) *Semiotics. An Introductory Anthology*. Bloomington: Indiana University Press.

Retzinger, Suzanne M. 1995. "Identifying Shame and Anger in Discourse." *American Behavioral Scientist*, 38: 1104.

Silverstein, Michael. 1996. "Indexical Order and the Dialectics of Sociolinguistic Life." Third Annual Symposium About Language and Society (SALSA III), Austin, 1996: 266–95. Proceedings of the Third Annual Symposium About Language and Society, Austin, 1995.

Steffgen, G. and M. Gollwitzer. 2007. *Emotions and Aggressive Behavior*: Hogrefe Publishing.

Stehle, M. (2006). "Narrating the Ghetto, Narrating Europe: From Berlin, Kreuzberg to the Banlieus of Paris." *Westminster Papers in Communication and Culture*, 3 (3): 48–70.

Toelken, Barre 1985. "'Türkenrein' And 'Türken, Raus!' – Images of Fear and Aggression in German Gastarbeiterwitze" in I. Basgöz (ed.) *Turkish Workers in Europe*: 150–64. Bloomington: Indiana University Turkish Studies.

Underwood, Marion K., John D. Coie, and Cheryl R. Herbsman. 1992. "Display Rules for Anger and Aggression in School-Age Children." *Child Development*, 63: 366–80.

Urciuoli, Bonnie. 1998. *Exposing Prejudice. Puerto Rican Experiences of Language, Race, and Class*. Boulder: Westview Press.

Woolard, Kathryn. 1985. "Language variation and cultural hegemony: toward an integration of sociolinguistics and social theory." *American Ethnologist*, 12 (4): 738–48.

Woolard, Kathryn. 1998. "Introduction. Language Ideology as Field of Inquiry" in B. B. Schieffelin, Kathryn A. Woolard, Paul V. Kroskrity, and P. Kroskrity (eds), *Language Ideologies. Practice and Theory*: 3–50. New York, Oxford: Oxford University Press.

Chapter 19

Emotion and conceptual metaphor

Cristina Soriano

Introduction: conceptual metaphor theory

Language is a powerful tool for the study of emotion. Scholars interested in how different languages express and represent affective experience have a variety of methods available to them. In this chapter I introduce one of the approaches frequently used in cognitive linguistics to study conceptual representation, including the representation of emotion concepts. The approach, Conceptual Metaphor Theory (CMT), has been applied to the study of emotion since the early 1980s, generating a large number of studies in languages from all over the world.

CMT is based on the observation that much of what we say in everyday language is figurative and fairly systematic. It contends that regularities in the way we speak figuratively about a domain (e.g., time or emotion) inform us about the way the domain is conceptualized (Lakoff and Johnson 1980). For example, time is conventionally talked about in terms of space and motion (e.g., time *flies*, Christmas will be here *soon*, we can't *go back* to those days), suggesting that space and motion are used in the conceptual representation of time—giving it shape and potentially constraining our reasoning about it. Cognitive linguists refer to such stable cross-domain mappings as conceptual metaphors.[1]

Notice that the figurative expressions instantiating conceptual metaphors may be very conventional ways of speaking, but they are figurative nonetheless. For example, English speakers conventionally refer to their feelings for a partner as being "in love," but love is hardly a physical thing one can be "in." The existence of this and many other similar expressions indicates that we represent states (including emotional states) as "locations" or "containers" that we can occupy, go to, abandon, and even fall into or out of, as illustrated in the metaphorical expressions (1–4) below:

1 *to be in a panic*
2 *to drive to despair*

3 *to abandon hope*
4 *to fall in/out of love.*

An increasingly large body of experimental evidence in psychology attests to the existence of these and other cross-domain associations uncovered by cognitive linguists, and to their influence on perception and reasoning. Additionally, there are other reasons why conceptual metaphor scholars claim that expressions like those in 1–4, above, are not mere accidents in language, but the manifestation of stable conceptual associations recurrently activated in thought. First, novel or colorful metaphorical expressions often reflect the same associations as the standard expressions (e.g., "*exile oneself from love*").[2] Second, patterns in polysemy and semantic evolution can be successfully explained through conceptual metaphor. Third, large metaphorical systems seem to govern our discourse in politics, advertising, economics, religion, and science. Finally, gestures, behavior, images, and the objects we create for everyday use also exhibit these conceptual patterns.

CMT is a well-established research paradigm in cognitive linguistics, with a wide range of applications. For example, conceptual metaphors have been used in the study of literature, grammar, specific discourses, and in second language teaching—where it has been argued that knowing the metaphor-based explanation for idiomatic and polysemic expressions can aid in their learning.

In the remainder of this paper I will illustrate the type of research done in the field, and its utility for the investigation of emotion—with examples from my own research and that of my collaborators on the conceptualization of (different types of) anger in English, Spanish, and Russian. In doing so I will address a number of relevant questions in CMT research:

- How can we know what conceptual metaphors underlie the representation of a particular emotional domain?
- What can we learn about the conceptualization of an emotion by looking at conceptual metaphors?
- Why is metaphor analysis useful in cross-linguistic emotion research?
- How is metaphor analysis useful for other disciplines?

Identifying conceptual metaphors

The question addressed in this part is mainly methodological: how do linguists identify the conceptual metaphors underlying the representation of a given emotion concept? The first works on emotion conceptual metaphor relied on introspection and dictionaries to collect examples of figurative language (e.g., Kövecses 1990). Contemporary research relies on large electronic corpora, i.e., collections of naturally occurring texts sampled from a number or written and oral sources to represent, to the extent possible, the nature of a given language. This kind of corpus can comprise hundreds of millions of words and is considered more comprehensive and accurate in "speaking for a language" than any one native speaker, however well trained.

Different methods can be used to probe a corpus for figurative expressions used to talk about emotion in a given language. One option is to focus on specific emotion words of the domain under scrutiny. For example, in order to study the domain of ANGER in English, one may select words like *anger, irritation, fury, indignation, frustration* or *resentment.* Once the target words are identified, we can retrieve from the corpus all the sentences in which those words are employed. This usually involves numbers too high for manual inspection, but a typical approach in the field is to analyze 1,000 of them randomly selected from the full list. The following are some examples for the word *anger* extracted from the British National Corpus (BNC):

5 Julius couldn't remember when he had last been hit by such a *wave of anger.*
6 *Anger was still simmering in him.*
7 He was also formidable, demanding, difficult—and *smoldering with anger.*
8 Once out of his presence he *vents his anger* for his dead friend on nature.
9 His occasional *outbursts of anger* shocked those around him.

The researcher would then identify the metaphorical expressions and classify them according to the metaphor they instantiate. As analysis method, my colleagues and I employ Metaphorical Profile Analysis (Ogarkova and Soriano 2014b). This method entails the rephrasing of the observed metaphorical expressions as metaphorical patterns. A metaphorical pattern is "a multi-word expression from a given source domain into which a specific lexical item from a given target domain has been inserted" (Stefanowitsch 2006: 66). For example, the metaphorical patterns in sentences (5–9) are *wave of* [emotion], [emotion] *simmer, smolder with* [emotion], *vent* [emotion], and *outbursts of* [emotion]. Then the metaphorical patterns are grouped according to source domain (e.g., FIRE, HOT FLUID), and the number of expressions in each group is counted. The resulting list of conceptual metaphors and their degree of exploitation for a given word constitutes the word's "metaphorical profile."

Some of the conceptual metaphors in the metaphorical profile of *anger* are presented in Table 19.1, with examples of the metaphorical patterns that instantiate these metaphors, and the number of occurrences of them, in a random sample of 1,000 citations from the BNC.

Table 19.1 Examples of conceptual metaphors and linguistic metaphorical patterns in the representation of ANGER in English

Conceptual metaphor (ANGER is a ...)	*Metaphorical patterns*	*N*
PRESSURIZED FLUID IN THE BODY-CONTAINER	[anger] rise in X, [anger] wells up in X, contain [anger], vent [anger], [anger] spill-over, outburst of [anger], explode with [anger]	60
FIRE	[anger] burn, flame of [anger], spark [anger], kindle [anger], stoke [anger], blaze with [anger], fume with [anger], [anger] scorch	30
WEAPON	turn/direct/cast [anger] against (/at, /on) Y, target of X's [anger], deflect [anger], [anger] be (sharp) like a knife	29
HOT FLUID	[anger] boil, [anger] simmer, [anger] bubble, [anger] seethe, [anger] sizzle	23
OPPONENT IN A STRUGGLE	fight [anger], conquer [anger], overcome [anger], imprison [anger], [anger] assail X	20
ANIMAL	leash/unleash [anger], rein in [anger], fierce [anger], [anger] roar inside X	13
FORCE OF NATURE	eruption of [anger], storm of [anger], [anger] engulfs X, wave of [anger], [anger] ebbs away, tide of [anger]	10
ILLNESS	spasm of [anger], festering [anger], suffer from [anger], chronic [anger]	6
INSANITY	fit of [anger], beside oneself with [anger]	3

Note
X = emoter, Y = third person, N = observed number of figurative expressions instantiating the metaphorical patterns.

What do conceptual metaphors tell us about emotion?

If emotions are represented conceptually in terms of more concrete domains like FIRE or ILLNESS, what does it tell us about the emotions themselves? A way to answer this question in a manner useful across disciplines is to resort to the notion of "semantic focus" originally proposed by Kövecses (2000: 40–6). Semantic foci are aspects of emotional experience foregrounded by metaphor. Kövecses mentions evaluation (i.e., the positive or negative axiology implied by many metaphors), intensity, and harm, among others. For example, emotions conceptualized as ILLNESS are represented as negative and harmful, and emotions conceptualized as FIRE are seen as intense. Other semantic foci are the self-regulation one may exert on one's feelings and/or their manifestation, the intrinsic controllability of the emotion, and its degree of expressivity (i.e., whether the emotion is conceptualized as openly visible or, on the contrary, as internalized) (see Soriano 2013; Ogarkova and Soriano 2014b). A look at semantic foci in the set of conceptual metaphors identified for the words *anger, irritation, fury, rage, frustration, indignation,* and *resentment* in English indicates that ANGER in this language is represented as being intense (e.g., FIRE, HOT FLUID), negative (e.g., OPPONENT, INSANITY), harmful for the person and others (e.g., ILLNESS, WEAPON), involving expressive behavior (e.g., ANIMAL), and requiring regulation (e.g., OPPONENT, PRESSURIZED FLUID), although the emotion is inherently difficult to control (e.g., FORCE OF NATURE). This overall characterization is coherent with descriptions of the category from psychology (e.g., Russell and Fehr 1994). But the important thing in this case is that we can use these semantic foci to compare different types of anger and the variants of the emotion in different languages, as will be shown next.

Why is metaphor analysis useful in cross-linguistic emotion research?

The metaphorical profiles constitute a semantic profile of the words, informing us of the ways the emotions designated by those words are conceptualized. Words can be compared within and across languages, in search for similarities and/or differences. For example, Spanish has two salient terms to label the ANGER category. One of them, *ira* ("anger," but also "wrath"), is the term typically used in emotion psychology. The other, *rabia* ("anger," but also "rabies"), is a term more frequently used by lay people to refer to the emotion.

An analysis of their metaphorical profiles using distributional statistics reveals important differences: *ira* is significantly more associated with the conceptual domains of FIRE, FORCE OF NATURE and WEAPON, while *rabia* is more associated with ILLNESS. This suggests that the preferred term in psychology refers to a more intense (FIRE), violent (FORCE OF NATURE) and aggressive (WEAPON) emotion, while the more popular term is more saliently associated with a disruption of normal body functioning.

Zooming onto the specific linguistic expressions that instantiate a conceptual metaphor also provides important insights. For example, both in English and Spanish ANGER IS A PRESSURIZED FLUID is a salient metaphor. However, it is not elaborated linguistically in the same way. The metaphor represents anger in both languages as a substance inside the body that increases in quantity, thus rising in the container and exerting pressure on it. In Spanish it is also conventional to express the idea that somebody is accumulating anger inside by saying that they (or parts of their body, like the nose) are "swelling" (10, see below). This is a possible inference afforded by the logic of the metaphor in English as well, but the inference has not given rise to any conventional expressions in this language. In English people do not typically "swell with anger" (although they do with pride).

10 *Me estás hinchando las narices* (Literally, "you are swelling my nose," i.e., "you are making me angry").

We have also found that the different use of "swelling" expressions in English and Spanish echoes a more general pattern: metaphors highlighting "containment" in general are more salient in the representation of anger in Spanish than in English (Ogarkova and Soriano 2014b). This, in turn, may be linked to socio-cultural traits, as will be further described below.

In sum, metaphorical profiles allow us to make useful distinctions between words in the same language or close words in different languages. This is undoubtedly useful for linguists and translators, but can metaphor research be useful to other disciplines as well?

How is metaphor analysis useful for other disciplines?

A way in which metaphor research can be brought to bear on neighboring disciplines is through the notion of semantic foci, earlier defined as aspects of emotional experience foregrounded by metaphor. Some semantic foci resemble well-known constructs in emotion psychology, like valence (akin to "evaluation"), and arousal (related to "intensity") (Soriano 2013). The semantic foci may thus be used as common currency by both disciplines. For example, cross-cultural psychology may be informed about the valence/evaluation of an emotion by looking at the axiology (positive versus negative) of its metaphorical expressions. In the case of ANGER, for example, negativity seems to be more salient in Spanish than in English (Ogarkova and Soriano 2014b).

Metaphor analysis can also reveal aspects of emotion salient for the speakers of a language, but potentially disregarded by emotion theorists. Two examples are the association of anger with irrational behavior (captured by the metaphor ANGER IS INSANITY), and the damage it can cause to the person him/herself (captured by ANGER IS AN ILLNESS) (Soriano 2013). The first aspect is overshadowed in emotion psychology by the tendency to emphasize the overall utility of emotions as adaptive mechanisms that prepare the organism for optimal interaction with the environment. And if anger prepares us to correct wrongs inflicted on our person, how can it be irrational? Indeed, in an analysis of English (1) psychology guides, and (2) websites, where lay people seek advice for their psychological problems, Beger and Jäkel (2009) found that experts hardly talk about anger resorting to the INSANITY metaphor, while this strategy is common among lay people. Our folk-representation of the emotion, as suggested by language, invites a more nuanced view: anger may be rational overall, but it often results in irrational reactions nevertheless. The second aspect, often disregarded by psychology (except in clinical contexts), is the potential damage of the emotion to the person. It is common in psychology to refer to anger as a "negative" emotion because it feels unpleasant, it is caused by something negative, and it leads to confrontation. But nothing is typically said (when justifying the "negativity" of anger) about the possible negative effects of the emotion for one's well-being. By contrast, metaphor highlights the "pain" inherent in anger, the disruption it causes to body functions, and its possible long-term negative effects. In sum, both aspects of the emotion (irrationality and damage) are present in expert theories of emotion to some extent, but a look at language can remind psychologists that these two factors are much more salient in the way lay people represent anger for everyday purposes.

Metaphorical profiles can also be relevant for cross-cultural studies. For example, Wierzbicka (1989) has observed that Russian "*duša*" (soul) and English "mind" are salient terms in their respective cultures to discuss intangible aspects of human life. Congruently with these observations, our analysis of metaphor across several terms revealed that when the body is conceptualized as a container for anger, the emotion is more frequently associated with the soul and heart in Russian, and with the head and mind in English (Ogarkova and Soriano 2014a).

Another example of cultural specificity is the pattern observed for the semantic foci of expression (the visibility of the emotion) and regulation (the willing control of the feeling). Significantly, more expressions related to containment are found in Spanish than in English for the metaphor ANGER IS A PRESSURIZED FLUID. Additionally, more Spanish expressions are related to pressure. The latter is also true for Russian. By contrast, English compared to Russian has a significantly larger number of metaphors highlighting expression—the coming out of the anger-fluid. It has been suggested (Ogarkova and Soriano 2014b) that these patterns may reflect the more collectivistic nature of Spain and Russia, compared to English-speaking communities like the USA and the UK—which score high on individualism. Cross-cultural psychology suggests that collectivistic communities experience a greater urge to repress the overt manifestation of intense negative emotions for the sake of harmony within the group. This would explain the relevance of containment metaphorical expressions in Russian and Spanish. Individualistic communities, on the contrary, would have a comparatively more positive evaluation of the open manifestation of anger, seen as an affirmation of the self. This is coherent with the comparatively greater number of expressions profiling the "coming out" of the anger-fluid in English.

Conclusions

The goal of this paper was to present and illustrate CMT, a popular approach to the study of conceptual representation in cognitive linguistics that can also be of use to the interdisciplinary field of the affective sciences. CMT is a theoretical framework in that it posits the existence in our minds of stable associations between different domains recursively employed to help us represent reality. CMT is also a methodology in the sense of proposing a way of looking at language to identify these stable associations. The theoretical paradigm introduced in the 1980s was applied from the very beginning to the study of emotion concepts, and continues to generate new studies all over the world. Cognitive psychology has also used metaphor research for the experimental investigation of embodied cognition. Furthermore, the paradigm has inspired cross-cultural and social psychology, which now advocate a "metaphor-enriched social cognition" (Landau *et al.* 2010).

In the middle of this interdisciplinary interest in metaphor, constructs like the semantic foci discussed here are particularly useful to compare findings across disciplinary domains. Another important development is the adoption of corpus-based quantitative approaches to metaphor analysis, which allow us to measure the relative significance of the observed patterns for different emotion concepts within and across languages. This has useful applications in linguistic research, but also in other disciplines. As illustrated in previous sections, patterns in metaphorical language use inform us of the way communities represent their emotional experiences and can reveal underlying cultural differences.

Emotion is a multifaceted phenomenon and its study requires a multidisciplinary approach. Linguistics, anthropology, and psychology look at it, respectively, from the standpoint of language, culture, and cognition. Conceptual metaphor research stands halfway between the three, providing a privileged vantage point on the phenomenon. This may be the greatest advantage of CMT for the affective sciences. The various disciplines involved in the study of emotion can communicate, quite literally, through metaphor.

Acknowledgments

This work was supported by grants from the Swiss Network for International Studies (SNIS) and the Swiss Center for Affective Sciences.

Notes

1 A conceptual metaphor comprises a target domain (i.e., the domain represented, like TIME) and a source domain (i.e., the domain invoked to represent the target, like SPACE). Their association is typically expressed in small capitals through the formula SOURCE IS TARGET (e.g., TIME IS SPACE). The label "metaphorical expression" is reserved for the specific linguistic instantiations of these conceptual patterns, like *time flies* or *we are approaching Christmas.* I follow the convention in CMT of writing concepts in small capitals and linguistic expressions in italics.

2 Due to space constraints only a few works in the metaphor literature concerning emotion can be mentioned. See Soriano (2012) for references on all these aspects and an overview of relevant research on conceptual metaphor in general.

References

Beger, A. and O. Jäkel. 2009. "ANGER, LOVE and SADNESS Revisited: Differences in Emotion Metaphors Between Experts and Laypersons in the Genre Psychology Guides," *Metaphorik.de*, 16: 87–108. Available at: www.metaphorik.de/sites/www.metaphorik.de/files/journal-pdf/16_2009_begerjaekel.pdf (last accessed June 23, 2014).

Kövecses, Z. 1990. *Emotion Concepts.* Berlin, New York: Springer Verlag.

Kövecses, Z. 2000. *Metaphor and Emotion. Language, Culture and Body in Human Feeling.* Cambridge: Cambridge University Press.

Lakoff, G. and M. Johnson. 1980. *Metaphors We Live By.* Chicago, London: University of Chicago Press.

Landau, M. J., B. P. Meier, and L. A. Keefer. 2010. "A Metaphor-Enriched Social Cognition," *Psychological Bulletin*, 136 (6): 1045–67.

Ogarkova, A. and C. Soriano. 2014a. "Emotion and the Body: A Corpus-Based Investigation of Metaphorical Containers of Anger Across Languages," *International Journal of Cognitive Linguistics*, 5 (2): 147–179.

Ogarkova, A. and C. Soriano. 2014b. "Variation Within Universals: The 'Metaphorical Profile' Approach to the Study of Anger Concepts in English, Russian and Spanish" in A. Mussolf, F. MacArthur, and G. Pagani (eds) *Metaphor and Intercultural Communication*: 93–116. London: Bloomsbury Academic.

Russell, J. A. and B. Fehr. 1994. "Fuzzy Concepts in a Fuzzy Hierarchy: Varieties of Anger," *Journal of Personality and Social Psychology*, 67 (2): 186–205.

Soriano, C. 2012. "La Metáfora Conceptual" in I. Ibarretxe-Antuñano and J. Valenzuela (eds) *Lingüística Cognitiva*: 97–121. Barcelona: Anthropos.

Soriano, C. 2013. "Conceptual Metaphor Theory and the GRID Paradigm in the Study of Anger in English and Spanish" in J. Fontaine, K. R. Scherer, and C. Soriano (eds) *Components of Emotional Meaning: A Sourcebook*: 410–24 Oxford: Oxford University Press.

Stefanowitsch, A. 2006. "Words and Their Metaphors. A Corpus-Based Approach" in A. Stefanowitsch and S. Gries (eds) *Corpus-Based Approaches to Metaphor and Metonymy*: 61–105. Berlin, New York: Mouton de Gruyter.

Wierzbicka, A. 1989. "Soul and Mind: Linguistic Evidence for Ethnopsychology and Cultural History," *American Anthropologist*, 91 (1): 41–58.

Chapter 20

The intensification and commodification of emotion

Declarations of intimacy and bonding in college field trips to the Global South

Gada Mahrouse

I have long been interested in the power and privilege dynamics within encounters in which people from the Global North travel to the Global South to learn, help, or somehow lend their support.[1] A particular subset of this travel that I have examined in recent years, is a specific educational program offered by a Canadian college[2] and involves students traveling to the Global South[3] on a month-long field trip to poor and rural regions in Nicaragua.[4] The trip is designed to help the students (the majority of whom are 16–19 years old) learn first-hand about the economic, social, and political conditions in developing countries; and to participate in the everyday lives of those who live in them. The trip was divided into two stays—each one two weeks in duration—in the homes of Nicaraguan families.

I was curious about this particular program because it was the most well thought out of the ones that I had come across. For instance, before they went on the trip, students were expected to study the history, current socio-political conditions, and cultural norms in Nicaragua; and many of them were encouraged to research topics relevant to the discrepancies between the Global South and the Global North.[5] The students were taught about the colonial histories of, and the neo-colonial dependencies created by, international development programs and aid. Unlike many educational programs involving this type of field trip component, this one impressed me because it sought to meaningfully address power imbalances head-on, not merely gloss over them. I also learned that the educators who coordinated the field trip and accompanied the students on it (hereafter referred to as "coordinators") were conflicted about the paradoxes of bringing a group of young people from the North into small, rural communities in Nicaragua to teach them about North/South power inequalities. Conscious of unintentionally exacerbating such inequalities, the coordinators tried to minimize the intrusive nature of the field trip by giving local Nicaraguan community leaders ongoing input into how the program was run. For these reasons, this program struck me as a rich site from which to explore the ways in which students might negotiate their privilege as Northerners venturing into the Global South.

As expected, the data I collected wielded significant insights with respect to how the students understood and negotiated their privilege during the trip. For instance, some of the responses I collected were embedded in what I have referred to elsewhere as discourses of equation or reversal—such as "while we have wealth, they have what truly matters: community, hope, and understanding" (Mahrouse 2011). While these findings were important insofar as they demonstrated a consistent dynamic that arises across various forms of alternative travel (one which, I have previously argued, serves to obscure power imbalances), my objective in this chapter is to draw attention to what I had *not* solicited—numerous articulations of intimacy and emotional bonding between the students and the host families, and in particular the seemingly exaggerated and intense ways in which these emotions were expressed.

Indeed, the responses I received from the students to the questions I put to them were distracting, puzzling, and surprising. Although I had set out to identify social and political themes related to their privilege, and their reflections on North/South power relations, I ended up with responses that were brimming with emotions. Furthermore, the sheer prevalence and centrality of these expressions rendered it impossible for me to overlook them. Like some of the other contributors to this volume, I found myself out of my analytical depth and suddenly having to grapple with the opaque and unfamiliar realm of emotions.

In what follows I will detail the methods and research design that I used, summarize some of the findings pertaining to emotions, and outline the analytic I developed for making sense of this emotional data—one especially pertinent to my overall objective of studying relations of privilege and power.

Methods and research design: emotions as an emergent theme

As a qualitative researcher interested in North/South power relations, and gaining insight into the complexities of the students' field trip experiences, I first needed to gain a full understanding of the program, as well as access to the students beforehand. My initial step was therefore to approach the program coordinators, first in a letter and then with telephone calls. The three coordinators enthusiastically and readily agreed to participate in the study because they thought it would provide the students with a chance to reflect upon their experiences in Nicaragua. Their responses were encouraging and indicated to me that they saw a need for such a study.

To gain an overall picture of the program and its field trip component, I began by conducting in-depth interviews with the coordinators.[6] The primary theme that emerged during these interviews was their above-mentioned ambivalence with respect to taking students on the trip. The interviews also revealed some of the ways by which the coordinators reconciled these contradictions—including encouraging the students to actively engage in the experience at a personal level. As one of the coordinators explained: "We're here to engineer a very specific kind of interaction" [Interview 1]. Recognizing the limitations of the material and physical help that their students might be able to offer in Nicaragua, another coordinator stated that he had learned to live with the contradictions because he believed that "the bottom line is that it [the trip] fosters a human connection" [Interview 2]. Similarly, while conceding that the trip was loaded with "contradictions and hypocrisy," the third coordinator said it would nevertheless open the students up to "a kind of generosity in the world that is not measured in material wealth ... one measurable in terms of their humanity" [Interview 3].

For the next stage of my research I needed the students' first-person accounts of their expectations, experiences, and reflections about the trip. Following discussions with the coordinators, and given the timing of an upcoming field trip, it was determined that two sets of open-ended questionnaires would be administered to students (to which they would respond in writing)—to be completed before and after their trip, approximately three-and-a-half months apart. With the coordinators' cooperation, and to ensure that the majority of students would take part, the questionnaires were completed as part of their college classes.

Before the questionnaires were distributed my research assistant and I gave the students a description of the project. We were candid about our particular interest in North/South encounters; and specifically how the students would negotiate their privilege and positioning as people from the Global North. We explained that participation was voluntary, and that they would be asked to complete a follow-up questionnaire. Students were also informed that they would be given a chance to ask questions about the study.[7]

The students completed the first questionnaire about a month before they left for their trip. It consisted of some general questions about their motivations and expectations:

1 Why did you enrol in this program?
2 What do you expect to gain from participating in this trip?
3 Do you have any concerns regarding this trip? If yes, please detail them.
4 As far as you are concerned, what is the objective of this trip?
5 What effect do you think your group's presence will have on the communities and people you interact with in Nicaragua?

6 Do you anticipate that you will be contributing something to these communities? If so, what/how?
7 What do you think is meant by privilege (for people from the North) in these types of North/South encounters?

The students completed the second questionnaire six weeks after they had returned. This time the questions asked them to reflect on their experiences on the trip:

1 Do you feel that this trip has changed you? Please give examples.
2 What effect(s) did this trip have on you?
3 What were some of the highs and lows of living with your host family?
4 Did anything happen that you had not anticipated? Please explain, using examples.
5 What impact do you think you (and your group) had on your host family and/or the local community?

On both occasions that the questionnaires were administered, students were given an opportunity to share additional comments. In all, 13 of the 18 students completed both questionnaires.[8]

The students' responses were subsequently read for content and thematic analysis. In particular—and given my primary concern about their negotiations as privileged people from the Global North—I combed through their responses looking for excerpts pertaining to their understanding of the North/South positioning. It was then that I began to see a clear pattern—one which indicated to me that an emotional dimension had inadvertently emerged through this research design. With this discovery, I realized that I would need to extend the original parameters of the study to consider the idea of power more broadly—especially its links with emotions.

Love and familial bonding in the encounter abroad

In response to the questions about the highs and lows of their trip, or about the experiences they had not anticipated, ten of the 13 students wrote about the strong bonds they had formed with their host families. For example:

> They called me their daughter and I really felt an incredible *bond*.
> (Nancy)[9]

> The highs included being able to talk and *bond* with them. I enjoyed just spending time with them and sharing our different cultures.
> (Rachel)

Most noteworthy in these types of response is their consistency, and the degree of intensity of the level of intimacy they express. Many of the students also described how the closeness that they developed extended to a level of feeling like they had become a member of their host family:

> The worst part of the trip was leaving them [host family] behind, knowing that I will probably never *be one of them* in this way again.
>
> (Kathy)

> The highs were to become *a true member* of that family and to develop a solid relationship with them in such a short period of time.
>
> (Kim)

Perhaps the best indicator of the intensity and extremity of emotion that was expressed by the students was the fact that as many as six (nearly half) of them used the word "love" to describe the mutual feelings between them and their host families. For instance:

> I *loved* my host family. I loved the connection between us.
>
> (Elizabeth)

> I have gained an extended family that I *love* and hope to see again.
>
> (Zoe)

> Now each family has one more child living abroad ... as a group I think we were *loved.*
>
> (Peter)

What puzzled me about the type and degree of emotions being expressed, was the fact that, on average, the students spent only two weeks with each family. Furthermore, in their responses to the questionnaires, nearly all of the students had expressed concern or frustration about their inability to speak Spanish—to the point that verbal communication with their host families would be very limited. Yet despite the short time-span and the language barrier, the majority of students believed that they formed significant emotional bonds with their host families.

Given what I had been told by the coordinators about their objectives for the field trip component of the program—to create an opportunity for personal bonds and relationships to be established—I determined that part of what was likely fueling the students' emotive responses was simply the fact that such interpersonal relations had been proactively encouraged. For instance, I had to take into consideration that long before their arrival in Nicaragua the hosting family members were referred to as "mother" and "father" (or "mama" and "papa"). This language of kinship (common in this type of program) is used to create a connection for the students with their host families from the start. Furthermore, recalling one of the coordinator's earlier statements about trying to "engineer" a certain type of interaction for the students, I first tried to dismiss their responses about bonding with their host families as somewhat "scripted"—and therefore not worthy of further examination. With respect to their expressions of "love," I needed to consider the possibility that I was reading too much into the students' responses. Certainly, one can argue that young people express themselves in exaggerated ways, and therefore their use of the word "love" could be easily understood as nothing more than a kind of colloquialism.

When I went back to back to the data, however, I concluded that these expression patterns *were* meaningful and did warrant attention—for two reasons. First, the students had responded in writing and had therefore had time to reflect on the words they chose. Second, I could see that many of them were choosing to use specific words deliberately; and in some cases the students seemed self-conscious about their responses being perceived as exaggerations. In fact, as the following excerpts reveal, many of them stated that they were surprised themselves by the intensity of the feelings they experienced, and by the strength of the bonds they established under such unlikely circumstances:

> I really didn't expect to fall *in love* with my first family the way I did. I really feel like they've become a part of me.
>
> (Ursula)

> I didn't expect to get so attached to my two families like I did. I got so close and I miss and think of them every day.
>
> (Helen)

It thus became clear that I needed to consider *why* the students felt such strong love and familial ties with people they had just met, had little in common with, and with whom they could hardly communicate. In highlighting the unlikely conditions in which this intense bonding took place, my aim was not to judge or cast doubt upon the emotions felt by the students. In fact, it was because I believed that these emotions were sincerely felt that I wanted to understand them.

Given my initial objectives, I wanted to make sense of these emotional responses vis-à-vis the students' positioning and power as members of the Global North. To this end, I borrowed from, and adapted, an analytical approach for studying emotions where they appear in the context of asymmetrical power relations — an approach largely inspired by the work of Helena Flam (2009; 2013). Specifically, this led me to develop a two-pronged analytic which drew on both historical and sociological writings on emotions to consider the contextually specific "feeling rules" (Hochschild 2003) that formed the students' experiences on this trip. Armed with this, I set out to consider the following: why do these emotions manifest themselves in a seemingly intense and exaggerated way? What does the feeling of emotional bonding *do* in such encounters abroad? And how do the material conditions of the encounter shape the specific feelings that emerged?

Charged emotions: Why the intensity? Why there?

What was I to make of such demonstrative and effusive expressions of intimacy and bonding given the context in which time and language barriers should have served to constrain the possibility of the emergence of such intense emotions? My first clue came from work on the notions of emotional and imaginative geographies, and specifically from seventeenth century travel writing.

The idea of imaginative geographies first gained currency through the work of Edward Said (1978), who sought to capture the ways in which Western travelers understand, experience, and represent the places they visit. He argued that these are all closely tied to their preconceptions of such places. Furthermore, and making "power" central to his analysis, Said argued that one must pay attention to questions of self/other knowledge that manifest through such encounters abroad. When applied to the field trip in question here, this means that one needs to consider how the students imagined what the place and the people would be like before they got there. The emotional aspect of their experience also needs to be contemplated alongside the idea popularized by geographers in recent years—that we must take into account the spatiality and locations in which such emotions appear (Anderson and Smith: 2001). In other words, and as I will discuss next, it was not incidental that the degree of intensity they experienced took place while they were "over there."

Although ideas of imaginative and emotional geographies have been variously examined by those interested in contemporary imperial relations in travel and tourism, for my purposes the most relevant application comes from the work of historian Chloe Chard (1999), who examined expressions of emotions by European travelers between 1600–1830. Her work shows that a recurring theme of this period, especially in seventeenth century travel writing, is hyperbole—or intensification—and a language of excess.[10] Chard explains that "the foreign" permitted emphatic expression without qualification or restraint, and supplied an element of drama which was greeted by the European traveler "as an effect produced by an unusual intensity, concentration, or extremity" (Chard 1999: 49). Importantly, she points out that this rhetorical device emphasizes differences of degree rather than kind. Chard also points out that expressions of hyperbole were seen as risky insofar as the narrator made her/himself open to accusations of naïvety.

When applied to the responses of the students in my study, Chard's (1999) work suggests that—just like it did for those seventeenth century European travelers—the trip to Nicaragua allowed them to feel things more intensely and express them more freely. In other words, although such expressions of intimacy and emotion may have seemed inappropriate or exaggerated in their usual surroundings and living spaces, experiencing and expressing this intensity became acceptable because it took place elsewhere. Interestingly, and just as it was for the seventeenth century travel writers before them, the students tried to fend off accusations of gullibility or of being too easily impressed by insisting that they, too, were surprised by the intensity of the feelings that they had experienced. In so doing, they emphasized that such feelings were unanticipated, thereby inscribing authenticity to their emotions. This suggests that although at first glance the intense bonds of intimacy felt by the Canadian students toward their Nicaraguan hosts may have seemed unlikely—given the vast differences between them—the simple fact that these encounters took place in Nicaragua made such feelings possible for them.

To further consider the emergence of emotions in the context of this vast asymmetry in power, it was also necessary to draw upon sociological work linking emotions with the social and economic structures in which they appear. Of particular relevance here is Arlie Hochschild's (2003) contention that expressions of emotion must be considered in terms of how they are driven by economic forces. To contextualize this part of the discussion it is first necessary to offer some background information concerning the economic conditions that the students' emotional bonding was embedded within.

Although it was difficult for me to obtain precise information about how the host Nicaraguan families were compensated for taking these young people into their homes, it became clear that there were significant material incentives for them. I learned that to be accepted as a host family for the program they had to meet rigorous criteria.[11] One of the students wrote that the father of her host family kept "thanking God" for her being there—implying that those who are deemed appropriate and eligible to host students consider themselves fortunate. Through my interviews with the program coordinators I also discovered that an informal monetary or material exchange often takes place between the students and their host families. For instance, I was told that although they are instructed not to, after they return to Canada some students send money and gifts to their host families. The point is that the Nicaraguan hosts (some of whom were described as "desperately poor") may be compelled to welcome Canadian students into their homes for practical and economic reasons, and that therefore they have a vested interest in creating a positive experience for their guests. More precisely, Hochschild's (2003) notion of "emotional labor" is key to understanding the students' experiences and expressions of love and intimacy; and in particular that this cannot be separated from the likelihood that their Nicaraguan hosts are in fact "working" to ensure that this emotional bond occurs. This is not to suggest that the Nicaraguan hosts are disingenuous; just that their experience of this encounter is very differently motivated. Indeed, given the informal monetary exchange and gift-giving that takes place between the students and their host families, it is easy to imagine that the families stand to benefit in very material ways by creating a positive experience for the students. Yet, paradoxically, the program coordinators insist that the program encourages a kind of non-material generosity; and that the benefits of the experience are, as one of them put it, "measured not in dollars but in terms of their humanity" [Interview 3].

Displaying love to reconcile power

Thus far, I have argued that being in Nicaragua permitted the college students to express themselves in seemingly exaggerated ways; and that the program was designed to engender such bonds of human connection. I now want to consider what emotional bonding with the "other" did for the students' understandings of themselves in these encounters abroad. Specifically, returning to the students' expressions of love, it is important to ask what such articulations do in geopolitical contexts of asymmetries of power? Sara Ahmed's (2004) writing was helpful here. She draws on Freud to argue that love can serve to make "the subject vulnerable, exposed to, and dependent upon another" (Ahmed 2004: 125). Extending this idea further would suggest that in experiencing and expressing love for their host families, the students may be trying to reduce the power differences between them. Indeed, such expressions of love appear to be a way for them to pay their respect, and suggest that these expressions are akin to what Hochschild (2003: 76–7) referred to as "bowing from the heart." As Hochschild (2003: 83) explains, in some circumstances "we may offer a tribute so generous that it actually transforms our mood and our thoughts to match what others would like to see."

I want to end by proposing that not only were such effusive expressions likely—given the geopolitical context in which they appeared—in some ways they were also necessary. That is to say, the emotional expressions help us to understand the student/host family encounter given the inherent inequality that characterizes it. Feelings and expressions of love helped the students to imagine themselves, and the world they inhabit, as less unequal and divided. In other words, one of the ways that the students learned to live with the inequalities they experienced in Nicaragua was to invest in human connections with the people there. These emotional connections helped them to reconcile the material disparities between them.

Conclusion: lessons learned about methods, power, and emotions

With the benefit of hindsight, I can see that the methodology and design that I used for this project was inadvertently useful for uncovering emotional data. This was especially true with respect to the fortuitous decision to collect written responses (as opposed to oral ones) and to use individual interviews (as opposed to focus group ones, which I had also been contemplating). By writing their responses down, the students were able to express themselves more freely and perhaps less self-consciously than might have been the case orally. In fact, had I conducted oral interviews, it is very likely that I would have intervened and redirected these emotional expressions since they were not what I had been seeking. In other words—albeit unintentionally—the written data collection method I used proved to be an effective means of gathering emotional data.

Thus, despite the significant challenges that these unexpected emotional expressions presented for me, their emergence certainly offered deeper insights into the tensions and contradictions of this type of travel; and prompted a more thoughtful analysis of such contemporary transnational encounters. Before this study, I, like many others, regarded emotional relations as something separate from the economic and/or as something private that extended beyond the scope of my interests in the political/social and public spheres (Anderson and Smith 2001: 3). What this data revealed to me is that power and emotions are inextricably linked, and therefore require particular methodological approaches. Furthermore, for my own purposes it was necessary to draw from both historical and sociological texts to offer a nuanced discussion of how emotional expressions do much more than simply capture sentiment. Indeed, I have shown that such expressions can reveal many insights about power and North/South relations. More specifically, the analytic I used helped to show how inequalities can be negotiated through emotional experiences and displays. This methodological finding has important implications for researchers who, like me, are committed to uncovering some of the insidious ways in which power manifests in encounters involving people from the Global North who have traveled to the Global South.

Notes

1 The conceptions of power and privilege I use in my work derive from the work of feminist, post-structural, and post-colonial theorists who link subject positions to histories and geopolitical histories and locations. For a longer description of this theoretical framework see Mahrouse (2014).

2 In Quebec the program-level is referred to as *Collège d'Enseignement Général et Professionnel* (or CEGEP) and represents the first stage of higher education.

3 The program spans two years. Graduates receive a certificate of specializations in International Development Studies, along with their College Diploma.

4 Once there, students assist in projects such as: helping to build houses, repairing the roofs of schools, or building cisterns. For such projects the college pays for materials and the fees of local experts, with the students providing some of the labor.
5 They are also encouraged to critically examine various communities' access to health, water, and education. Although the students are taught about a number of geographic contexts in the developing world, the program focuses mostly on Central and South America.
6 These interviews were conducted face-to-face and lasted 60–120 minutes. The interviews were audio taped and then transcribed. These interviews were semi-structured as a means of encouraging the coordinators to contribute any ideas or concerns they felt would be relevant to the study at any point during the interview.
7 Students were asked to sign a detailed informed consent form.
8 Of the 13, 11 were female and two were male. Those who only completed one of the two questionnaires were not analyzed in this study.
9 Throughout, the italics emphasis is mine. All of the names are pseudonyms.
10 Chard (1999: 48–9) explains that a typical rhetorical strategy was to highlight the difference of the foreign space by setting it in direct, symmetrical, opposition to the familiarity of home. She demonstrates that these types of expression have survived various transformations in travel writing style that have taken place in the nineteenth and twentieth centuries—and have since become naturalized.
11 Families were selected via an informal process carried out by the Canadian coordinators and the local Nicaraguan community partners with whom they had developed the program over the years.

References

Ahmed, S. 2004. *The Cultural Politics of Emotion.* New York: Routledge.

Anderson, K. and S. J. Smith. 2001. "Editorial: Emotional Geographies," *Transactions of the Institute of British Geographers*, 26 (1): 7–10.

Chard, C. 1999. *Pleasure and Guilt on the Grand Tour: Travel Writing and Imaginative Geography, 1600–1830.* Manchester: Manchester University Press.

Flam, H. 2013. "The Transnational Movement for Truth, Justice and Reconciliation as an Emotional (Rule) Regime?" *Journal of Political Power*, 6 (3): 363–83.

Flam, H. 2009. "Extreme Feelings and Feelings at Extremes" in D. Hopkins, J. Kleres, H. Flam, and H. Kuzmics (eds) *Theorizing Emotions: Sociological Explorations and Applications*: 73–93. Frankfurt, New York: Campus.

Hochschild, A. R. 2003. *The Managed Heart: Commercialization of Human Feeling.* 20th anniversary edition. Berkeley: University of California Press.

Mahrouse, G. 2011. "Feel Good Tourism: The Ethical Option for Socially-Conscious Westerners," *ACME: An International E-Journal of Critical Geographies*, 10 (3): 372–91.

Mahrouse, G. 2014. *Conflicted Commitments: Race, Privilege, and Power in Solidarity Activism.* Montreal: McGill Queen's University Press.

Said, E. 1978. *Orientalism.* London: Routledge.

Part V

Emotions in visuals

Chapter 21

Visuals and emotions in social movements

Helena Flam and Nicole Doerr

Visual methods have been attracting many researchers interested in social movements[1] and public protest. This text, heavily modified by Helena Flam and extended to consider emotions, takes as its starting point an excerpt from a forthcoming text by Nicole Doerr, and offers a short "how-to" introduction to the field of visual analysis. It also suggests how to address the emotions that visuals convey.

Visual analysis refers to the development of concepts and methods to study visual elements generated and/or spread by social movement activists. Visual iconography focuses on photographs, posters, or material visuals in newspapers and media—tracing them back to their historical precursors and the emotions they evoked (Müller 2003). Focal in this volume are the emotions these precursors were meant to evoke and the question of whether the present-day visuals that echo these precursors still generate similar or other emotions (see Falk, and further down). A broader approach, inspired by socio-linguistics and discourse analysis, focuses on mentally constructed images expressed in different discursive forms as visual images (Kress and van Leeuwen 2006). Research on emotions suggests that those who generate specific visuals or texts expect their viewers to feel or at least be already familiar with them; or, alternatively, wish to impose specific feeling rules or an emotional regime on their viewers (Hochschild 1979; Reddy 1997). For example, Billig (1995) argues that love for one's country and a general preparedness to make sacrifices for it is evoked by everyday images and symbols—such as the national flag, currency, stamp, or a media photo or a text about the national football team. From a true patriot the same bi-modal emotional rule regime requires that a visual or text representing a national enemy evokes hatred and preparedness for combat—even if the battlefield is the local playground or the supermarket (Flam and Beauzamy 2008). Next we propose a few methodological instruments that help "to see visuals."

Visuals and social movements

We can distinguish three broad areas of research on social movements which lend themselves to visual analysis (Doerr *et al.* 2012: xii). Each is capable of generating a research project in its own right, and each is associated with a distinct methodological question:

1 what is the "visual expression" of issues and self-images important to a social movement?
2 what is, or what are, the "visual representation(s)" of a social movement by external actors?
3 how visible is this social movement in a given society?

The selection of visual material should start with consideration of a broad range of image categories—including visuals and representations that pop up in discourses on a specific topic—in order to consider what the focus should be. Before starting the analysis, prepare a checklist asking: which images, metaphors, pictures, or symbols have to be included—and which can be ignored—to answer the main research question. Is the visual analysis to be combined (triangulated) with other investigative methods? To pursue the question of which emotions specific images, metaphors, or symbols evoke, make a parallel decision about which of them must be included to represent the feeling rules or the emotions they convey. If a specific emotion or emotional constellation is of interest, material suggesting its various expressions has to be selected.

Next, write down elements which will help to contextualize the material to be analyzed, asking: (1) how does, or did, the central image to be studied interact as a symbol with its representations in pictures, paintings, flyers, videos, or photographs; (2) who created the original image(s), and which brokers have been engaged in the process of diffusion; and (3) which audiences are addressed by an image, and, if you have material on this, how do these audiences interpret the image(s).

A parallel effort should go into tracing if, and how and why, the initial feeling rules and emotion(s) conveyed by the original image became modified in the subsequent versions of it. The images themselves should call forth empathetic irritation in the researcher (Bauer 2013; on critical visual literacy, see Kress and van Leeuwen 2006). This term stands for engaging with the object of study at both a symbolic and emotional level, without becoming its captive or losing critical distance and reflection. Knowing who created, who reproduced, or who recreated the images—just as knowing which audiences these were directed at—assists the reflective-empathetic, yet critical distancing processes. It enables the very first educated guesses about the feeling rules and emotions mediated by the series of images at hand.

To ease into the analysis one can start either with public discourses about visuals, or the official visuals themselves. The next step would be to look for contrary or "hidden transcripts" (Scott 1990), and the "hidden visuals"[2] generated by social movements. This enables us to analyze how these reproduce, but also how they challenge the official discourses and symbols. Crises, catastrophes, and public controversies make it easier for normally-submerged discourses and images to be taken up by the official mass media—so if cleavages and creases in the otherwise-smooth social fabric are of interest, then focusing on these guarantees good research results. Depending on the research objective, the collected material might only cover the time of their duration, or it might—for comparative, contrasting purposes—also include material gathered during a few "regular" days/weeks before and after the crisis, controversy, or catastrophe in question.

Taking the "Eurozone" crisis as an example: juxtaposing news images of EU politicians during one of their meetings, with those of German shoppers; or the visuals depicting burning Athens or Spanish students staging a sit-in, would very effectively show the official, mass media image of the EU split during the crisis. The selection confirms that in times of "crisis" the mass media—which normally focuses on the more official EU representation of events—makes an effort to capture protest activities, and in the process renders hitherto invisible movements and discourses visible. A closer look at these images and captions/commentaries would reveal whether the EU politicians looked happy, or worried and irritated; whether the German shoppers appeared happy-go-lucky, or desperate; and whether images of a burning Athens were meant to represent a national tragedy, or the work of mere rowdies. The analytical work would consist of selecting and sharpening indicators, applying them systematically to the material, and thinking through various interpretations to construct a compelling argument about the EU-imposed financial-political regime with its accompanying emotional regime and the emotional suffering it causes (Reddy 1999: 272). Arguably, the emotional regime imposed by the mass media visuals and discourses attributes blame to the amoral, fiscally irresponsible, or economically unsuccessful European South, and calls for antipathy, contempt, and hate towards it; while portraying protesters as empty-headed or destructive, and anti-European. Systematic analysis of visuals would show whether this is true, and possibly also reveal alternative discursive and emotional constructs.

To find "hidden" images of the same crisis, one could, for example, collect (from contrasting geographical areas) protest posters, buttons, or visuals represented by dissenting fly-posters. But the internet and social media are probably the most frequent starting points for research on political mobilization; and we turn next to the issue of how to do research that relies on these sources.

Challenges of data collection from online sites

For most topics, social media homepages, alternative media sites, or indeed Google, offer visuals and discourses that are excluded and run counter to those presented in official media. Any material that challenges official discourses and visuals is of interest. To stay with the "Eurozone" example, any visuals reversing the political and emotional regime by portraying international organizations, states, and decision-makers as powerful predators causing much unnecessary suffering in the European periphery—and featuring protesters as heroes—would confirm a challenge to the official version of reality propagated by the official mass media. The search should continue until social media reveal alternative political and emotional regimes, or force a conclusion that none can be found.

Social media

Facebook is obviously an attractive site for gathering new images from personal networks. However, a disadvantage here is that mainstream search engines—such as those operated by Google or Facebook—are subject to ever-changing user policy and privacy rules, as well as to an individualistic network design. These constitute an obstacle to media research—which requires standardized sources. Social media generate their own selection bias, just as newspaper analysis does. For example, if one is not part of a campaign and lacks access to the network that spread it, it is hard to track the career of specific images or to know if one's information is reliable.

Nevertheless, some interesting research results can be produced. Olesen (2013), for example, worked with online images depicting the torture and murder of Khaled Said by the Egyptian police in 2010. Olesen identified a series of visuals which turned Said into a symbol of the Arab Spring. In contrast to the defamation campaign launched by the authorities, Said's passport picture showed him as a typical, innocent, young urban Egyptian middle class person. The picture taken by his family in the morgue after a series of brutal police beatings showed Said's face disfigured out of all recognition. Olesen argues that protesters "appropriated" Said for their movement when they photographed themselves juxtaposed against his image. In this manner they transformed the visual, while spreading the message of universal victimhood. Olesen documented the online production of alternative visibilities among Egyptians, demonstrating that the photographs resonated with, and amplified, the existing injustice frames prevalent within that society. He concluded that it was not the post mortem photograph of Said itself which caused the powerful moral and emotional reaction; rather it was the photograph's sophisticated visual manipulation, and its diffusion by activists.

Analyzing a visual

There is considerable literature on how to learn to look closely at an image to see it fully—what is portrayed, and how it is portrayed (Müller 2003). Our examples focus instead on explicating emotions by closely inspecting the images, while relating them to discourses, movements, and myths.

A good start is to look at the visual in question and ask what it says to its viewers, and wherein lies its power. This first analytical step draws on our everyday knowledge of the world, its symbols, and its feeling rules. "All" we have to do is to see and to associate. This first step is intensely personal: it calls for emotional and interpretative engagement, and may produce very idiosyncratic results.

Banksy, the activist street graffiti artist, drew a young male figure caught in a moment of throwing—his left arm is stretched forward, aiming at a target, his head is turned in the same direction; his right arm is behind him, bent, holding the object about to be thrown. We only see a body caught in a movement. We are left to imagine the target, the surroundings, and the context. The upper part of the body is mostly black, the pants represented only by a few lines. Only the object about to be thrown is colorful.

The image generates a mild shock because it counters several expectations. The thrower's thin body, basketball cap, and the bandanna partly covering up his face compel the association with an urban guerrilla, a gang member, a terrorist, or a protester caught by a press photograph in

Figure 21.1 Banksy's flower thrower, © Scott Smith/Submedia.

the act of throwing. This thrower, however, does not hold a Molotov cocktail or a stone in his hand. Instead we see a bouquet of flowers. By putting flowers where a stone or a bomb would be, Banksy subverts the usual representations. He draws on, and simultaneously questions, the mass media and their portrayal of the young as the causers and wielders of violence. He lets this thrower make a statement against violence and for peace. But how? The visual features a young, frail body. It thus evokes David fighting against Goliath, and asks the viewer to sympathize with the pacifist David, engaged in an uneven struggle with the warmongering Goliath. But only David is in sight. Who is the Goliath here? A specific occupier or a nation? Or rather the military, the weapons industry, the politicians? The grown-ups? The visual leaves it to the viewer to answer this question. We can guess that the symbolic power of the visual stems from the decades, even centuries-long, pacifist movement. The thrower's flowers echo the joy of the flower children's movement and evoke the slogan "Make Love not War." But their flowers were free, anarchistic. Social Democratic parties' ads and campaign posters often feature flowers, but in a simple bunch. Banksy begs to differ. His colorful flowers are encased by the wrapper, and thus evoke a strong association with formal gifts and civilized social gatherings. Now it appears that the visual juxtaposes the beauty stemming from the constraints of civilization with the rampages of war. Is the thrower hoping to disarm the opponent with this typical Western gesture of gift-bearing; is he challenging his enemy to respond in kind? If so, he is as touching in his naïveté as the flower children were, making us both feel for him and saddened at the same time. Now he seems to be the bearer of lost causes. The sketch of the thrower's frail, young body possibly disarms our emotional defenses also because in the contemporary West we have a feeling rule that we are to love peace and be very sensitive towards children and young adults, their wishes, and their suffering. Here we see a young boy who—even in this seeming gesture of aggression—wishes for peace. Yet his bodily posture is assertive, not bent in supplication. He is not pleading for our compassion. This makes it harder to respond generously, with empathy. It irritates. It is much easier to agree to unconditional peace when seeing an image of an "innocent child" wounded or maimed by land mines. This was well understood by the worldwide anti-landmine campaign which swept the West in the 1990s. Instead this young man is demanding, looking challengingly ahead of himself—into the future? By disallowing any easy compassion, the visual prompts reflection. Can we deny the call for violence to end that is communicated by this youth? If we identify with his target, we feel discomfort or disdain. If we identify with the thrower, the graffiti possibly imbues us with hope; after all, the biblical David was victorious.

When one shares the worldview of the discourse and visual that one is investigating, it is relatively easy to associate it with the symbols, discourses, and myths it evokes. Arguably, one feels good about oneself and about the world when engaging in this type of self-confirming analysis, even if it frustrates and challenges from time to time. But looking deeper is necessary: both to discover elements that are beyond the reach of one's immediately accessible knowledge; and to highlight what otherwise would be lost due to one's own longstanding familiarity with specific arguments, words, or visuals—a familiarity which makes them "too obvious" to explicate. Pursuing single elements of a discourse or a visual using etymological and idiom dictionaries, encyclopedias, or other scientific/artistic literature, until one reaches a kind of investigative saturation point, helps formulate a more deeply rooted and convincing argument. Discussing one's interpretation with others is also helpful, as is the case with interview or discursive material. An intermediate or final step could be to interview the producers and/or viewers about what they "see."

Analyzing the discourses and visuals of those whose worldviews one does not share demands more in terms of knowledge acquisition. But the analytical steps are the same: free associations while drawing on one's everyday knowledge, first, intensive research, second. Some might also find it emotionally difficult to deal with deeply upsetting material day after day. It can be helpful to read about how others handle such upset (Brink 2000).

For example, Nicole Doerr (2010) found that while left wing activists working in the field of migration used cosmopolitan images of "Euroland" to criticize the EU's neoliberal political agenda, right wing political parties such as the "Swiss People's Party" (SVP) manipulated photographs of immigrants as "criminals" or used "black sheep" cartoons to visualize European nationalists pitted against the immigrants.

By combining the stereotype of the "black sheep" with the idea of immigrants as "criminal" and therefore deserving of deportation, the SVP propaganda effectively attached two different racist images to the entire population of immigrants living in Switzerland (Wodak 2013). The SVP's public campaign relied on an image that did not directly use a racist discourse, but at a visual level was meant to invoke strong feelings of hatred towards immigrants.

The "black sheep" poster constructed by the Swiss SVP rapidly spread across Western Europe on the blogs of the sympathizers of the German extreme right wing party, the NPD, and the Italian party, Lega Nord. Visual content analysis showed that Lega Nord had reproduced the original Swiss strong black sheep image—and simply replaced the Swiss national flag in the background with its own symbols and flag. The bloggers of the NPD went a step further. They constructed a shared racist European identity of the NPD, SVP, and Lega Nord—styled as "white sheep"—kicking out a black sheep from an imaginary European space. This, then, was the visual language of racism—a symbol for the EU space occupied by white sheep, kicking out the black sheep. "Google images" enabled researchers to find variations on the "black sheep" poster. Analysis of these, and a content analysis of extreme right wing texts, provided a first overview of how transnational solidarity works among extreme right wing movements and parties that are bent on communicating a multilingual message of hate.

How do visuals communicate contents and emotions? Let us take the many white and one black sheep image as an example. Which visual elements are important? What stereotypical associations pop into one's mind?

The distinction between an imagined "Swiss majority"/new fascist majority and the "immigrant minority" is expressed in the contrasting colors: white and black; and evoked by numbers: many white and just one black sheep. A dividing line between the white and black sheep implies disapproving group emotions and the implicit act of separation, rejection, or ostracism that they lead to. The in-group situated *within* the borders defines itself by its "whiteness"—understood as a positive property, since it is usually associated with innocence and purity in Western, Christian iconography. It defines the object of its exclusion or ostracism by its "blackness"—understood as a negative attribute, since it is usually associated in the West with being evil and threatening. By combining several layers of familiar cultural iconography, the cartoon's racist political idea can be easily recognized by Western audiences without any explicit recourse to racist discourses. Using only a few elements, the claim is effectively conveyed that whiteness is superior, and should remain privileged, supremacist—cultivated and celebrated at a distance from other "races." The cartoon in an early, probably Swiss, version evokes this demand without requiring any further explanation. It does not depict exactly *how* the black sheep threaten or are rejected by the white sheep. It does not have to. It can rely on our tacit knowledge of familiar arguments and cultural stereotypes. Most onlookers will already be aware of the discourse that suggests a minority of migrants seek to contaminate, ruin, deprave, or outnumber the native majority—which is therefore justified in taking measures to protect itself.

At first glance the cartoon seems rather innocent. It merely asserts the difference of color that should be sustained by separation. But since the cartoon is publicized as part of a political campaign for votes, and since the flag of Switzerland is near white sheep, it relies on the everyday association between "white/Swiss/good" and "black/migrant/evil" to convey its message to voters that they should feel threatened and mobilize for the party willing to remove the threat.

Unlike this (presumably) earlier SVP poster, (presumably) subsequent posters of the SVP and of the new fascist bloggers' make explicit and radicalize the original visual and emotional message. In the (presumably) later

Figure 21.2 Image of an SVP election campaign poster (reproduced with kind permission of the photographer, Claude Longchamp. www.flickr.com/photos/stadtwanderer/1114522237).

posters, one white sheep is actually kicking out the black sheep beyond the Swiss/EU borders. The act of "kicking out" makes hatred in action visible to all. The poster of the new fascist bloggers transposes the same idea to the EU.

The intent of making the new fascist movement, and its demands, seem innocent—even though it engages in the sort of hate propaganda and racial discrimination that is illegal in many European countries and in the EU— becomes evident when we reflect upon the fact that the cartoon sheep look sweet, cute, and cuddly. This makes us want to embrace them. Endless other ways of portraying them could have been chosen, but were not. This is surely intentional; although, paradoxically, the new fascists behind these posters are indeed the proverbial wolf in sheep's clothing.

The cartoon does not show how the black sheep feels. The implicit feeling rule is: you should empathize with your likes but the fate or emotions of the "unlikes" is none of your concern. Care about your likes, feel indifference toward all others beyond the borders of your nation and/or of the EU. At first sight it might seem ironic that the cartoon evokes the image of a "black sheep in the family"—which implicitly defines the strange/deviant/different as somehow belonging. But perhaps this is not ironic, but rather intentional. Since migrants of various skin colors have become part of everyday life in all European countries—which has in turn led to policies being adopted throughout the EU to facilitate their integration—the extreme right wing parties have, in their own way, recognized migrants' advanced state of "belonging" and are now calling for disengagement. Online "counter-cartoons" saying "I am the black sheep of the family and proud of it," or "Even black sheep of the family need love," underline that a black sheep, even if criticized and frowned upon, is still a family member. The new fascist cartoons implicitly recognize, then, that the EU and many of its member states have become familiar with that which the extreme right still insists on defining as "foreign" and therefore in need of being removed. But the extreme right is not interested in how rejection, exclusion, and ostracism feel to the black sheep. Theirs is a promotion of a self-centered, unbiblical feeling rule: love thyself and thyself only.

Even without the necessary second research step—which would involve perusing other sources—this snapshot analysis of just two visuals demonstrates that this process can be very helpful in deciphering vital parts of the political message generated by the extreme right. The fact that the expression "black sheep" is known in Afrikaans, Bosnian, Czech, Dutch, French, German, English, German, Greek, Polish, Portuguese, Romanian, Serbian, Slovak, Swedish, and Turkish, and that it has its roots in the Old Testament, and that there are almost countless literary and visual elaborations upon it, goes a long way towards accounting for its rapid adoption and diffusion by the European extreme right wing parties. It speaks for itself.

Conclusion

This chapter has shown how visual analysis of images produced by both official sources and social movements can contribute to interdisciplinary research on emotions. After discussing the problems of data selection, we offered several examples of visual analysis to show how one can find out which feeling rules or emotions they are likely to evoke. We proposed a multi-step analysis of visual images that focuses on the context of image production and the content of the image itself—including its complicated aesthetic, political, and emotional messages. Our analysis has not focused on the audiences, or on the variety of interpretations that a single image can provoke among sympathizers, opponents, and bystanders, or in different national and political contexts. However, we were still able to suggest why a specific pacifist image surprises, delights, and imbues with hope like-minded individuals; and why two new fascist images in support of racial hatred are able to travel easily across national borders.

Notes

1 Visual analysis seconds research on movement-framing, mobilization, and impact in digitalized public arenas.

2 We should distinguish between the official, hidden, and borderline visuals, just as we distinguish between white, black (censored), and gray (border-crossing) literature in repressive regimes.

References

Bauer, J. 2013. "Empathie und historische Alteritätserfahrungen" in J. Bauer and M. Lücke (eds) *Emotionen, Geschichte und historisches Lernen*: 75–92. Göttingen: V&R unipress.

Billig, M. 1995. *Banal Nationalism*. London: Sage.

Brink, C. 2000. "Secular Icons: Looking at Photographs from Nazi Concentration Camps," *History & Memory*, 12 (1): 135–50.

Doerr, N. 2010. "Politicizing Precarity, Producing Visual Dialogues on Migration: Transnational Public Spaces in Social Movements," *Forum: Qualitative Social Research*, 11 (2). Available at: www.qualitative-research.net/index.php/fqs/article/view/1485 (last accessed December 29, 2014).

Doerr, N., A. Mattoni, and S. Teune. 2012. "Introduction," *Special Issue on 'Advances in the Visual Analysis of Social Movements' of Research on Conflict, Social Movements, and Political Change*, 35: xi–xxvi.

Flam, H. and B. Beauzamy. 2008. "Symbolic Violence" in G. Delanty, R. Wodak, and P. Jones (eds) *Identity, Belonging and Migration*: 221–40. Liverpool: University of Liverpool Press.

Hochschild, A. 1979. "Emotion Work, Feeling Rules and Social Structure," *American Journal of Sociology*, 85 (3): 551–75.

Kress, G. R. and T. van Leeuwen. 2006. *Reading Images: The Grammar of Visual Design*. London: Routledge.

Müller, M. 2003. *Grundlagen der visuellen Kommunikation. Theorieansätze und Analysemethoden*. Konstanz: UVK Medien/UTB.

Olesen, T. 2013. "'We are all Khaled Said': Visual Injustice Symbols in the Egyptian Revolution, 2010–2011" in N. Doerr, A. Mattoni, and S. Teune (eds) *Advances in the Visual Analysis of Social Movements* (Research in Social Movements, Conflicts and Change, Volume 35): 3–25. Bradford: Emerald Group Publishing Limited.

Reddy, W. M. 1997. "Against Constructionism: The Historical Ethnography of Emotions," *Current Anthropology*, 38 (3): 327–51.

Reddy, W. M. 1999. "Emotional Liberty: Politics and History in the Anthropology of Emotions," *Cultural Anthropology*, 14 (2): 256–88.

Scott, J. 1990. *Domination and the Arts of Resistance: Hidden Scripts*. New Haven: Yale University Press.

Wodak, R. 2013. "'Anything Goes' – The Haiderization of Europe" in R. Wodak, M. Khosravinik, and B. Mral (eds) *Rightwing Populism in Europe: Politics and Discourse*: 23–38. London: Bloomsbury.

Chapter 22

Evoking emotions

The visual construction of fear and compassion[1]

Francesca Falk

In 1992 Oliviero Toscani chose a photograph of an overcrowded boat for his provocative Benetton campaign.[2] Interestingly, however, it was not only Benetton that used this imagery—various right wing parties also chose to use it. In the 1990s the German right-wing party Die Republikaner used a poster of a "Noah's Ark"-type vessel overcrowded with immigrants; and in 2002 Lega Nord used a similar motif for an anti-migration campaign (Pagenstecher 2008: 610).[3] Today, boat people clambering ashore at Europe's borders are frequently portrayed by the European media; yet most of the numerous victims who die at sea during these crossings remain invisible. It is usually the survivors who are depicted in the media, not the dead or dying, or the actual sinking of the boats. On the other hand, "successful" and therefore unobserved passages also go "undocumented."

The image of the over-full boat can vary: Noah's Ark could in fact have a positive connotation in a Christian context; while a ship full of Albanian refugees waving happily upon arrival in Italy may transport another message—as is the case in the example mentioned above.[4] Such pictures are often polyvalent—their meaning and emotional charge can change according to the context since they contain a multiplicity of possibilities. The viewer can feel, for instance, compassion, pity, or fear—or a combination of all of these. However, generally speaking, packed ships have the potential to evoke a feeling of threat and thus fear. Given such ambiguities, it is necessary to propose a framework for defining how concrete images relate to their iconic lineage, and to wider discourses beyond the visual realm. This will allow for an analysis of the emotionality of each particular image.

However, the image of the "cramped boat" is not limited to the visual domain. During World War II, Eduard von Steiger, a member of the Swiss government, referred to Switzerland as being a proverbial lifeboat in distress, with scarce supplies and restricted room (Häsler 1989: 180). By claiming that there was a lack of space and resources in Switzerland, he wanted to legitimize a policy of highly restrictive admission of refugees. Many of those refugees who were refused entry as part of this tightening up of admission procedures later died in German extermination camps. Nevertheless, after the war, Switzerland imagined and presented itself as a humanitarian haven that had afforded protection to those who had needed it—as depicted in a huge two-part poster designed by Victor Surbek in 1946.

The poster, portraying Switzerland—and especially the Swiss army—in a heroic light, was used as part of an exhibition that was displayed in several Swiss cities just after the war. The aim of the poster was to help raise money for the war-damaged countries of Europe. Even though Switzerland is shown here as an almost full lifeboat, there is still room for one more person—and so a strong man is depicted as unhesitatingly reaching out to rescue another drowning man. In actual fact, during the war Switzerland for a long time granted asylum only to refugees who were under personal threat owing to their political activities, and not to those who were in danger as a result of their religion or ethnicity. More than 20 years later, in 1967, Alfred Häsler initiated a critical discussion about Swiss refugee politics during the World War II in his book *The Boat Is Full.* Some 12 years later, in 1979, the same author wrote an article about refugees coming from Indochina. Häsler urged Switzerland to accept more fugitives; the title of his article was: *Our Boat Is Not Full.* It was at this time that the term "boat people" came into common usage with the mass departure of Vietnamese refugees.

Today, the European icon for "illegal immigration" seems to be condensed to cramped boats full of male Africans. But the term "icon," as it is used here, doesn't designate a particular photograph. In fact, similar pictures circulate widely. These images constitute a visual place of memory. However, this does not mean that such pictures are effective only on a visual level. In Byzantine times, icons were already characterized by an interrelation between the picture and the inscription. Furthermore, the boundary between words and images has fluctuated in the course of history (Foucault 1997). Icons do not possess a stable status: an icon does not stand for all time, and its meaning can change according to the context (Perlmutter 1998: 10). For example, cramped boats can recall memory of the overcrowded ships that transported slaves—but such a connection is not necessarily made in modern times since the colonial context of immigration has been rendered invisible.

Strikingly, in photos of boat people arriving in Europe, they are often received by people wearing masks. In such pictures, migration meets medicine—and the military. This is the case in a photograph by the European Pressphoto agency. The caption reads:

> In the early hours of Monday, 20 October 2003, Carabinieri assist a severely dehydrated and starving immigrant Somali man as he is brought to the Lampedusa island harbor—an island midway between

> Tunisia and Sicily. Coastguards counted 13 dead bodies on the wooden vessel when it was spotted last night off the island.

The situation shown and described here clearly differs from the image of the cramped boat. We see a fragile individual, who arrived, as the caption says, in a wooden vessel and not in a big fishing cutter. Some of his fellow passengers have died on the way. The flabby arm and the drooping hand reveal the weakness of the Somali—a weakness that contrasts with the strong body of the man supporting him who is also wearing a white glove and a mask. This composition recalls countless representations of the *Pietà*. Meaning "pity" or "compassion" in Italian, a *Pietà* depicts the pain and grief of the sorrowful Virgin Mary and other bystanders as they lament the suffering and death of Christ. One example is the painting by

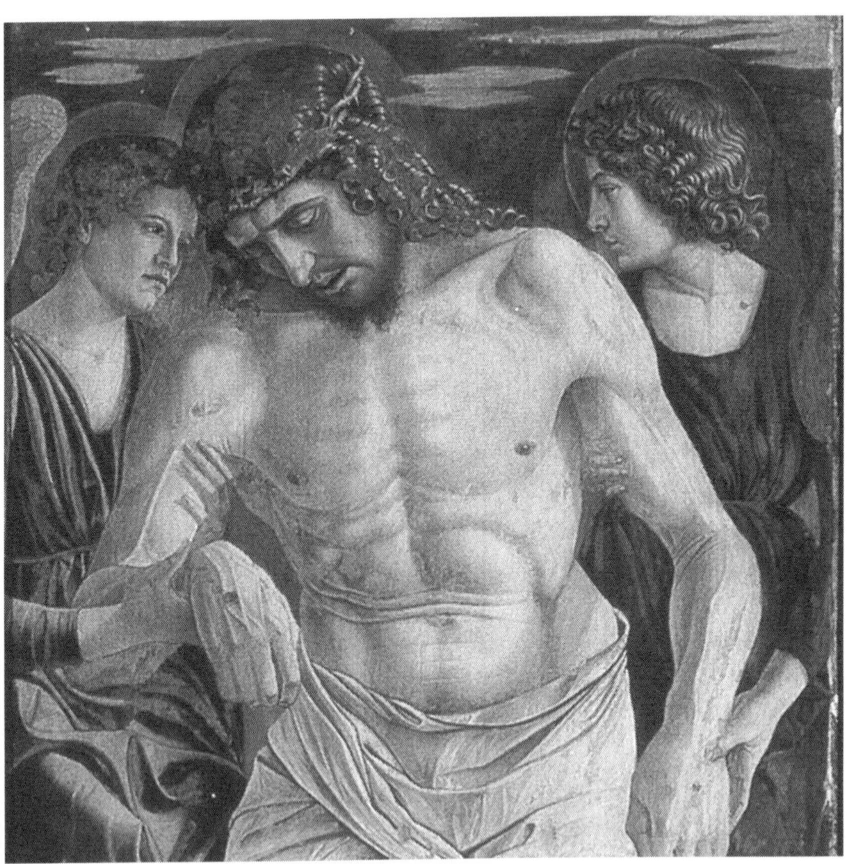

Figure 22.1 Giovanni Bellini, polyptych of St Vincent Ferrer, 72/67 cm, Basilica of St John and St Paul in Venice, 1465–8.

Giovanni Bellini in the Basilica of St John and St Paul in Venice.[5] On a polyptych of St Vincent Ferrer, a Spanish Dominican, Jesus is supported in a very similar way to the Somali refugee in the picture taken at the harbor of Lampedusa. An angel holds the bent arm of Jesus, so that the stigmata of Christ become visible. We can find the same posture, though as a reversed image, in the photograph of the Somali refugee.

I have no way of telling whether the photographer or someone at the European Pressphoto agency consciously had the image of the *Pietà* in mind when selecting this particular picture from a number of possible alternatives. However, a visual tradition can cause a déjà vu effect (Leggewie 2000: 156), thereby influencing the way a photo is perceived, even unconsciously (Assmann 1998: 30). In particular, visual traditions have a constitutive effect on the emotional content that viewers find in an image. The immigrant from Somalia thus appears here in visual imitation of the *Pietà*: as an innocent victim. Images of refugees in the tradition of Christian iconography are in fact widespread. For instance, you can find a motif recalling the Madonna with her child on the cover of Seyla Benhabib's book *The Right of Others* (2004), in which the author argues for the ideal of porous borders.[6] And in the poster by Surbek, see especially how the upper part of one refugee's body is depicted in reference to Michelangelo's famous *Pietà*. But iconology always requires a certain amount of shared understanding and feeling.

Aby Warburg employed the term "iconology" as early as the beginning of the twentieth century. His work was also important for the interpretation of emotions, suffering, and passion conserved in images.[7] Iconology was subsequently developed by Erwin Panofsky (1975 [1955]).[8] Regarding our example of the full boat, it cannot be assumed that everyone viewing Surbek's image will make such an association with the *Pietà*. We are therefore dealing here with a particular way of looking at a picture that is generated by a specific cultural context. Images refer to other images and in so doing produce specific meanings and emotions.

To identify such image references, research of online picture archives[9] and collaboration with art historians can often prove very fruitful. The interpretation of reproduced gestures and facial expressions can also vary considerably. It can therefore be rewarding to conduct an empirical analysis of the reception of such images by interviewing viewers (who have been selected using specific criteria) about how *they* interpret them. An image will be viewed quite differently by a migrant, a civil rights activist, and a supporter of the right wing Lega Nord movement. It is therefore necessary to reflect the synergy of internal and external images, since mental pictures not only form our view of external images, but also determine to whom or to what we direct our attention and emotions in the first place.

Photographs are always taken from a specific perspective, and representations that show immigrants as victims are one-sided insofar as migrants are active agents and not merely passive victims without agency (see here Fassin 2001: 5; Bleiker and Kay 2007: 149). They act in order to change their situation, even if the price is very high. There is, however, an important difference between the pictures of the polyptych of St Vincent Ferrer and the Somali refugee—the latter is alive and staring right at us, thus breaking out of his role as a passive victim. At the same time, the picture of the Somali can evoke not only pity or compassion, but also fear—the mask hinting at the possibility of infection. This fear is born of the discursive and iconic connection between infection and immigration. Here, territorial borders are superimposed on the boundaries of the body; migration appears at the same time as an assault upon the integrity of one's own body and on that of Europe. Such images become part of our collective and cultural memory and thereby shape the perception of immigration as a threat. What is perceived as familiar or unfamiliar, as being part of the community or not, is very often the result of mental and material images: communities are imagined and thus constituted among others by shared feeling, often constructed through certain kinds of visualization.

In this paper I contrasted two types of picture portrayed by the European media, and featuring boat people. Immigration, here, is depicted either as an invasion, with refugees appearing as an anonymous and threatening mass—or an individual refugee is portrayed as a victim, following the tradition of Christian iconography and evoking compassion in the process. The analyzed image of the cramped boat, and the image showing a victim, are thus connoted differently and evoke different feelings. Nevertheless, both share some common features. For a European public, such pictures evoke a clear distinction between "us" and "them"—the threatened or compassionate Europeans, and the "others" (the refugees), who either have to be helped or expelled. In both kinds of representation—the one that generates compassion and the one that evokes fear—the reasons for leaving the country of origin remain invisible, and with them the context that shows in what way this migration is linked to our history and present.

List of images mentioned in the text

Several pictures mentioned in the text could not be reproduced here for copyright reasons. Readers can find them online:

Oliviero Toscani, Benetton Group Campaign 1992. www.pubenstock.com/2012/benetton-les-annees-toscani (last accessed October 10, 2014).

Victor Surbek, lithograph, 1946, 127/182cm, Basler Plakatsammlung, available at the Swiss Poster Collection online at: http://ccsa.admin.ch/cgi-bin/gw/chameleon?skin=affiches&lng=de&inst=consortium&host=biblio.admin.c

h%2b3603%2bDEFAULT&patronhost=biblio.admin.ch%203603%20DEFAULT&search=KEYWORD&searchid=H4&function=CARDSCR&sourcescreen=INITREQ&pos=3&itempos=1&rootsearch=KEYWORD (last accessed October 10, 2014).

Franco Lannino, Italian Carabinieri assist a severely dehydrated and starving immigrant Somali man, October 20, 2003. Photograph: EPA/Keystone, available at: www.epa.eu/politics-photos/migration-photos/immigrant-boat-deaths-photos-00072473 (last accessed October 10, 2014).

Notes

1 This article is based on Falk (2013, 2010a, 2010b).
2 This picture was taken in August 1991 in the Albanian town of Durrës; see Pagenstecher (2008: 610).
3 See also www.leganord.org/ilmovimento/manifesti2002.asp (accessed March 5, 2010).
4 See: www.corbisimages.com/Enlargement/Enlargement.aspx?id=TL017003&caller=search (accessed March 5, 2010).
5 This piece of art was created in 1460, but the attribution is contested. However, for the point I am making here the question of authorship is immaterial.
6 The photo recalling a Madonna was taken by Sebastian Bolesch in Afghanistan in 2002.
7 See Warburg http://warburg.sas.ac.uk/photographic-collection/iconographic-database.
8 Today his approach is criticized as being sometimes too text-oriented, too much focused on the Renaissance, and doing too little justice to the imagery contained within the images.
9 See for example http://prometheus-bildarchiv.de.

References

Assmann, A. 1998. "Frauenbilder im Männergedächtnis bei Pater, Proust und Joyce" in M. Strunk (ed.) *Bildergedächtnis, Gedächtnisbilder*: 24–65. Zürich: Edition Howeg.

Benhabib, S. 2004. *The Rights of Others. Aliens, Residents, and Citizens.* Cambridge: University Press.

Bleiker, R. and A. Kay. 2007. "Representing HIV/AIDS in Africa: Pluralist Photography and Local Empowerment," *International Migration Review*, 51: 139–63.

Falk, F. 2010a. "Europe – A View from the Margins. Boat People and the Memory of Images" in B. Drechsel and C. Leggewie (eds) *United in Visual Diversity. Images and Counter-Images of Europe*: 180–5. Innsbruck: Studienverlag.

Falk, F. 2010b. "Invasion, Infection, Invisibility: An Iconology of Illegalized Immigration" in C. Bischoff, F. Falk, and S. Kafehsy (eds) *Images of Illegalized Immigration. Towards a Critical Iconology of Politics*: 83–100. Bielefeld: Transcript.

Falk, F. 2013. "Öffentliche Bilder analyiseren" in C. Bischoff, W. Leimgruber, and K. Oehme (eds) *Empirisches Arbeiten in der Kulturanthropologie. Ein Studienbuch.* Bern: Haupt.

Fassin, D. 2001. "The Biopolitics of Otherness," *Anthropology Today*, 17: 3–7.

Foucault, M. 1997. *Dies ist keine Pfeife.* München: Carl Hanser.

Häsler, A. A. 1989. *Das Boot ist voll: Die Schweiz und die Flüchtlinge 1933–1945.* Zürich: Diogenes.

Leggewie, C. 2000. *Amerikas Welt: Die USA in unseren Köpfen.* Hamburg: Hoffmann und Campe.

Pagenstecher, C. 2008. "'Das Boot ist voll.' Schreckensvision des vereinten Deutschland" in G. Paul (ed.) *Das Jahrhundert der Bilder. 1949 bis heute*: 606–13. Göttingen: Vandenhoeck & Ruprecht.

Perlmutter, D. D. 1998. *Photojournalism and Foreign Policy: Icons of Outrage in International Crises.* Westport, Connecticut: Praeger.

Part VI

Documented emotions

Chapter 23

"My heart belongs to daddy"

Emotion and narration in early modern self-narratives

Claudia Jarzebowski

> So I want to warn you laddie
> Though I know that you're perfectly swell
> That my heart belongs to Daddy
> Cause my Daddy, he treats it so well
>
> (Cole Porter, 1938)

This song, sung by artists such as Mary Martin as early as 1938, and by Pat Kirkwood and Marilyn Monroe in 1960, has been iconic ever since. It is still one of the most played songs at wedding parties! To turn down love relations for the love of one's father might appear an outdated concept; however, it worked (tongue-in-cheek) on stage. Memoirs, too, serve as stages for one's life narration and, as we will see below, "daddy" remains equally important as a point of reference in self-justification. But while musicals and movies create artificial figures, autobiographical writings refigure one's own life. Self-narratives as a life-staging source reveal the ambiguous entanglements of the narrated life, as well as its narration. This is all the more true in early modern history—when this type of narration was more popular than it would be nowadays. In particular, members of the political elite—kings, queens, dukes, and duchesses—had a strong inclination to "keep the record straight." Many sovereigns chose to write their own memoirs or put together autobiographical compilations. Today historians refer to these as self-narratives.

Memoirs and autobiographies authored during the nineteenth century typically addressed the writer's own descendants. The author claimed to bear witness to his or her family's fate, and his or her own more-or-less successful life. The intended audience was clearly one's own family. In contrast, in early modern history, authors of self-narratives seem to have anticipated a wider public as their readership. Early modern narratives present a challenge of interpretation since they attempt to bridge literary ambition, autobiographical input, anticipated responses, and the reconstruction of historical "reality."

In this text I will show that one of the distinctive features of pre-modern self-narrations is how they interweave narration and emotion. Thus, emotions can be grasped in a two-fold manner: as a topic of narration, and as a narrative strategy. My argument runs contrary to the modern historiography of feeling. Still, my novel perspective on emotions, their meanings, and functions in a text written in the early modern period reveals a promising yet unexplored approach.

According to historians of the modern era, emotions were a substantial ingredient in bourgeois family life as it evolved from the late eighteenth century onwards. For a long time, however, a parallel but false image of a non-emotional pre-modernity prevailed. In fact, emotions were not invented in modern history, not even as a distinguishing mark of the bourgeois family (Karant-Nunn 2010). It is true that emotions did undergo a significant shift of paradigms in the symbolic order, but they were exiled into the sphere of femininity, privacy, and nature—and posited as the very opposite of the putative male sphere of reason, public politics, and culture. This dichotomy is itself an invention of the late eighteenth and nineteenth century,[1] and therefore lacks any legitimacy for understanding how emotions worked in early modern history. The same invention casts emotions as intensely connected to feelings, and feelings as intensely connected to the inner life of an individual—be they alone, or situated among a stable or accidental transitory collective. The notion of the "inner feeling" has become very influential. It refers to, and concomitantly establishes, a universal notion of an individual sufficiently coherent to embody and to constitute a "container of feeling." Scholars of transcultural history have contested the notion of a coherent individual constant over a lifetime, as universalizing. Indeed, upon closer examination, this notion referred to white, Christian, middle-class men of the nineteenth century becoming "universalized" against all odds.

Recent contestation and findings pose the question of how, then, early modern men and women of different social status perceived and constructed themselves—through narration, portraits or state documents—for the afterworld. Natalie Zemon Davis is one of the very few early modernists to have spelled out the add-on-value of transcultural, and what she calls—tellingly—decentered perspectives:

> Rightly done, such history is always relational: the history of women involves men, the history of peasants involves proprietors; the history of workers involves employers. But even while describing all the parties, the decentering historian may let the subalterns and their practices and beliefs carry the narrative.
>
> (Davis 2011: 190)

This approach justifies my choice of Christina of Sweden, and her memoirs, as a starting point for my investigation of emotions in pre-modern self-narratives.

Her *Memorabilities* are at the same time exemplary and exceptional. They are exemplary in that they belong to the genre of memoirs frequently left behind by political leaders of this period. They are exceptional in that they have been authored by a queen—a queen of northern Europe who abdicated her throne in order to convert to Catholicism and turn to a poor, monastic lifestyle. Only Charles V before her had dared do this—in 1556. Christina's voice is representative and subaltern at the same time.

Christina of Sweden is one of the most enigmatic figures in early modern European history (Atkinson 1989). Born in 1626, she was the only heir of the then fledgling Swedish monarchy.[2] Her father, Gustav Adolph, a famous and fierce defender of Protestantism during the Thirty Years' War (1618–48), died in a battle in 1632, leaving young Christina with great responsibility. She was named queen by a guardian committee previously selected by her father, two months after his death. The committee had been assigned the task of taking care of Christina's education and upbringing. Having spent her younger years in the care of her late father's sister, she now moved to the Swedish court and—according to her own writings—had a fabulous time among such learned men of honor. When she turned 18 years old, in 1644, she officially took over the monarchy, keeping the committee at her side. But just 11 years later Christina abdicated, converting to Catholicism soon after. She left Stockholm and Sweden, and headed for Rome. There she lived intermittently until her death in 1689, at the age of 62.

Christina's life has raised many suspicions among historians, and from an interested public. These suspicions center on the issue of her non-marriage and reports of her wearing manly attire following her abdication.[3] They also appear to be based on her on-off relationship with her companion Ebba Sparre up to 1662, with queer history positing Christina as an icon of lesbianism.[4] In broader historical debates, however, her memoirs—*La Vie de la Reine Christine Faite par Elle-Même, Dédiée à Dieu*—attract attention because the extensive reflections on gender and marriage have resulted in an intense methodological and historical debate about patchwork identities and identity-building (Aurelius 1997).

As I will show, at the very center of Christina's (self-)reflections, emotions emerge as a legitimizing force for her decisions and for her conduct. Emotions come to the fore also as a narrative strategy, building up the drama of the text in such a way as to garner support for her view of things. If one looks closely at where, when, and how emotions feature strongly, one sees that they help structure the narrated life as much as the narrative-writing itself.

In order to lead the modern reader through the thicket of early modern history and self-narratives, let me first introduce Christina's memoirs according to her life stages: from her birth, to her education, through to her reign and eventual abdication. The aim is to (re)create a rudimentary narrative (self-)construction—to which, step by step, further analytical elements can be attached. In this particular case the focus will be on emotions and the question of when, and for what purposes, they surface in the narrative. I will show how one can answer this question by taking a closer look at two narration patterns: the narrative marker of divine love, and the construction of narrative spaces where various dimensions of life, and issues of central importance, cross over. Finally, I will present Christina's "language of tears" as a political language.

Life stages

It is a peculiarity of early modern self-narratives that the authors remember their own birth as if they had been capable of witnessing it from a distant perspective. In Christina's case, after her mother had miscarried twice, astrologers had foretold a boy. This prediction was confirmed by her mother's dreams. But:

> I was born cauled from the head to the knees, with only my face, arms, and legs free. I was completely hairy, I had a deep and strong voice. All these things made the midwives believe that I was a boy. They filled the palace with a false joy, which deceived the king himself for a while. Hope and desire helped mislead everybody, but it caused great consternation for the women when they realized that they were wrong. They were at a loss how to disabuse the king. Princess Catherine[5] ... carried me in her arms in such a position for the king to see me and to make him perceive what she did not dare say to him.... That great prince did not express any surprise at all; he took me in his arms and made me as welcome as if he had not been wrong in his expectation. He said to the princess: "Let us thank God, my sister. I hope that this girl will be worth a boy to me. I ask God to preserve her for me, since he has given her to me."
>
> (Atkinson 1989: 414)[6]

Christina's life, according to her own account, started with a tremendous misunderstanding that involved everybody but her father. He was able to see her—to perceive her beyond her mere physiological appearance as a girl—as the future ruler of Sweden, thus cutting through the gender issue. In her words, this insight was inextricably attached to God's agency, expressed through the figure of Gustav Adolph who ordered the celebration of her birth as the birth of the future sovereign.

Father the king thus stages Christina's gender as being of God's choice, and as a choice of love. In her narration Christina distinguishes several types of love: the love that attaches her to her father, and her father to her, all sparked by divine inspiration. Gustav Adolph is able to love Christina as she is, because God's love reaches her through her father's capacity for opening his heart. Christina thus grants herself a dual descent—from God, and from her father, the king. This narrative strategy leaves no room for a mother. While comparing her mother's and her father's feelings towards their newborn child, Christina makes this very clear:

> The queen, my mother, who had all the weaknesses as well as all the virtues of her sex, was inconsolable. She could not abide me, because she said that I was a girl and ugly; and she was not greatly in the wrong, because I was as swarthy as a little Moor. My father loved me very much, and I responded accordingly to his love in a manner that surpassed my age. It seemed that I perceived the differences in their merits and their feelings, and that I began to do justice to them from the cradle.
>
> (Atkinson 1989: 414)

Christina links the capacity to perceive and receive divine love (as a means of ascent to worldly power) to gender. She portrays her mother as a typical woman—both weak and virtuous, and unable to transcend the limits of her gender. As such she is not able to perceive and receive divine love. This pattern reappears throughout the *Memorabilities*. It reverberates also at the very end when Christina expresses her gratitude to those who prevented her mother from taking over the guardianship of her underage daughter—as was the case, for example, with Catherine de Medici of France.[7] Her rejection of the confines to which women of her time were sentenced could not be clearer.

As well as gender, Christina attributes age as being important in defining her "elect" status. Her inclination to present herself as God's agent on earth follows, for her, also from the fact that part of her personality is apparently ageless. This, too, reverberates on many occasions throughout the text—as, for example, when Christina refers to her teachers' admiration for her capacity to learn, "so rare in a child of my age" (Atkinson 1989: 419). Christina ascribes to herself a notion of divine love that makes her body appear ageless and genderless.

My analysis suggests that for an early modern text it is fruitful to look for emotions as narrative markers. A narrative marker—in this case, divine love—emerges to account for the special qualities and/or special status of the narrator. These qualities and status have political implications—they set the stage for subsequent developments. In *Memorabilities*, divine love emerges as a narrative marker with its own logic, one that affects only the "elect." Even at birth it sets action into motion.

When Christina turns to her personality, emotions also play a substantial role. Christina describes herself as almost free of physical needs. This includes, explicitly, erotic desire. But still, she complains about her corrupt nature and her failure to tame her temperament:

> I was mistrustful, suspicious, and also ambitious to excess. I was irascible and hotheaded, vain and impatient, scornful and jeering.... I know well that I can suppress them when I wish. But I do not know if I had ever tried seriously to tame them completely. It is your grace alone, Lord, which has prevented them from carrying me away.... [M]y hot and impetuous temperament did not give me less inclination for love than for ambition.
>
> (Atkinson 1989: 419)

It is important to note that Christina's thinking is in line with Cartesian notions of the body, emotions, and temper (see, for example, her letters to Descartes, in Descartes 1909). According to Descartes, the body is an ambiguous territory as far as temper and self-control are concerned. The red line is marked by the heart. If one's heart belongs to God, one is—in the context of early modern terms—bound for heaven. The red line is crossed if temper reigns the heart. Christina attributes to God her capacity for not crossing this line. She says her heart has always belonged to God; or, alternatively, that God had always kept it for her:

> You gave me a heart which should not be occupied except by you.... You were to be the sole object of my desires. This heart was yours from the moment it beat in my being.... You alone did miracles in this heart, which make you so much more glorious because they have you alone for spectator and witness.... I contributed nothing to all that except my unworthiness and nothing more remains for me but to let you act and admire you.
>
> (Atkinson 1989: 420)

Concerning emotion and narration, I suggest that these, and similar passages, have to be read as building blocks which serve to construct specific narrative spaces in which multiple subjectivities (Somers 1994: 630) can cross over. On the one hand, these narrative spaces posit a hot tempered, physically deprived Christina beyond the reach of erotic desires of any kind. On the other hand, they posit her as the sole instrument of God. This narrative strategy opens space for a discussion of two fundamental issues in her life: her non-marriage, and her abdication and conversion. These interweave. A marriage, argues Christina, would have made her a woman, and as such subject to her husband's will. She frankly anticipates that she would have loved her kingdom more than any child she might have had (Atkinson 1989: 420, 423).[8] Here she returns to her main theme: God, rather than a kingdom or a child, has been the leading master of her life. He filled her heart with His love. He filled her father's heart with love for his newborn child, converting her father the King into the Lord's own instrument. His will was to install Christina as his messenger on earth.

However unconvincing these arguments might sound to modern ears, Christina legitimizes her conversion as an act of God—His will acted upon her and drove her to religious conversion.

We know that Christina worked on and modified *Memorabilities* continuously, until her death. By creating narrative spaces Christina bridges her life, and her narration of it. These spaces allow her to retrospectively express doubts and hesitations about key decisions. This becomes clear, too, when she describes her teachers' and tutors' absolute devastation about her abdication and conversion. These people were her father's closest companions. Their disappointment brings her late father back to her because it echoes his likely disappointment. Christina's capacity to abandon the Protestant confession by following her heart elevates her to a spiritual level that was unachievable for her father—even though he came close when he proclaimed her as the successor to his throne. In her act of converting to Catholicism, God-father trumps father trumps mother, to cut a long story short.

The language of tears

The distinction between different kinds of love that are categorized by their source and direction (ego—God—heart—body), resurfaces in the language of tears.[9] Gustav Adolph had been one of the most important leaders of the Protestant forces during the Thirty Years' War (1618–48). As Christina recalls, at one time she went up to him as a six-year-old girl in order to bid her farewells since he was bound to leave for another battle. Instead of listening to her recitation he

> took me in his arms and embraced me and could not hold back his tears.... [W]hen he left, I cried so hard for three whole days without stopping that it did so much damage to my eyes that I was on the verge of losing my sight.... My tears were taken as evil omens, especially because I normally cried little and rarely.
>
> (Atkinson 1989: 417)

Since Gustav Adolph never returned, this scene conveys the close bond between father/king and daughter/future queen. Tears here become the fluid of empowerment. Everybody present, as Christina points out, noted and remembered this event. Court's attention highlights the exceptionality of their crying together. Neither were known as cowards, which links the tears to a future to come rather than at the sadness of parting. The king's tears emerge as the language of God speaking through his heart and his eyes—tears that were shared by Christina and her father. The tears serve the narrative and supra-narrative purpose of embodying the power of God as a distinguishing feature for those who are able to feel it, and let

Him act through oneself. In this scene of shared emotion and prescience, Gustav Adolph passes down dynastic power, as embodied by his and Christina's shared tears. Unsurprisingly, her mother's tears represent the mere physical language of tears—as opposed to a shared spiritual language. When the mother comes to court in order to bury her husband (two years after his death—Christina was eight years old at this point), the burial becomes an (at this time unheard of) celebration in terms of grandeur and (staged) grief. Her mother, Maria Eleonora, according to Christina's account, drowned her daughter in tears—unable to overcome this apparent need to shed tears she cried night and day for many weeks (Atkinson 1989: 422).

As we have come to know by now, Christina was not telling her story just for the sake of it, but to make a political statement. Only a few pages later she informs the reader that women should never be allowed to reign over a country (Atkinson 1989: 423). This harsh statement has led future generations of historians to label her a misogynist. Upon closer examination, however, one becomes aware of this scene as just another example of Christina's continuous attempts at self-degendering in order to establish her body as spiritual. In all her attempts to establish her spiritual non-gendered body as a container for her multifaceted personality—which she contrasts with the then prevalent concept of destiny—emotions serve as a narrative marker of distinction. Following Christina's thoughtfully demonstrated ways of God, enables historians to improve their understanding of the meaning and the function of tears in the language of politics and emotion in early modern history.

Emotions: narrative markers and narrative spaces

Emotions by themselves—as expressed emotions, or narratively vivified markers of royal court politics or religious affection—cannot serve as a silver bullet for historical investigations. However, as I have shown, considering emotions' functions in narration as modes of building social and political relations will add substantially to our understanding of early modern history. An approach that identifies emotions as narrative markers in early modern texts helps us to tease out their social and political implications. Narrative spaces constructed in self-narrations serve the function of helping to resolve conflicting life dimensions and discursive threads. They serve as bridging and productive links. As we can see by following Christina in her *Memorabilities*, these genuinely important narrative spaces are constructed with the help of emotions. They constitute a space for opening and dismissing claims about gender, but also about the legitimacy of spiritual and worldly power and life. Beyond reflections, they also entail decisions and actions—including those looked upon retrospectively by Christina and prospectively by her political and spiritual contemporaries.

In these two ways—i.e., looking at emotions as narrative markers and as narrative spaces—my text has shown how to reintegrate emotions into the political history of early modern Europe (see Jarzebowski and Kwaschik 2013), and thus how to reach this rather unexpected, novel, understanding. From Christina's point of view, her heart belonged to at least two "daddies"—the spiritual one and the worldly one. This is why she was able to become a leader without descendants, a convert, and a royal dropout.

Acknowledgments

I have discussed earlier versions of this paper at the Early Modern History and Renaissance Study Group at the University of Western Australia; and at the TEEME-colloquium at the Free University in Berlin. I want to thank those who participated in these discussions and helped to push forward the ideas in this paper. Concerning Swedish research literature, and the history of the various editions and translations, I am deeply indebted to Francisca Hoyer.

Notes

1 Pierre Bourdieu has termed this as "la division de monde."
2 In 1523 Gustav Wasa I was been elected as the first King of Sweden.
3 Upon closer inspection, this manly attire is meant to reflect the habitus of a scholar—alluding to her longed for self-perception (see Cavalli-Bjoerkman 1997).
4 This reading had been sparked by movies such as *Queen Christina* (1933), starring Greta Garbo as Christina.
5 The sister of Gustav Adolph.
6 Atkinson's translation is based on the German edition of Johan Arckenholtz: *Historische Merckwürdigkeiten die Königinn Christina von Schweden betreffend*, 4 volumes, Leipzig and Amsterdam, 1751–60. The so-called Arckenholtz edition is based on one of three manuscripts available at that time. One of these manuscripts is kept in Paris at the Bibliotheque Nationale, the others are available at the Riksarkivet of Sweden in Stockholm as part of the Azzolino Collection. A full edition is expected for 2015 (www.sol.lu.se/en/project/394). I compared the English quotations with the German and French precursors, and marked possible disparities.
7 Catherine de Medici occupied the French throne intermittently for many years, each time functioning as legal guardian for her young sons.
8 She emphasizes the slave-like character of any wife.
9 For a fundamental contribution to the language of tears in eighteenth century writings, see Ulbrich (2012).

References

Atkinson, J. L. 1989. "Queen Christina of Sweden. Sovereign Between Throne and Altar" in K. M. Wilson and F. Warnke (eds) *Women Writers of the Seventeenth Century*: 405–27. Athens, London: University of Georgia Press

Aurelius, H. E. 1997. "The Great Performance. Roles in Queen Christina's Autobiography" in M.-L. Rodén (ed.) *Politics and Culture in the Age of Christina*: 55–67. Stockholm: Astrom

Cavalli-Bjoerkman, G. 1997. "Christina Portraits" in M.-L. Rodén (ed.) *Politics and Culture in the Age of Christina*: 93–107. Stockholm: Astrom

Davis, N. Z. 2011. "Decentering History: Local Stories and Cultural Crossings in a Global World," *History and Theory*, 50: 188–202.

Descartes. R. 1909. *La Princesse Élisabeth et la Reine Christine. D'Après des Lettres Inédites.* Paris: F. Alcan.

Jarzebowski, C. and A. Kwaschik. 2013. *Performing Emotions. Zum Verhältnis von Politik und Emotion in der Frühen Neuzeit und in der Moderne.* Göttingen: Vandenhoeck & Ruprecht Unipress.

Karant-Nunn, S. 2010. *The Reformation of Feeling. Shaping the Religious Emotions in Early Modern Germany.* Oxford: Oxford University Press.

Somers, M. R. 1994. "The Narrative Construction of Identity. A Relational and Network Approach," *Theory and Society*, 23: 605–49.

Ulbrich, C. 2012. "Tränenspektakel. Die Lebensgeschichte der Luise Charlotte von Schwerin (1731) zwischen Frömmigkeitspraxis und Selbstinszenierung," *L'Homme. Zeitschrift für feministische Geschichtswissenschaft*, 23 (1): 27–42.

Chapter 24

How to detect emotions?

The cancer taboo and its challenge to a history of emotions

Bettina Hitzer

In 1977, Chicago journalist Jory Graham confronted her readers with the extremely upsetting story of the parents who discovered their 13-year-old daughter's diary after she had died from cancer. The diary revealed that, unbeknown to them, their daughter had known about her terminal diagnosis all along—but had kept it a secret because she believed that her parents were unaware of the seriousness of her condition. The girl wrote about her fear of dying and her despair at having to cope alone. Her parents had known of their daughter's condition but had kept this truth hidden to protect her from the terrible reality of impending death. Jory Graham, who had herself undergone breast cancer surgery and radiation treatment, wanted to shake up her readers with the story and "break through the emotional isolation and unparalleled aloneness of all who are living with and dying of cancer" (*Milwaukee Journal* 1983). She pursued the same goal when she promised readers of her fortnightly column "Time to Live" that she would let them know if and when her illness became terminal. She kept her promise. Six years later, shortly before her death, she wrote: "That time [to die] has come, and you and I need to begin the painful, yet necessary, process of learning to say goodby [*sic*]" (*Milwaukee Journal* 1983).[1]

Cancer studies mark the post-World War II years as an era of keeping silent about cancer, using metaphors and allegories about it—thus contributing to the social isolation and stigmatization of cancer patients. Jory Graham's story is part of a shift that began in the early 1960s and gained widespread momentum in the 1970s.[2] Described as a taboo-breaking development in cancer studies history, it entailed an offensive, often polemical and provocative campaign against the secrecy surrounding cancer and death. Talking about cancer openly, and discussing the illness in its specific physical manifestations, became regarded as the healthiest and most honest way of dealing with the disease, both on a personal and political level.[3]

The issue of cancer as taboo poses a series of methodological problems. Skeptical historians point out that it is hard to identify inner, hidden emotions—in contrast to overt, expressed ones—even if the expressed emotions are accessible through archival documents. Using this argument, mainstream historians often dismiss the history of emotions as unfeasible. As far as the cancer taboo is concerned, the problem is even more acute, since the silence imposed about the disease itself makes the expression of emotions related to it even less likely to appear, and thus even more problematic for study—available documentation may itself be evasive regarding the emotions attached to it. As long as cancer remained taboo, the feelings of the cancer patients themselves were like a void: perceived but not filled.

How, then, did I, as a historian, go about examining these possibly-felt but not-communicated emotions? First, I had to learn what the cancer taboo meant, how it worked, and in what ways it was relaxed in order to capture the context in terms of classical hermeneutics. Archive and secondary literature research provided the essential contextual information which revealed that the so-called cancer taboo has a long history (Aronowitz 2007; Kauz 2010). Here I will confine myself to the 1940s and 1950s, and to a Western world in which—as I found out—cancer, despite all the taboo-related talk, was not actually so until the point of diagnosis. In most Western countries, prevention campaigns provided information about the early symptoms of many different types of cancer, as well as possible therapies. With the promise "early caught—curable," all adults were encouraged to examine themselves and go for regular check-ups. Even in the remotest corners of the Western world it was apparently known that cancer might show no symptoms in its early stages. A poem, written by the Austrian dialect poet Hannes Grabher, tells about *Kreäbsangscht* (fear of cancer) in a conversation between two village women, and concludes: "Ich abr han jôhrwils/ko Schmeärzo mi g'ha/und dies ist das Gföhrli [I do not suffer pain and that's dangerous]."[4]

The silence began after diagnosis. Only in rare cases did families share with friends and acquaintances that someone in their midst was suffering from cancer. Hospital stays and follow-up treatment were usually concealed or attributed to other ailments (Dornheim 1983). Relatives were often afraid that their loved ones would be stigmatized (since there was a widespread belief that cancer was spread by germs); and that touching the sick and the dying was at the very least awkward, and perhaps also dangerous in the sense of "summoning death." But during the course of my research I began to doubt that this was the only reason. As several contemporary surveys confirmed,[5] doctors seldom told patients that they had been diagnosed with cancer. Instead, cancer patients were usually told that they had a benign tumor that would need to be operated upon to prevent further degeneration. In West Germany, numerous doctors were opposed to the foundation of specialist cancer clinics on the grounds that they might jeopardize patient confidentiality, while health insurance and pension funds used shared code words and numbers to avoid use of the word "cancer" in their records and documents.[6] Doctors would share their diagnosis with a patient's next of kin, but the vast majority of physicians were convinced that it was an unnecessary (even dangerous) cruelty to tell patients the truth about their condition.

Even though most people diagnosed with cancer were kept in the dark, I found out that they were not completely unaware of their condition. When I turned to medical journals, psychology, theology, law literature, and the popular press, I found a discussion about the so-called "truth on the sickbed." There seemed to be a general consensus that many, if not most, patients guessed the seriousness of their condition as a result of the public campaigns that were raising awareness about different types of cancer and its therapeutic options. Unlike the later generation of "taboo-breakers," however, a large number of physicians found this state of ignorance or uncertainty among their patients both positive and helpful. They argued that suspicion was easier for the patients to handle than certainty. They claimed that certainty was synonymous with a feeling of hopelessness and despair, while mere guesswork about their true condition allowed for optimism and hope.

But when I began to analyze the cancer stories, which were increasing in number during the 1960s and 1970s, I learned that patients and their families felt that this professional opinion was itself cruel. Many cancer stories adopted this perspective, which contributed towards a shift in "cancer as taboo" to "cancer as an issue." The stories of the patients themselves highlighted the emotional significance of this shift. Turning cancer into an issue helped the victims move away from despair and loneliness—with professional support—towards an honest, authentically felt, and empathetically accompanied, emotional coping strategy.

Working on these stories, I realized that I, too, was deeply influenced and shaped by the norm of authenticity and emotional expressiveness. I was convinced that expressing and working on "negative" feelings was therapeutic and promoted spiritual balance. Like many other historians before me, I was (and am) inclined to naturalize my own emotions and refrain from perceiving them as historically and culturally influenced. Nevertheless, adopting the same perspective on emotions as the one expressed in cancer stories which are still current today is methodologically risky. Arguably, the moral judgments associated with the silence that surrounded cancer in the 1950s had changed by the 1970s—when medical paternalism gave way to a destigmatizing openness about cancer and death. The new style of emotional expressiveness, and the psychoanalytical view that repressed or suppressed emotions could be both physically and psychologically harmful, were not only drivers of change—they also influenced how this secrecy was interpreted and felt (Biess 2008).

How, then, can one read the growing number of later personal testimonies that describe the suffering felt as a result of the cancer taboo—testimonies which advocate for an open approach to the disease? This question prompted me to reflect some more about a basic assumption in the history of emotions and mentalities that implies the existence of a rather slow rate of transformation of feelings—a process that requires decades, if not centuries, to take place.

In contrast, I would argue that one should not take this assumption of a *longue durée* in emotional transformation for granted; but rather ask how quickly or how slowly changes in emotions and emotional norms—what Stearns calls emotionology (Stearns and Stearns 1985; Harré 1986)—could and did take place. Those personal testimonies of the 1960s and 1970s provided information about what many cancer patients remembered feeling when dealing with their illness, and the secrecy that surrounded it. But I realized that deciding whether such testimonies revealed what cancer patients had felt (but not dared express) before, or whether they described emotions that changed in parallel with the changing times and attitudes towards cancer itself, could not be established using the testimonies alone. Oral history interviews with the few people who were diagnosed with cancer in the 1950s, and were still alive today, would be possible—but this process would present a major and perhaps insurmountable methodological challenge, since the drastic shift in norms pertaining to cancer and cancer-related emotions might have influenced their retrospective narration (Gammerl 2009). In any case, since contemporary eye-witnesses (i.e., surviving cancer patients) from the 1950s would be scarce (or hard to trace), corroboration would be almost impossible to achieve.

In the end I opted for two different methodological approaches that opened a path—albeit a rocky one—for tracing the feelings of cancer patients of the 1940s and 1950s. William Reddy's concept of emotive, as well as the emphasis on praxeological and artefactual dimensions of emotions (Reddy 1997; Scheer 2012; Reckwitz 2012), led me down this path.

Based on Reddy's views, I assumed that emotions are initially just activated thought material, and that they become relevant only once they are named. Naming emotions is rarely without consequences, be it by triggering an introspection process ("do I really feel what I just said I did?"), or by giving what is felt a particular direction and meaning, or by comparisons triggering emotional responses. Reddy uses the term emotive to refer to a mix of the constative (universally descriptive expressions such as "the table is white") and performative (universal, condition-altering statements such as "I do," as in the case of a couple exchanging marriage vows). This means that the emotive only rarely fully encompasses the emotion. What is felt provides a potential. Different discourses and habitual changes affect this potential—they override some and highlight other feelings (Reddy 1997).

Inspecting professional discourses suggests that the representatives of those professions that dealt with cancer patients saw these patients as particularly harmonious and altruistic. They understood these positive emotions as a legitimation of their choice to keep the truth about their impending death from them.

There are numerous reports by physicians, psychologists, and hospital chaplains describing daily encounters in hospitals and focusing on the psychological state of cancer patients. These reports must be read critically, or with what Jan Plamper calls the "hermeneutics of silence" (Plamper 2012). The aim is to discover the taboo by deciphering the micro-logic of texts, taking into account local emotional cultures. Furthermore, one should pay special attention to the metaphors used in the texts since they could offer a kind of "secret" pathway into the otherwise hidden emotions (Kövecses 2000).

When analyzing the micro-logic of these texts, one discovers that the reports did not intend to justify the secrecy or concealment of cancer-related feelings. On the contrary, they often advocated more truthfulness towards the patients, and highlighted a critical attitude towards hiding the diagnosis and avoiding talking about cancer and the feelings related to it. Even though the authors had different interests in writing such reports—either they wished to advertise their medical success, or were interested in the psychological profile of cancer patients, or they probed the doctor/patient relationship or searched for psychosomatic explanations for carcinogenesis—most shared a feeling of amazement when observing the apparent emotional "balance" and optimism demonstrated by most cancer patients.

In 1946, two neurologists wrote about the "psyche of cancer patients":

> For many cancer patients there is a pronounced dissimulation. They are inclined to attribute even severe disease symptoms to trivial causes.... In hospitals, cancer patients are the quiet, silent patients.... Cancer patients are good-natured, mostly pleasant, and easy to open up. They act mostly in good faith, have an optimistic outlook on life, and demonstrate a simple and straightforward way of thinking.
>
> (Kretz and Pötzl 1946: 20)

Some ten years later, a hospital chaplain continued in the same vein:

> You would think that with their physical condition, and their less obvious psychological and mental condition, cancer patients would display a certain despair, bitterness, and depression. Actually, this is not the case. Anyone dealing with cancer patients wonders again and again over the peace and serenity that they display. One marvels at the bravery, the utmost patience and strength with which cancer patients cope with their severe pain.... In my experience, cancer patients are very sociable, even altruistic. We find people who speak with great

> concern about their families, care about their loved ones, and whose love and compassion are extended to the other patients in the ward.
> (Bolech 1958: 355–6)

According to hospital staff, at least, the felt and expressed emotions were not fear, despair, and emotional isolation, but rather emotional balance, empathy, and compassion, i.e., "active" emotions, related to other people. Returning to Reddy's model of emotives: can it be assumed that, at least in the late 1940s and 1950s, the taboo—as well as the emotional expectations in accordance with a certain more general emotional style of self-composure and fear-avoiding optimism—help the suspecting (but unknowing) patients to "produce" mental balance through a life of sympathy and affection that leaves all other feelings (like fear and despair) unnamed and thus unperceived? And did emotional balance as emotive consequently lead to an emotional practice of love and compassion? But how can the perceived shift in "feeling cancer" be explained?

A different methodological perspective might help to approximate the answer, taking into account the role of spaces and artifacts in structuring emotional practices. Based on this line of thought, Andreas Reckwitz proposes extending the usual assumption of praxeological intersubjectivity to the concept of interobjectivity (Reckwitz 2012). Adopting this perspective helps to explore the socially relevant emotions in the tabooed space between experience and expression. In the 1950s a new space and a new artifact related to cancer treatment were invented: the so-called cobalt gun, and the room in which it was located. These turned out to be of crucial importance for the "new," or at least newly expressed, feeling of emotional isolation. Tumors have been treated with radiotherapy since the beginning of the twentieth century, but cobalt was employed and became widely used in the 1950s. The gammatron, as it was formally known, was almost always located in the basement of hospitals due to the strong radiation it produced. Relatives were not allowed to accompany patients to treatment. Even radiologists and nurses would only stay in these rooms for as long as it took to help patients assume the right position under the gammatron's gigantic arm. The gammatron rotated for several minutes as if steered by an invisible hand, passing over patients underneath who were abandoned in the bare, concrete-lined room. The press, presenting the gammatron as a technical innovation of the West in the Cold War era, drew parallels between the cobalt gun and the atom bomb (see, for example, *Der Spiegel* 1958; Leopold 2008).

Patient diaries, which often mentioned gammatron radiation therapy, described feelings of abandonment and helplessness—feelings that became even stronger and were combined with fear, despair, and anger when it later turned out that cobalt radiation was hard to control and resulted in burns to the skin's surface or even deeper skin layers.[7] As a new artifact, as well as a new area of cancer treatment, the gammatron had a decisive role in enabling the feeling and experience of emotional isolation, named and expressed in a powerful way. The practice of gammatron radiation supports the argument that the feeling of emotional isolation—which may have existed before but only in an indefinite and non-specific form—came to be felt much more sharply, and in a way that could be actually experienced, named, and expressed.

In this short text it has been demonstrated that the cancer taboo poses a particular methodological challenge for the history of emotions since it accentuates the much-discussed problem of a possible distance between feeling as an inner experience and feeling as an outward expression. The methodological assumption that only feelings that are *communicated* in some manner bear social importance is, in this context, particularly problematic. Where personal accounts are not available—although they might have existed as a form of emotional practice—questions remain. Projections of later self-narratives into the past follow a very difficult path, methodologically, since the rate and speed of the changes of emotions in question remain unclear, and bear no relation to previously conceived notions of a slow rate of emotional change. A precise context reconstruction is the prerequisite for opening up new paths that are more relevant to the history of emotions. An approach based on the "hermeneutics of silence" concept, as suggested by Jan Plamper, is one such path to address narrative, logical, and other "textual disturbances." A praxeological approach that places particular emphasis on the constitutive importance of the emotive—as well as the objectivity of the human/space/artifact interaction—allows for a plausible convergence of the experienced and expressed emotions. Additionally, it allows us to formulate research questions that are not based on the experience/expression dichotomy, but rather focus on observable practices.

Acknowledgments

I would like to thank Benno Gammerl, Jan Plamper, Monique Scheer, as well as the editors of this book—Helena Flam and Jochen Kleres—for their constructive criticism and invaluable insights.

Notes

1 Jory Graham's column "Time to Live" appeared between 1977–83, first in the *Daily News* and then in the *Sun Times* (both based in Chicago). The column was then reprinted in a series of American dailies. Jory Graham's column, and particularly the story of the young cancer sufferer, attracted attention even in Germany—see *Der Spiegel* (1977).

2 Sociologists, anthropologists, as well as psychiatrists and psychologists, contributed to the shift in talking about, and researching, cancer and death. A

groundbreaking study in sociology was Barney Glaser and Anselm Strauss's *Awareness of Dying* (1965), which analyzed the interactions between healthcare personnel and terminally ill patients. Their main argument was that terminally ill patients were surrounded by silence, or euphemisms, concerning their impending death—despite their efforts to get factual information about their health situation. In a similar vein, psychiatrist Elisabeth Kübler-Ross conducted a study based on interviews with dying people, later published as the classic text, *On Death & Dying* (1969). She advocated a more truthful and open approach, arguing that facing death openly would initiate the psychological process of grieving and dying that consisted (ideally) of five stages, and would eventually lead to acceptance by the victim. An important contribution to this shift was also made by Erving Goffman. Goffman, in his influential *Asylums* (1961), did not consider cancer or terminally ill patients in the study, but rather psychiatric patients. Goffman—among others—explored how hospitalization affected patients' (or inmates') notion of self, as well as their behavior towards personnel working in what he defined as total institutions. As part of the anti-psychiatry movement of the 1960s, he bolstered a critical attitude towards the then commonly accepted doctor/patient relationship—which was conceived of as patriarchic, and which therefore forced patients into the role of being a "good patient."

3 Sontag's *Illness as Metaphor* (1978) represents a multitude of taboo-breaking press articles, personal testimonies, and columns.
4 The poem is written in the dialect of Vorarlberg, the westernmost federal state of Austria. See Grabher (1963: 116–17).
5 For the USA see Fitts and Ravdin (1953: 901–4), and Oken (1961: 1120–8).
6 See the following statement: "To avoid unpleasantness, personnel are advised to avoid the term 'cancer' in all circumstances when talking or writing to patients and their relatives … and to ensure that no documents contain this term." (Director of the Rhineland Regional Council, Department of Social and Health Services III, clause for the Chief Executive Officer to combat cancer (NRW), Dr Spohr. Düsseldorf, June 23, 1958, Bundesarchiv BArch B 142/3434: 311–13 (p. 313)).
7 In fact, burns were among the side-effects of all radiation therapy, but not on this scale. It was with good reason that one of the first "informed consent" trials concerned the side-effects of radiation therapy. See Natanson versus Kline [1960] in Leopold (2008: 42–58).

References

Aronowitz, R. A. 2007. *Unnatural History. Breast Cancer and American Society*. Cambridge: Cambridge University Press.

Biess, F. 2008. "Die Sensibilisierung des Subjekts: Angst und 'Neue Subjektivität' in den 1970er Jahren," *Werkstatt Geschichte*, 49: 51–71.

Bolech, P. 1958. "Die seelsorgerliche Betreuung der Krebskranken als besondere Aufgabe," *Der Krebsarzt*, 13 (8): 353–60.

Der Spiegel. 1958. "Krebs: Die Kobalt-Kanone." 17 December, p. 51.

Der Spiegel. 1977. "Voll Bitterkeit." December 12: 207–9.

Dornheim, J. 1983. *Kranksein im dörflichen Alltag. Soziokulturelle Aspekte des Umgangs mit Krebs*. Tübingen: Tübinger Vereinigung für Volkskunde e.V.

Fitts, W. and I. S. Ravdin. 1953. "What Philadelphia Physicians Tell Patients with Cancer," *Journal of the American Medical Association*, 153 (10): 901–4.

Gammerl, B. 2009. "Erinnerte Liebe. Was kann eine Oral History zur Geschichte der Gefühle und der Homosexualitäten beitragen?" *Geschichte und Gesellschaft*, 35 (2): 314–45.

Glaser, B. G. and A. L. Strauss. 1965. *Awareness of Dying*. Chicago: Aldine Publishing Company.

Goffman, E. 1961. *Asylums. Essays on the Social Situation of Mental Patients and Other Inmates*. New York: Doubleday.

Grabher, H. 1963. "Kreäbsangscht" in *So is's Läobo*, Lustenau: 116–17, published by the author.

Harré, R. (ed.). 1986. *The Social Construction of Emotion*. Oxford: Basil Blackwell.

Kauz, D. 2010. *Vom Tabu zum Thema? 100 Jahre Krebsbekämpfung in der Schweiz 1910–2010*. Basel: Schwabe Verlag.

Kövecses, Z. 2000. *Metaphor and Emotion. Language, Culture, and Body in Human Feeling*. Cambridge, New York: Cambridge University Press.

Kretz, J. and O. Pötzl. 1946. "Die Psyche des Krebskranken," *Der Krebsarzt*, 1 (1): 19–29.

Kübler-Ross, E. 1969. *On Death & Dying*. New York: Simon & Schuster.

Leopold, E. 2008. *Under the Radar. Cancer and the Cold War*. Chapel Hill: Rutgers University Press 2008.

Milwaukee Journal. 1983. "Jory Graham took time to live," May 13.

Oken, D. 1961. "What to Tell Cancer Patients. A Study of Medical Attitudes." *Journal of the American Medical Association*, 175 (13): 1120–8.

Plamper, J. 2012. *Geschichte und Gefühl: Grundlagen der Emotionsgeschichte*. München: Siedler.

Reckwitz, A. 2012. "Affective Spaces" in *Emotional Styles – Concepts and Challenges* (special section of *Rethinking History*, 16 (2): 241–58, edited by B. Gammerl.)

Reddy, W. M. 1997. "Against Constructionism. The Historical Ethnography of Emotions," *Current Anthropology*, 38 (3): 327–51.

Reddy, W. M. 2001. *The Navigation of Feeling. A Framework for the History of Emotions*. Cambridge: Cambridge University Press.

Scheer, M. 2012. "Are Emotions a Kind of Practice (And Is That What Makes Them Have a History)," *History and Theory*, 51 (2): 193–220.

Sontag, S. 1978. "Illness as Metaphor," *New York Review of Books*, 24 (21–2): 10–16.

Stearns, P. N. and C. Z. Stearns. 1985. "Emotionology. Clarifying the History of Emotions and Emotional Standards," *The American Historical Review*, 90 (4): 813–30.

Chapter 25

The geography and temporality of emotions

Helena Flam

John Cheever suffered from constant, "incontinent" desire. It never let him be. It made him yearn for both objects and people: a chalice noticed during a Sunday sermon, a random woman seen in the street. He tried to attend to it, but found it unruly, capricious, urging—a source of much excitement, anxiety, fear, and deepest sadness in his life. There is no doubt that at the very center of Cheever's emotional geography stood his desire.

John Cheever (1912–82) was a much-acclaimed, award-winning American writer, a contemporary of Saul Bellow, Philip Roth, and Vladimir Nabokov. After his death, Cheever left behind his journals in 29 loose-leaf notebooks, and a wish to have them published (Cheever 2008: vii)[1]—even though he was perfectly well aware that this would forever ruin his respectable public image. It is on these edited journals that this text builds.[2]

My purpose with the analysis of John Cheever's emotional geography is to suggest how one can investigate emotions expressed by a single person over a longer period to time in, for example, journals and diaries. Arguably, these are a way for a person to take their own emotional pulse, or keep their own emotion logs. In contrast to memoirs, letters, or emails—which represent as part of a dialog more of a public image-shaping endeavor that entails a considerable dose of justification or self-aggrandizement (Jarzebowski, this volume), journals and diaries are more self-focused. Unlike autobiographic, narrative interviews that rely on recollections, journals take note of concurrent emotions. They constitute a free space in which their authors form and sustain their selves by engaging in an inner dialog. Being in control, they have a chance to tell their "truth." The claim of my text is that it fairly accurately and succinctly reproduces quite a bit of John Cheever's "truth"—his emotional geography. I owe this in part to Cheever's obsessions, reiterated in many beautiful notes. Only in conclusion do I address "the objective truth about John Cheever."

In Lacan's linguistic theory of the unconscious, desire assumes a central role. It is the energy invested by human beings in search of fulfillment and recognition in and against a world of symbolic distortions. Desire stands also for a void within—a distance of oneself from oneself that can only be satisfied by the recognition by and/or possession of the other. Since in the world of symbolic distortions the other exists merely as the signifier of something else, the moments when "desire appears to cohere with its objects [are] fugitive and transitory"—desire can never be satisfied (Thomas 2013: 1–4). Thomas Hardy apparently anticipated Lacanian theory in exploring the role of desire in the conception of the self and the subjectivity. Hardy stressed "the persistent, obsessive, frustrating and essentially narcissistic nature of desire; its necessary objectification in forms that ultimately fail to satisfy the desiring subject; and its fundamental importance as the energy behind creative endeavor" (Thomas 2013: 3).

When, for the purposes of this analysis, I reread these pages, my first inclination was to contrast Lacan's or Hardy's all-encompassing concepts of desire with John Cheever's reductionist experience of it. Sometimes his desire amounted to no more than a desire for sex. Still, it was much more than this. Often it implied a wish for a ritual consecrating life, a creative explosion, or a promise of creativity. It dovetailed with the great issues raised by human existence, and of his own substance and contours. John Cheever's *Journals* help to highlight the role desire plays in the constitution of the self. But in addition they help clarify how emotions can and do constrain desire.

For much of his life John Cheever experienced desire as a painful longing for sex, and for human touch—for a heart-warming embrace of the beloved. *The Wapshot Scandal* (2003b: 161, 171) has as its refrain his own dream of: "Oh, the wind and the rain and to hold in one's arms a willing love!" Indeed, Cheever saw himself as suffering from a permanent "earth-shaking, back-breaking, binding, grinding need for love" (Cheever 2003b: 301). He conflated sex and love as can be seen from the following passage: "I don't know what to do. I must sleep with someone, and I am so hungry for love" (p. 234).

Cheever was often both perturbed by, and ponderous about, his desire. He found it unruly, comparable to a misbehaving child or a turbulent river (see Soriano, this volume). He experienced it as nagging and urging, constantly pressing its demands against his will. It took his mind on "sinful"—sometimes pleasant, sometimes dangerous and scary—(day) dreaming escapades. Cheever often disowned his incontinent, presumptuous, and disconcerting desire. It was a stranger or an enemy that had to be watched and contended with. Still, he found it fascinating. First I will show that Cheever's emotional geography served both to contain and discipline his unruly desire. Then I will ask whether Cheever ever accepted his desire. For my answer I rely on a simple form of text analysis.

Cheever's emotional geography and desire

Cheever was a fanatical believer in the traditional family, with the wife as home-maker:

> When I was a young man, I woke one morning in the unclean bed-sheets of squalid furnished rooms, poor and hungry and lonely, and thought that some morning I would wake in my own house, holding in my arms a fragrant bride and hearing from the broad lawn beyond my window the voices of my beloved children. And so I did.
>
> (p. 348)

His personal emotional geography posited a heart-warming, family-embracing home situated close to invigorating, morality-restoring nature and community. He associated health, moral purity, and happiness with a life filled with simple pleasures such as swimming, hiking, ice-skating, fishing, or cycling, and basic tasks, such as watering the flowers or taking the children to school. He believed in the soothing, restorative power of his home-making wife: "… at home Mary takes me in arms, kindly, tenderly, and I am myself" (pp. 144, 16, 186). Cheever was thrilled by seemingly prosaic community rituals—part of the American way of life that his fiction depicted:

> Is there anything more wonderful than the Monday morning train: the 8:22?.… On Sunday … [w]e see the darkness end the weekend without any regret—it has all been so pleasant.… You water the grass, tell the children a story, take a bath, and get into bed. The morning is brilliant and fresh. Your wife drives you to the train in the convertible. The children and the dog come along. From the minute you wake up you seem to be on the verge of an irrepressible joy. The drive down … to the station seems triumphal … and when you kiss your wife and your children goodbye and give the dog's ears a scratch and say good morning all around the platform and unfold the *Tribune* and hear the train, the 8:22, coming down the tracks, it seems to me a wonderful thing.
>
> (pp. 8–9)

Three short sentences crack the image of a happy family and the wholesome American way of life that Cheever portrays: "I am tired, but this will pass. I love my wife's body and my children's innocence. Nothing more" (p. 19). These sentences raise the question of why Cheever needed to declare his love and its limits. And why did he not simply declare his love for his family, rather than alluding to his wife's body and his children's innocence?

For a long time, and with unabated fervor, he attributed to his wife, his children, nature, and simple life pleasures and tasks, the power to buttress his "true" self and keep him attached to the normal, moral, safe world beyond which loneliness, depression, destruction, and death threatened. They constituted the "only thing [he] had to proceed on"—the "invisible thread" (p. 45)—that helped him fight his self-doubts, opt for the forces of good against those of the evil, and steer clear of the abyss.[3]

He felt exposed and vulnerable: "I resent it that there should be parts of the world that have the power to do me so much harm" (p. 46). His central worry was his desire—which threatened to undo his delightful dreams of family and home. He found this contrary to the natural and moral order of things, a cause of "deepest sadness": "there are speculations and desires that seem contrary to the admirable drift of the clouds in heaven, and perhaps the deepest sadness that I know is to be absorbed by these" (p. 122). Desire kept him traveling "through some erotic purgatory" (p. 61).

Cheever's desire did not have any single location. Instead, his "I" felt it, or it marked or sprang from his mind, or body, or penis, or the atmosphere of specific places. Few of his formulations expressed taking responsibility for his desire—some are a curious blend of distantiation and self-attribution. He wrote of

- feeling "very libidinous"/"feeling lewd" (p. 58); "horny in a disgusting way" (p. 120)
- his unruly "mind ... stained with desire" (p. 61)
- his body being a "fool ... philandering, complaining, demanding, the gullible dupe of con men and subversive agencies, capricious, cowardly, the essence of inconstancy" (p. 88); "enflamed with fruitless desire when a stranger rubs witch hazel between my toes" (p. 61)
- "his male member, bristling with usefulness and self-importance, [which] takes the center of the stage" (p. 69); his "muscle [that] keeps up its nagging and complaining" (p. 108)
- his mind: "I do not understand the capricious lewdness of the sleeping mind" (p. 52)
- places: "[with their] erotic misdemeanor" (p. 60) and "a sort of erotic darkness" (pp. 207, 272, 632, 642).

Pitted against Cheever's desire were other areas—frightful, rather than uplifting and heart-warming—of his emotional geography. These were occupied by his experiences as an adolescent, living in his estranged parents' cold, bitter, and lonely home (pp. 44, 77, 152), as well as his experiences as a young man who lived in "cold, ugly, and forsaken places yearning for a house, a wife, the voices of my sons" (p. 190, see also p. 61).

The fantasy of acting on desire outside marriage immediately evoked these early experiences of loneliness, as well as of sordid, squalid, cold, hotels: “I am afraid of living in hotel rooms and eating in cafeterias” (p. 93). He wrote:

> [T]he soul of man is reflected ... in fourth-string hotel rooms, malodorous and obscure. This is all there is. There is nothing. Tired but sleepless, lewd but alone, hopeless, drunk ... this is the image of man.... Here is the soul of man, venereal, forlorn, and uprooted
>
> (p. 169)

He recalled how he “tasted,” “for the first time the strangeness of ... hotel rooms in which you will, as a grown man, find yourself frightened and alone” (p. 214). He feared that “after the laughter and open fires, I will end up cold, alone, dishonored, forgotten by my children, an old man approaching death without a companion” (pp. 190, 219, see also Cheever 1978).

That is why, even though his desire tugged at him, even though boredom reigned, and even though family bliss turned into family hell, he would jot down: “I don’t have [the] guts, spine, vitality ... to sell my house and start wandering” (p. 234, see also pp. 18–20, 33, 36, 57–8, 144, 163 and Bailey 2009: 297, 312). Loneliness, and fear of loneliness, were Cheever’s constant companions: “I experience a loneliness as painful as intestinal flu” (Bailey 2009: 374, 410, 581, 603, 611).

Cheever also associated desire with the no-go areas carved out by hoodlums, criminality and homosexuality. These he feared since they constituted a real danger to property, life, and limb:

> [T]he hoods ... strange and predatory and truly dangerous, car thieves and muggers ... jeopardize all our cherished concepts, even our self-esteem, our property rights, our powers of love, our laws and pleasures. The only relationship we seem to have with them is scorn or bewilderment, but they belong somewhere on the dark prairies of a country that is in the throes of self-discovery.
>
> (p. 52, Cheever 2003b: 246–7)

His “throes of self-discovery” revealed his own “dark prairies”: “I do have trouble with the dead hours of the afternoon without ... sexual discharges and drink” (p. 372). Cheever’s journal is dotted with self-disparaging remarks about his “violent drunkenness and disgusting venereal embroilments” (Bailey 2009: 287). He also repeatedly associated his desire for strangers with the police and with scandal: “The stranger’s cheek is fair and round, but if I caress it I will end up in the police station” (p. 66). Aged nearly 50, Cheever felt both threatened and fascinated by two men he witnessed in the toilets at Grand Central Station in New York—the applecart-upsetting potentiality of a single opportunity-suggesting word, gesture or sight: "I seem threatened by an erotic abyss" (p. 140). Infatuated with a young man, he only knew to compare him to death (p. 143). The persecutions of the McCarthy era produced an unprecedented homophobia—the atmosphere was such that one suspected even one's own shadow of homosexuality (Bailey 2009: 207, 286). Cheever picked up on this anxiety and fear. Looking back, he recalled: "Homosexuality seemed to me a lingering death" (pp. 219, 208).

Thus far I have shown that Cheever's central preoccupation—his desire—was disciplined both by his (programmatic) loves, and by his fears. I will next see if I can trace emotional changes in John Cheever's journals over time, in order to find out whether he ever became more accepting of his desire.

Temporality of feelings

How can I prove that Cheever has become more accepting of his unruly desire? One indication of growing self-acceptance in an autobiographical account would be a shift from a very vague, limited, and rigid vocabulary to a richer and/or more playful vocabulary concerning those aspects of the self that one views as problematic. Can this be demonstrated with regard to John Cheever?

Cheever's penis

Cheever was always preoccupied with the antics of his penis, and sometimes he pondered those of his acquaintances and friends. When inspecting the journals one last time, he was "shocked at the frequency with which [he] referred to his member" (Bailey 2009: 669). At first he referred to the penis with only a few, repetitive words—"my cod sore," "[u]p goes his cod again," or "his capricious cod" (pp. 65, 69, 131); and to sexual acts as "fleshly things" or "lewd follies" (p. 52). His distantiation was communicated by reference to such acts as "things," or "follies." The word "lewd" indicates that he viewed sexual acts as immoral, even if in jest.

Just a few pages later, however, his sexual-erotic vocabulary becomes richer and more playful. Some words are, or become, common at the time; others are his own—distantiated-ironic, or complaining-embittered—inventions, such as:

my sport (p. 74)
my muscle [that] keeps up its nagging and complaining, my groin, my love muscle (pp. 108–9)
my old dick stirs in the sunlight like a hyacinth (p. 150)
my groin smarting like a wound (p. 151)

my itchy member (p. 171)
my flower stiff as a horn (p. 173)
itchiness in my crotch (p. 177)
naked and unaccommodated (p. 183)
sad and illicit stirring (p. 214)
my capricious dick (p. 226)
my poor, poor cock (p. 232)
my cock, my hard-on (pp. 252–3)
very fucky but no cigar (p. 268)
very happily horny (p. 273)
longing into a pussywussy, a yummy snatch (p. 277)
in ... acute erotic discomfort (pp. 293, 295)
the mounting hots (p. 331)
my carnal drives (p. 338)
my wayward cock (p. 344)
me, horny (p. 347)
my carnal sport (p. 364)
delights and engorges my sexuality (p. 379)
stiff pricks (p. 387).

His vocabulary seems equally imaginative and playful over time, suggesting that his sexual-erotic vocabulary does not indicate any change, or is a poor tracer of change. An in-depth study could perhaps reveal semantic and emotional shifts.[4]

Issue-related wishes, gestures and (inter-)actions

Another indication of a person's increasing self-acceptance of his or her self-defined "problem" would be a shift from very vague to more detailed and explicit descriptions of issue-related wishes, gestures, and interactions. In Cheever's case, descriptions of sexual desire and sexual encounters—whether real, dreamed, or imagined, with women or with men—became more frequent, more in-depth, and more explicit.

Early in the journals Cheever notes:

> (1952) ... I can remember walking around the streets of New York on a summer night some years ago ... it was torment, crushing torment and frustration. I was caught under the weight of some great door. The feeling always was that if I could express myself erotically I would come alive.... Then ... a bar ... [a] conversation ... the crushing weight was lifted; it was merely a summer night in the city. I put this down because I think it all belongs to the past. Most of the aberrations seem to belong to the past.
>
> (pp. 11, 5)[5]

In this excerpt Cheever's "torment, crushing torment and frustration" is underscored by the metaphor of being trapped under a heavy door that prevents his erotic expression and the sense of feeling alive. At the end of the quote, the "aberrations" that "seem to belong to the past"—the only other word suggesting eroticism/sex—are left very vague. He relegates these "aberrations" to the past, implying a tentative ("I think") sense of relief and a need for self-assurance that "it all" (dismissive) belongs to the past. His uncertainty resurfaces in the last sentence ("seem to"). The repetition—"it all belongs to the past" and "seem to belong to the past"—indicates the need to assure himself that this is indeed the case.

Some years later, Cheever jots down his desire for an orgy that comes unaccompanied by remorse, repulsion, or guilt:

> (1960) ... I fancy a very lewd orgy but without any sense of shock or revulsion. I seem to have come to terms with my bones and these courses of speculation and I hope it does not mean any loss of moral awareness.
>
> (p. 125)

He provides a highly ironic snapshot of himself, bordering on self-ridicule—ridicule being a self-distancing yet self-embracing feat of the self-confident:

> (1960) ... I stand by the bed with the telephone in my right hand and a stiff cock in my left and this is I.
>
> (p. 126)

In a longer note, the homosexual nature of his reveries becomes explicit. Cheever dismisses this as inconsequential, since it is unreal; yet at the same time it is interesting because it belongs to an "infantile country of irresponsible sexual indulgence" in his head. Still—and revealing of his churchgoer's habitual take on sex—he describes "having his way" as "dirty" in this reverie. He then ponders the emotions—crushing shame, self-esteem, confidence—that accompany his homoerotic dreams, and wonders if he suffers from having an "uncured image" of violent women:

> (1960) ... I think, walking with [my son] on a spring day, that I will walk with X, find some cold lake[,] ... swim in it ballocksy, and have my dirty way with his rotund arse. I let the reverie spend itself, and what does it matter? There is no X, and ... I would not want to swim or do the other things I seem to want, but there does seem to be in my head some country, some infantile country of irresponsible sexual indulgence that has nothing to do with the facts of life as I know them. But what interests me is the contradictions of my nature, in anyone's

> nature, their grandioseness: that in a space of a few minutes I experience crushing shame and then swim into some pure source of self-esteem and confidence that wells up like a spring in a pond. And half asleep I wonder if I do not suffer from some uncured image of women, those creatures of morning, as predators, armed with sharp knives.
>
> (p. 129)

In another note, for all his to-ing and fro-ing about the merits and demerits of extra-marital sex, Cheever's anxiety about, and fear of, actual physical encounters with (wo)men outside his marriage—or with the state of his morals—seem to have evaporated:

> (1962) ... It is my wife's body that I most wish to gentle, it is into her that I most wish to pour myself, but when she is away I seem to have no scruple about spilling it elsewhere.... I am determined ... not to be compromised by my instincts[,] ... there are the spiritual facts: my high esteem for the world ... a passionate wish to honor the vows I've made to my wife and children. But my itchy member is unconcerned ... and I am afraid that I may succumb to its itchiness. We are urged to take things as they come ... to upset the petty canons of decency and cleanliness, and yet if I made it in the shower I could not meet the smiles of the world ... he ... a gentle object of sensual convenience. And yet I have been in this country a hundred times before and it is not, as it might seem to be, the valley of the shadow of death.... But I have been here before, and in the end it may be nothing, nothing. Why should I be tempted to throw away the vast delights of love for a chance shot in a shower?
>
> (pp. 171–2)

With much self-irony Cheever interrogates his attraction to both women *and* men: "Would I sooner nuzzle D.'s bosom or squeeze R.'s enlarged pectorals?" (p. 213) He seems to arrive at a clear position, yet a few pages later he questions why it is that he should blame himself for having such feelings:

> Why do I blame myself for this? Homosexuality seems to be a commonplace in our time—no less alarming than drunkenness and adultery—but my anxiety on the matter is very deep and seems incurable. I suffer, from time to time, a painful need for male tenderness, but I cannot perform with a man without wrecking my self-esteem.
>
> (pp. 245, 219)

No valuations, however, are attached to the subsequent, very explicit descriptions of his joyous sexual couplings—one with a woman, another with a man:

> (1968) ... finger-fucking, sucking, tongue-eating, arse-kissing ... with my cock in her mouth and my tongue up her cunt.
>
> (p. 254)

> (1978) ... [W]hen we met here, not long ago, we sped into the nearest bedroom, unbuckled each other's trousers, groped for our cocks in each other's underwear, and drank each other's spit. I came twice, once down his throat ...
>
> (p. 347)

Cheever could hardly be more explicit about the sexual acts. He affirms and underscores gestures that earlier on in his journal were either unnamed, or labeled lewd, obscene, or dirty.

At some point, he makes light of his various worries by listing them next to one another. His "brooding" suggests that there *is* a line he is unwilling to cross—the line separating him from public, open, homosexuality:

> I want to sleep.... I am tired of worrying about constipation, homosexuality, alcoholism, and brooding on what a gay bar must be like.
>
> (p. 289)

He seems to turn assertive, yet remains hesitant about his homosexuality. He writes: "I am queer, and happy to say so" (p. 344), only to add in the next sentence: "At the same time, the waitress is so desirable that I could eat her hands, her mouth."

Still, rather than feeling trapped or self-incarcerated, he finally is "his own house":

> I experience the arrogance of a man committed to a wayward cock. This morning, eating bacon and toast, my galling otherness has been conquered.... I am my own house. That I will suffer all these agonies again is likely, but, having come through them so many times, I know that they are not a destination.
>
> (pp. 344–5)

But his self-assurance does not last. Self-doubt is always near, but is expressed in a more detached, less painful, manner: "I thought: I am gay, I am gay, I am at last free of all this. This did not last for long" (p. 347).

Old, sick, and nearing death from cancer and acutely aware of it, Cheever still wrestles wearily with his desire: "I have done my obscenities, which seems to me of some importance, but which this morning bore me....The voyage has, from time to time, been serenely free from the unconscionable boredom of unwanted lewdness" (p. 388).

Cheever's ... skin!

A final way in which I want to show that—despite all his ambivalence and periodic returns to pejorative-repressive vocabulary—Cheever became more accepting of his "wayward desire," focuses on how he talked about his skin. There is a great contrast between the time when he still embraced the churchgoers' condemnation of sexuality and desire, and a later time when he is more affirmative of his desire.

For years "his skin seems lacerated" by the world:

> (1954) ... how can I take pride in my skin when my skin seems lacerated?... [T]his painful feeling of laceration was felt years and years ago.
>
> (p. 36)

But then Cheever proposes that his "capricious skin" is a "blessing":

> (1957) ... if my hands tremble with desire they tremble likewise when I reach for the chalice on Sunday.... What can this capricious skin be but a blessing?
>
> (p. 89)

He asserts that he has gained control over his "indiscreet and capricious skin," and its "ridiculous and romantic yearnings":

> (1960) ... I know my skin, indiscreet and capricious, and can cope cheerfully with all of its ridiculous and romantic yearnings.
>
> (p. 129)

Finally, he is jubilant about his "skin ... filled with ardor":

> (1978) ... So the grail, the grail; and anyone who thinks of this in terms of genitalia is a contemptible noncombatant. The grail, the grail! It fills one's mind in the early morning as one's skin is filled with ardor. There is no question of compromise or defeat.
>
> (p. 350)

Only the less evident formulations and words in the last three citations indicate that he is still struggling: "What can [it] be but a blessing?" implies that there are negative alternatives which the question challenges. And if something is not an issue there is no need to assert: "I know ... and can cope"; "cheerfully" again implies the opposite possibility; and speaking of "ridiculous ... yearnings" expresses some need for distantiation and domestication, and thus felt implicit threat. Finally, the last quote imposes a spiritual war as a metaphor on the reader, disparagingly dismissing its opposite. Cheever emerges as a victorious combatant from this war. But once the morning is over, as the *Journals* tell, he has to wage this war over and over again.

Final remarks

Although this text was intended as an exercise in methods, it suggests that John Cheever—even though he did not leave behind the denotative hesitancy (Clair 1998) that is typical of members of social groups who are experiencing enormous pressure to think and feel in terms of hegemonic discourses and emotional regimes that are prevalent at the time—became somewhat more relaxed about his unrelenting desire and homosexuality some years before the gay movement emerged. His sexual liaisons—whether imagined or real—began with his first publishing successes of the late 1950s, and never stopped. By 1968 he was making money and could fully live up to his single breadwinner model (Bailey 2009: 430). His persistent, shocking (even to his drinking buddies) daily alcohol consumption dampened his moral self-condemnation and restraints. When the opportunities presented themselves during his stays abroad, in Hollywood, or as a guest professor, he followed his desire—both with men and with women. Bailey (2009: 290 note*, 605 note*, 657) underlines the fact that Cheever only ever permitted men to perform fellatio *on him*—he therefore remained "manly" until the end. Although he did learn to wake up in the morning in a loving embrace with another man (Bailey 2009: 574–5), he never dared to enter a gay bar. He never became a publicly gay person.

Knowing how homophobic the McCarthy era was, and how tormented and puzzled Cheever felt by his "incontinent" desire, it comes as a big surprise to see that an entire chapter of *The Wapshot Chronicle* (1957) is devoted to homosexuality. In Chapter 34 its hero, Coverly

> felt a dim rumble of homosexual lust in his trousers. This lasted for less than a second. Then the lash of his conscience crashed down with such force that his scrotum seemed injured.... Then the lash crashed down once more, this time at the hands of a lovely woman who scorned him bitterly ... and whose eyes told him that he was now shut away forever from a delight in girls—those creatures of morning.
>
> (Cheever 2003a: 290)

Perturbed by this and other events, Coverly writes a letter to his father, who replies: "Man is not simple.... Life has worse troubles" (Cheever 2003a: 298–9).[6]

In the text above I have used several "indicators"—such as Cheever's notes on his penis/sexual desire, his sexual activities, and his skin—to explore whether, over time, he became more accepting of his "unruly" and "incontinent" desire. I then went through his journal notes, selecting excerpts. These showed that until his last days Cheever remained ambivalent about his desire, although he became a bit more accepting of it.

At the same time I proposed that a person feeling their way against social taboos, and anxious not to cross the boundaries they impose, remains silent, vague, or very rigid about taboo-related acts. Only the vagueness could be asserted, however. I also suggested that a greater level of self-acceptance is expressed via the explicit references to tabooed feelings and acts, and the adoption of a richer and more flexible language in reference to taboo-related body parts and acts. However, only the explicitness could be demonstrated. The task of linking these hunches to the theories of emotions and affect remains.

Acknowledgments

I presented these ideas at the 11th Congress of the European Sociological Association in Torino in 2013. I thank Falk Eckert, Jochen Kleres, Kate Davison, and Eva Köppen for enduring the onset of my obsession with John Cheever's *Journals*; Benno Gammerl for enduring several bouts of it; and Alina Strugut and Jocelyn Pixley for taking me through the (for now) final phase. Jochen suggested the final, curative cuts.

P.S.:

> I . . . have a horrendous dream in which Mary is made president of the college. . . . I retaliate by having a homosexual escapade, unconsummated, with Ronald Reagan.
>
> (p. 223)

Notes

1 When I cite from Cheever's *Journals*, I provide just the page number. Since Cheever ruminates, I sometimes cite more than one page on the same topic, though without being exhaustive.

2 The *Journals of John Cheever* were published for the first time in 1990 by his friend and editor, Robert Gottlieb (2008). They span the time period between the late 1940s and the time of Cheever's death, but this represents only a twentieth of the original journal—which ran to a length of up to four million words. Bailey (2009) argues that the *Journals* cannot be relied for its chronology. But where I address Cheever's ruminations, this is irrelevant, except for the question of when, exactly, Cheever began to act on his desires. However, both the *Journals* and Bailey agree on this point. Bailey's (2009) biography filled in many facts, but did not change my analysis. For reasons of space I could not dwell on Cheever's phobias, imposter fears, and envy. Nor could I discuss his relationship with his wife or to women in general.

3 See also:

> So there are, I suppose, two faces to this: my fear of being caught in a world that bores me, and the sexual richness of my marriage. I think—foolishly but, nonetheless, with pleasure—of the house, of greeting guests, of pointing out the river view from the terrace. I am back in my own jolly country. Now the image of death is laid ... I am unafraid.
>
> (p. 144)
>
> [again] I have been drunken, dirty, unkind, embittered, and lewd.
>
> (p. 160)

4 Just one example: Cheever referred to penises as "cod"—perhaps this was popular vernacular in the New England he grew up in. Moreover, Cheever was an enthusiastic fisherman, and in his journals and fiction he devoted much space to the masculine ritual of going fishing. He often took his sons, by boat, to an abandoned hut, from where they would then go fishing. The hut, he understood as a domain of masculinity in which man's right to chaos as well as unwashed bodies and dirty socks could assert itself, and where contempt for women's love of hygiene and order could be expressed. *Journals* and Bailey (2009) often mention Cheever going fishing, but never for cod. Still, cod could have played an important role in Cheever's self-conception: both his idea of masculinity and his self-image as a New England aristocrat. The cod species is a dominant-looking fish with a white line that bestows on it some elegance:

> [Its] courtship [ritual] involves fin displays and male grunting ... [then] [t]he male inverts himself beneath the female, and the pair swim in circles while spawning.... The Atlantic cod has two distinct color phases: gray-green and reddish brown.... Cod has been an important economic commodity in international markets since the Viking period.... The fish was so important to the history and development of Massachusetts, the state's House of Representatives hung a wood carving of a codfish, known as the Sacred Cod of Massachusetts, in its chambers.... In 1733, Britain tried to gain control over [the] trade.... In addition to increasing trade, the New England settlers organized into a "codfish aristocracy" ... [and] rose up against Britain's "tariff on an import."

See http://en.wikipedia.org/wiki/Cod (last accessed February 18, 2014).

5 Another example:

> I seem, after half a lifetime, to have made no progress, unless resignation is progress. There is the erotic hour of waking, which is like birth.... There is euphoria, the sense that life is no more than it appears to be, light and water and trees and pleasant people that can be brought crashing down by a neck, a hand, an obscenity written on a toilet door. There is always, somewhere, this hint of aberrant carnality. The worst of it is that it seems labyrinthine; I come back again and again to the image of a naked prisoner in an unlocked cell, and to tell the truth I don't know how he will escape. Death figures here, the unwillingness to live. Many of these shapes seem like the shapes of death; one approaches them with the same amorousness, the same sense of terrible dread. I say to myself that the body can be washed clean of any indulgence; the only sin is despair, but I speak meaninglessly in my own case. Chasteness is real; the morning adjures one to be chaste. Chasteness is waking. I could not wash the obscenity off myself. But in all this thinking there is lack of space, of latitude, of light and humor.
>
> (pp. 8, 64)

6 Bailey (2009: 756 and 560 note*) misses this fact.

References

Bailey, B. 2009. *Cheever – A Life.* New York. Vintage Books.

Cheever, J. 1978 [1964]. "The Swimmer" in *The Stories of John Cheever.* New York: Alfred A. Knopf.

Cheever, J. 2003a [1957]. *The Wapshot Chronicle.* New York: HarperCollins Publishers.

Cheever, J. 2003b [1964]. *The Wapshot Scandal.* New York: HarperCollins Publishers.

Cheever, J. 2008 [1990]. *The Journals of John Cheever.* Edited by Robert Gottlieb. New York: Vintage International.

Clair, R. P. 1998. *Organizing Silence.* Albany: State University of New York Press.

Gottlieb, R. 2008. "Editor's Note by Robert Gottlieb" in R. Gottlieb (ed.) *The Journals of John Cheever.* 397–9. New York: Vintage International.

Thomas, J. 2013. *Thomas Hardy and Desire: Conceptions of the Self.* Houndmills, Basingstoke: Palgrave Macmillan.

Part VII

Surveying emotions

Chapter 26

Triangulation as data integration in emotion research

Sylvia Terpe

In the 1970s Norman Denzin defined the idea of triangulation in the social sciences as the examination of a research phenomenon "from as many different methodological perspectives as possible" (Denzin 1970: 297). Nowadays it is emphasized that the potentials of methodological triangulation can be utilized only if theoretical triangulation and data triangulation are considered as well (see Flick *et al.* 2012). This advice also applies to emotion research: different methods in the study of affective phenomena build on different theoretical conceptions, and produce different kinds of data. Hence, for any kind of triangulation it is necessary to reflect which level and aspects of emotionality the chosen theoretical perspectives and methods address. In this article I will focus on two forms of triangulation which aim at an integration of qualitative and quantitative data on emotional phenomena. While other forms of triangulation analyze these data separately and then compare their respective findings (see Bryman 2006), the two forms presented here require a "conversion of data from one type to another" (Bazeley 2006: 66) in order to analyze them jointly. First, I will show how to proceed in quantitizing qualitative data on emotional phenomena, and which matters should be considered in matching them with respondents' information from standardized instruments. Then I will show how to proceed in qualitizing quantitative data on emotionality in order to merge them with qualitative data of respondents' narratives. Both types of triangulation require qualitative and quantitative data for every unit of analysis. The first triangulation type experienced an upswing due to advancements of qualitative data analysis software in recent years (Bazeley 2006; Fielding 2012). I will emphasize the unique benefits of the second, rare variant of triangulation.

Quantitizing qualitative data on emotionality and matching them with quantitative ones

This kind of triangulation aims at conducting statistical analyses in order to explore patterns and correlations in one's data or test effects for significance (see Cohen 1988). Since this requires large samples, studies with a predominantly quantitative design—e.g., surveys with mostly closed and some open-ended questions—are best suited for this approach. In such surveys open-ended questions usually address emotions in one of the following three ways: respondents are asked to describe a situation in which they experienced a particular emotion selected by the researcher (see Fontaine *et al.* 2006 for shame and guilt); respondents are asked to describe their emotions in a particular situation characterized by the researcher (see Turner and Schutte 1981 for situations in which a person felt her "true self"); or respondents are asked to describe how they would act and feel in a hypothetical situation (see Malti *et al.* 2013 for moral conflicts).

When it comes to quantitizing such qualitative data—transforming texts into countable entities—one has to decide from which perspectives the material will be examined, or, in other words: which codes or categories are suitable for capturing (emotional) meanings expressed in texts. Basically, the quantitizing of qualitative data on emotional phenomena follows the same logic as any other qualitative content analysis (Mayring 2004; Schreier 2012). Which codes or dimensions one chooses will depend on the research questions, on the existing knowledge about the research phenomenon, and on the theoretical inclinations of the researcher. Besides following a deductive, theory-driven strategy, a researcher can also employ inductive, data-driven strategies to generate categories. In practice no deductive procedure gets by without inductive elements, and no inductive procedure is completely without theoretical considerations (see Dewey 1986 [1938]: Chapter 21).

A main challenge in quantitizing qualitative data on emotional phenomena consists in dissecting the "emotionality" of a text—uncovering the "emotional messages" inherent in it. Two complementary ways of doing this can be distinguished. The first approach builds on explicit emotion terms to be found in the respondents' answers, and assigns corresponding codes to them.[1] Here the first task of the researcher is to determine those emotions which are relevant for one's research question. Take for instance a study which explores the phenomenon of conscience (see Thome and Terpe 2012), and in which respondents were asked to describe their situation, thoughts, and feelings when they had experienced their conscience. Since theoretical reflections point to the association of conscience with guilt and shame in particular one can start with a coding frame which contains two separate categories for these emotions. One would attach the code "guilt" to an answer if it contains words with the root *guilt**, and one would assign the code "shame" if it contains words with the root *shame** or *ashamed**. Furthermore, one would assign both codes if the answer contains words with roots for guilt and shame at the same time, and one would assign none of these codes if these roots are not used or if they are used in a negative way, as, for example, in "I didn't feel guilty." In the latter case one might introduce a code called "negation of guilt."

Next the researcher may also want to categorize other emotion terms as synonyms for guilt and shame. For instance, the "affect label coder" (see endnote 1) treats remorse as a synonym for guilt. While this accords with the approach of Tangney and her colleagues, who add regret as yet another synonym (Tangney *et al.* 2007: 349–50), Gabrielle Taylor (1996) emphasizes the fundamental difference between guilt, remorse, and regret. In turn, the "affect label coder" treats regret as a synonym for the emotion of longing. An obvious remedy bypassing such disagreements typical for other emotions as well, is to treat every emotion term in its own right at first, and use a coding frame with separate codes for each additional term. This procedure generates frequencies with which each emotion was named, but in order to conduct statistical analyses one has to have a fairly large number of cases for each code. Hence, often it will be necessary to put together codes to create more inclusive categories with larger case numbers. This merging is a result of a more-or-less theoretical or data-informed process entailing interpretations, and should be documented carefully.

The second way to approach the emotionality signaled by a text takes into account that respondents do not always use explicit emotion terms to describe emotional experiences. For instance, respondents often describe an experience of conscience by using phrases like: "I still ask myself why I did that/it's gnawing at me/I wish I could turn back time/I still stay out of her way." These phrases seem to have an emotional meaning which is conveyed by metaphors, wishful thinking, actions, and self-questioning. Jochen Kleres calls this the "essentially narrative nature" of emotional experiences, and recommends several "analytical tools that allow dissecting a text's emotionality" in terms of its semantic, syntactic, and structural features (Kleres 2011: 188).

Just as in other qualitative studies, this process, and the coding that follows, is "the product of a highly complicated series of interpretive moves" (Sandelowski *et al.* 2009: 211) since it is difficult to assign phrases unequivocally to one specific emotional state. For example, one might interpret "I still ask myself why I did that" as a sign of surprise and astonishment, as an expression of regret or guilt, or as an indicator of rumination—a particular kind of reflection. Each of these interpretations would result in another coding and hence produce different results. In order to reach a compelling interpretation, one should apply the principles of hermeneutics, analyzing the text "sequentially, extensively and in detail" (Reichertz 2004: 294), engaging in a group discussion to generate an intersubjective agreement.

The focus on the narrative structure of open-ended answers has the virtue of sensitizing to all those dimensions of emotionality which were "measured" with a specific question, but do not reveal themselves at first glance. A researcher usually has theory-derived assumptions about these dimensions. The hermeneutic approach helps to confirm, to refute, or to modify these assumptions, revealing dimensions not considered before. For instance, as a result of her hermeneutic analyses and theoretical reflections, a researcher might wish to introduce a code which captures how respondents articulate their emotional experiences, adding sub-codes such as "use of explicit emotion terms," or "use of metaphors." Additional codes may discriminate between various affective phenomena, their causal roles and intensities, various kinds of objects, causes and valences of emotions, or standards by which affective phenomena are evaluated. It is advisable to create only few, well-motivated sub-codes, since for lack of sufficient cases most of them will have to be merged to create larger categories suitable for statistical analysis.

The process of quantitizing qualitative data on emotionality is completed when the emotional meanings in all answers have become assigned to suitable codes and categories. These can be used as variables in statistical procedures relying on categorical data (see Agresti 2007). However, one can speak of data triangulation first when these quantitized qualitative data are merged with information from standardized instruments into one common data set. The researcher then has to consider how variables and codes can be related to each other in a meaningful way.

Depending on the research question and statistical procedure necessary to answer it, the researcher will also have to decide which data on emotionality are to be used as dependent variables, which as independent variables, and which "as a covariate, mediator, or moderator of the effect of some other variable" (Sandelowski *et al.* 2009: 211). Take, for instance, the open question on experiences of conscience. One's coding frame may contain a category which discriminates between three groups of emotions: "guilt," "shame," and "pleasure." If the questionnaire also contains a standardized instrument which measures a person's disposition to experience guilt and/or shame (e.g., the TOSCA by Tangney and Dearing 2002), one may treat this instrument as the independent variable to see if it predicts the emotions the respondent indicates as experiences of conscience. Or one might explore whether dispositions to guilt and/or shame measured by standardized questions correlate with dispositional statements, such as "I always blame myself/I am a shy person," given in the open answers. However, one should be aware that one is never measuring the same thing with two different instruments.

Qualitizing quantitative data and matching them with qualitative ones

The triangulation presented in the previous section combines data measured by standardized and non-standardized instruments in the context of a quantitative analysis. The other kind of triangulation proposed now requires a transformation of quantitative into qualitative data in order to put them into dialog with other qualitative data in the context of a qualitative analysis. Hence, again, one has to have both kinds of information for every unit of analysis. The starting point for this type of triangulation is a single unit of analysis; for example, the narrative of a respondent derived from the questionnaire or the face-to-face interview subject to the hermeneutic analysis outlined in the previous section (Kleres 2011).

In a next step the answer of this respondent to a standardized question of interest and the distribution of this variable are added. The distribution of the variable may stem from one's small qualitative or large quantitative sample, but also from another survey which used the same instrument. The standardized answer of the respondent in the context of the variable's distribution reveals how typical or atypical it is. The guiding assumption in this step of the analysis is that of the quantitative logic, according to which items and preset answers have a common meaning for all respondents. The researcher tries to make sense of the respondent's narrative in light of the standardized answer and its assumed shared meaning.

This assumption of a shared meaning is abandoned in a further step, the central element in the qualitizing procedure: the researcher begins to put the standardized answer of the respondent into dialog with her narrative. The point of reference is the respondent's context of meaning, worked out during the hermeneutic analysis of her narrative. In other words: the standardized item and the answer to this item are now interpreted from the perspective of the respondent. In this way not only the narrative but also the standardized instrument becomes an object of hermeneutic analysis. This procedure of moving between the general and the particular may confirm the previously assumed meaning of the item, but it can also concretize it or uncover new meanings. The answer by a respondent may be typical from a statistical point of view insofar as the majority of respondents chose the same option. Yet the hermeneutic analysis of the item from the perspective of the respondent may reveal a singular meaning this item has for this particular respondent. If this procedure is repeated several times with further respondents (who should be sampled according to the usual criteria for qualitative studies, see Sandelowski 1995, 2000), it may turn out that more than one meaning can be attached to one and the same answer.

Benefits of qualitizing quantitative data for triangulation in emotion research

The kind of triangulation sketched in the last section brings several benefits to emotion research. It advances and enlarges one's repertoire of instruments for the study of affective phenomena, while expanding the knowledge about the emotional repertoires of the respondents.

Many standardized instruments in emotion research, such as the TOSCA, do not measure emotionality directly by the use of explicit emotion terms. They instead consist of items and preset answers with scenarios that tell stories or describe behavior and thoughts. Respondents are asked to rank these, or choose between them. These instruments utilize the narrative character of emotionality, but they are built on the assumption that a particular story is a more-or-less clear-cut indicator of a particular emotion or emotional disposition. Take, for instance, a scale which is measuring various kinds of guilt- and shame-proneness (Suslow *et al.* 1999), and which treats the following items as indicative of a disposition to "punitive guilt," defined as fear of punishment and social rejection:

"It seems to me that everybody reproaches me"
"I always worry about being punished for something"
"I can't bear it to get criticized for a mistake."

If a respondent rejects the first two items, but agrees with the last one, the hermeneutic analysis of this person's narrative may reveal how she understood the last item. The person may have agreed to it because she realizes she turns angry sometimes when she is criticized. Hence, the interpretation of the item through the eyes of the respondent would disclose that her agreement does not indicate a proneness to "punitive guilt," but rather a self-awareness of a disposition to become angry when criticized. To be accepted as final, this interpretation would have to be supported or rejected analyzing other self-assessments of the same person.

This procedure, repeated several times with further respondents and additional items of interest, would also improve statistical analyses because the hermeneutic interpretation of an item may result in group- or situation-specific hypotheses which take into account two or more meanings. Furthermore, this procedure could complement factor analyses (Mulaik 2009) and reliability tests (Sijtsma 2009) which reveal items that do not "fit" in statistical terms, but cannot explain deviations.

Exploiting the narrative character of emotionality, one can also reveal emotional meanings attached to standardized instruments which were originally designed to measure other phenomena. In this way one's methods repertoire suitable for the empirical study of affective phenomena widens. A necessary requirement for this is, again, a decidedly hermeneutic attitude towards standardized instruments, leaving behind the assumption that each item or preset answer has only one unambiguous meaning.

Let me illustrate this with the internal conversation indicator developed by Margret Archer (2007) which aims at measuring the dominant style of a person's self-reflection. While some items meant to reveal the self-reflection style directly address emotions and ways of emotional thinking, other items do not include emotions. Imagine two persons in a sample who agree with the item "Being decisive does not come easily to me," and who evoke emotions when describing decision-making situations when asked to remember an experience of conscience.

The first person sees herself confronted with many expectations with which she cannot comply simultaneously—caring for her old mother, looking after her mother-in-law, attending to her school-age son, being a dependable colleague at work. She reports feeling guilty about not meeting all these expectations in a way she would be content with. Her agreement to the standardized item "Being decisive does not come easily to me" may be interpreted as a confirmation that she is certain about, and feels positively attached to, the moral claims placed upon her; yet uncertain about how to rank and decide between them. The second person reports conflicting emotions about being honest to his wife who suffers from Alzheimer's disease. He realizes that in moments of honesty he is troubling his wife, but when he restrains his wish for being honest in favor of his wife's well-being, he feels uneasy. His agreement to the item "Being decisive does not come easily to me" may be interpreted as a confirmation of his belief in the value of honesty: he cannot decide easily because he knows that he would violate a principle he feels attached to. Yet his agreement may also indicate emerging feelings of doubt with respect to the unconditional validity of the principle of honesty: he cannot be decisive easily because he is uncertain about whether occasionally refraining from honesty would actually do some good.

For both respondents the standardized item addresses a specific set of emotions, called "epistemic feelings" in philosophy (de Sousa 2011: Chapter 9). In particular, the feelings of certainty and doubt refer to a particular quality of one's knowledge which—as the examples showed—may be about the validity of moral values. Whether this also applies to other respondents, and whether one can formulate clear hypotheses about the relationship between the item and these feelings, would have to be explored in further hermeneutic analyses. The key point is that one can utilize standardized instruments developed for other purposes for the study of affective phenomena when these are combined with the hermeneutic analysis of narratives and are interpreted in light of these narratives.

A final benefit of the triangulation method proposed here is that it reduces limitations inherent in using either qualitative or quantitative approaches to emotional phenomena. It is not always easy for respondents to describe the emotional facets of their experiences; sometimes they have difficulties in finding adequate words, sometimes they cannot or just do not want to express feelings. To have an elaborated vocabulary for the articulation of one's emotional experiences may be a feature of the *homo sentimentalis* typical of selected social milieus (Illouz 2007).

Researchers should be aware that the ability and readiness to talk explicitly about one's emotional life may be distributed unequally between and within societies. Narrative analysis offers one way of revealing hidden emotional meanings, while standardized questions about specific emotions may constitute pragmatic alternative solutions. For some respondents it may be easier to characterize their emotional experiences by just marking a box. In such cases standardized instruments provide valuable information which might have escaped a researcher otherwise. However, the value of the information provided by the respondent will depend on the researcher's awareness of the limitations which inhere in standardized data collection techniques: they restrict the emotional facets of a phenomenon to those dimensions the researcher has in mind when constructing a questionnaire, thus reducing the complexity of an emotional experience to a plain statement. Standardized items also assume a shared meaning attached to emotional terms or a common emotional meaning attached to specific scenarios.

As I have argued so far, the limitations inherent in standardized questions and working with large quantitative samples may be compensated to some extent by a hermeneutic approach towards standardized data, and by its integration with qualitative data where relevant. In this manner a dialog between quantitative and qualitative data may expand our knowledge about the world of emotionality.

Note

1 See the list of emotion terms and the "affect label coder" of the Swiss Center for Affective Sciences at www.affective-sciences.org/researchmaterial.

References

Agresti, A. 2007. *An Introduction to Categorical Data Analysis.* Hoboken: Wiley-Interscience.

Archer, M. 2007. *Making Our Way Through the World.* Cambridge: Cambridge University Press.

Bazeley, P. 2006. "The Contribution of Computer Software to Integrating Qualitative and Quantitative Data and Analyses," *Research in the Schools,* 13 (1): 64–74.

Bryman, A. 2006. "Integrating Quantitative and Qualitative Research: How is it Done?" *Qualitative Research,* 6 (1): 97–113.

Cohen, J. 1988. *Statistical Power Analysis for the Behavioral Sciences.* New York: Erlbaum.

Denzin, N. 1970. *The Research Act: A Theoretical Introduction to Sociological Methods.* Chicago: Aldine.

de Sousa, R. 2011. *Emotional Truth.* Oxford: Oxford University Press.

Dewey, J. 1986 [1938]. *Logic. The Theory of Inquiry.* Carbondale: Southern Illinois University Press.

Fielding, N. G. 2012. "Triangulation and Mixed Methods Designs: Data Integration With New Research Technologies," *Journal of Mixed Methods Research*, 6 (2): 124–36.

Flick, U., V. Garms-Homolová, W. J. Herrmann, J. Kuck, and G. Röhnsch. 2012. "'I Can't Prescribe Something Just Because Someone Asks for it…': Using Mixed Methods in the Framework of Triangulation," *Journal of Mixed Methods Research*, 6 (2): 97–110.

Fontaine, J. R. J., P. Luyten, P. de Boeck, J. Corveleyn, M. Fernandez, D. Herrera, A. Ittzés, and T. Tomcsányi. 2006. "Untying the Gordian Knot of Guilt and Shame: The Structure of Guilt and Shame Reactions Based on Situation and Person Variation in Belgium, Hungary, and Peru," *Journal of Cross-Cultural Psychology*, 37 (3): 273–92.

Illouz, E. 2007. *Cold Intimacies: The Making of Emotional Capitalism*. Cambridge: Polity Press.

Kleres, J. 2011. "Emotion and Narrative Analysis: A Methodological Approach," *Journal for the Theory of Social Behaviour*, 41 (2): 182–202.

Malti, T., M. Keller, and M. Buchmann. 2013. "Do Moral Choices Make Us Feel Good? The Development of Adolescents' Emotions Following Moral Decision-Making," *Journal of Research on Adolescence*, 23 (2): 389–97.

Mayring, P. 2004. "Qualitative Content Analysis" in U. Flick (ed.) *A Companion to Qualitative Research*: 266–9. London: Sage.

Mulaik, S. A. 2009. *Foundations of Factor Analysis*. London: Chapman and Hall.

Reichertz, J. 2004. "Objective Hermeneutics and Hermeneutic Sociology of Knowledge" in U. Flick (ed.) *A Companion to Qualitative Research*: 290–5. London: Sage.

Sandelowski, M. 1995. "Sample Size in Qualitative Research," *Research in Nursing and Health*, 18 (2): 179–83.

Sandelowski, M. 2000: "Combining Qualitative and Quantitative Sampling, Data Collection, and Analysis Techniques in Mixed-Method Studies," *Research in Nursing and Health*, 23 (3): 246–55.

Sandelowski, M., C. I. Voils, and G. Knafl. 2009. "On Quantitizing," *Journal of Mixed Methods Research*, 3 (3): 208–22.

Schreier, M. 2012. *Qualitative Content Analysis in Practice*. Los Angeles: Sage.

Sijtsma, K. 2009. "On the Use, the Misuse, and the Very Limited Usefulness of Cronbach's Alpha," *Psychometrika*, 74 (1): 107–20.

Suslow, T., V. Arolt, G.-F. Marano, M. W. Batacchi, and M. Hönow. 1999. "Zur Reliabilität und Validität einer deutschsprachigen Version der Scham-Schuld-Skala," *Psychologische Beiträge*, 41: 439–57.

Tangney, J. P. and R. L. Dearing. 2002. *Shame and Guilt*. New York: Guilford.

Tangney, J. P., J. Stuewig, and D. J. Mashek. 2007. "Moral Emotions and Moral Behaviour," *Annual Review of Psychology*, 58: 345–72.

Taylor, G. 1996. "Guilt and Remorse" in R. Harré (ed.) *The Emotions: Social, Cultural and Biological Dimensions*: 57–73. London: Sage.

Thome, H. and S. Terpe. 2012. "Das Gewissen – (k)ein Thema für die Soziologie?" *Zeitschrift für Soziologie*, 41 (4): 258–76.

Turner, R. H. and J. Schutte. 1981. "The True-Self Method for Studying the Self-Conception," *Symbolic Interaction*, 4 (1): 1–20.

Chapter 27

Missing values

Surveying protest emotions

Dunya Van Troost

This chapter offers a fieldwork tale on the ins and outs of quantifying the emotions of protesters. In the Fall of 2009 a team of researchers, operating under the name "Caught in the Act of Protest, Contextualizing Contestation" (the CCC Project), set out to administer the first of a survey series among demonstrators. Four items in this survey concerned the emotions that demonstrators experienced in relation to the issue that brought them out into the street. The role of emotion in social movement research has convincingly been argued over the last two decades (Goodwin and Jasper 2006). However, the empirical examination of emotion within the context of protest remains challenging. The measurement of emotion has been deemed "one of the most vexing problems" (Mauss and Robinson 2009) by psychologists and social movement scholars alike. Conducting the fieldwork during demonstrations, to get these measurements from protesters, does little to alleviate this challenge. Three years prior to the first CCC survey Goodwin and Jasper (2006: 617) made the following observation:

> [M]ethodological barriers to getting at emotions in social movements persist, since the rigorous questionnaires favored by social psychologists who study emotions are not always appropriate or feasible in studies of protest. The result is that emotions have remained unrecognized and untheorized, even as they have supplied much of the causal force behind some of the key mechanisms identified in recent years.

That same year Van Stekelenburg (2006) published pioneering work—using the instrument of the questionnaire—to measure anger among protesters. The method that Van Stekelenburg used[1] shows that the administration of a questionnaire *is* feasible in studies of protest.

Which leaves the question: how appropriate it is to measure emotion through a survey? This chapter focuses specifically on the issue of missing values—a pervasive problem when using self-administered surveys. It is important to understand the mechanism of how the data are missing since this can lead to biased parameter estimates—which is particularly hazardous when the data are used for inferential statistics (Graham 2009). I will start by explicating the current state of research regarding emotion within the context of social movements, and explore how survey research is employed among demonstrators. Thereafter I explain the rationale behind the emotion question in the CCC survey, and the way this question was answered by respondents.

Conceptualization of protest emotions

In order to reliably measure the emotions of protesters we need to define our understanding of "emotion." Sociological studies about emotion among protesters tend to deal with it as part of the affective processes that occur within a social unit, e.g., groups or social movement organizations. As such, a range of phenomena—including feelings, moods, and long-standing affects[2]—have been studied. Social movement scholars, however, have failed to produce a firmly bounded definition of "emotion"—which leads to difficulties when operationalizing emotion, and to an inability to reliably compare research results across studies.

Looking at psychological literature it becomes clear that emotions can be distinguished from feelings or moods because emotions have objects—"they are about something, be it fact or belief" (Scherer 2005), whereas for feelings or moods this is not necessarily the case. Goodwin and Jasper (2006) continue on this path and distinguish between three objects of emotion: the opponent, the in-group, and contentious issues. Protesters are likely to experience negative emotions towards their opponent and the contentious issue, while they most likely feel positive emotions towards the group they identify with. This distinction does not equal a definition, but it does provide a tool to pull emotion aside from other affective processes described in social movement studies. This objects-of-emotion paradigm falls in line with a componential model of emotion. This is a psychological model in which emotion is described as a feeling associated with distinctive thoughts, psychological and biological states, and action tendencies in reaction to personally meaningful stimuli (Mauss and Robinson 2009). It is this model that is used here.

In order to select which emotions to include in the survey I narrowed the array of possible emotions down to those that are considered modal or frequently experienced (Scherer 2005), namely: happiness, sadness, fear, and anger (Ekman *et al.* 1987). Positive emotions such as happiness will not be experienced frequently in relation to protest issues. Prompting positive emotions might be seen as insensitive or strange, thus jeopardizing the overall reliability of answers. Sadness is a possible reaction to protest issues; but it is less likely that this emotion will be experienced by protesters since the associated action tendency is inaction rather than action (Smith *et al.* 2008). In this manner I decided that fear and anger responses would be prototypical in relation to protest issues (Van Troost *et al.* 2013). Anger had already been shown to reinforce the motivation to protest (Van Zomeren *et al.* 2004) and seems to function as an accelerator or amplifier of instrumental and ideological motives (Van Stekelenburg and Klandermans 2007). One of the results gained by measuring the emotions of protesters has been that "worry" appears to be a second relevant protest emotion. Particularly in situations where protesters feel less efficacious—for instance when the protest issue concerns racism, or the use of nuclear energy—they feel worried rather than angry about the issue they are protesting about.

Emotion measures

For the study at hand I needed to find out what people were feeling, and approach them while they were part of a large and vociferous crowd. Thus far psychologists have used autonomic measures, brain states, behavioral measures, and self-reported measures to assess emotions (see Mauss and Robinson 2009 for a systematic review of the use of these methods for emotion research). Autonomic measures and brain states may allude to the idea of an objective measurement of emotion; however, emotions are intrinsically subjective in nature. Scherer therefore maintains that "there is no access other than to ask the individual to report on the nature of the experience" (Scherer 2005: 712). Interview and survey methods are among the regularly applied instruments used by social movement scholars, and both allow for self-reported measures of emotion. The methodology that I will elaborate on here is that of measuring the emotions of protesters through a survey—with the individual as the unit of analysis.

Sampling procedure

Data was collected as part of the CCC Project. The idea behind this project has been the compilation of a data set that makes it possible to compare demonstrations and demonstrators across different contextual settings. The method used was a postal survey that local research teams distributed during large demonstrations taking place in Sweden, the UK, the Netherlands, Belgium, Switzerland, Spain, and Italy. Very important was the standardization of data collection. Each event was covered according to the same sampling rules[3] in order to ensure that differences in responses could be attributed to differences in the composition of the demonstration population rather than changes in the way that protesters were sampled while they were demonstrating.

There were two sampling steps—the first concerned the choice of demonstration; the second the selection of respondents. In choosing which demonstrations to include we had two requirements. Eligible demonstrations needed to have an expected size of at least 3,000 participants, plus the expectation that the demonstration would be non-violent in character. With these requirements in mind the teams attended more than 70 demonstrations between 2009–13, spread across the aforementioned countries.

Within a single selected demonstration a total of a 1,000 demonstrators were selected, at random, as respondents. A standardized sampling procedure, developed by Walgrave and Verhulst (2011), was used to approach respondents and obtain reliable, valid, and comparable data about demonstrators. Two principles are crucial to guaranteeing a representative sample: (1) a strict division of labor between selectors and interviewers, and (2) a systematic sampling procedure. The method that was used to administer the survey is fully described in a paper by van Stekelenburg *et al.* (2012).

The survey question

The four emotion items were formulated as a statement that respondents were asked to complete. "Thinking about ... makes me feel: Angry"—and repeated for "Worried," "Fearful," and "Frustrated." The space after "Thinking about" is used in each survey to mention the issue of the demonstration. So, the full statement might read: "Thinking about the use of nuclear power makes me feel: Angry." Answers were given on a five-point Likert scale, ranging from "not at all" to "very much." The basic design of this question makes it applicable to pretty much every imaginable protest topic, while still remaining specific. The question was posed relatively early on in the survey booklet.

In order to achieve reliable data using a self-reporting approach, respondents should at least know how they themselves feel about the issue they are protesting about. There are individual differences in awareness of emotion—for instance due to alexithymia, and willingness to report on emotional states. People with alexithymia—the inability to put their feelings into words—have difficulty identifying, analyzing, and verbalizing their feelings (Van der Velde *et al.* 2013). Besides these individual differences the test-retest reliability[4] of self-reported emotions decreases when there is a time lapse between the lived experience and the moment of reporting (Mauss and Robinson 2009). By relating the emotion question to the issue of the demonstration—and not the act of participation—I secure the reliability of this emotion measure.

Responses

On average, respondents felt quite angry, worried, frustrated, and somewhat fearful (Table 27.1). The responses for worry, anger, and to a lesser

Table 27.1 Descriptive statistics of emotion items

Emotion	*Mean*	*SD*	*Skewness*	*SE*	*N*	*% Missing*
Anger	4.23	1	−1.31	0.02	14,141	7.41
Frustration	4.00	1.18	−1.04	0.02	13,722	10.15
Worry	4.21	0.96	−1.22	0.02	14,109	7.62
Fear	3.06	1.28	0.02	0.02	13,239	13.31

Note
Emotion items were measured on a scale of 1–5, and positively scored. Total sample size is 15,272.

extent frustration, are negatively skewed—meaning that the distribution of values is non-symmetrical and violates the basic statistical principle of normality. What should be taken into account, however, is that this is not only true of this sample—it is also most likely the case for the total population of demonstrators.[5]

Non-response

Data were gathered on 15,272 respondents. However, not everyone was equally diligent in answering all four of the emotion items. The percentage of missing values (Table 27.1) is comparable to the result of other studies that use a quantitative measure of emotion (e.g., Pressman *et al.* 2013). For the generalizability of the findings, from respondent to demonstration crowd, it is important to assess any bias in non-response to the emotion question. Due to the large sample size of this particular study I can compare those who did answer with those who did not.

By counting the number of missing values across the four emotion items I am able to identify three groups: (1) respondents who answered all four items (85 percent), (2) respondents who selectively answered some of the emotions items (13 percent), and (3) respondents who answered none of the four emotion items (2 percent). Little's MCAR was significant (Chi-Square (28) = 646.59, $p < 0.001$), meaning that the unanswered items were not missing completely at random. This leaves two options: the data are missing at random (MAR), or missing not at random (NMAR).[6]

The 2 percent of respondents with four missing values provided no information about the dependent variable, and for this reason I will have to drop these respondents in further analyses. At this point, however, I do want to know more about this 2 percent of the sample to see if this leads to a bias in the sample. In comparison to the group without missing values—where half of the sample is male (51 percent)—men are more dominant (60 percent) among the group with four missing values, t (247) = –2.84, $p < 0.01$. This group of non-responders is older (M = 49 years of age, SD = 15.43) than respondents who answered all four question

(M = 44 years of age, SD = 15.54), t (14,964) = –4.88, $p < 0.001$). There is also inter-country variation, but this does not have great implications because the range of "four missing values" is between 1–3 percent (F (6, 15,265) = 10.03, $p < 0.001$).

From here on I focus solely on the 14,939 respondents who answered *at least one* emotion item. The respondents with no missing values are compared[7] to the 13 percent (N = 1,936) of respondents who returned some missing values. Almost two-thirds (63 percent of the 1,936 respondents who answered some but not all items) responded with the highest value possible—i.e., they recorded 5 on the 1–5 point scale on the items that they *did* answer. This is an indication that some of the missing values could be the result of a scoring pattern in which respondents only answer the emotion items that they feel very strongly about; and leave a blank on items that they feel less strongly about. If this *is* the case it leads to inflated mean scores for the overall sample, and contributes to the negative skewedness of the data. To further examine this idea of a scoring pattern—top (5) score, or missing—I look at the missing values of a closely related question about the motives for participating in the demonstration in the first place, which also uses a Likert scale. The emotion question was asked just before the motives question. Among the respondents who had missing values and a scoring pattern on the emotion questions, 43 percent repeated this pattern on the motive question. Among the respondents who answered all four emotion questions this scoring pattern on motives only occurred among 1.5 percent.

The following section provides a more detailed outline of the basic demographic differences between thorough and less thorough respondents. The men and women in the entire sample seem equally thorough, 13 percent had some missing values, t (14,400) = 1.14, $p = 0.25$. To examine how respondents' age (M = 44.23, SD = 15.43) matters, I opted to compare the occurrence of missing values across four generations: the Silent Generation (born before 1945); the Baby Boomers (born 1945–64); Generation X (born 1965–80); and the Millennial Generation (born after 1980). The result of this comparison, using a One-Way ANOVA (F (3, 14,718) = 483, $p < 0.001$), and Turkey's b post-hoc comparisons, showed that respondents from the older Silent Generation more frequently had missing values on the emotion question than Baby Boomers. The Baby Boomers had more missing values than the respondents from Generation X, who in turn had more missing values than respondents from the youngest Millennial generation (Table 27.2).

The next step is the level of education of the respondents. Most of them held the equivalent of bachelor's degree, or higher (Table 27.2). As the respondents' level of education increases, so too does the frequency of answering all four emotion items, as indicated by the negative correlation (r (14,548) = –0.12, $p < 0.001$) between level of education and having

Table 27.2 One-way ANOVA percentage of missing values per generation and educational level

Educational level (N)	*Silent Generation*		*Baby Boomers*		*Generation X*		*Millennial Generation*		*Total*	
	%	N	%	N	%	N	%	N	%	N
Not more than lower secondary	50[a]	167	27[a]	582	14[a]	199	3[a]	183	8	1,131
Upper secondary	45[a]	203	22[b]	1,496	8[b]	750	2[a]	635	21	3,084
Post-secondary, BA, MA, or PhD	32[b]	654	17[c]	3,893	5[b]	3,020	2[a]	2,692	71	10,259
Total	**38**	**1,024**	**19**	**5,971**	**6**	**3,969**	**2**	**3,510**		**14,474**
F Value Generation 483**										
F Value Educational level 107**										

Notes
Results of ANOVA post-hoc analysis. All differences in incidence-level between generations, within the same educational level, are statistically significant at $p < 0.05$. Differences in incidence-level between educational levels, within the same generation, are marked by a different letter in superscript and statistically significant at $p < 0.05$. ** = $p < 0.001$.

missing values. Among respondents of the Silent Generation this negative correlation is at its strongest (r (1,024) = –0.15, $p<0.001$). Table 27.2 shows that the missing value rate per level of educational attainment is—approximately—reduced by half for the Baby Boomers and Generation X. Within the cohort of Millennials the level of education is no longer related to having missing values (r (3,510) = –0.02, p = n.s.).

The final step is a comparison between the different countries where the demonstrations were held. This is not an individual characteristic of the respondents, but a characteristic at the level of the demonstration. The results of the One-Way ANOVA (Table 27.3) show that the southern European countries of Spain and Italy have a relatively high rate of missing values, while the more northern European countries of the Netherlands, Sweden, and the UK have a much lower rate. The scoring pattern of only the highest value being scored, and of missing values, is also more prevalent in the South than the North (Table 27.3). This apparent variation between countries may be the result of local differences in the socio-demographic composition of the demonstrators themselves. Therefore, to complete the story, I opt for a regression analysis to see how both country and demographic characteristics influence the number of missing values that respondents record in response to the emotion question (Table 27.4). It now becomes clear that the main difference between countries follows a North-South divide, after controlling for demographic variables. The more northern European countries fall in line with the low number of missing

Table 27.3 One-way ANOVA percentage of missing values on the emotion question and scoring pattern across countries

	% of respondents with missing values out of N		*% with scoring pattern out of N respondents with missing values*	
UK	7[a]	2,567	51[a]	181
Sweden	10[b]	2,027	60[abc]	204
Netherlands	10[bc]	2,832	57[ab]	297
Switzerland	13[cd]	1,910	65[bc]	255
Belgium	13[d]	1,500	61[abc]	193
Spain	19[e]	2,515	69[bc]	488
Italy	20[e]	1,588	70[c]	318
Total	**13**	**14,939**	**63**	**1,936**
F Value ANOVA	46.33***		5.48***	

Notes

Results of One-way ANOVA comparing group percentages on missing values across countries. Post-hoc results on the differences in incidence values between countries are marked by a different letter in superscript and statistically significant at $p < 0.05$. Incidence values marked "a" are significantly different from values marked "b" and other letters.

Table 27.4 Linear regression analysis for variables predicting the number of missing values on the emotion question

	B	*SE B*	*B*	*SE B*
Sweden	0.04**	0.01	0.02*	0.01
Netherlands	0.04***	0.01	0.02	0.01
Switzerland	0.06***	0.01	0.03**	0.01
Belgium	0.05***	0.01	0.04***	0.01
Spain	0.15***	0.01	0.13***	0.01
Italy	0.12***	0.01	0.10***	0.01
Male			–0.04***	0.01
Age			0.30***	0.00
Basic education			0.08***	0.01
Secondary education			0.04***	0.01
Constant	0.05	0.01	0.06	0.01
Adjusted R^2	0.02		0.12	

Note
Data are from 14,332 respondents. The dependent variable number of missing values ranging between 0 and 3 was rescaled between 0 and 1. Predictor variables coded as 1 for male, and 0 for female. Age is in years and centered around the mean. Education is dummy coded with the highest completed level of education coded as 1; holding a college degree (BA, MA, PhD) or equivalent is the reference category. Country in which the demonstration was held is dummy coded with the UK as the reference category. *$p = 0.05$. **$p < 0.001$. ***$p < 0.001$.

values recorded in the UK, while the southern European countries of Spain and Italy still have a large impact on the number of missing values of respondents. Older and less well educated respondents are more like to have missing values for the emotion question, confirming the previous results. After controlling for age, education, and differences between countries, gender then comes into play—and we find that within the same country, generation, and level of educational attainment, female respondents have more missing values than male ones.

Concluding remarks and discussion

How appropriate is it to use a survey to measure emotion among protesters? Given that the field in which demonstration research takes place is dynamic and far removed from any clinical laboratory setting, a flexible and swift approach is needed. The field survey methodology offers just that, and there is recognition by social movement scholars that such methods are necessary, so that current theories on emotion in protest politics can be empirically examined.

The CCC Project has demonstrated that it is feasible to administer an emotion questionnaire among protest participants. Based on the analysis presented in this chapter I see two concerns that require some additional thought. First, the responses given tend to be skewed. Not because our sample was skewed in relation to the population, but rather because the population that we are interested in is not normally distributed. A five-point Likert scale might not be the optimal way of measuring emotion among a highly engaged population. The lower end of the scale is hardly used, while the top end leaves too little room for variability between the responses; therefore it is worth considering using the seven-point version of the scale.

Second, non-response on the emotion question was not MCAR. However, certain variables in the data could account for the "missingness" and therefore I assume MAR. Respondents with missing values are likely to be older and less well educated than respondents without missing values. I found the occurrence of missing values to be more common in Italy and Spain than in the northern European countries included in this study—a finding that runs counter to the prejudicial supposition that southern Europeans are more emotional than their northern counterparts.[8] In addition to this, I observed quite a distinct scoring pattern among respondents with missing values. Arguably, this scoring pattern occurs because of respondents' tendency to report intense emotions but then leave a blank where they do not feel any particular emotion. Since they treat the item as irrelevant, and ignore the lower values on the scale, the observed means become inflated. Leaving out cases with missing values means losing valuable data from specific demographic groups. For this study it would mean dropping a disproportionally large part of the Silent Generation and the less well educated respondents—groups that are already less prevalent in this data set.

An avenue for future research would be to consider posing two rather than one emotion question: one asking whether specific emotions are experienced, the other asking about the experienced emotions. An online administered survey will be the most suitable method for this as respondents will only have to indicate the intensity of the emotion that they feel for those emotions that they actually experience. The use of a feeling thermometer that runs from 0–100 to measure the intensity of each emotion would thwart the skewedness of responses. Both suggestions, however, are space-consuming and perhaps also require more cognitive work on the part of the respondent than the single question examined here.

Emotional experience is an intra-personal process—this means that if we only study emotions by observation, this process remains unexplored. Observing norms and values which give shape to emotion within a specific social movement, or observing behavior that is a result of emotion, provides information about the cognitive and motivational components of emotion. However, we have to include the internal processes to gain insight into the subjective feeling component of emotion. That said, emotions are complex in nature and the appropriateness of a self-assessment tool still leaves much to be desired.

I believe that all-too-often social scientists forgo the biological building blocks that are also part of the emotional experience. Methodologies such as in-depth interviews and surveys—commonly used for studying movement activists—simply do not accommodate the measurement of the biological or physiological aspects of emotions. We should incorporate the knowledge that is available on these aspects—knowledge that is documented in other fields of research—into our work. I do not proclaim that a questionnaire grasps the full emotional experience, but I do consider it a good starting point for mapping out the emotional landscape across demonstrations and social movements.

Notes

1 The method was developed by van Aelst and Walgrave, and is also used in the CCC Project (Van Stekelenburg *et al.* 2012).
2 Goodwin and Jasper count "love" and "hate"—but also "trust" and "respect"—as long-standing affects. To this I would add "solidarity" as being especially relevant to social movements.
3 These rules are discussed and documented in a manual which is available to other research teams wanting to replicate the original study in different countries and in later time periods. The website www.protestsurvey.eu contains a form under the heading "Survey" that provides access to this manual.
4 Test-retest reliability can be obtained by administering the same test twice over a period of time on the same sample.
5 Based on the ratio between skewness and SE, which runs from –52 to –66 for the skewed items.
6 MAR entails that "missingness" data is dependent only upon observed variables, and that after controlling for these variables, any remaining "missingness" is completely random. With MNAR "missingness" depends on unobserved data, which yields biased parameter estimates (Graham 2009: 552).
7 I created a dummy variable—whereby 0 = no missing values, and 1 = some missing values—to serve as the dependent variable in the comparison of means analyses.
8 In order to fully substantiate this observation an analysis of per country means would be necessary. However, this goes beyond the scope of this chapter.

References

Ekman, P., W. V. Friesen, M. O'Sullivan, A. Chan, I. Diacoyanni-Tarlatzis, K. Heider, R. Krause, W. A. LeCompte, T. Pitcairn, P. E. Ricci-Bitti, K. R. Scherer, M. Tomita, and A. Tzavaras. 1987. "Personality Processes and Individual, Universal and Cultural Differences in the Judgments of Facial Expressions of Emotion" in *Journal of Personality and Social Psychology*, 5 (4): 712–17.

Goodwin, J. and J. M. Jasper. 2006. "Emotions and Social Movements" in J. E. Stets and J. H. Turner (eds) *Handbook of the Sociology of Emotions*: 611–35. New York: Springer.

Graham, J. W. 2009. "Missing Data Analysis: Making it Work in the Real World," *Annual Review of Psychology*, 60: 549–76.

Mauss, I. B. and M. D. Robinson. 2009. "Measures of Emotion: A Review," *Cognition and Emotion*, 23 (2): 209–37.

Pressman, S. D., M. W. Gallagher, and S. J. Lopez. 2013. "Is the Emotion-Health Connection a 'First-World Problem'?" *Psychological Science*, 24 (4): 544–9.

Scherer, K. R. 2005. "What are Emotions? And How Can They be Measured?" *Social Science Information*, 44 (4): 695–729.

Smith, H. J., T. Cronin, and T. Kessler. 2008. "Anger, Fear, or Sadness: Faculty Members' Emotional Reactions to Collective Pay Disadvantage," *Political Psychology*, 29 (2): 221–46.

Van Stekelenburg, J. 2006. *Promoting or Preventing Social Change. Instrumentality, Identity, Ideology and Group-Based Anger as Motives of Protest Participation*. Vrije Universiteit, Amsterdam, Psychology and Pedagogy.

Van Stekelenburg, J. and B. Klandermans. 2007. "Individuals in Movements: A Social Psychology of Contention" in B. Klandermans and C. Roggeband (eds) *Handbook of Social Movements Across Disciplines*: 157–204. New York: Springer.

Van Stekelenburg, J., S. Walgrave, B. Klandermans, and J. Verhulst. 2012. "Contextualizing Contestation. Framework, Design and Data," *Mobilization. An International Journal*, 17 (3): 249–62.

Van Troost, D., J. Van Stekelenburg, and B. Klandermans. 2013. "Emotions of Protest" in N. Demertzis (ed.) *Emotions in Politics. The Affect Dimension in Political Tension*: 186–203. Basingstoke, New York: Palgrave Macmillan.

Van der Velde, J., M. N. Servaas, K. S. Goerlich, R. Bruggeman, P. Horton, S. G. Costafreda, and A. Aleman. 2013. "Neural Correlates of Alexithymia: A Meta-Analysis of Emotion Processing Studies," *Neuroscience and Biobehavioral Reviews*, 37 (8): 1774–85.

Van Zomeren, M., R. Spears, A. H. Fischer, and C. W. Leach. 2004. "Put Your Money Where Your Mouth Is! Explaining Collective Action Tendencies Through Group-Based Anger and Group Efficacy," *Journal of Personality and Social Psychology*, 87 (5): 649–64.

Walgrave, S. and Verhulst, J. 2011. "Selection and Response Bias in Protest Surveys," *Mobilization*, 16 (2): 203–22.

Index